Language and Music as Cognitive Systems

1. Is music's expressivity an appropriate object of evolutionary study?

2. ~~Regular~~ Conventional approaches to music's expressivity reveal a deficit in levels 3/4 analysis.

3. ~~Relevant evidence~~ Evidence relevant to these analysis is emerging and has the potential to further our understanding of music's expressivity

Language and Music as Cognitive Systems

Edited by

Patrick Rebuschat
Bangor University, UK

Martin Rohrmeier
Freie Universität Berlin, Germany

John A. Hawkins
University of Cambridge, Cambridge, UK
University of California, Davis, USA

Ian Cross
University of Cambridge, Cambridge, UK

OXFORD
UNIVERSITY PRESS

Great Clarendon Street, Oxford OX2 6DP

Oxford University Press is a department of the University of Oxford.
It furthers the University's objective of excellence in research, scholarship,
and education by publishing worldwide in

Oxford New York

Auckland Cape Town Dar es Salaam Hong Kong Karachi
Kuala Lumpur Madrid Melbourne Mexico City Nairobi
New Delhi Shanghai Taipei Toronto

With offices in

Argentina Austria Brazil Chile Czech Republic France Greece
Guatemala Hungary Italy Japan Poland Portugal Singapore
South Korea Switzerland Thailand Turkey Ukraine Vietnam

Oxford is a registered trade mark of Oxford University Press
in the UK and in certain other countries

Published in the United States
by Oxford University Press Inc., New York

British Library Cataloguing in Publication Data
Data available

Library of Congress Cataloging in Publication Data
Data available

Typeset in Minion by Cenveo, Bangalore, India
Printed in Great Britain
on acid-free paper by
CPI Group (UK) Ltd,
Croydon, CRO 4 yy

ISBN 978–0–19–955342–6

10 9 8 7 6 5 4 3 2 1

Contents

Contributors

Mireille Besson
Institut de Neurosciences
Cognitives de la Méditerranée
CNRS – Marseille Universités
Marseille, France

Jamshed Bharucha
Department of Psychology
Tufts University
Medford, MA, USA

Ian Cross
Centre for Music and Science
University of Cambridge
Cambridge, UK

Meagan Curtis
School of Natural and Social Sciences
Purchase College, State University of New York
Purchase, NY, USA

Zoltán Dienes
School of Psychology and Sackler Centre for Consciousness Science
University of Sussex
Brighton, UK

Laura Dilley
Department of Communicative Sciences & Disorders
Michigan State University
East Lansing, MI, USA

Nigel Fabb
Department of English
University of Strathclyde
Glasgow, UK

W. Tecumseh Fitch
Department of Cognitive Biology
University of Vienna
Vienna, Austria

Usha Goswami
Centre for Neuroscience in Education
Faculty of Education
University of Cambridge
Cambridge, UK

Jessica A. Grahn
Centre for Brain and Mind
Department of Psychology
University of Western Ontario
London, ON, Canada

Xiuyan Guo
Department of Psychology
East China Normal University
Shanghai, China

Morris Halle
Department of Linguistics and Philosophy
Massachusetts Institute of Technology
Cambridge, MA, USA

John A. Hawkins
Research Centre for English & Applied Linguistics
University of Cambridge
Cambridge, UK

Catherine Jones
School of Psychology
University of Sussex
Brighton, UK

Simon Kirby
Language Evolution and Computation Research Unit
School of Philosophy, Psychology and Language Sciences
University of Edinburgh
Edinburgh, UK

Stefan Koelsch
Cluster of Excellence "Languages of Emotion"
Freie Universität Berlin
Berlin, Germany

Nina Kraus
Auditory Neuroscience Laboratory
Department of Communicative Sciences & Disorders
Northwestern University
Evanston, IL, USA

Gustav Kuhn
Department of Psychology
Brunel University
Uxbridge, UK

Justin London
Department of Music
Carleton College
Northfield, MN

J. Devin McAuley
Department of Psychology
Bowling Green State University
Bowling Green, OH, USA

Steven Mithen
Department of Archaeology
University of Reading
Reading, UK

Iain Morley
Institute of Cognitive & Evolutionary Anthropology
University of Oxford
Oxford, UK

Neil Myler
Department of Linguistics
New York University
New York, NY, USA

Kaivon Paroo
Department of Neuroscience
Brown University
Providence, RI, USA

Aniruddh D. Patel
The Neurosciences Institute
San Diego, CA, USA

Isabelle Peretz
Laboratory for Brain, Music, and Sound Research (BRAMS)
Department of Psychology
Université de Montréal
Montréal, QC, Canada

Brechtje Post
Department of Theoretical and Applied Linguistics
University of Cambridge
Cambridge, UK

Patrick Rebuschat
Department of Linguistics
Bangor University
Washington, DC, USA

Ian Roberts
Department of Linguistics
University of Cambridge
Cambridge, UK

Martin Rohrmeier
Cluster of Excellence "Languages of Emotion"
Freie Universität Berlin
Berlin, Germany

Daniele Schön
Institut de Neurosciences Cognitives de la Méditerranée
CNRS – Marseille Universités
Marseille, France

Erika Skoe
Auditory Neuroscience Laboratory
Department of Communication
Sciences & Disorders
Northwestern University
Evanston, IL, USA

Elizabeth Tolbert
Peabody Institute
Johns Hopkins University
Baltimore, MD, USA

Leigh VanHandel
College of Music
Michigan State University
East Lansing, MI, USA

Bert Vaux
Department of Linguistics
University of Cambridge
Cambridge, UK

Jennie Wakefield
Department of Learning Technologies
University of North Texas
Dallas, TX, USA

Geraint A. Wiggins
Department of Computing
Goldsmiths
University of London, UK

Wendy K. Wilkins
New Mexico State University
Las Cruces, NM, USA

John N. Williams
Research Centre for English &
Applied Linguistics
University of Cambridge
Cambridge, UK

Introduction

The past 15 years have witnessed an increasing interest in the comparative study of language and music as cognitive systems. Language and music are uniquely human traits, so it is not surprising that this interest spans practically all branches of cognitive science, including linguistics, psychology, cognitive neuroscience, education, anthropology, and computer science (see e.g. the contributions in Avanzini, Faienza, & Minciacchi, 2003; Avanzini, Lopez, & Koelsch, 2006; Bigand, Lalitte, & Dowling, 2009; Dalla Bella et al., 2009; Hallam, Cross, & Thaut, 2009; Hardon & Purwins, 2009; Peretz & Zatorre, 2003; Peretz, 2006; Spiro, 2003; Wallin, Merker, & Brown, 1999). Underlying the study of language and music is the assumption that the comparison of these two domains can shed light on the structural and functional properties of each, while also serving as a test case for theories of how the mind and, ultimately, the brain work.

Language and music share many properties, which makes them particularly suitable for comparison (see Besson & Schön, 2006; Jackendoff, 2009; McMullen & Saffran, 2004; Patel, 2008, for overviews). For example, both domains rely primarily on the auditory modality and involve the perception and production of sound. They require memory capacity for storing representations (words, chords, etc.) and the ability to combine these representations by means of a system of rules or structural schemata (Jackendoff, 2009). In both cases, some aspects are universal and thus shared across cultures, whereas other aspects are culture-specific. Moreover, we are not born with the ability to comprehend a specific language or appreciate a specific tonal system. Instead, both abilities are formed through a prolonged learning process that results predominantly in implicit knowledge.

The present volume contributes to the study of language and music by bringing together researchers from a variety of scientific disciplines. The book spans a wide range of fields, including archaeology, anthropology, cognitive psychology, computer science, cognitive neuroscience, education, linguistics, and musicology. The purpose is to provide a snapshot of the different research strands that have focused on language and music, to identify current trends and methodologies that have been (or could be) applied to the study of both domains, and to outline future research directions. We also hope that the volume will promote the investigation of language and music by fostering interdisciplinary discussion and collaboration.

Background

This volume is based on an eponymous conference which was organized by the editors. It took place in Cambridge, UK, between 11–13 May 2007 and was co-hosted by the Centre for Music & Science (CMS) and the Research Centre for English & Applied Linguistics (RCEAL), both University of Cambridge. The conference was originally planned as a one-day event, with two or three invited speakers and about eight paper presentations. We quickly realized, however, that there was an extraordinary amount of interest in the topic and that the demand greatly outnumbered the available slots for presentations. Our small, local symposium thus quickly developed into a three-day international conference, with five keynote presentations, four panel discussions, seven paper and three poster sessions, as well as receptions, music performances, and a formal hall at Jesus College. In the end, the conference featured 172 presenters, who travelled to the UK from 21 different countries, ranging from Australia and Austria via Greece and Israel to Singapore and the United States.

Like the present volume, the conference was structured around four core areas in which the study of music and language has been particularly fruitful: (1) structural comparisons, (2) evolution, (3) learning and processing, and (4) neuroscience. For each research strand, we invited outstanding researchers to serve as keynote speakers or panellists. Since one of our objectives was to encourage collaboration and discussion across disciplines, we decided to follow each keynote presentation with a panel discussion. The keynote speakers were asked to send their presentations to their respective panellists several weeks before the conference so that the latter could prepare a 10-minute commentary. After each panellist had presented their commentary, the session concluded with an open discussion, in which members of the audience could join in.

In the structural-comparisons strand, the keynote was delivered by Nigel Fabb and Morris Halle ('Grouping in the stressing of words, in metrical verse, and in music') and followed by commentaries from Laura Dilley and Devin McAuley, Brechtje Post, Bert Vaux, and Ian Roberts. In the evolution strand, Tecumseh Fitch's keynote ('The evolution of rhythm: Embodiment and musical syntax') was followed by commentaries from Simon Kirby, Steven Mithen, and Iain Morley. The learning-and-processing strand featured a keynote address by Jamshed Bharucha ('Musical communication as alignment of non-propositional brain states') and commentaries from Ted Briscoe, Zoltán Dienes, Geraint Wiggins, and John Williams. The neuroscience strand featured two keynote presentations, the first by Aniruddh Patel ('Language, music, and the brain: a resource-sharing framework'), the second by Isabelle Peretz ('Comparisons between music and language as tests of modularity'). Patel's keynote was followed by commentaries from Jessica Grahn, Larry Parsons, and Stefan Koelsch. Peretz's keynote was intended as a concluding address, so there was no panel discussion.

This volume

The feedback we received from the conference presenters and delegates was very positive throughout. When we were approached by Oxford University Press regarding the possibility of producing an edited volume inspired by the conference we readily agreed to do so. We have decided to maintain the four core areas that provided the structure for the conference because these continue to be areas in which much of the research on language and music concentrates. And because our conference format—a keynote address, followed by a panel discussion—proved very successful, we decided to apply this to the volume as well. The current volume thus consists of four sections, each of which contains a target article, several commentaries on the target article, and a response to the commentaries by the author(s) of the target article. Our fourth section (neuroscience) is the exception, as it contains two target articles and two sets of commentaries. Each of the sections is preceded by a short introduction from the editors.

Our keynote speakers agreed to convert their presentations into much expanded and updated chapters, and all panellists, with two exceptions, agreed to produce a commentary on their respective target articles. We also recruited several commentators who were not involved in the original conference. In the case of Isabelle Peretz's contribution, this was necessary because her keynote address had not been followed by a panel discussion. In other cases, we believed that the discussion would benefit from the addition of contributors with different research backgrounds.

The target article for Section 1 (Structural comparisons) was co-authored by Nigel Fabb and Morris Halle ('Grouping in the stressing of words, in metrical verse, and in music'). It is followed by commentaries from Laura Dilley and Devin McAuley, Brechtje Post, Bert Vaux, Neil Myler, and Ian Roberts. The target article for Section 2 (Evolution) is written by Tecumseh Fitch ('The biology and evolution of rhythm: unravelling a paradox') and followed by commentaries from Simon Kirby, Steven Mithen, Iain Morley, and Elizabeth Tolbert. Section 3 (Learning and processing) features a co-authored target article by Jamshed Bharucha, Meagan Curtis, and Kaivon Paroo. This is followed by commentaries from Zoltán Dienes, Gustav Kuhn, Xiuyan Guo, Catherine Jones, Geraint Wiggins, and John Williams. Section 4 (Neuroscience) features two target articles. Aniruddh Patel's contribution ('Language, music, and the brain: a resource-sharing framework') is followed by commentaries from Stefan Koelsch, Jessica Grahn, and Justin London. Isabelle Peretz's target article ('Music, language, and modularity in action') is followed by commentaries from Erika Skoe, Nina Kraus, Mireille Besson, Daniele Schön, Usha Goswami, Leigh VanHandel, Jennie Wakefield, and Wendy Wilkins. The volume concludes with a chapter by Ian Cross ('Music as a social and cognitive process') that ties together many of the topics covered in the other sections of the volume.

The chapters in this volume were carefully read by the editors and the contributors. In addition, the first drafts were also used as readings in an undergraduate course on Language and Music taught by the first editor at Georgetown University. This enabled us to gain feedback on the readability of the texts and on the clarity of the arguments expressed by the contributors. The final product is a volume that is written in an accessible and engaging fashion and that gives readers a glimpse into the exciting research that is being conducted on language and music.

Acknowledgements

The volume, and the conference which inspired it, would not have been possible without the extensive help of many people.

We would like to thank our invited speakers, presenters, and delegates for making it such a unique event. We are very grateful to the members of our scientific committee, who diligently evaluated a substantial amount of submitted abstracts: Theresa Biberauer, Alan Blackwell, Ted Briscoe, Eric Clarke, Zoltán Dienes, Jessica Grahn, Sarah Hawkins, Simon Kirby, Stefan Koelsch, David MacKay, William Marslen-Wilson,

Steven Mithen, Iain Morley, Larry Parsons, Isabelle Peretz, Pierre Perruchet, Brechtje Post, Ian Roberts, Carson Schuetze, Mark Steedman, Dan Tidhar, Bert Vaux, Graham Welch, and Geraint Wiggins. Henkjan Honing, Francis Nolan, Ted Briscoe, Stefan Koelsch, and William Marslen-Wilson served as session chairs and/or panel moderators, for which we are also very grateful.

We would like to thank Mary Jacobus, Catherine Hurley, Gemma Tyler, Philippa Smith, and Anna Malinowska at the Centre for Research in the Arts, Social Sciences and the Humanities (CRASSH) as well as Susan Rolfe, Barbara Jones, and Mike Franklin at RCEAL for their help in several important administrative aspects of this conference. Many student volunteers helped by manning the registration desk, setting up the audiovisual equipment, carrying chairs, tables, and poster boards, and we are very grateful for their assistance and support.

Finally, the organization of this event, and thus the publication of the present volume, would not have been possible without substantial funding. We would like to acknowledge the generous financial support of CRASSH, the Society for Education, Music and Psychology Research (SEMPRE), the Arts & Humanities Research Council (AHRC), the Faculty of Music, Cambridge, and Oxford University Press.

With regards to the volume, we would like to thank our authors for their excellent contributions and their patience with inevitable delays. At Oxford University Press, we would like to thank our editor, Martin Baum, for suggesting this project and for his continued support, as well as Charlotte Green, Carol Maxwell, Kate Wilson and Priya Sagayaraj for their assistance with the logistics. At Georgetown, we are grateful to the students of Language and Music (Ling 370) for their valuable feedback on the texts and to Phillip Hamrick and Elizabeth Kissling, who provided editorial assistance during the final stages of this project. We hope the volume will stimulate further interest in the comparative study of language and music and encourage discussion across scientific boundaries.

Patrick Rebuschat, Washington, DC
Martin Rohrmeier, Berlin
John A. Hawkins, Cambridge and Davis, CA
Ian Cross, Cambridge

References

Avanzini, G., Faienza, C., & Minciacchi, D. (Eds.) (2003). The neurosciences and music [Special issue]. *Annals of the New York Academy of Sciences, 999.*

Avanzini, G., Lopez, L., & Koelsch, S. (Eds.) (2006). The neurosciences and music II: From perception to performance [Special issue]. *Annals of the New York Academy of Sciences, 1060.*

Besson, M., & Schön, D. (2006). Comparison between language and music. *Annals of the New York Academy of Sciences, 1060,* 232–58.

Bigand, E., Lalitte, P., & Dowling, W. J. (Eds.) (2009). Music and language: 25 years after Lerdahl & Jackendoff's GTTM [Special issue]. *Music Perception, 26*(3).

Dalla Bella, S., Kraus, N., Overy, K., Pantev, C., Snyder, J. S., Tervaniemi, M., *et al.* (Eds.) (2009) The neurosciences and music III: Disorders and plasticity [Special issue]. *Annals of the New York Academy of Sciences, 1169.*

Hallam, S., Cross, I., & Thaut, M. (Eds.) (2009). *Oxford handbook of music psychology.* Oxford: Oxford University Press.

Hardon, D. R. & Purwins, H. (Eds.) (2009). Music, brain and cognition [Special issue]. *Connection Science, 21*(2–3).

Jackendoff, R. (2009). Parallels and nonparallels between language and music. *Music Perception, 26*(3), 195–204.

McMullen, E., & Saffran, J. R. (2004). Music and language: A developmental comparison. *Music Perception, 21*(3), 289–311.

Patel, A. D. (2008). *Music, language, and the brain.* Oxford: Oxford University Press.

Peretz, I. & Zatorre, R. (Eds.) (2003). *The cognitive neuroscience of music.* Oxford: Oxford University Press.

Peretz, I. (Ed.) (2006). The nature of music [Special issue]. *Cognition, 100*(1).

Spiro, J. (Ed.) (2003). Music and the brain [Special issue]. *Nature Neuroscience, 6*(7).

Wallin, N. N., Merker, B., & Brown, S. (Eds.) (1999). *The origins of music.* Cambridge, MA: MIT Press.

Section 1

Structural comparisons

Chapter 1

Introduction

A central property of both language and music is their 'structure', which we can characterize roughly as the grouping of individual items into phrases or larger units at different levels of analysis. Borrowing Ferdinand de Saussure's key insight (in his 1916 *Cours de linguistique générale*) these items combine with one another 'syntagmatically' within their respective groups, and are 'paradigmatically' related and opposed to alternative items that are permitted within the same groupings. In discussing language structure and musical structure the papers in this section focus primarily on phonological structure, i.e. on items that ultimately involve units of sound and their groupings, and they compare them with sound units and their groupings in music. The target article by Nigel Fabb and Morris Halle, 'Grouping in the stressing of words, in metrical verse, and in music', also adds poetic metre to the discussion and proposes a system of metrical grids that is common to three domains: the assignment of stress contours to words and phrases; the determination of rhythm in music; and the well-formedness of lines of metrical poetry. Metrical grids are abstract structures assigned to the respective linear units within these three domains and the same computational system is shown to apply to them all. Stress and poetic metre are properties assigned to sequences of syllables; musical rhythm is a property of sequences composed of musical pitches and silences.

In their commentary to the target article, Laura Dilley and Devin McAuley contextualize and discuss this approach by Fabb and Halle to 'metrical stress theory' and consider an alternative that seeks a perceptual basis for commonalities between music and language. Brechtje Post argues in her commentary that the stress-assignment rules of French are very different from those of English and that they point to a different weighting of prosodic constraints, leading to cross-linguistic variation, and that a prosodic hierarchy needs to be added to Fabb and Halle's metrical constraints. Bert Vaux and Neil Myler's commentary is critical of Fabb and Halle's assumption that metrical structure is projected from the surface syllables of a linguistic text and they argue for an alternative approach that maps linguistic structures onto a predetermined metrical template. Finally, Ian Roberts extends the discussion and the parallels between language and music beyond phonology and into syntax and into questions of language evolution, arguing that language and music share the same computational system in general. The section concludes with Fabb and Halle's response to two of the more critical points made in the commentaries.

Reference

de Saussure, F. (1916) *Cours de linguistique générale*, publié par C. Bally et A. Sechehaye avec de A. Riedlinger. Lausanne: Payot.

Chapter 2

Grouping in the stressing of words, in metrical verse, and in music

Nigel Fabb and Morris Halle

In this chapter we argue that computations of the same kind determine the well-formedness of certain structures in language, metrical verse, and music. In all three domains, elements are organized into groups (pairs and triplets) which are themselves organized into groups (and so on). When stress is placed in words, syllables are grouped; syllables are also grouped when the metricality of a line is determined; and in the metrical organization of music, timing slots are grouped. Grouping is accomplished by a set of iterative rules, which generate a bracketed grid from the initial material. Specific aspects of the word, metrical line, or piece of music are controlled with reference to particular features of the metrical grid. In the first three parts of the paper we introduce the iterative rules, and show how they explain the distribution of stress in a word, and how in metrical verse they both control the length of the line as well as its rhythm. In the fourth part of the paper, we discuss the grids assigned by Lerdahl and Jackendoff to music, and show that these grids can be generated by the same iterative rules as are used in language and poetic metre.

On the stress of words and on prosody in general

It is well known that our perception of physical stimuli goes well beyond the simple recording of the signals that impinge on our sense organs. For example, the perceptual effects which are often termed 'visual illusions' imply that our visual sense is somehow deceived into an incorrect judgement about the 'true' nature of the stimuli. In fact, when the matter is looked into with some care it appears that very few of our perceptions are direct records of the signals impinging on our peripheral sense organs; almost everything we perceive is a complicated construct quite remote from the physical—visual or acoustic—signals that impinge on our peripheral sense organs.

Perhaps the most striking example of a physical signal that evokes elaborate mental construction is our perception of speech. When we hear an utterance in a language we know, we normally perceive not only an acoustic signal, but also—and more importantly—a meaningful message that informs us about an aspect of this world or instructs us to perform an action of some kind. Although at this time we have only limited understanding of how a meaning is extracted from a noise, important advances have been made in the understanding of how certain aspects of language are processed. There is, for example, general agreement that although the speech signal is quasi-continuous, humans perceive these acoustic signals as sequences of discrete sounds (phonemes, segments). The phonemes, moreover, are grouped simultaneously into two parallel kinds of units: morphemes and syllables.

Both morphemes and syllables are sequences of phonemes, but of a totally different kind. Viewed in terms of the morphemes that compose it, the English noun *con-fid-ent-ial-ity* is composed of five morphemes separated here by hyphens. The morphemes, moreover, are combined into a series of nested constituents as shown in (1).

```
(1)    con - fid - ent - ial - ity
        |     |     |     |     |
       pref-stem-suff-suff-suff
         \   /    /    /    /
           V     /    /    /
            \   /    /    /
              A     /    /
               \   /    /
                 A     /
                  \   /
                    N
```

The tree in (1), however, represents only one aspect of the structure of the word. Simultaneously with being perceived as the nested object in (1), an utterance of the word *confidentiality* is also perceived as a sequence of the seven syllables shown in (2).

```
(2)    con.fi.den.ti.a.li.ty.
```

While the principles of grouping morphemes as in (1) are the domain of syntax and morphology, the very different principles of grouping syllables as seen in (2) are the domain of prosody.

When English speakers pronounce a sequence of syllables like that in (2), they do not pronounce all syllables in the same way, but differentiate them with respect to prominence or stress, as shown in (3), where the asterisk columns reflect different degrees of prominence. (The columns could be written either above or below the word; this makes no difference.)

```
(3)    con.fi.den.ti.a.li.ty
        *   *   *   *  *  *  *
        *       *      *
        *              *
                       *
```

In the normal pronunciation of the word *confidentiality*, the odd-numbered syllables are more prominent than the even-numbered (except for the odd-numbered syllable at the end of the word), and the antepenultimate (the third from the end) syllable has greater stress than the rest.

Having established that differences in prominence are an important phonetic feature of English words, we are immediately faced with the necessity of providing a plausible mechanism that might account for the noted differences in prominence. It was suggested by Mark Liberman (1975) that the differences in prominence are the result of grouping the syllables. Liberman's suggestion was followed by a series of investigations into the nature of stress systems (e.g. Liberman and Prince, 1977; Hayes, 1981; Prince, 1983; Halle & Vergnaud, 1987; Hayes, 1995). These studies culminated in Idsardi (1992), where a powerful new mechanism for expressing prosodic facts of all kinds (not only the word stress) was first described. It is this mechanism that we now explain.

In the Idsardi account, the syllables of an utterance are projected as a sequence of asterisks, where each asterisk stands for a single syllable.[1] The theory also disposes of two junctures, represented here by ordinary parentheses, '(', the left parenthesis, and ')', the right parenthesis. The junctures are inserted among the asterisks, and this has the effect of grouping the syllables in accordance with principle (4).

(4) A left parenthesis groups the syllables on its right; a right parenthesis groups the syllables on its left. A syllable that is neither to the right of a left parenthesis, nor to the left of a right parenthesis is ungrouped.

Thus, in (5a) all syllables (asterisks) constitute one group, but in (5b) all asterisks are ungrouped.

```
(5)   (a) (* * * * * * *
      (b)  * * * * * * *(
```

In both examples in (5) only a single juncture (left parenthesis) was inserted at one of the edges of the sequence. More than one juncture can be inserted and junctures can be inserted elsewhere than at the edges: junctures may freely be inserted anywhere into the asterisk sequence, thus turning a sequence of syllables into a sequence of groups of syllables. These groups have traditionally been called feet.

The groups are not just sub-sequences of syllables; our theory of groups says that they also possess the additional intrinsic property that one of the two syllables that terminates (i.e. begins or ends) the sub-sequence is the head of the group, and is projected to form a new sequence of asterisks. In addition to stipulating the nature of the parenthesis that is inserted into the asterisk sequence, it is necessary to stipulate whether the left-most or right-most asterisk in the group is the head. In (6) we illustrate the only two possible head locations in the group (5a). In (6a) the head is the left-most asterisk in the group, in (6b), the head is the right-most asterisk.

1 In some rare stress systems, more than one asterisk is projected from certain of the syllables in the sequence. No such cases will be considered below.

```
(6)    (a)  (* * * * * * *
             *

       (b)  (* * * * * * *
                         *
```

Although we have shown some effects of parenthesis insertion, we have as yet not provided any information on the mechanism that carries out the insertion. In (5) and (6), the parenthesis is inserted by an ordinary rule in the phonology, which recognizes the left edge of a sequence. Perhaps the most important innovation of Idsardi's study was the discovery that parentheses are inserted not only in the same environments as those visible to ordinary phonological rules, but that parenthesis insertion is often due to a special iterative rule that starts at one edge of the sequence and ends at its opposite edge. Such iterative rules, which are not otherwise available in the phonology, insert parentheses at fixed intervals, and the intervals are of two kinds: binary or ternary. Iterative parenthesis-insertion can thus generate feet of only two lengths. We recall that head location in the groups also is subject to a binary choice: the left-most or the right-most asterisk in the group is the head. As a consequence the rule of iterative grouping of syllables can generate feet of only four basic kinds, the two binary feet called trochee (left-headed) and iamb (right-headed), and the two ternary feet, dactyl (left-headed) and anapaest (right-headed).

An account for the prominence distributions in (3) might begin with an iterative rule inserting right parentheses at binary intervals starting at the left edge. The effects of this rule are shown in (7), where we have labelled the two sequences of asterisks gridline 0 and gridline 1 respectively. This demonstrates the significant difference between the two types of parenthesis.

```
(7)    con.fi.den.ti.a.li.ty
       )*   *)  *   *)*  *) *    gridline 0
        *       *     *          gridline 1
```

We note that if we had inserted left, instead of right parentheses from left to right in (7), we would have generated the four feet in (8), and implied, contrary to fact, that the word *confidentiality* has four, rather than only three prominences.

```
(8)    con.fi.den.ti.a.li.ty
       (*   * (*   *(*  * (*    gridline 0
        *       *     *     *    gridline 1
```

The rest of the prominence pattern of (3) can be generated by positing for gridline 1 an iterative rule inserting left parentheses at binary intervals starting at the left edge and generating left-headed groups.[2] This is shown in (9).

---

[2] By analogy with the term feet on gridline 0, we might use the traditional terms metra for the groups on gridline 1, and cola for those on gridline 2.

```
(9)    con.fi.den.ti.a.li.ty
       )*   *)  *   *)*  *) *     gridline 0
       (*       *   (*            gridline 1
        *            *            gridline 2
```

As shown in (10), the derivation of the prominence pattern of *confidentiality* is completed by the generation of a right-headed group on gridline 2 with the help of the (non-iterative) insertion of a right parenthesis at the right edge of the asterisk sequence.[3]

```
(10)   con.fi.den.ti.a.li.ty
       )*   *)  *   *)*  *) *     gridline 0
       (*       *   (*            gridline 1
        *            *)           gridline 2
                     *            gridline 3
```

We summarize in (11) the formal rules, both iterative and other, that have been posited in the discussion of (3) above in order to assign the asterisk array in (10) to the word *confidentiality*.

(11)
(a) Project each syllable as an asterisk forming gridline 0.
(b) Gridline 0. Starting at the L edge, insert a R parenthesis, form binary groups, heads L.
(c) Gridline 1. Starting at the L edge, insert a L parenthesis, form binary groups, heads L.
(d) Gridline 2. At the R edge, insert a R parenthesis, head R.

We use the term 'metrical grid' to name asterisk arrays like that in (10). It is to be noted that the grid of itself does not assign stress to the syllables of the word. To this end we require the rule (12).

(12) Assign different degrees of prominence (of high pitch) to the syllables in direct proportion to the height of their asterisk column in the metrical grid.

It is the goal of the linguist to discover which combination of grid-building rules, and which stress-assigning rules, are required to explain the pattern of stresses which we find in the words of a specific language.

The need for rule (12) in addition to the rules of grid construction (11) is due to the fact that languages differ not only with respect to their rules of grid construction, but also

[3] The three rules stated above are simplified versions of the actual rules required for the assignment of stress to English words. For a discussion of the actual rules, see Halle (1998).

with respect to such rules of stress assignment as (12), which can vary from language to language.

An instructive example of the latter fact is provided by the stress system of the American Indian language Creek (our data is drawn from Haas (1977)). In a subset of the words of this language, only one syllable carries stress; this is the rightmost even-numbered syllable. In (13) we show two words which illustrate this pattern; we write numbers under the syllables to make it evident that it is the rightmost even-numbered syllable in each word which carries stress.

```
(13)
  (a) imahicíta  'one to look after' (4th syllable stressed)
      1 2 3 4 5
  (b) isimahicitá  'one to sight at one' (6th syllable stressed)
      1 2 3 4 5 6
```

The rules which generate grids for these words are stated in (14).

```
(14)
  (a) Project each syllable as an asterisk forming gridline 0.
  (b) Gridline 0.  Starting at the L edge, insert a R parenthesis, form
  binary groups, heads R.
  (c) Gridline 1.  At the R edge, insert a R parenthesis, head R.
```

These rules generate the grids in (15) from the unstressed sequence of syllables.

```
(15)
  (a)
      imahicita
     )* *)* *)*     gridline 0
        *   *)      gridline 1
            *       gridline 2
  (b)
      isimahicita
     )* *)* *)* *)  gridline 0
        *   *   *)  gridline 1
                *   gridline 2
```

The main difference between stress in Creek and English is not due to different metrical grids, but rather to different rules assigning stress. In English stress is assigned by rule (12) to syllables that project to a gridline above gridline 0. In a long English word, like *confidentiality* above, there may be many stressed syllables with different degrees of stress. By contrast, in this subset of words in Creek no matter how long the word, only one syllable is stressed, namely, the right-most even-numbered syllable. But in order to locate this syllable, the metrical grids in (15) must be constructed. It is via these grids that stress is assigned by rule (16).

```
(16) Assign main stress (extra high pitch) to the syllable projecting to
  gridline 2.
```

The grid assigned to the word in Creek by the rules in (14) is periodic: gridline 0 projections of syllables are grouped into pairs (from left to right), and the rightmost syllable in each pair projects to gridline 1. This does not directly represent the stress pattern, or rhythm, of the word, which is not periodic. Instead, this grouping is required in order to locate the single syllable which projects to gridline 2 and to which stress is assigned. The grid in Creek is more complex (abstract) than the stress pattern of the word: in Creek the grid does not represent the rhythm of the word in any direct way, but only via a condition. In this, the grids for word stress are similar to grids for lines in metrical verse, where the grid is again more complex and more structured than the rhythmic pattern it controls.

Metrical verse

The cardinal difference distinguishing a text in verse from a text in prose is that verse is composed of lines. In this section we review the major formal aspects of metrical verse, which is the most common kind of spoken verse, and we leave aside poetry based on syntactic parallelism, like that of the Old Testament, or free verse (*vers libre*), which has enjoyed great popularity in Western Europe and America since the end of the nineteenth century. In all types of poetry the text is invariably split into lines: absent the line, the text is prose, no matter how 'poetic'.[4]

Lines in metrical verse are subject to two kinds of restriction: they are restricted in length, and they exhibit different kinds of restrictions on the placement of marked syllables—e.g. syllables bearing the word stress, or syllables with particular rhymes. Thus, lines in the English trochaic tetrameter, like those in (17), are eight or seven syllables in length, with a strong tendency of placing syllables with word stress in odd-numbered positions (counting from left to right).

```
(17)
  Slaves to London I'll deceive you;
  For the country now I leave you.
  Who can bear and not be mad,
  Wine so dear and yet so bad?
```

(Pierre Antoine Motteux, 'A Song', 1696.)

The most important result of our book on metrical verse (Fabb and Halle, 2008) was to show that these restrictions, as well as all restrictions encountered in other types of metrical verse, require the assignment of metrical grids to the syllable sequences that make up the line. The grids are of the same kind as those that were encountered in stress placement in the preceding section. In the case of the lines in (17) we explain the connection between the restrictions on line length and the restrictions on the

4 For further discussion see Fabb (2002, chapter 5), and Fabb and Halle (2008, chapter 1).

placement of stressed syllables with the help of rules which generate a grid from the line, rules (18) and (20) below.

Rule (18) projects an asterisk from each syllable in the line. The result is shown in (19).

(18) Project each syllable as an asterisk forming gridline 0.

```
(19)
  Slaves to London I'll deceive you;
   *     * * * *    * *    *      gridline 0

  Wine so dear and yet so bad?
   *    * *   *   *   * *         gridline 0
```

Next, the set of iterative rules (20), which are specific to the trochaic tetrameter, is applied to generate the grids in (21).

(20) Rules for English trochaic tetrameter
(a) Gridline 0: starting just at the L edge, insert a L parenthesis, form binary groups, heads L.
i. Incomplete groups are admitted.
(b) Gridline 1: starting just at the L edge, insert a L parenthesis, form binary groups, heads L.
(c) Gridline 2: starting just at the L edge, insert a L parenthesis, form binary groups, heads L.

```
(21)
  Slaves to London I'll deceive you;
   (*    * (* * (*    *(*    *(    gridline 0
   (*      *    (*     *(          gridline 1
   (*           *(                 gridline 2
    *                              gridline 3

  Wine so dear and yet so bad?
   (*    * (*   *   (*   * (*      gridline 0
   (*      *        (*     *(      gridline 1
   (*                *(            gridline 2
    *                              gridline 3
```

What necessarily limits the length of the line is that there are iterative rules on each gridline, that each of the three iterative rules in (20) inserts parentheses at binary intervals, and that the gridline which is the last to be generated (bottom-most in our grids) must have exactly one asterisk. We state the latter requirement formally in (22).

(22) The last-to-be-generated gridline in a well-formed metrical grid must contain a single asterisk.

In addition to line length, metrical verse in English places specific restrictions on the location of stressed syllables in the line, and it is these restrictions that provide the line with its characteristic rhythm. In a metre in which every odd-numbered syllable was stressed and every even-numbered metre unstressed, we would have the condition in (23).

(23) A stressed syllable must project to gridline 1, and a gridline 1 asterisk must project from a stressed syllable.

But this is not the right generalization, and hence not the right condition for English verse. Though the grid is fully periodic, the rhythm is not fully periodic, so the pattern of stressed and unstressed syllables cannot be fully controlled by a condition on the grid. It is true that it is possible to pronounce the line with a fully regular rhythm, for example stressing *I'll* in (21) because it is odd-numbered, but this is a performance practice rather than a fact about how the metre controls the composition of the line. It is also possible to perform the line with a more regular rhythm (in which *I'll* is not stressed), and this is just as metrical.

A better condition, which accounts more generally for the distribution of stressed syllables in English metrical verse requires a definition of the relevant type of syllable in (24) and a condition formulated as in (25).

(24) The syllable bearing the word stress in a polysyllabic word is a maximum, if it is preceded and followed in the same line by a syllable with less stress.

(25) Maxima must project to gridline 1.

Though stressed monosyllables tend to project to gridline 1, they do not have to; only the stressed syllable in a polysyllabic word must project to gridline 1, and this only when it is a maximum or 'peak' relative to surrounding syllables. There are two maxima in the first scanned line in (21) (the stressed syllables in *London* and *deceive*), and both project to gridline 1. Since there are no maxima in the second scanned line, the rule does not control the distribution of stressed and unstressed syllables at all in this line. Note that there is not a complementary requirement that gridline 1 asterisks must project from stressed syllables or from maxima. The line might in principle have no stressed syllables at all, and though this would be linguistically odd the line would not be unmetrical (so long as it had the right number of syllables).

It is important to note that conditions such as (25) which control for the presence of stressed syllables in the metrical line are not part of the grid-building process. The grid has already been generated from the line by the iterative rules (which know nothing of differences between syllables) at the point when the condition is checked. The job of the metrical analyst is to discover which combination of iterative and other rules, and which conditions on the resulting grid, best explain the characteristics of the metrical line.

It should now be clear how iterative rules such as those in (20) explain both why the metrical line has a specific length and how the syllables are patterned. We further illustrate our approach with the lines in iambic pentameter shown in (26).

(26)

Hungarians! Save the world! Renew the stories
Of men who against hope repelled the chain,
And make the world's dead spirit leap again!
On land renew that Greek exploit, whose glories
Hallow the Salamanian promontories,
And the Armada flung to the fierce main.

(Matthew Arnold, 'Sonnet to the Hungarian Nation', lines 9–14, 1849.)

The rules which generate a grid for iambic pentameter are given in (27).

(27) Rules for iambic pentameter

(a) Gridline 0: starting (just at the edge OR one asterisk in) at the R edge, insert a R parenthesis, form binary groups, heads R.

(b) Gridline 1: starting just at the R edge, insert a R parenthesis, form ternary groups, heads R.

i. The last (leftmost) group must be incomplete -- binary.

(c) Gridline 2: starting just at the L edge, insert a L parenthesis, form binary groups, heads L.

In (28) we show the effect of the rules (just rule (27a) the second to sixth lines). We have indicated which syllables we think are likely to be stressed in a performance of the line, and we have underlined the maxima. Stressed syllables in general are not subject to a constraint on their location; only the subset of stressed syllables which we have identified as maxima must project to gridline 1. Because it is a grammatical word, 'against' does not contain a word stress, and hence not a maximum.

(28)

```
    '        '        '        '        '
Hungarians! Save the world! Renew the stories
)*  *) *     *)    *  *)     * *)   *   *) *    gridline 0
    *        *)       *        *        *)      gridline 1
            (*                          *(      gridline 2
             *

     '         '     '      '           '
 Of men who against hope repelled the chain,
)*   *)   * *) *     *)   * *)      *   *)      gridline 0
     *      *        *      *           *       gridline 1
```

```
        '       '       '     '     '      '
 And make the world's dead spirit leap again!
)*     *)     * *)       *      *)*    *)  * *)      gridline 0
       *      *                 *      *     *       gridline 1

      '      '         '        '         '
 On land renew that Greek exploit, whose glories[5]
)*   *)    * *)    *    *)   *    *)     *     *)*   gridline 0
     *     *            *         *            *     gridline 1

 '              '      '
Hallow the Salamanian promontories,
)*  *)    *  *)* *) *    *)* *)*                     gridline 0
    *        *  *        *  *                        gridline 1

               '     '            '      '
 And the Armada flung to the fierce main.
)*     *) * *)*   *)    *    *)  *        *)         gridline 0
       *   *      *          *            *          gridline 1
```

We note that parentheses on gridline 0 are inserted from right to left. There are two kinds of evidence for this. We have seen that the last group generated by an iterative rule can be incomplete, and in a trochaic metre this is the rightmost group; in an iambic metre the leftmost group can sometimes be incomplete (indicating that groups are formed from right to left). Furthermore, the rightmost syllable in the line can be 'extrametrical' (as seen in the first, fourth, and fifth lines of (28)). This arises because the iterative rule (27a) may skip the first asterisk encountered.

This is one way in which the line can have an extra syllable. But extra syllables can also appear within the line, which cannot be accommodated by skipping the first asterisk of gridline 0 in applying rule (27a). This is illustrated by some 11-syllable lines in iambic pentameter by John Donne in (29), where we indicate the syllables by writing the letter s below the line.

```
(29)
 And gluttonous death, will instantly unjoynt
 s    s s s    s      s  s  s  s s s
 My body, and soule, and I shall sleepe a space,
  s  s s  s   s      s  s   s      s   s  s
 But my ever-waking part shall see that face,
  s  s s s  s s   s     s    s   s   s
```

(John Donne, 'Holy Sonnet 6' lines 5–7.)

In some metrical theories extra syllables within the line are accommodated by treating a pair of syllables as a single metrical element. In contrast, we never allow two syllables to project as a single asterisk. In our theory, syllables are projected onto

[5] The noun *exploit* is given final stress in *Walkers Pronouncing Dictionary* of 1852.

gridline 0 by rule (18), but poets may (occasionally) violate rule (18) and not project a given syllable, so where two syllables appear to project as one asterisk in fact one syllable projects and the other does not.[6] In the first and second lines the third syllable does not project as an asterisk, and in the third line the fourth does not project; this is shown in (30), where the syllables which do not project are marked by Δ (for the convenience of the reader: this symbol has no formal status). Gridline 0 in each case consists of ten asterisks, even though the line has 11 syllables.

```
(30)
  And gluttonous death, will instantly unjoynt
 )*     *) Δ  *     *)      *    *)  *    *)*  *)      gridline 0
 My body, and soule, and I shall sleepe a space,
 )*  *)Δ  *     *)      *    *)  *       *)    *    *)  gridline 0
 But my ever-waking part shall see that face,
 )*   Δ *)*    *)*     *)      *       *)   *    *)      gridline 0
```

Projection of an asterisk on gridline 0 is governed by rule (18); if this rule does not apply then a syllable will not project as an asterisk, and we have seen that this is a possibility. However, no rule permits an asterisk to appear on gridline 0 if it is not projected from a syllable; that is, an asterisk cannot project from a pause or rest, but only from an actual syllable. (As we will see, music differs in this regard.)

The iterative rules in words and in metrical lines

There is a deep similarity between the computations of stress in a word, which we discussed in the first part, and the computations that test the metricality of a line, which we discussed in the second part of this chapter. The metrical grid is generated in both domains by an iterative (repeating) rule which inserts parentheses into a sequence of asterisks; the rule also projects a new line of asterisks, and the set of asterisks comprises the grid. Each iterative rule involves a choice from the following five parameters, of which all but the first involve a choice between two alternatives.

(31)
(i) Insertion starts either just at the edge of the gridline, or one asterisk in, or two asterisks in.
(ii) Edge of the sequence (Left (L) / Right (R)) at which insertion begins.
(iii) Nature of parenthesis inserted (L/R).
(iv) Interval between consecutive insertions (2/3 asterisks).
(v) Location of head in each group (L/R).

[6] There is no general principle in English poetry determining which syllables cannot project, but there are some tendencies (e.g. syllable ending in a vowel preceding a syllable beginning with a vowel, as in (29, 30)). By contrast, the non-projection of syllables in lines of Romance poetry is subject to strict rules. (For discussion, see Fabb and Halle (2008)).

However, there are two important differences between the assignment of stress in words and the ascertaining of metricality of a line. First, the metrical rules do not alter the phonetic form of the line in any way; instead, the rules generate a grid from the phonetic form, and test whether certain phonetic characteristics of syllables match the position of the syllable in the grid (e.g. that it projects to an asterisk on a specific gridline). In contrast, by assigning stress to particular syllables in the line, the stress rules alter the phonetic form of the line after generating a grid from the line.

The second important difference in the use of iterative rules in metrical verse and in words is that the rules function to limit line length in metrical verse. This is because in metrical verse every gridline is subject to iterative rules (this is not true in words, as we saw above), and by virtue of condition (22), the final gridline must contain one asterisk. The conjunction of these two facts means that a well-formed grid can be generated only from a line with a specific number of gridline 0 asterisks. In comparison, the rules (14) for Creek words can generate a well-formed grid from a word of any length (because gridline 1 asterisks are grouped by a non-iterative rule). We noted earlier that metrical verse is divided into lines, and that lines are not linguistic entities. Now we see another way in which a line is not a linguistic entity: it is limited in length. Linguistic entities are not controlled in their length by linguistic rules; for example, the length of words or sentences is not so controlled.

In this and the previous sections the same kinds of iterative rules were used to generate grids both for metrical lines of verse, and for words (in the assignment of stress). Though the two domains are distinct, similar computations are employed in both domains. In the next section, we see that metrical structure in music is also generated by the same kind of rule.

Metre in music

In their pioneering book *A Generative Theory of Tonal Music*, Lerdahl and Jackendoff note that music also has metre and describe the metrical structure as involving those aspects of music that relate to the 'regular alternation of strong and weak beats at a number of hierarchical levels' (1983, p. 8). We show below that the beat pattern of music is the result of grouping the timing slots. In this we differ from Lerdahl and Jackendoff (1983), for whom 'beats do not possess inherent grouping' (p. 28).

The metre of music is traditionally represented by an array of dots which in its essentials is identical with the metrical grids that were studied above. For Lerdahl and Jackendoff, the grid is not generated from the piece of music, but instead comes into existence independently, and represents the rhythmic organization of the music. The asterisks (dots) on the lowest gridline represent beats (defined by them as points without duration, which are equidistant in time); beats which project to a higher gridline are experienced as stronger than beats which project to a lower gridline. The rule system itself places no limit on the number of gridlines, but, as Lerdahl and Jackendoff note, there is a practical limit based on human auditory perception of rhythm.

We accept the general principle that metrical structure in music is represented as a grid. However, this is a grid not subject to condition (22), which requires that the last generated gridline contain one asterisk: this condition helps control the length of the line in poetic metre. This means that the last-to-be-generated gridline may contain any number of asterisks, depending on how long the musical piece lasts. We suggest further that gridline 0 is projected not from the timeless beats, but from the time intervals between beats, with a defined, minimal time interval projecting as one asterisk. Both pitches and silences are assigned to time intervals. As a consequence, in music, a gridline 0 asterisk can project from a rest or silence, which is not possible in the metrical structure of verse.

However, we propose a major change in the explanation of why some grids are possible and others are not. Since for Lerdahl and Jackendoff any two-dimensional array of dots (asterisks) constitutes a potential grid, their major problem is to rule out the many arrays that are not possible as representations of musical form. For example, the grids in (32) are possible musical grids, but the grids in (33) are not.

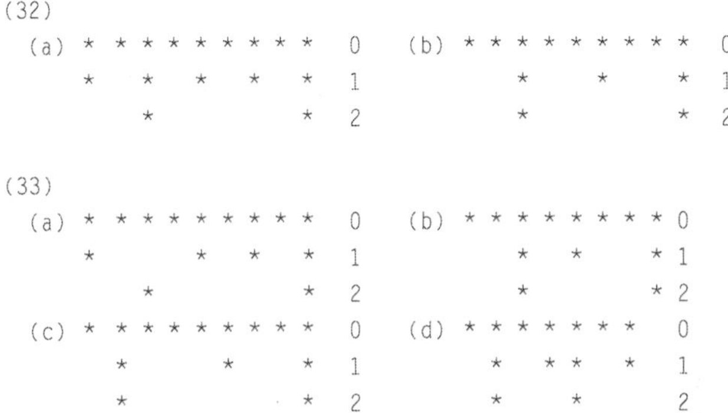

To rule out all the impossible grids, Jackendoff and Lerdahl (1983) formulate the metrical well-formedness rules (MWFRs) in (34).

(34)

MWFR 1 Every attack point must be associated with a beat at the smallest metrical level present at that point in the piece.

MWFR 2 Every beat at a given level must also be a beat at all smaller levels present at that point in the piece.

MWFR 3 At each metrical level, strong beats are spaced either two or three beats apart.

MWFR 4 The tactus and immediately larger metrical levels must consist of beats equally spaced throughout the piece. At the subtactus metrical levels, weak beats must be equally spaced between the surrounding strong beats.

(Jackendoff and Lerdahl, 1983, p. 97.)

Each note has an 'attack point', and a beat on the smallest metrical level corresponds to a gridline 0 asterisk in our grid. We have said that each timing slot projects as a gridline 0 asterisk; we can restate MWFR1 as this projection rule if we require that a note fully occupy a set of one or more timing slots. This is little more than a notational variant, but a more substantial difference can be seen when we consider the other three metrical well-formedness rules. In our account, the iterative rules take the place of the metrical well-formedness rules. None of the grids in (33) can be generated by iterative rules alone.

As we show below, all of the MFWRs are redundant if metrical grids are constructed with the help of the iterative rules of grid construction in the manner discussed in the preceding section. In particular, we assume that each note or pause has a duration that is a multiple of some minimal duration (most commonly, a 1/64 note) and we represent the minimal timing slot in a piece of music with a gridline 0 asterisk. Notes and pauses of duration longer than the minimum are assigned several consecutive timing slots. This is our equivalent of MFWR1.

MWFR2 filters out a grid such as (33a) where there is an asterisk on gridline 2 which does not have a vertically corresponding asterisk on gridline 1. In our account, such a grid cannot be generated because asterisks can appear on gridline n+1 only by being projected from gridline n. We do not need a filter such as MWFR2 to rule them out since our formalism generates only continuous asterisk columns.

MWFR3 filters out a grid such as (33c) where a pair of asterisks on gridline 1 is four (gridline 0) beats apart, or (33d) where a pair of asterisks on gridline 1 is one beat apart. Neither possibility can be generated by our rules, which generate asterisks on gridline n+1 by projecting one asterisk per group from binary groups on gridline n or from ternary groups on gridline n; but neither four-asterisk nor one-asterisk groups are possible on gridline n. Our theory does not need to invoke MWFR3 to exclude (33c).

MWFR4 filters out a grid such as (33b) where gridline 1 asterisks project from asterisks which on gridline 0 are sometimes two and sometimes three asterisks apart. We achieve this result by projecting gridline 1 asterisks as heads of groups of asterisks on gridline 0; the gridline 0 groups must be either consistently binary or consistently ternary, because parentheses are inserted by the iterative rule either at binary or at ternary intervals (but never a mixture).

Thus according to our account, all and only the well-formed grids can be generated by the iterative parenthesis-insertion rules which are based on setting the parameters in (31) and which are a part of universal grammar. In contrast the MFWRs do not have universal status, but instead function as ad hoc conditions which rule out some logically possible arrays of asterisks and parentheses. Our proposal that binary and ternary grouping is shared with the groupings in the assignment of stress to words and in the characterization of metres in metrical verse suggests a closer relationship between language and music than is found in Lerdahl and Jackendoff's account (1983, p. 85). (This gap between music and language is extended further in Lerdahl (2001, p. 285) who argues that this metrical grouping is related to grouping principles found in other aspects of musical form such 'pitch space'.)

We conclude this comparison by noting that Jackendoff and Lerdahl use the term 'grouping' to mean something different than we do. Their 'grouping structure' is the organization of the music into motives, themes, and so on (1983, p. 13); and they distinguish it from metrical structure. They consider grouping to be accessible to consciousness, and note that the elementary units of music (the notes and pauses) are perceived as being grouped together. It is largely for this reason that they insist that the metrical structure does not involve grouping: they say that there is no perception of a strong beat as grouped with the preceding weak beat but not grouped with the following (or vice versa). We agree with this claim about perception, while nevertheless holding that metrical elements are grouped, where grouping is implemented by the insertion of parentheses as sketched above. A metrical grid is a structure which explains certain aspects of the organization of syllables in the words of a language, or in the lines of metrical verse, and also of timing slots in music. There is no conscious access to the rules which generate the grid or to the grid itself, and so no consciousness of the grouping of elements. The parentheses and the grouping of elements are part of the algorithm which generates the grid, but the grouping is not directly perceived in any of the three modalities: music, language, or poetry.

In (36) below, we show two lines of a song by George Peale, set to music by John Dowling. Above the line we indicate the notes,[7] and the musical grid; the musical grid is generated by the rules in (35). Gridline 0 asterisks project from timing slots corresponding to half-notes. The musical grid should be thought of as continuous over the two verselines. The last gridline to be generated, gridline 2, is ungrouped and contains any number of asterisks (it is not subject to condition (22)). (Below the lines we write the grid for the metrical structure of the poetry, which we return to shortly.)

(35)

(a) Gridline 0: starting just at the L edge, insert a L parenthesis, form ternary groups, heads L.

(b) Gridline 1: starting just at the L edge, insert a L parenthesis, form binary groups, heads L.

(36)

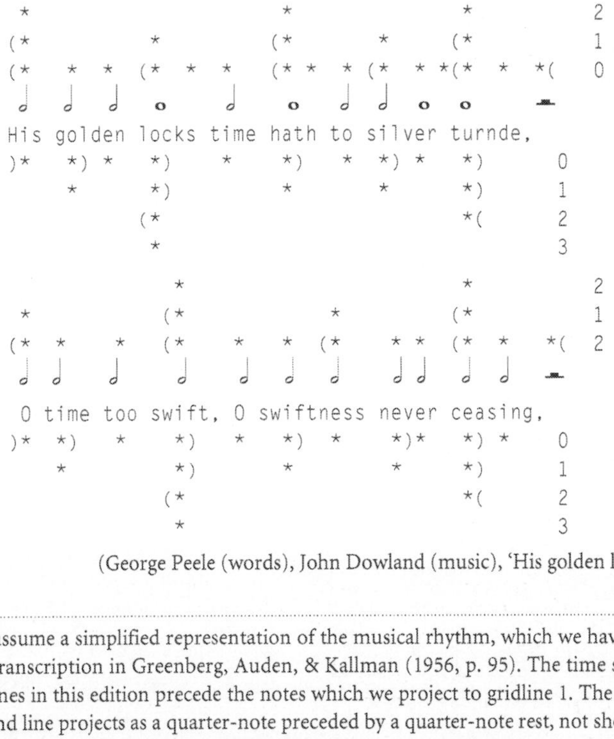

```
*                          *                   *            2
(*          *              (*          *       (*           1
(*    *   *   (*   *   *   (*  *   *  (*   *  *(*   *   *(  0
His golden locks time hath to silver turnde,
)*    *)  *   *)       *   *)     *   *)  *    *)       0
      *       *)           *          *        *)       1
            (*                                 *(       2
              *                                         3

                *                              *            2
*             (*              *               (*            1
(*  *     *   (*       *   *  (*       * *    (*   *    *(  2
O time too swift, O swiftness never ceasing,
)*  *)    *    *)    *    *)   *      *)*     *) *      0
    *          *)         *           *       *)        1
             (*                               *(        2
               *                                        3
```

(George Peele (words), John Dowland (music), 'His golden locks', 1587.)

7 We assume a simplified representation of the musical rhythm, which we have adapted from the transcription in Greenberg, Auden, & Kallman (1956, p. 95). The time signature is 3/2; barlines in this edition precede the notes which we project to gridline 1. The word 'O' in the second line projects as a quarter-note preceded by a quarter-note rest, not shown here.

The relation between the musical grid and the rhythm of the music is captured formally by the rule (37).

(37) A note projecting to gridline n+1 is assigned greater prominence than the nearest note projecting to gridline n.

Below each of the lines of the poem we show the metrical grid that characterizes their metre, where each gridline 0 asterisk projects from a syllable; the lines are in iambic pentameter, and the grid is generated by the rules in (27).

The musical grid above the line and the poetic metrical grid below the line are both generated by rules based on the parameters in (31). This identity reflects a deep connection between music and language, but in almost every other respect, the musical and poetic representations are different. Though the rules are of the same kind, the actual rules used to generate the respective musical and metrical grids are different. The syllables which project (via their notes, and timing slots) to higher-numbered gridlines in the musical grid are not always the syllables which project to higher-numbered gridlines in the metrical grid of the poem. (The two lines of the song differ in that the first line has a closer correlation between text and tune than the second.) Note in particular that the words *golden* and *swiftness* contain maxima which must project to gridline 1 in the poetic metrical grid, but do not project as prominent in the musical grid.

For poetic metre, the grid functions to fix the length of the line, and this is achieved by a combination of requiring iterative rules on every gridline and the condition (22) requiring the last-to-be-generated gridline (the bottom-most in our grids) to have one asterisk. The first of these requirements is relaxed in the assignment of stress to words, which can therefore have groups of any length on certain gridlines and so no overall control on size. The second of these requirements is relaxed in music, where the last-to-be-generated gridline can contain any number of asterisks; unlike metrical poetry, musical pieces are not divided into metrical sections (lines) of pre-set lengths.

Conclusion

Above we examined three very different sets of data—the stress of words, metre in poetry, and metre in music—and we showed that these different bodies of fact are accounted for by grouping elements in a linear sequence into the hierarchical pattern of the metrical grid. In all three cases the elements were grouped into either pairs or triplets, marking one of the elements as head. The heads constitute a new (and sparser) sequence of elements, which in turn is subject to the further grouping. In the assignment of stress to words and in the construction of poetic metre the elements subject to grouping are syllables, whereas in music, it is timing slots that are grouped.

Metrical structure in all three cases is not a characteristic of the acoustic signal, but part of a mental representation of words or lines of verse, or sequences of music. Since language, poetry, and music are all products of the human mind it is perhaps not surprising that we find the same mechanism operating in these three domains. What is new here is the detail, namely that the entities subject to grouping are syllables in language, but timing slots in music; that grouping is implemented everywhere by junctures of the same kind (which we have represented by ordinary parentheses), and that grouping is recursive; i.e. that the heads of groups are projected on a separate gridline and are themselves subject to grouping.

Underlying the various groupings there must be specific neurobiological mechanisms, the nature of which is a mystery at this time. In view of the rapid advances that biology has achieved during the last fifty years, it can be hoped that this mystery will be solved in the not too distant future.

References

Fabb, N. (2002). *Language and literary structure. The linguistic analysis of form in verse and narrative.* Cambridge: Cambridge University Press.

Fabb, N., & Halle, M. (2008). *Meter in poetry. A new theory.* Cambridge: Cambridge University Press.

Greenberg, N., Auden, W. H., & Kallman, C. (1956). *An Elizabethan song book. Lute songs madrigals and rounds.* Garden City, N.Y.: Doubleday Anchor Books.

Halle, M. (1998). The stress of English words. *Linguistic Inquiry, 29,* 539–68.

Halle, M., & Vergnaud, J-R. (1987). *An essay on stress.* Cambridge, MA: MIT Press.

Haas, M. R. (1977). Tonal accent in Creek. In L. Hyman (Ed.), *Studies in stress and accent* (Southern California Occasional Papers in Linguistics vol. 4, pp. 195–208). Los Angeles, CA: University of Southern California.

Hayes, B. (1981). *A metrical theory of stress rules* (PhD dissertation). MIT, Cambridge, MA.

Hayes, B. (1995). *Metrical stress theory.* Chicago, IL: University of Chicago Press.

Idsardi, W. (1992). *The computation of prosody* (PhD Dissertation). MIT, Cambridge, MA.

Lerdahl, F. (2001). *Tonal pitch space.* New York: Oxford University Press.

Lerdahl, F., & Jackendoff, R. (1983). *A generative theory of tonal music.* Cambridge MA: MIT Press.

Liberman, M. (1975). The intonational system of English (PhD dissertation). MIT Department of Linguistics, Cambridge, MA.

Liberman, M., & Prince, A. (1977). On stress and linguistic rhythm. *Linguistic Inquiry, 8,* 249–336.

Prince, A. (1983). Relating to the grid. *Linguistic Inquiry, 14,* 19–100.

Chapter 3

The Fabb–Halle approach to metrical stress theory as a window on commonalities between music and language

Laura Dilley and J. Devin McAuley

The world's languages are universally characterized as involving alternations of relatively stronger and weaker prosodic units or events; these alternations of more and less prominent events are often described as rhythmical in nature. The elegant framework for describing these prosodic alternations put forward by Fabb and Halle in Chapter 2 in this volume fits within a general theoretical approach that has come to be known over the last 30 years as *metrical stress theory*. In this chapter, we situate the Fabb–Halle approach within the wider context of metrical stress theory and within linguistics more broadly, while responding to some of the specific claims made in Fabb and Halle's chapter. Taking this broader perspective makes possible an appreciation of the differences between the Fabb–Halle approach to metrical stress theory (hereafter, FH) and other approaches within the same theoretical framework.

The chapter is organized as follows. First, we describe metrical stress theory and how it has evolved over the years. Second, we review claims made by FH and evaluate whether their approach provides a reasonable and better description of basic similarities between music and language than other approaches, such as Lerdahl and Jackendoff (1983), hereafter LJ. Third, we address the descriptive versus explanatory adequacy of the theory, with particular emphasis on the question of whether the theory affords an *explanation* of the various patterns of prosodic prominence and grouping associated with the world's linguistic prosodic systems. Finally, we consider an alternative approach that seeks a perceptual basis for commonalities between music and language.

The origins of metrical stress theory and its role in the study of language

This article aims to provide perspective on (1) how the particular theoretical framework advanced in FH fits into the more general theoretical framework of metrical stress theory, as well as (2) how the specialty area of linguistics represented in FH fits in with the study of language overall. With respect to the former point, FH is one instantiation of metrical stress theory, a theoretical approach which has sought generally to account for word- and phrase-level stress patterns and other prosodic phenomena in terms of hierarchical constructs involving metrical grid and tree structures similar to those used in music to account for relative prominence. The seminal ideas behind metrical stress theory were first advanced by Liberman (1975) in his PhD dissertation; since then many variations on the central ideas of this original work have been put forward. Liberman's proposals, elaborated in Liberman and Prince (1977), centred on the idea that variations in stress level are due to underlying hierarchical structures of prominence or grouping. Liberman's proposals provided a counterpoint to the dominant theoretical approach at the time, which was to treat stress as a type of segmental distinctive feature. (See Jakobson, Fant, & Halle, 1952; Stevens, 2000 for a discussion of distinctive features.) The treatment of stress as a distinctive feature had built on the work of the American structuralist school of linguistics (e.g. Trager & Smith, 1951) and had culminated in *The Sound Pattern of English* (Chomsky & Halle, 1968), often abbreviated *SPE*. Liberman's insight was that variations in word stress can be explained by hierarchical structures (e.g. grid structures) similar to those found in music. The observations afforded under Liberman's approach made word stress appear much more regular than it seemed under competing accounts and obviated the need for assuming linguistic mechanisms such as cyclic rule application and stress subordination proposed in *SPE*.

The inherent connection between music and language has remained a running theme throughout much, but not all, subsequent work that has modified and refined the original ideas behind metrical stress theory. Significant debates in the 1980s centred on the relative importance for linguistic accounts of prosodic phenomena of two sorts of interrelated mechanisms for accounting for metrical prominence introduced in Liberman (1975). The first was the metrical grid, in which discrete events (e.g. syllables) were represented by X's; these X's indicate time slots, and the degree of prominence is represented by the height of a column of X's. The second was a tree structure, an example of which is shown in Figure 3.1. The nodes of a tree are labelled *s* (strong) and *w* (weak) to mark relative prominence, and grids (patterns of relative prominence) can then be read off the tree.

Early work in metrical theory (e.g. Hayes, 1984; Liberman, 1975; Liberman & Prince, 1977) emphasized tree formalisms while also making use of grids; many subsequent arguments centred on whether both grids and trees were necessary to account for prominence patterns and related phenomena across languages. Noteworthy proponents of a 'grid-only' approach were Prince (1983) and Selkirk (1984), while the charge for a 'tree-only' approach was led by Giegerich (1985). Hybrid approaches

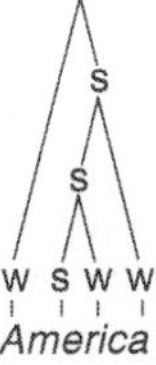

Fig. 3.1 An example of a tree structure used in some versions of metrical stress theory.

of various sorts incorporated both a mechanism for grouping (e.g. trees), as well as a mechanism for relative prominence (i.e. a grid of some kind) (Halle & Vergnaud, 1987; Hammond, 1984; Hayes, 1983, 1984). Hammond (1984) and Halle and Vergnaud (1987) in particular developed a structure that has come to be called a 'bracketed grid', in which X's are grouped by parentheses; this type of structure survives to populate the FH paper. Connections between music and language have played a role in various instantiations of metrical theory to varying degrees, from not at all to substantial.

The second consideration which provides perspective on FH is that this work and almost all of the work on metrical stress theory falls within a specialty branch of linguistics known as *theoretical phonology*. Researchers working in this area aim to develop broad, theoretical accounts for similarities and differences in the sound patterns of the world's languages, focusing largely on theoretical constructs and linguistic abstractions. Many theoretical phonologists do not focus on details of sound signals or properties of human perception and cognition which might shape linguistic knowledge and intuition; experiments involving manipulation of sound stimuli also fall largely outside of theoretical phonology.[1] Given that many subdisciplines of linguistics and psychology deal in some way with the study of language-based sound systems, it is noteworthy that certain statements made in FH apply narrowly to the subdiscipline of theoretical phonology, for example: 'It is the goal of the linguist to discover which combination of grid-building rules, and which stress-assigning rules, are required to explain the pattern of stresses which we find in the words of a specific language'. In this statement, FH are clearly equating 'linguist' with 'theoretical phonologist'; researchers working in other subdisciplines might well state the goals of their inquiries into sound systems differently.

Having considered the history of metrical stress theory and the field of linguistics generally, it is now possible to better appreciate particulars of the FH approach. The account proposed in FH permits a description of variations in stress systems of many languages using a combination of bracketed grids, iterative rules, and other types of rules. FH claim that this theoretical approach is simpler than that of LJ, who propose a series of metrical and grouping well-formedness rules which act to rule out impossible grid structures. Moreover, FH claim that in their theory music and language are more closely linked than in the work of LJ. FH provides an elegant description of stress patterns, and its ability to account for data from a variety of languages, as well as different types of structure (e.g. prose vs. poetry), is provocative. In the remainder of the chapter, we consider two issues. First, to what extent does FH provide a reasonable description of basic similarities between music and language? Second, to what extent does the theory afford an explanation of the various patterns of prosodic prominence and grouping associated with the world's linguistic prosodic systems?

[1] Note that the distinct but related sub-area of linguistics known as *laboratory phonology* integrates theoretical work with empirical data from experiments. See Pierrehumbert et al. (2000) for more information on this approach.

The FH approach as a reflection of the 'closeness' of music and language

Does the FH account entail a description that reflects the basic similarities between music and language? Stated differently, does FH's claim that their theory more closely links music and language than that of LJ stand up? In the following we consider three ways in which the FH instantiation of metrical stress theory presents a view of language that makes it seem relatively more dissimilar to music than might be otherwise envisioned.

First, consider that in FH and in many other versions of metrical theory, strong and largely a priori restrictions are assumed on types of grouping structures that can be formed from syllables in a word, leading to the appearance of greater dissimilarity between linguistic and musical structures than if these restrictions were not assumed. For example, FH assume that parses of metrical events on a given line of the grid must be all-binary or all-ternary. That is, for a given line of the grid, parsing rules apply iteratively such that all (complete) groups have exactly the same number of syllables (two or three). In other words, a group of two can't occur adjacent to a group of three or vice versa. This presents a view of language which suggests deviation from music in several respects. In music, there is no prohibition against alternations of binary and ternary groupings—groupings of two can follow groupings of three without penalty.

Perhaps of more concern for whether metrical theory reflects similarities in music and in language is the fact that the assumption in FH of all-binary or all-ternary parses entails an adjunct assumption of something called *extrametricality*. Extrametricality is assumed to cause a syllable not to belong to *any* group; such a mechanism is useful in theories which seek to limit the number of possible grouping structures by permitting rules for stress assignment to 'skip over' certain syllables in counting, treating them as if they were invisible. The notion of extrametricality has a long and rich history in theoretical phonology (Halle & Vergnaud, 1987; Hayes, 1979, 1981; Ito, 1986; Liberman & Prince, 1977; Roca, 1992); see Hayes (1995, pp. 58–60) for an overview. To illustrate how this mechanism works, consider that the word *extrametricality* seems to surface as a sequence of two binary feet plus a ternary foot, i.e. (s w) (s w) (s w w); this word would be parsed under FH and related approaches as three binary feet plus a final extrametrical syllable, i.e. (s w) (s w) (s w) w. A notion of extrametricality is critical to the FH account and much related work in metrical stress theory. While FH assumes that ternary feet exist in the inventory of possible structures, other so-called parametric versions of metrical theory take the hard line of assuming that ternary feet are not part of the possible inventory of grouping structures across languages. For example, Hayes (1981; 1995) dispenses with ternary feet entirely, instead assuming the existence of only binary (or unbounded) feet. Under associated supporting assumptions, Hayes accounts for attested ternary linguistic stress systems (i.e. languages in which stresses occur every three syllables within words, including Cayuvava, Pacific Yupik, and Sentani), as repeated sequences of a binary foot, plus an extrametrical syllable. (See Hayes, 1995, Chapter 8, for a discussion of these systems.) While these parametric versions of metrical theory comprise elegant descriptions with clever mechanisms for deriving stress patterns of words in many languages, the constraining nature of parametric assumptions of all-binary or all-ternary parses, combined with notions of extrametricality, seem to imply a wider divide between language and music than in an alternative theory which does not place such restrictions on ternary groupings.

In music, there is no such thing as extrametricality, and elements in a closely connected musical sequence do not occur 'ungrouped'. Rather, closely connected musical elements tend to be heard as grouped into twos and threes. (See Handel, 1989 for a review.) If fewer restrictions were placed on foot inventories of languages in under parametric metrical theories (e.g. the assumption that parses are all-binary or all-ternary), there would be no clear need for an adjunct notion of extrametricality, at least to account for prosodic phenomena.[2] These restrictions do not occur in music, and LJ do not assume a priori all-ternary or all-binary parses, nor a notion of extrametricality, to account for musical data; hence, the LJ approach seems to present a window in which music and language are more closely linked than under FH and related linguistic work.

A second respect in which the FH approach seems to cast a wider chasm between music and language has to do with the mechanism(s) associated with parenthesis insertion. The proposed mechanism in language for metre and grouping is an 'iterative' rule which inserts either a left or right parenthesis at regular intervals (every two or every three syllables). Such an iterative grouping mechanism (consisting of insertion of either right or left parentheses in sequences of abstract timing events) does not have any clear parallel in music. In essence, the mechanism assumes two different types of juncture ('right' and 'left'). The distinction in parenthesis type, together with the ability to count iteratively from either the left or right side of the word, permits the theory to render extrametrical a syllable either at the beginning or at the end of a string. But what does a distinction in type of parenthesis mean? What is the difference between a juncture of a 'left' parenthesis vs. a 'right' parenthesis? It is not clear what these correspond to in terms of phonetic characteristics, perceptual or structural conceptualizations, etc. The explanatory power of these distinctions is unclear when considered in a broader context. Again, the distinction in parenthesis type, together with the notion of extrametricality, are unnecessary if it is simply assumed that groups can be a mixture of binary and ternary feet.

Third, there are problems with the notion of 'iterativity'. The iterative application of grouping of events into twos and threes is a cornerstone of the FH account and related work (e.g. Idsardi, 1992). Yet, there is no clear corresponding notion of iterativity in music. Iterativity might or might not be likened to 'hysteresis'—however, the strictness of structure implied by the iterativity mechanism is not the case for music. Variations in timing, accentuation, etc. are readily adapted to, undercutting a strict notion of 'iterativity' in music. FH note that the notion of iterativity is controversial

[2] The notion of extrametricality has also been applied to segments (i.e. phonemes) comprising a syllable, in addition to syllables themselves. For example, extrametricality is invoked to explain certain facts about syllabification, i.e. how segments are arranged into syllables (Ito, 1986). Such arguments are often brought up in support of the notion of extrametricality generally, thereby bolstering its role in prosodics.

from the standpoint of linguistics as well, in that iterative rules do not otherwise occur in linguistic or musical sound systems. (See also Halle, 1990; Halle & Vergnaud, 1987).

Descriptive versus explanatory adequacy of the FH approach

It is important to consider what the FH approach does and does not attempt to do. In this regard, while the FH approach describes the data, it does not seek to explain how linguistic communication by sound works. Indeed, it considers only a limited set of structures which humans arguably might be thought to have in their heads. Moreover, it does not seek to describe, nor to explain, how differences of sound structure (e.g. the loudness level of syllables) might physically convey prosodic differences, nor how listeners might interpret these differences of detail of the speech signal in terms of underlying structures. FH assume that their system operates at a wholly separate level of description from the principles which are operational for physical, linguistic sound systems. Moreover, it seems unreasonable that FH should be held to the standard of explaining nuances of perception, and how sound systems convey prosodic grouping and prominence through details of physics. However, there are compelling reasons to consider whether other types of explanations might afford greater, or at least complementary, insight into how speakers and listeners communicate the nuances of prosodic properties in language.

One noteworthy aspect of the FH view and much other work in metrical phonology is the explicit assumption that linguistic structures making up grids are not privy to introspection. Moreover, FH assume that individuals' perceived sense of grouping may or may not correspond to underlying linguistic groups. By taking this tack FH assume that behavioural judgements and other types of experimentation aimed at uncovering the structures which individuals have in their heads bear no definable relationship to the types of structures in their metrical theory. As a result, the FH approach is moved into a realm in which it cannot reasonably be tested by most, if not all, behavioural methods. The assumption of a lack of connection between listeners' surface perceptions and behaviour and the underlying linguistic structures leads to an increase in complexity in any overarching theory of linguistic communication via prosodic sound systems. This is because such an approach requires a wholly separate mechanism to be posited to explain *perceived* groupings, as separate from the underlying ones. A theory which proposes (or implicitly assumes) two types of grouping—one implicit and the other explicit, where the implicit (linguistic) grouping might have an inherently different structure that the explicit grouping, is not very parsimonious.

A common perceptual basis for musical structure and prosodic patterns in language

An alternative approach which is being pursued by a number of researchers is to assume as a starting point the likelihood of shared mechanisms for processing music and language which might be responsible for both perception and production of metrical patterns in both domains (e.g. Cummins & Port, 1998; Dilley & McAuley, 2008;

Fedorenko, Patel, Casasanto, Winawer, & Gibson, 2009; Patel, 2005). For example, work by Dilley (2005; 2008) builds on traditional metrical stress frameworks and facts about English intonation while positing a strong connection between music and language. Other recent work (Dilley & McAuley, 2008) aims to identify whether specific properties of sound (amplitude, frequency, duration, timbre, etc.) lead to similar perceptions about grouping and metre in speech and non-speech auditory perception, a finding which would support shared processing mechanisms for speech and non-speech perception. This work builds on a relatively large literature on non-speech auditory perception illustrating effects of frequency, duration, and amplitude patterning on perceived organization of auditory sequences. In general, when individuals hear simple tone sequences, the frequency, duration and amplitude patterning of sequence elements (i.e. tones) conveys a sense of sequence organization and structure. Perceived organization includes the sense that some sequence elements belong together (i.e. they are grouped), that within a group some elements are accented, while others are not, and that accent patterns tend to repeat. For example, in an isochronous sequence of tones of equal amplitude and duration alternating between a fixed high (H) and fixed low (L) frequency, e.g. HLHLHL, listeners tend to hear repeating strong-weak binary groupings of tones with either the high or low tone as accented and beginning each group, i.e. (<u>H</u>L)(<u>H</u>L)(<u>H</u>L) or (<u>L</u>H)(<u>L</u>H)(<u>L</u>H) (Woodrow, 1909, 1911). Similarly, repeating strong-weak binary patterns of accents induced by distal (i.e. remote, distant, or non-local) frequency, duration, and/or amplitude patterning of sequence elements tends to generate periodic expectations about the grouping and perceived accentuation of later sequence elements, even when there are no explicit proximal (i.e. local) acoustic cues to groupings and accents in those elements (Boltz, 1993; Jones, 1976; Jones & Boltz, 1989; Large & Jones, 1999; McAuley & Jones, 2003; Povel & Essens, 1985; Thomassen, 1982).

Our experiments used lexically ambiguous syllable sequences (e.g. *footnote bookworm, foot notebook worm*) to examine how distal frequency and timing cues would affect segmentation of these proximal syllable strings into words. The acoustic characteristics of the final three syllables in our target experimental strings were held constant with H, L, and H pitch, and the pitch and durational pattern of the preceding, distal syllables was manipulated using computer speech resynthesis techniques. We showed that perception of grouping of syllables into words depended on the preceding prosodic context in precisely the way expected if listeners were applying principles to speech that they apply to non-speech auditory sequences alternating in pitch and/or duration (Dilley & McAuley, 2008), even though the acoustic characteristics of the syllables were identical. Support was found for a perceptual grouping hypothesis in which distal prosodic characteristics established perceived patterns of pitch and rhythm that affected the grouping of syllables into prosodic units in just the manner expected for non-speech auditory perception, thereby influencing word segmentation and lexical processing. This work fits into a growing body of interdisciplinary findings demonstrating evidence for shared processing resources in music and in language. We feel that such interdisciplinary experimental lines of work are likely to be profitable in terms of coming to understand how and why speakers perceive and produce prosodic patterning as they do in language. In this regard, it seems useful to pursue interdisciplinary research agendas in which experimental techniques as well as descriptive linguistic apparatuses such as those afforded in FH and related work can be brought to bear in understanding linguistic processing.

A variety of approaches are being pursued to uncover evidence of common processing mechanisms for music and speech. For example, Patel and colleagues are actively pursuing the question of shared processing mechanisms for music and language using a wide range of techniques. These include investigations of pitch, timing, and structural processing deficits in individuals with acquired or congenital amusia (Patel, 2005; Patel, Foxton, & Griffiths, 2005; Patel, Iversen, Wassenaar, & Hagoort, 2008), comparisons of human and nonhuman rhythm perception and production ability (Patel & Iversen, 2006; Patel, Iversen, Bregman, Schulz, & Schulz, 2008), investigations of processing demands in normal speakers using standard psycholinguistic tasks (Fedorenko et al., 2009; Slevc, Rosenberg, & Patel, 2008), and comparisons of temporal and pitch properties of speech and music from different cultures (Patel & Daniele, 2003; Patel, Iversen, & Rosenberg, 2006). Moreover, additional work aims to identify production constraints on rhythmic sequences in speech which affect both linguistic and musical performance similarly, while building alternative linguistic theoretical frameworks to accommodate such findings (Cummins & Port, 1998; Port, 2003). Perspectives on music and language processing are also greatly aided by developmental work (Hannon & Johnson, 2005; Hannon & Trehub, 2005) and by use of electrophysiological measures comparing processing of speech and music (Magne, Schon, & Besson, 2003; Snyder & Large, 2005).

We can envision the outline of a theory which builds on many core insights of metrical stress theory, including those embraced in FH, but in which principles of perception and cognition would play a central role to jointly explain facts about music and language. In this respect, we agree with FH that research is presently far from this goal, but that it is a desirable one to try to achieve. To this end, a theoretical perspective which both strives for parsimony and holds high the aim of reflecting commonalities between music and language seems most likely to afford the greatest insight into sound-based human communication systems.

References

Boltz, M. (1993). The generation of temporal and melodic expectancies during musical listening. *Perception and Psychophysics, 53*(6), 585–600.

Chomsky, N., & Halle, M. (1968). *The Sound Pattern of English*. New York: Harper & Row.

Cummins, F., & Port, R. F. (1998). Rhythmic constraints on stress timing in English. *Journal of Phonetics, 26*, 145–71.

Dilley, L. C. (2005). *The phonetics and phonology of tonal systems* (Unpublished PhD dissertation). MIT, Cambridge, MA.

Dilley, L. C. (2008). On the dual relativity of tone. In *Proceedings of the 41st Meeting of the Chicago Linguistics Society (2005)* (Vol. 41, pp. 129–144). Chicago, IL: CLS.

Dilley, L. C., & McAuley, J. D. (2008). Distal prosodic context affects word segmentation and lexical processing. *Journal of Memory and Language, 59*(3), 294–311.

Fedorenko, E., Patel, A. D., Casasanto, D., Winawer, J., & Gibson, E. (2009). Structural integration in language and music: Evidence for a shared system. *Memory and Cognition, 37*(1), 1–9.

Giegerich, H. J. (1985). *Metrical Phonology and Phonological Structure: German and English.* Cambridge: Cambridge University Press.

Halle, M. (1990). Respecting metrical stucture. *Natural Language and Linguistic Theory, 8*, 149–76.

Halle, M., & Vergnaud, J.-R. (1987). *An Essay on Stress.* Cambridge, MA: MIT Press.

Hammond, M. (1984). *Constraining metrical theory: A modular theory of rhythm and distressing* (Unpublished PhD dissertation). University of California, Los Angeles.

Handel, S. (1989). *Listening: An Introduction to the Perception of Auditory Events.* Cambridge, MA: MIT Press.

Hannon, E. E., & Johnson, S. P. (2005). Infants use meter to categorize rhythms and melodies: Implications for musical structure learning. *Cognitive Psychology, 50*, 354–77.

Hannon, E. E., & Trehub, S. E. (2005). Tuning in to musical rhythms: Infants learn more readily than adults. *Proceedings of the National Academy of Sciences (USA), 102*, 12639–43.

Hayes, B. (1979). Extrametricality. *MIT Working Papers in Linguistics, 1*, 77–86.

Hayes, B. (1981). *A metrical theory of stress rules* (Unpublished PhD dissertation). MIT, Cambridge, MA.

Hayes, B. (1983). A grid-based theory of English meter. *Linguistic Inquiry, 14*, 357–394.

Hayes, B. (1984). The phonology of rhythm in English. *Linguistic Inquiry, 15*, 33–74.

Hayes, B. (1995). *Metrical Stress Theory.* Chicago, IL: University of Chicago Press.

Idsardi, W. (1992). *The computation of prosody* (Unpublished PhD dissertation). Massachusetts Institute of Technology, Cambridge, MA.

Ito, J. (1986). *Syllable theory in prosodic phonology* (Unpublished PhD dissertation). University of Massachusetts, Amherst, MA.

Jakobson, R., Fant, G., & Halle, M. (1952). *Preliminaries to Speech Analysis.* Cambridge, MA: MIT Press.

Jones, M. R. (1976). Time, our lost dimension: Toward a new theory of perception, attention, and memory. *Psychological Review, 83*(5), 323–55.

Jones, M. R., & Boltz, M. (1989). Dynamic attending and responses to time. *Psychological Review, 96*(3), 459–91.

Large, E. W., & Jones, M. R. (1999). The dynamics of attending: How people track time-varying events. *Psychological Review, 106*(1), 119–59.

Lerdahl, F., & Jackendoff, R. (1983). *A Generative Theory of Tonal Music.* Cambridge, MA: MIT Press.

Liberman, M. (1975). *The intonation system of English* (Unpublished PhD dissertation). MIT, Cambridge, MA.

Liberman, M., & Prince, A. (1977). On stress and linguistic rhythm. *Linguistic Inquiry, 8*(2), 249–336.

Magne, C., Schon, D., & Besson, M. (2003). Prosodic and melodic processing in adults and children: Behavioural and electrophysiological approaches. *Annals New York Academy of Sciences, 999*, 461–76.

McAuley, J. D., & Jones, M. R. (2003). Modeling effects of rhythmic context on perceived duration: A comparison of interval and entrainment approaches to short-interval timing. *Journal of Experimental Psychology: Human Perception & Performance, 29*(6), 1102–25.

Patel, A. D. (2005). The relationship of music to the melody of speech and to syntactic processing disorders in aphasia. *Annals of the New York Academy of Sciences, 1060*, 59–70.

Patel, A. D., & Daniele, J. R. (2003). An empirical comparison of rhythm in language and music. *Cognition, 87*, B35–B45.

Patel, A. D., Foxton, J., & Griffiths, T. D. (2005). Musically tone-deaf individuals have difficulty discriminating intonation contours extracted from speech. *Brain and Cognition, 59*, 310–13.

Patel, A. D., & Iversen, J. R. (2006). A non-human animal cam drum a steady beat on a musical instrument. In M. Baroni, A. R. Adessi, R. Caterina & M. Costa (Eds), *Proceedings of the 9th International Conference on Music Perception & Cognition* (p. 477). Bologna, Italy.

Patel, A. D., Iversen, J. R., Bregman, M. R., Schulz, I., & Schulz, C. (2008). 'Investigating the human-specificity of synchronization to music.' Paper presented at the 10th International Conference on Music Perception and Cognition, Sapporo, Japan.

Patel, A. D., Iversen, J. R., & Rosenberg, J. C. (2006). Comparing the rhythm and melody of speech and music: The case of British English and French. *Journal of Acoustical Society of America, 119*, 3034–47.

Patel, A. D., Iversen, J. R., Wassenaar, M., & Hagoort, P. (2008). Musical syntactic processing in agrammatic Broca's aphasia. *Aphasiology, 22*, 776–89.

Pierrehumbert, J., Beckman, M., & Ladd, D. R. (2000). Conceptual foundations of phonology as a laboratory science. In N. Burton-Roberts, P. Carr & G. J. Docherty (Eds), *Conceptual and Empirical Foundations of Phonology* (pp. 273–303). Oxford: Oxford University Press.

Port, R. F. (2003). Meter and speech. *Journal of Phonetics, 31*, 599–611.

Povel, D. J., & Essens, P. (1985). Perception of temporal patterns. *Music Perception, 2*(4), 411–40.

Prince, A. (1983). Relating to the grid. *Linguistic Inquiry, 14*, 19–100.

Roca, I. (1992). Constraining extrametricality. In U. Dressler, H. Luschützky, J. Rennison & O. Pfeiffer (Eds.), *Phonologica 1988* (pp. 239–48). Cambridge: Cambridge University Press.

Selkirk, E. O. (1984). *Phonology and Syntax: The Relation Between Sound and Structure.* Cambridge, MA: MIT Press.

Slevc, L. R., Rosenberg, J. C., & Patel, A. D. (2008). Language, music and modularity: Evidence for shared processing of linguistic and musical syntax. In K. Miyazaki, Y. Hiraga, M. Adachi, Y. Nakajima & M. Tsuzaki (Eds), *10th International Conference on Music Perception and Cognition* (pp. 598–605). Sapporo, Japan.

Snyder, J. S., & Large, E. W. (2005). Gamma-band activity reflects the metric structure of rhythmic tone sequences. *Cognitive Brain Research, 24*, 117–26.

Stevens, K. N. (2000). *Acoustic Phonetics.* Cambridge, MA: MIT Press.

Thomassen, J. M. (1982). Melodic accent: Experiments and a tentative model. *Journal of the Acoustical Society of America, 71*(6), 1596–605.

Trager, G. L., & Smith, H. L. (1951). *An outline of English structure.* Washington, DC: American Council of Learned Societies.

Woodrow, H. (1909). A quantitative study of rhythm. *Archives of Psychology, 14*, 1–66.

Woodrow, H. (1911). The role of pitch in rhythm. *The Psychological Review, 18*, 54–77.

Chapter 4

Metrical structure and the prosodic hierarchy

Brechtje Post

A steadily growing body of evidence supports the key insight of Lerdahl and Jackendoff's seminal work that language and music share the same kind of hierarchical structuring of the incoming sound stream (Lerdahl & Jackendoff, 1983). In both domains, elements can be grouped together into larger chunks, segmenting the sound stream into hierarchically organized constituents of varying sizes. Hierarchical structuring also becomes apparent when elements are contrasted, for instance through prominence differences, and such differences can be insightfully expressed in terms of metrical grids (Lerdahl & Jackendoff, 1983; Jackendoff & Lerdahl, 2006; Fabb & Halle, Chapter 2, this volume).

Fabb and Halle's proposal takes the analogy further. They argue that word stress as well as metre in verse and music are all governed by the same computational principle, which groups elements into the hierarchical pattern of the metrical grid. In language, the principle accounts for differences in prominence between syllables, explaining the pattern of stresses in words by means of a combination of rules for grid-building and prominence-assignment. In poetry, it accounts for length restrictions and the placement of marked syllables in metrical grids, and in music, the grouping of timing slots in the metrical grid accounts for its beat pattern. This implies that the parallels between language, poetry and music run much deeper than has so far been suggested (Fabb and Halle, Chapter 2, this volume), which tallies with recent claims that different forms of temporally ordered human behaviour all show strong parallels in the way in which they are structured, reflecting the sharing of cognitive and neural resources (e.g. Gilbers & Schreuder, 2006).

However, the grid does not suffice to account for prominence distribution in language. In some languages, like French, the relation between word stress and patterns of prominence in speech is rather tenuous—so tenuous, in fact, that the existence of lexical stress is called into question (Coustenoble & Armstrong, 1934, p. 4; Pulgram, 1965, pp. 132–33; Rossi, 1979). I will argue that mechanisms for hierarchical grouping above the level of the word are required to account for the facts. In language, interface constraints that regulate syntax–phonology mappings interact with well-formedness constraints on constituency length and accent distribution, including the metrical grouping principle of Fabb and Halle's proposal (cf. Post, forthcoming). The effects of the interaction between these constraints are akin to time-span reduction in music in Lerdahl and Jackendoff's work (Lerdahl & Jackendoff, 1983; Jackendoff & Lerdahl, 2006). They propose that time-span reduction is a notational variant of prosodic structure in language, in that both are based on a segmentation of the surface string into a layered hierarchy, which is governed by prosodic well-formedness constraints (Lerdahl & Jackendoff, 1983, pp. 314–21). Taken together, the metrical and prosodic grouping mechanisms could provide the tools to develop a more generalized model of temporal ordering encompassing the domains of language, poetry, and music.

Hierarchical grouping in prosodic phonology

In prosodic phonology (Selkirk, 1986; Nespor & Vogel, 1986), the formalization of the mapping relations between syntax and phonology at different levels of the prosodic hierarchy allows us to describe how constituents in syntactic structure constrain phonological processes. In (1), an example of the different levels of constituency in the prosodic hierarchy is given, ranging from the mora to the Intonation Phrase (example adapted from Truckenbrodt, 2007; it illustrates a consensus model based on Liberman & Prince, 1977; Selkirk, 1980; Hayes, 1995). The dashed box in (1) indicates the levels in the hierarchy that are relevant to word stress, equivalent to gridlines 0 to 3 in Fabb and Halle's metrical grid. In the example, the alternating pattern of prominences that underlie word stress are accounted for in terms of the metrical constituents of the mora, the foot, and the Prosodic Word (the shaded box marks the metrically strong syllable which serves as an anchor for the pitch accent in this Intonation Phrase; other stressed syllables could have been accented). Moraic constituency expresses the weight of the feet, which are left-headed, and do the work of parenthesis insertion at gridline 0 in Fabb and Halle's metrical grid (Fabb and Halle, Chapter 2, this volume: 5).[1] Grouping at the level of the Prosodic Word is right-headed, reflecting parenthesis insertion at gridline 2 or 3 in Fabb and Halle's account, where the corresponding gridline depends on the number of syllables in the word (in a language like English; Fabb and Halle, Chapter 2, this volume: 7).[2]

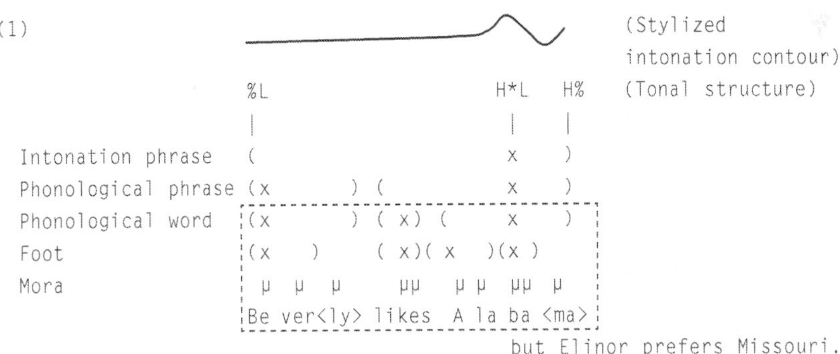

[1] The syllables *ly* and *ma* in (1) are extrametrical, i.e. they do not contribute to grid building, and are not parsed into feet (e.g. Hayes, 1995).

[2] The three Prosodic Words in this example exhaustively parse the three lexical words, but Prosodic Words would normally include any preceding function word with the lexical word.

Two differences between the consensus model adopted in (1) and Fabb and Halle's proposal are immediately apparent. First, the grid arrays that relate to word stress are projected from morae and feet rather than syllables in (1), and second, the brackets in (1) mark left and right junctures of constituents which are exhaustively parsed into higher-level constituents at the next level of structure, unlike Fabb and Halle's parentheses. Although these differences could have interesting implications for phrasing, they do not affect the main point made here, and will therefore be ignored in the following discussion.

The difference of interest to the discussion here is that two further levels of constituency above the word have been added in (1), showing how Prosodic Words (PW) group into Phonological Phrases (PP) which in turn form Intonational Phrases (IP).[3] For PPs, the mapping algorithms refer to syntactic phrases (XPs, e.g. Noun Phrases and Verb Phrases), but a number of other factors interact with syntactic phrasing in the mapping mechanism, such as length in number of syllables (e.g. for French: Verluyten, 1982; Delais, 1995; Post, 2000b), and speaking style and rate (Fougeron & Jun, 1998 for French). In other words, within the constraints imposed by syntactic structure, some variation in prosodic grouping is possible.

The same factors affect grouping at the level of the IP, which refers to root clauses in the syntax (2a), but they can also optionally map onto embedded coordinated clauses (2b), certain left- and right-peripheral constituents (2c), and incidental constituents (2d) (Selkirk, 2005).[4]

```
(2) (a) [Peter learns French]IP [and Mary watches TV]IP
    (b) [I think Peter learns French]IP [and Mary watches TV]IP
    (c) [Peter]IP [he will never learn French]IP
    (d) [Peter]IP [I think]IP [learns French]IP
```

As for PPs, length, rate, and style affect phrasing into IPs, but information structure also plays an important role in IP-formation. In (3), for instance, *Jean-Pierre* is in contrastive focus, and it is demarcated by an IP boundary on the left (Delais & Post, 2008).

```
(3) A: Frédérique est-il allé au cinéma hier?
    B: [Jean-Pierre]IP est allé au cinéma.
    'Did Frédérique go to the cinema yesterday?
    'Jean-Pierre went to the cinema'
```

Although groupings above the level of the word have traditionally been placed in a different component of the grammar (the postlexical component), it is generally

[3] The PP and the IP are not the only levels of phrasing above the level of the word that have been proposed in the literature (e.g. the clitic group and the intermediate phrase; see e.g. Nespor and Vogel (1986) for further levels of structure).

[4] IP formation follows the same principles in French (Delais-Roussarie forthcoming).

accepted that prosodic structure above the level of the word conforms to the same principles that apply at lower levels (e.g. Truckenbrodt, 2007).

Prominence distribution constrained by grouping

A range of phonological phenomena can be accounted for if the constituents of the prosodic hierarchy can be referred to as their domain of application (Nespor & Vogel, 1986). For instance, IPs are the domain of the full intonation contour; this is a rising-falling-rising contour in the case of the IP *Beverly likes Alabama* in (1), where the peak of the first rising movement is reached on the accented syllable *–ba-*, and the second rise is realized on the IP-final syllable *–ma*. The contour can be analysed as a combination of a falling pitch accent (H*L) which is associated with a stressed syllable, and a rising boundary (H%) which is associated with the right edge of the Intonation Phrase (as in the tonal grammar for Southern British English proposed in Gussenhoven, 2004).[5] In the French example of (3), a rising-falling contour on *Pierre*—which could be analysed as LH*L%—would be appropriate (Post, 2000b).

An example of a process that applies at the level of the PP is Clash Resolution, which describes the removal of prominence under clash conditions (also referred to as Iambic Reversal, the Rhythm Rule, or Stress Shift; cf. Giegerich, 1985). A clash can arise between metrically strong syllables when they are combined in connected speech. As is shown in (4), the clash between the immediately adjacent prominent syllables *–tique* and *chair* can be resolved by removing the prominence on *–tique*. In the example, the earlier syllable in the item *an-* is made prominent instead.

(4) He bought an anTIQue CHAIR → He bought an ANtique CHAIR

The process is bounded by the Phonological Phrase. That is, Clash Resolution applies within the PP, as in (5a), but it does not apply across PP boundaries (5b) (see e.g. Gussenhoven, 2005 for a recent discussion).

(5) (a) JapaNESe RAILways and MOtorways in FRANCE
→ [JApanese RAILways]PP [and MOtorways in FRANCE]PP
(b) JapaNESe RAILways and MOtorways
→ [JapaNESe]PP [RAILways and MOtorways]PP
but not *[JApanese]PP [RAILways and MOtorways]PP

The process has been accounted for as a shift or a reduction of stress in the clash item, expressed in terms of shifting asterisks in a metrical grid (Liberman & Prince, 1977;

5 The crucial point in this example is that intonation contours can be decomposed into elements which associate with the edges of prosodic domains (the IP here) and elements which associate with stressed syllables, not whether these elements should be analysed in terms of tones or contours (see e.g. Ladd, 1996 for a discussion). The tonal analysis in (1) is couched in the Autosegmental-Metrical framework (Pierrehumbert, 1980), which is currently the predominant model in the field, but an analysis in terms of contours could also have served the purpose of illustrating the relevance of the IP to the mapping between intonational and prosodic structure.

Hayes, 1984), but more recent proposals account for shifted and non-shifted patterns in terms of phrase level pitch accent placement rather than metrical prominence (Bolinger, 1981; Gussenhoven, 1991, 2005; Shattuck-Hufnagel, 1989). In Gussenhoven's view, the apparent stress shift underlying Clash Resolution in English results from the deletion of the first accent in the clash item, with an optional accent on an earlier syllable in the item. The pitch accent-based account has received empirical support from a number of studies on English (Horne, 1990, Grabe & Warren, 1995; Vogel, Bunnell, & Hoskins, 1995; Shattuck-Hufnagel, 1995; Shattuck-Hufnagel, Ostendorf, & Ross 1979; Ostendorf, Price, & Shattuck-Hufnagel, 1995), but it has also been shown to be better able to handle clash context data in French (Post, 1999, 2000a).

In French, Clash Resolution applies obligatorily to resolve clashes within the PP (Verluyten, 1982; Delais, 1994; Post, 1999, 2000a). The production experiment reported in Post (2000a) showed that Clash Resolution is produced whenever a Phonological Phrase-final accent was immediately followed by a preceding accent (6a), but it did not apply when a Phonological Phrase boundary intervened between the accents (6b). Clash Resolution resulted in a two-accent pattern in the majority of cases, but patterns with only one PP-final accent were also observed; the two patterns are illustrated in (6a) (French prenominal adjectives cannot function as the heads of Phonological Phrases, and therefore *jolis* in (6a) does not form a Phonological Phrase on their own; Verluyten, 1982; Nespor & Vogel, 1986; Selkirk, 1986).

```
(6) (a) de joLIS AIRS
        /də-ʒoli-z-ɛʀ/
        'pretty tunes'
                  → [de JOlis AIRS]PP
                  → [de jolis AIRS]PP
    (b) des hiVERS AUTRES qu'en aFRIQUE
        /de-z-ivɛʀ-otʀ-kɑ̃n-afrik/
        'winters different from (those) in Africa'
                  → [des hiVERS]PP[AUTRES qu'en aFRIQUE]PP
                  → [des hiVERS]PP[autres qu'en aFRIQUE]PP
```

A subsequent analysis based on native speaker judgements and acoustic measurements of fundamental frequency and duration confirmed that, as in English, French Clash Resolution is characterized by the absence of a pitch accent in the clash context rather than the presence of an accent that is shifted to an earlier syllable (Post, 1999). Clash Resolution appears to be a 'true phrasal' rule, i.e. a postlexical rule that adjusts the distribution of pitch accents with reference to a prosodically defined constituent, the PP.

These findings confirmed claims in the literature that the Phonological Phrase is the domain of pitch accent distribution in French (Verluyten, 1982; Delais, 1995).[6]

[6] The grouping of words into larger domains has long been recognized as a determining factor in pitch accent distribution in French (referred to as the *Groupe de Sens*, Coustenoble & Armstrong, 1934; Delattre, 1966b; *Groupe Rhythmique*, Fouché & Dauzat, 1935; Grammont, 1966; Delattre, 1966a; Ashby, 1975; *Breath Group* Pulgram, 1965; Vaissière, 1992; *Elément*

That is, PPs are obligatorily marked by a pitch accent at the right edge, and additional accents can optionally occur word-initially or word-finally elsewhere in the PP (Verluyten, 1982; Post, 2000b; see Di Cristo (2000) for a comprehensive overview of French accentuation). This is not to say that pitch accent placement cannot vary. Apart from differences in focus, which fall beyond the scope of this discussion, pitch accent distribution is variable because PP formation can be variable under certain conditions. More precisely, PPs can variably align with X' or X' heads in the morpho-syntactic structure (referred to as Small PP and Maximal PP respectively, Selkirk, 1986, 1995), and hence, the material that is incorporated in the PP can vary if the maximal projection contains more than one X' projection. Such differences in phrasing are reflected in differences in accent distribution, as is illustrated in (7).

```
(7) des enFANTS}X' SAGES}X')XMax →
    (a) Small PPs: [des enFANTS]PP [SAGES]PP
    (b) Maximal PP: [des enfants SAGES]PP or [des ENfants SAGES]PP
        'well-behaved children'
```

Second, speaking rate and style have been found to have an effect on pitch accent distribution. Speakers produce slightly fewer phonological phrases in (semi-)spontaneous than in read speech, with correspondingly fewer PP-final accents, and they produce considerably fewer accents in non-final position in the PP (Post, 2003). In a follow-up of the study reported in Post (2003), speaking rate was introduced as an orthogonal factor to directly compare the effects of rate and style on the number and location of pitch accents and PP and IP boundaries, as well as their phonetic realization. The results showed comparable effects for faster rates and more spontaneous speech, although they were stronger for rate. Acoustic analyses revealed—in line with earlier findings for rate effects (Fougeron & Jun, 1998)—that the phonetic realization of accents and boundaries is also affected, with significant reductions in duration and fundamental frequency for faster and more spontaneous speaking styles. Crucially, though, rate and speaking style did not affect the prosodic structure itself, since PPs were always aligned with X' or X' projections, and they were always demarcated by a phrase-final pitch accent.

A role for metrical structure in French?

The co-occurrence of accents and domain boundaries has led to claims that French is in fact a language without accent (Rossi, 1979; Féry, 2001), or alternatively, that French does not have lexically determined stress (e.g. Coustenoble and Armstrong, 1934, p. 4; Pulgram, 1965, pp. 132–33; see Di Cristo (2000) for a discussion). In these

Rythmique Grammont, 1966; *Syntagme prosodique* Di Cristo & Hirst, 1997; and *Accentual Phrase* Jun & Fougeron, 2002), but the group was never formally defined on independent grounds, and therefore, no unequivocal way of decomposing an utterance into accentual groups was available. Since Phonological Phrases are derived from the morpho-syntactic structure by phrase-formation algorithms, the constraints on pitch accent distribution that are imposed by grouping can be independently formalized.

accounts, there is no role for the metrical grid in explaining patterns of prominence in French, which could weaken the parallels drawn by Fabb and Halle (Chapter 2, this volume).

However, a number of counter-arguments can be brought forward to support the view that metrical structure is relevant to prominence (or accent) distribution in French after all. First, as Dell (1984) points out, utterances that end in a final full syllable and those in which the final syllable is a schwa show different alignments of intonation contours. For instance, the peak of a rise-fall realized at the end of an IP will be located in the syllable with the full vowel, and not in the following schwa if there is one. This implies that the pitch movement is not an edge-marking phenomenon which is blind to the internal structure of the PP, but rather that it is anchored to a specific (heavy) syllable in the word. Second, the optional accents mentioned above are also sensitive to structure. The examples in (8) illustrate the distribution of the optional accent in polysyllabic words (cf. Di Cristo, 2000). The accent usually occurs word-initially, as in (8a) and (8b), but when the word starts in a vowel, the second syllable will be accented instead (8c), unless this leads to a clash (Mertens, 1992; Pasdeloup, 1992). An account in terms of edge-marking would make the right predictions for cases like (8a) and (8b) if it can refer to word edges, but (8c) cannot be accounted for in this way. As the example in (8d) shows, the accent is invariably located on the first syllable in consonant-initial words, and on the second in vowel-initial words (provided clashes are avoided), regardless of the number of syllables in the word.[7]

(8) (a) C'est NEcesSAIRE 'It's necessary'
(b) C'est IMposSIBLE 'It's impossible'
(c) L'imPOSsibiliTE 'The impossibility'
(d) C'est DEcouraGEANT It's discouraging'

We have to conclude that prominence distribution is constrained by grouping as well as by metrical constraints which reflect factors such as syllable weight.

The account of French pitch accent distribution in Post (2000b) captures these facts by distinguishing between metrically strong syllables (structural positions) and pitch accents (phonological tones), where the former can function as the landing sites for the latter (cf. Bolinger, 1965; Gussenhoven, 2004; Hayes, 1995), but where the distribution of the latter is further constrained by factors like prosodic phrasing, the avoidance of clashes and lapses, the length of syntactic constituents, speaking rate, etc.

It is debatable whether metrical strength is determined at the lexical level in French, as in languages with dynamic stress, but the distinction between metrical strength and accentuation has been independently supported for Dutch (Rietveld, Kerkhoff, & Gussenhoven, 2004). A study of primary and secondary stress in minimal pairs like *ˌkameˈraadje* 'comrade' (+diminutive)–*ˈcameˌraatje* 'camera' (+diminutive) showed

[7] An alternative approach in which metrical prominence is described in terms of an alternating pattern from the right (Verluyten, 1982; Tranel, 1986) would also have to be rejected (Post, 2000b).

that, if the words are pronounced without a pitch accent (e.g. by embedding them in a compound noun like *FILMkameraadje–FILMcameraatje*), the syllable with the primary stress is significantly longer than the one with the secondary stress, independent of accentual and phrasal lengthening. As Gussenhoven (2004, p. 21) argues, this implies that the distinction in metrical strength must be phonologically represented independent of the presence of a pitch accent on the word.

Conclusion

Prominence distribution in French is determined by a number of interacting prosodic constraints which regulate the association of accents with the segmental string. I have argued that, in addition to metrical constraints of the type discussed in Fabb and Halle's proposal, the French data require a hierarchical grouping mechanism which accounts for the effects of word grouping on prominence patterns. More specifically, under this view, French prominence distribution is governed by the interaction of mapping constraints that are part of a prosodic phrasing system at the interface of different representational components in the grammar. As in other languages, the system mediates between syntax, phonology (segmental, metrical, and intonational), and semantics/pragmatics (including discourse and information structure), and it deals with competition and trade-offs between constituent length, focus, illocution, edge alignments, and tree configuration interactions (Post, 2011; cf. Selkirk, 2000; Fodor, 2002; Delais-Roussarie & Post, 2008). Cross-linguistic differences arise when the relative weight of the constraints, which varies between languages, leads to different mappings between the structures. In this way, prominence distribution can be modelled in a language with dynamic stress like English which is more dependent on patterns of lexically determined metrical strength, as well as in a language with fixed stress like French in which post-lexical factors such as prosodic phrasing are more prominent.

Apart from constraining prominence distribution in language, the hierarchically organized phrasing system may allow for a further parallel with the domain of poetry to be drawn, since it constrains constituency length in language, a function that is carried by the metrical grid for poetry in Fabb and Halle's proposal (Chapter 2, this volume). However, further parallels with music are probably more straightforward to pursue (cf. Lerdahl & Jackendoff, 1983). For instance, hierarchical phrasing is directly relevant in the domain of rhythm, since edge-marking phenomena like phrase-final lengthening (which is cumulative over levels of representation in the hierarchy) contribute to the rhythm percept. A prosodic phrasing system like the one outlined here could perhaps be used to further explore the parallels in hierarchical structuring in the domains of language, poetry and music.

Acknowledgements

The work discussed here was supported by the EC Marie Curie Network *Sound to Sense* (MRTN-CT-2006-035561), *Categories and gradience in intonation* (Economic and Social Research Council grant RES-061-25-0347), and *Pro-Gram* (Agence Nationale de la Recherche).

References

Ashby, W. (1975). The rhythmic group, liaison, nouns and verbs of French. *Studia Linguistica, 29*, 110–16.

Bolinger, D. (1965). Pitch accent and sentence rhythm. In I. Abe & T. Kanekyo (Eds.), *Forms of English: Accent, morpheme, order* (pp. 139–80). Tokyo: Hokuou.

Bolinger, D. (1981). *Two kinds of vowels, two kinds of rhythm.* Distributed by Indiana University Linguistics Club, Bloomington, Indiana.

Coustenoble, H., & Armstrong, L. (1934). *Studies in French intonation.* Cambridge: W. Heffer and Sons.

Delais, E. (1994). Rythme et structure prosodique en français. In C. Lyche (Ed.), *French generative phonology: Retrospective and perspectives* (pp. 131–50). Salford: AFLS/ESRI.

Delais, E. (1995). *Pour une approche parallèle de la structure prosodique* (Doctoral dissertation). Université de Toulouse-Le Mirail.

Delais-Roussarie, E. (forthcoming). La structure prosodique. In A. Abeillé, F. Gadet, & D. Godard (Eds.), *Grande grammaire du français.* Paris: Bayard.

Delais-Roussarie, E., & Post, B. (2008). Unités prosodiques et grammaire de l'intonation: vers une nouvelle approche. *Actes des XXVIIème Journées d'Études sur la Parole (JEPTALN 2008), Avignon, Juin 2008.* Retrieved from http://www.llf.cnrs.fr/Gens/Delais-Roussarie/delais_post.pdf.

Delattre, P. (1966a). Les dix intonations de base du français. *The French Review, 40*(1), 1–14.

Delattre, P. (1966b). *Studies in French and Comparative Phonetics.* The Hague: Mouton.

Dell, F. (1984). L'accentuation dans les phrases en français. In F. Dell, D. Hirst, & J.-R. Vergnaud (Eds.), *La forme sonore du langage* (pp. 65–122). Paris: Hermann.

Di Cristo, A. (2000). Vers une modélisation de l'accentuation du français. *French Language Studies, 10*, 27–44.

Di Cristo, A., & Hirst, D. J. (1997). L'accentuation non-emphatique en français: stratégies et paramètres. In J. Perrot (Ed.), *Polyphonie Pour Ivan Fónagy: Melanges Offerts En Hommage a Ivan Fónagy* (pp. 71–101). Paris: l'Harmattan.

Féry, C. (2001). Focus and phrasing in French. In C. Féry & W. Sternefeld, (Eds.), *Audiatur Vox Sapientiae. A Festschrift for Arnim von Stechow* (pp. 153–81). Berlin: Akademie-Verlag.

Fodor, J. D. (2002). Psycholinguistics cannot escape prosody. In B. Bel & I. Marlien (Eds.), *Proceedings of the 1st International Conference on Speech Prosody* (pp. 83–8). Retrieved from http://aune.lpl.univ-aix.fr/sp2002/pdf/fodor.pdf.

Fouché, P., & Dauzat, A. (1935). La prononciation actuelle du français. In A. Dauzat (Ed.), *Où en sont les études de français* (pp. 11–62). Paris: D'Artrey.

Fougeron, C., and Jun, S.-A. (1998). Rate effects on French intonation: prosodic organization and phonetic realization. *Journal of Phonetics, 26*, 45–69.

Giegerich, H. (1985). *Metrical Phonology and Phonological Structure.* Cambridge: Cambridge University Press.

Gilbers, D., & Schreuder, M. (2006). Language and music in optimality theory. *Rutgers Optimality Archive*, 571. Retrieved from http://roa.rutgers.edu/view.php3?roa=571.

Grabe, E., & Warren, P. (1995). Stress shift: do speakers do it or do listeners hear it? In Connell & Arvaniti (Eds.), *Phonology and phonetic evidence: Papers in Laboratory Phonology IV* (pp. 95–110). Cambridge: Cambridge University Press.

Grammont, M. (1966). *Traité pratique de la prononciation française.* Paris: Delagrave.

Gussenhoven, C. (1991). The English rhythm rule as an accent deletion rule. *Phonology, 8*, 1–35.

Gussenhoven, C. (2004). *The Phonology of Tone and Intonation*. Cambridge: Cambridge University Press.

Gussenhoven, C. (2005). Procliticized phonological phrases in English: Evidence from rhythm. *Studia Linguistica, 59*, 174–93.

Hayes, B. (1984). The phonology of rhythm in English. *Linguistic Inquiry, 15*, 33–74.

Hayes, B. (1995). *Metrical stress theory: principles and case studies*. Chicago, IL: The University of Chicago Press.

Horne, M. (1990). Empirical evidence for a deletion analysis of the rhythm rule in English. *Linguistics, 28*, 959–81.

Jackendoff, R., & Lerdahl, F. (2006). The capacity for music: What is it, and what's special about it? *Cognition, 100*, 33–72.

Jun, S.-A., & Fougeron, C. (2002). Realizations of accentual phrase in French intonation. *Probus, 14*, 147–72.

Ladd, D. (1996). *Intonational phonology*. Cambridge: Cambridge University Press.

Lerdahl, F., & Jackendoff, R. (1983). *A Generative Theory of Tonal Music*. Cambridge MA: MIT Press.

Liberman, M., & Prince, A. (1977). On stress and linguistic rhythm. *Linguistic Inquiry, 8*, 249–336.

Mertens, P. (1992). L'accentuation de syllabes contiguës. *ITL International Journal of Applied Linguistics, 95/96*, 145–63.

Nespor, M., & Vogel, I. B. 1986. *Prosodic phonology*. Dordrecht: Foris.

Ostendorf, M., Price, P.J., & Shattuck-Hufnagel, S. (1995). *The Boston University Radio News Corpus (ECS Technical Report)*. (Report No. ECS-95-001). Boston, MA: Boston University. Available by anonymous ftp from raven.bu.edu.

Pasdeloup, V. (1992). A prosodic model for French text-to-speech synthesis: A psycholinguistic approach. In G. Bailly, C. Benoit & T. Sawallis (Eds.), *Talking machines: Theories, models, and designs* (pp. 335–48). Amsterdam: Elsevier Science Publishers.

Pierrehumbert, J. (1980). *The phonetics and phonology of English intonation* (Doctoral dissertation). MIT, Cambridge, MA.

Post, B. (1999). Restructured phonological phrases in French. Evidence from clash resolution. *Linguistics, 37*(1), 41–63.

Post, B. (2000a). Pitch accents, liaison and the phonological phrase in French. *Probus, 12*, 127–64.

Post, B. (2000b). *Tonal and phrasal structures in French intonation*. The Hague: Holland Academic Graphics.

Post, B. (2003). Evidence for a constraint-based account of French phrasing and accentuation in different speaking styles. In M. Solé, D. Recasens, & J. Romero (Eds.), *Proceedings of the 15th International Congress of the Phonetic Sciences* (pp. 1309–12). Barcelona: Universitat Autònoma de Barcelona.

Post, B. (2011). The multi-facetted relation between phrasing and intonation in French. In C. Lleo & C. Gabriel (Eds.), *Hamburger Studies on Multilingualism 10: Intonational Phrasing at the Interfaces: Cross-Linguistic and Bilingual Studies in Romance and Germanic* (pp. 44–74). Amsterdam: John Benjamins.

Pulgram, E. (1965). Prosodic Systems: French. *Lingua, 13*, 125–44.

Rietveld, T., Kerkhoff, J., & Gussenhoven, C. (2004). Word prosodic structure and vowel duration in Dutch. *Journal of Phonetics, 32*, 349–71.

Rossi, M. (1979). Le français, langue sans accent. *Studia Phonetica, 15*, 13–51.

Selkirk, E. (1980). The role of prosodic categories in English word stress. *Linguistic Inquiry, 11*, 563–605.

Selkirk, E. (1986). On derived domains in sentence phonology. *Phonology Yearbook, 3*, 371–405.

Selkirk, E. (1995). The prosodic structure of function words. In J. Beckman, L. Walsh Dickey, & S. Urbanczyk (Eds.), *Papers in Optimality Theory* (pp. 439–69). Amherst, MA: GLSA.

Selkirk, E. (2000). The interactions of constraints on prosodic phrasing. In M. Horne (Ed.), *Prosody: Theory and Experiment* (pp. 231–61). Dordrecht: Kluwer Academic.

Selkirk, E. (2005). Comments on Intonational Phrasing in English. In S. Frota, M. Vigario, M., and J. Freitas (Eds.), *Prosodies: Selected papers from the Phonetics and Phonology in Iberia Conference, 2003 (Phonetics and Phonology Series)* (pp. 11–58). Berlin: Mouton de Gruyter.

Shattuck-Hufnagel, S. (1989). Stress shift as the placement of phrase-level pitch markers. *Journal of the Acoustic Society of America, 86*, 493.

Shattuck-Hufnagel, S. (1995). Pitch accent patterns in adjacent-stress vs. alternating stress words in American English. *Proceedings of the 13th International Congress of Phonetic Sciences, 3*, 656–59.

Shattuck-Hufnagel, S., Ostendorf, M. & Ross, K. (1979). Stress shift and early pitch accent placement in lexical items in American English. *Journal of Phonetics, 22*, 357–88.

Tranel, B. (1986). French liaison and extrasyllabicity. In O. Jaeggli & C. Silva-Corvalan (Eds.), *Studies in Romance Linguistics* (pp. 283–305). Dordrecht: Foris.

Truckenbrodt, H. (2007). The syntax-phonology interface. In P. de Lacy (Ed.), *The Cambridge Handbook of Phonology* (pp. 435–56). Cambridge: Cambridge University Press.

Vaissière, J. (1992). Rhythm, accentuation and final lengthening in French. In R. Carlson, L. Nord, & J. Sundberg (Eds.), *Proceedings of the 1990 Wenner-Gren Center Conference on Music, Language, Speech and Brain* (108–20). New York: Macmillan.

Verluyten, S. (1982). *Recherches sur la prosodie et la métrique du français* (Doctoral dissertation). Universiteit Antwerpen, Antwerp.

Vogel, I., Bunnell, T., & Hoskins, S. (1995). The phonology and phonetics of the Rhythm Rule. In B. Connell & A. Arvaniti (Eds.), *Phonology and phonetic evidence: Papers in Laboratory Phonology IV* (pp. 111–27). Cambridge: Cambridge University Press.

Chapter 5

Metre is music: a reply to Fabb and Halle

Bert Vaux and Neil Myler

Introduction

The theory of metrification presented by Fabb and Halle in Chapter 2 (henceforth F&H) seems to us to be flawed in a number of respects. At the root of the problem is F&H's assumption that metrical structure is projected from the surface syllables of a linguistic text. We argue that an alternative view not discussed by F&H is superior. This view, shared in its essentials by Deo (2007), Hanson (2006), J. Halle (2008), Kiparsky (1991), Lerdahl (2001) among others, holds that metrification proceeds via the mapping of linguistic structures onto a pre-determined metrical template. We show that this view leads to more natural accounts of many of the relevant phenomena, especially with regard to mismatches between text and metrical structure, such as catalexis, anacrusis, anceps, and syncopation. Our alternative has the advantage of allowing for poetic and musical metre and performance to be accounted for with a unified set of straightforward mechanisms. We argue, contra the fourth section of F&H, that this is a desirable and feasible move.

Summary and critique of F&H's arguments

The first section of F&H consists of a summary of approaches to stress in Generative Phonology, and an exposition of Idsardi's (1992) theory of prosodic organization as applied to word stress. While F&H's views on these matters are not defended in the contribution under discussion, they are extensively documented in Halle's previous publications and in the references F&H cite, and we tend to concur with the theory of stress they outline. For this reason, we concentrate our summary and critique of F&H's arguments on the second section onwards ('Metrical verse'), and will say no more about the first section.

The second section contains F&H's discussion of metrical verse, which they claim is to be distinguished from prose in that it is composed of lines. As they put it, 'absent the line, the text is prose, no matter how "poetic"'.[1] Two important properties of lines for F&H are that they are restricted in length and that they differ in the principles

[1] It should be noted that this curious assertion is a matter of subjective definition rather than fact, and that many scholars and practitioners of poetry would not agree with it.

which determine the placement of marked syllables. Fabb and Halle (2008) argue that these principles and restrictions can be accounted for using the same grid formalism and grouping rules as are employed in Idsardi's stress theory. They cite this as 'the most important result' of their book. F&H demonstrate this idea by elaborating the rules for generating English trochaic tetrametre, as exemplified by Pierre Antoine Motteux's 'A Song' of 1696. F&H's first assumption is that syllables project on to line 0 of the metrical grid as asterisks; hence, their approach is one in which metre is projected from linguistic syllable structure. They then formulate three rules specific to trochaic tetrametre. Applying these to Motteux's first line yields the parse in (1) (their (21)):

```
(1)
  Slaves to London I'll deceive you;
   (*     * (*  * (*     *(*     *(    gridline 0
   (*       *     (*       *(          gridline 1
   (*               *(                 gridline 2
    *                                  gridline 3
```

They stipulate the condition on well-formed grids for metrical poetry in (2) (their (22)):

(2) The last-to-be-generated gridline in a well-formed metrical grid must contain a single asterisk.

F&H argue that this condition derives the requirement that lines be limited in length. Given that the bracketing rules are applied iteratively and can only form binary or ternary groups, the claim is that only lines of a certain length can possibly conform to the condition in (2). But in fact, this condition can only derive such a constraint on the assumption that there is an absolute limit on the number of gridlines for which there are rules. In F&H's examples there are never more than three rules, and thus a practical maximum of four gridlines (0, 1, 2, 3), but nowhere in their argument do they make explicit any theoretical limit on the number of gridlines, much less explain why such a limit should hold. This being the case, we must assume that the number of gridlines is simply stipulated, which is no better than stipulating the requirement that lines be limited in length.

Note that the grid shown in (3) is periodic, but the actual rhythm of the piece need not be. As F&H put it, '[i]t is true that it is possible to pronounce [the line "slaves to London I'll deceive you"] with a fully regular rhythm, for example stressing "I'll" because it is off-numbered, but this is a performance practice rather than a fact about how the metre controls the composition of the line. It is also possible to perform the line with a more regular rhythm (in which "I'll" is not stressed), but this is just as metrical'. They conclude from this that no condition on grids can constrain the distribution of stressed and unstressed syllables correctly, and instead introduce the notion of 'maximum', along with the condition below (their (24) & (25)):

(3) The syllable bearing the word stress in a polysyllabic word is a maximum, if it is preceded and followed in the same line by a syllable with less stress.

```
(4) Maxima must project to gridline 1.
```

This means that stressed monosyllables need not project to gridline 1, although they will tend to do so. Such projection is only compulsory for maxima. This is an intriguing proposal, whose strong predictions need to be tested against the ample literature on this topic.

Within this general framework, metrical analysis becomes the task of discovering 'which combination of iterative and other rules, and conditions on the resulting grid, best explain the characteristics of the metrical line'.

F&H move on to provide a further illustration of their theory using a piece in iambic pentametre. It is here that F&H present their responses to some of those (frequent) circumstances in which linguistic material and metre fail to match perfectly, obviously an important issue for an approach in which the former is claimed to be a projection of the latter. F&H's rules for generating iambic pentametre (their (28)) are exemplified using an excerpt from Matthew Arnold's 'Sonnet to the Hungarian Nation' of 1849. Here we repeat only the second line used by F&H, illustrating the full grid for it. Interestingly, F&H have indicated using accents the syllables which '[they] think are likely to be stressed in a performance of the line'; note that this does not always coincide with where prominence is assigned on the grid (maxima are underlined):

```
(5)
     ‘        ‘     ‘      ‘           ‘
 Of men who against hope repelled the chain,
)*   *)   * *)*     *)   * *)     *    *)   gridline 0
     *      *       *      *           *    gridline 1
           (*                          *(   gridline 2
            *
```

In this case, for example, the syllable assigned most prominence by the grid is likely to receive no stress at all in performance. F&H would presumably attribute this to a performance convention not relevant to the theory of the structure of the underlying metre; at any rate they do not comment on it. Before considering their mechanisms for deriving other forms of text-metre mismatch, however, it is worth noting that F&H's algorithm inserts parentheses on gridline 0 from right to left. They claim that there are two arguments for this: one is that 'in an iambic metre the leftmost group can sometimes be incomplete'. The other is that the rightmost syllable is sometimes skipped by the grouping algorithm. However, it seems to us that at least the second of F&H's arguments here is undercut by the fact that their theory also allows for the non-projection of syllables (see below). There is nothing that prevents non-projection of syllables from occurring at the periphery of a line, and so apparent 'skipping' of a peripheral syllable cannot be taken to show anything about the directionality of parenthesis insertion. Nonetheless, F&H take this evidence as indicating that such syllables are extrametrical. They argue that this is what happens in the line below, also from Arnold's 'Sonnet to the Hungarian Nation':

```
(6)
  ‘                    ‘          ‘

  Hallow the Salamanian promontories
  )*  *)   *  *)* *) *    *)* *)*   gridline 0
      *       *   *       *   *     gridline 1
```

Allowing extrametricality is one way in which F&H can account for circumstances in which a syllable appears to be ignored by metrical structure whilst maintaining their view that the latter is projected from syllables. However, extrametricality can only be invoked in the case of syllables that are peripheral to a line. The problem is that 'extra' syllables are also found in the midst of lines. F&H recognize this, citing the following example from John Donne's 'Holy Sonnet 6' (their (29)); we have bracketed the 'extra' syllable:

```
(7) And gluttonous death, will instantly unjoynt
     s     s [s] s   s      s   s   s   s s  s
```

Since in F&H's approach only individual syllables can project onto gridline 0, they cannot solve this difficulty by allowing two syllables to correspond to a single unit of metre. Instead, they propose that 'poets may occasionally violate [the rule forcing syllables to project to gridline 0] and not project a given syllable'. As for when this non-projection option can be invoked, F&H assert that '[t]here is no general principle in English poetry determining which syllables cannot project, but there are some tendencies'. This is held to contrast with the situation in Romance, where 'the non-projection of syllables [. . .] is subject to strict rules' (footnote 6). Crucially, while the projection of an asterisk to Gridline 0 may occasionally be absent in the presence of a syllable, the converse can never hold. As F&H put it, 'no rule permits an asterisk to appear on gridline 0 if it is not projected from a syllable; that is, an asterisk cannot project from a pause or rest, but only from an actual syllable'. They add that music differs from poetic metre in this regard.

There are a number of things to say about these proposals. One is that F&H are able to deal with hypersyllabicity (surfeit of syllables relative to the canonical number), but only at the cost of introducing two separate mechanisms—extrametricality and non-projection. Effectively, these two mechanisms are there to account for the same phenomenon, differing only in the position in the word of the syllables affected. This redundancy is surely undesirable, and is in no way mitigated by the fact that the two mechanisms occur at different levels of analysis in F&H's framework: in the case of extrametricality an asterisk is ignored, in the case of non-projection no asterisk is visible in the first place.[2] Worse still, there is a serious flaw in F&H's requirement that asterisks cannot be projected from a pause or a rest in metrical poetry. This requirement, which is fundamental to the architecture of F&H's projection-based theory,

---

[2] Furthermore, extrametricality implies that the affected syllable entirely fails to participate in the metrical structure. We believe that this is false—the alternative approach to metrification that we expound below shows that the relevant beats are not in fact outside of the metre.

seems to us to leave them with no way of accounting for catalexis[3]—the appearance of obligatory silences before, within or after lines. Such gaps participate fully in metrical structure, and yet have no linguistic material associated with them.

Deo (2007) provides an impressive generative metrics account of the metrical repertoire of Classical Sanskrit verse, a tradition that had previously seemed chaotic and problematic from the point of view of formal metrical theory. The account makes crucial use of catalexis in order to bring out the underlying unity of metres which had traditionally been categorized separately. For instance, Deo (2007) compares the metres known as Jalaughavegā and Cāruhāsinī (p. 99; Deo's (41)):

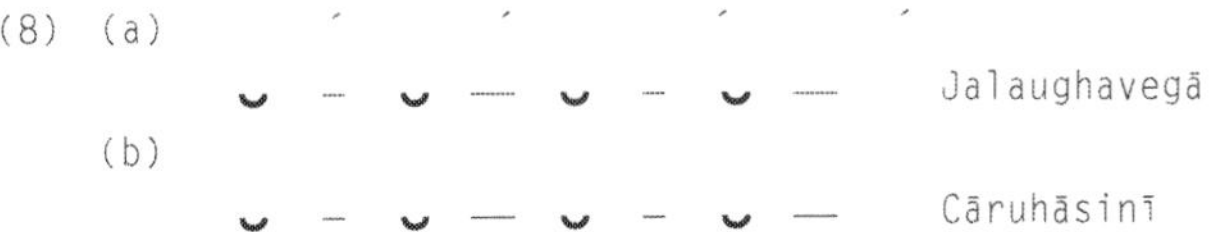

Deo points out that 'Cāruhāsinī is exactly like Jalaughavegā except that it lacks the final syllable' (p. 99). By assuming that Cāruhāsinī has a final catalectic foot, Deo is able to assign the same parse to Cāruhāsinī as to Jalaughavegā, one with four iambic feet (p. 99, her (42b)):

Deo is able to show that no fewer than ten Sanskrit metres can be seen as instantiating this parse if catalexis is assumed. While the data from Sanskrit verse are argument enough for the importance of catalexis, we would like to emphasize that the phenomenon is by no means restricted to this metrical tradition. Catalexis has been crucially invoked for Japanese by Kawakami (1973) and Asano (2002) (where five-mora lines have three catalectic moras and seven-mora lines have one catalectic mora), for Persian by Hayes (1979), for Spanish by Flores (2004), for modern and Classical Greek by Parker (1976), and for Classical Arabic by Golston and Riad (1997). In English too use of catalexis in verse has been noted, for instance in the work of Larkin (Groves, 2001), in trochaic verse in English (Deo, 2007, p. 92), in some American folk verse (Hayes & MacEachern, 1998), in short lyrics such as those of Emily Dickinson and Robert Frost (Lerdahl, 2001), and in Shakespeare, who often has nine-syllable lines in iambic pentametre sections, including initial catalexis (Groves, 2007, pp. 130, 134). Ironically, what we take to be the correct solution to this problem, a greater exploitation of the

[3] There are other types of mismatch between text and metre which seem problematic for F&H but are readily resolvable by the alternative view that we set out below, such as anacrusis, syncopation and anceps. For space reasons we restrict ourselves to a discussion of catalexis.

parallelism between poetic metre and musical metre, is closed off by the analytical wall that F&H erect between the two in their fourth section ('Metre in music').

In this section, F&H propose to extend the grid formalism to the analysis of music. However, as anticipated above, there are major analytical differences between poetic metre and musical metre for F&H. Firstly, they recognize no musical entity equivalent to the line in poetry. Music is thus held to be exempt from condition (22), 'meaning that the last-to-be-generated Gridline may contain any number of asterisks, depending on how long the musical piece lasts'.[4] Secondly, F&H propose that rather than being projected from beats, gridline 0 in music is projected from the silences between beats. This draws a fundamental analytic divide between poetry and music, because on this account 'in music, a gridline 0 asterisk can project from a rest or silence, which is not possible in the metrical structure of verse'. Of course, allowing for such projection in metre as well would allow for an analysis of catalexis, yet we have already seen that this would go against an architectural imperative of F&H's approach. Not only does this lead to descriptive inadequacy with regard to metre itself, it also misses an enlightening parallel between music and metre. Silent beats, uncontroversially a staple of musical rhythm, are a precise analogue for catalexis.[5] The parallelism cannot be captured by F&H because of their assumption that metrical structure is projected from linguistic structure. We suggest that this notion needs to be replaced by one in which linguistic structure is mapped onto a pre-existing abstract metrical template. The format of such templates, we suggest, is fundamentally the same in the case of both metre and music (see also Deo, 2007; Hanson, 2006; J. Halle, 2008; Kiparsky, 1991). Since the mapping of linguistic material to metrical units is not obligatorily 1:1, this idea avoids the flaws we have identified in F&H's approach. There is no need to invoke two separate mechanisms to capture hypersyllabicity—this phenomenon is the result of a many-to-one mapping between syllables and a metrical time slot.[6] Catalexis is merely the result of a timing slot being unfilled. We shall see that this view allows more abstract regularities in metrical structure to be brought out. In addition, it allows music and metre to be accounted for using the same mechanism.

Let us illustrate these points via a comparison of the analyses that the two approaches offer of the nursery rhyme 'Hickory Dickory Dock'.

---

4 It is not at all clear to us that this assertion is well motivated—much seems to depend on one's definition of line here. We leave this issue aside for space reasons.

5 We believe that the same could be said for some of the other phenomena mentioned in note 3, but we cannot explore this here.

6 The opposite sort of many-to-one relation, in which a single syllable corresponds to several metrical time slots, is also attested, as when syllables are lengthened to fit the metre (Annis (2006) notes cases of melismata in Greek, where vowels can be lengthened for this reason; an example is *oulomene:n* for *olomene:n*, from the Iliad 1.2). Note that such many-to-one and one-to-many relationships between linguistic material and timing slots precisely mirror the possibilities of autosegmental analyses of ordinary phonology. Hence, our approach preserves the most attractive aspect of F&H's theory by allowing linguistic and metrical phenomena to be described with the same formalism.

```
(10) Hickory dickory dock,
  The mouse ran up the clock,
  The clock struck one,
  The mouse ran down,
  Hickory dickory dock.
```

Notice that an analysis in F&H's terms is forced to assume one parse for the first and final lines of the rhyme (dactylic trimetre) and another for the other lines (iambic trimetre):

```
(11) Hickory   dickory dock
     (*  * *   (*  * *  (*
     (*         *       (*
     (*                  *
      *

     The mouse ran up the clock
     )*   *)    *  *)  *    *)
         (*        *       (*
          *
```

On the other hand, a single parse can be assigned to this nursery rhyme if the metre is assumed to consist of a template with the sort of regular rhythmic structure familiar from western music theory. Note that the placement of columns in this representation indicates metrical timing slots, and their relative height depicts their relative prominence—the text here is mapped onto these metrical slots, rather than the latter being projected from the former.

(12) 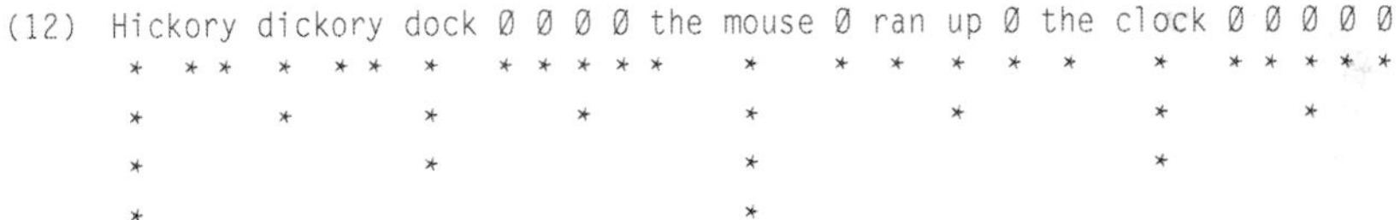

We can see from this representation that in fact the nursery rhyme has a completely predictable repeating 3/4 or 6/8 rhythm which is entirely missed by an F&H-style analysis. Prominences occur on the first beat and every third beat after that. The prominences in turn can be grouped into repeating sets of four where the most intense prominence is the first, the second and fourth have weakest prominence, and the third is an intermediate one. Here we see yet another defect of F&H's approach—the primacy of syllables in their account leads to an overly surface-oriented approach to metre. An abstract template which admits the existence of silent beats, on the other hand, can bring out deeper regularities of metrical structure.

We agree with Deo (2007) that what F&H consign to the nebulous domain of performance actually constitutes an essential component of the rhythmic competence of both composer and listener.

Conclusion

While we applaud F&H's attempt to employ similar analytical devices in the analysis of stress, poetic metre, and music, we feel that their projection-based approach leaves them unable to account for many important aspects of metre. Ironically, one of the major causes of this is the fact that assuming the primacy of linguistic syllable structure bars them from giving a more unified account of music and metre than they would otherwise be able to achieve. We have argued that a mapping approach avoids the descriptive inadequacies of projection by allowing the fundamental similarities of music and metre to be brought out. The notion of mapping of linguistic structures onto timing slots preserves an analytical link between ordinary autosegmental phonology and the analysis of music and metre, this being one of the most attractive features of F&H's proposals.

References

Annis, W. (2006). *Introduction to Greek Meter.* Retrieved online from http://www.aoidoi.org/articles/meter/intro.pdf [Accessed 29 May 2011].

Asano, M. (2002). Metrical pauses and the prosodic structure of Japanese poetry. *Proceedings of WECOL*, 36–52.

Deo, A. (2007). The metrical organization of Classical Sanskrit verse. *Journal of Linguistics, 43*, 63–114.

Fabb, N. & Halle, M. (2008). *Meter in poetry: A new theory.* Cambridge: Cambridge University Press.

Flores, M.-B. (2004). The role of catalexis in Spanish rhythm structure: a phonological and phonetic study of catalexis in Spanish syllable-timed poetry (Magister Thesis in General Linguistics). Department of Linguistics and Phonetics, Lund University.

Golston, C. & Riad, T. (1997). The phonology of Classical Arabic meter. *Linguistics 35*, 111–32.

Groves, P. (2001). What music lies in the cold print: Larkin's experimental metric. *Style, 35*, 703–23.

Groves, P. (2007). Shakespeare's Pentametre and the End of Editing. *Shakespeare, 3*(2), 126–42.

Halle, J. (2008). *'Text Setting and Prosodic Form.' Paper delivered at Tufts University Conference on Music and Language*, 13 July 2008. Retrieved online at http://www.johnhalle.com/musical.writing.technical/halle.ac.metrical.form.pdf [Accessed 29 May 2011].

Hanson, K. (2006). Shakespeare's lyric and dramatic metrical styles. In B. Elan Dresher & Nila Friedberg (Eds.), *Formal approaches to poetry: recent developments in metrics.* Berlin: Mouton de Gruyter.

Hayes, B. (1979). The rhythmic structure of Persian verse. *Edebiyat 4*, 193–242.

Hayes, B., & MacEachern, M. (1998). Quatrain form in English folk verse. *Language, 64*, 473–50.

Idsardi, W. (1992). *The computation of prosody* (Doctoral dissertation). MIT, Cambridge, MA.

Kawakami, S. (1973). *Nihongo onshuuritu no saikentoo. Onishi hakushi kiju kinen onseigaku taikai ronbunshuu* (pp. 665–71). Tokyo: Phonetic Society of Japan.

Kiparsky, P. (1991). 'Catalexis.' Ms., Stanford University, CA.

Lerdahl, F. (2001). The sounds of poetry viewed as music. In R. Zatorre and I. Peretz (Eds.), The Biological Foundations of Music. *Annals of the New York Academy of Sciences, 930*, 337–54.

Parker, L. (1976). Catalexis. *The Classical Quarterly, New Series, 26*(1), 14–28.

Chapter 6

Comments and a conjecture inspired by Fabb and Halle

Ian Roberts

Introduction

In this paper, I will begin by pointing out some fairly obvious and mostly well-known similarities between music and language, and specifically how aspects of Fabb & Halle's proposals reflect these. Observing, then, that the similarities between language and music appear to run quite deep, I will speculate on what the reason for this might be. This leads to a brief introduction to the detailed conception of the faculty of language put forward by Hauser, Chomsky & Fitch (2002). In terms of their approach, I will suggest that language and music have in common the core computational system: in other words, at root, the relation between these two human cognitive capacities is not one of similarity or shared evolutionary origin, as has often been suggested, but rather identity. Language and music differ in that the single computational system common to both relates to distinct interfaces in each case: most importantly, language has a propositional or logical interface which music does not have (the same point is made by Cross & Woodruff (2008, pp. 4, 14) and Cross, Bisphan, Himberg, & Swaine (n.d., p. 2)). I conjecture that both the richness of the natural-language lexicon and the duality of patterning characteristic of natural language may be indirect consequences of this; hence music has a relatively impoverished lexicon and does not appear in any obvious way to show duality of patterning.

My very tentative conclusion is thus: natural language and music share the same computational system. In the case of natural language, however, the system's outputs subserve reasoning and fixation of belief; the outputs of music lack this function. I will very briefly speculate on the extent to which the other interfaces (those involving 'externalization' of cognitive outputs) are similar or different between music and language; it seems likely that they are somewhat similar overall, although the importance of dance in relation to music should not be underestimated.

Fabb and Halle: the grid in linguistic, metrical, and musical structure

In their paper, Fabb and Halle (F&H) show that linguistic structure and musical structure are the same in the cases of word stress, poetic metre, and musical grouping. As they say in their conclusion 'these different bodies of fact are accounted for by grouping elements in a linear sequence into the hierarchical pattern of the metrical grid. In all three cases the elements were grouped into either pairs or triplets, marking one of the elements head. The heads constitute a new . . . sequence of elements, which in turn is subject to the further grouping'. The units grouped are different (syllables in language, but timing slots in music), but the grouping algorithm is the same in two major respects: 'it is implemented everywhere by junctures of the same kind . . . and is recursive; i.e. . . . the heads of groups are projected on a separate gridline and are themselves subject to grouping'. The claim is, then, that a mental computational system imposes a particular form of discrete, recursive hierarchical structure on a linear sequence of units.

For example, the word *confidentiality* has the stress structure in (1) (F&H's (10)):

```
(1)  con.fi.den.ti.a.li.ty
     )*   *) *   *)*  *) *    gridline 0
     (*      *   (*           gridline 1
      *           *)          gridline 2
                  *           gridline 3
```

This structure is the result of the (possibly iterated) output of the following rules (F&H's (11)):

(2)
  (a) Project each syllable as an asterisk forming gridline 0.
  (b) Gridline 0. Starting at the L edge, insert a R parenthesis, form binary groups, heads L.
  (c) Gridline 1. Starting at the L edge, insert a L parenthesis, form binary groups, heads L.
  (d) Gridline 2. At the R edge, insert a R parenthesis, head R.

Stress is assigned by the rule in (3) (their (12)):

(3) Assign different degrees of prominence (of high pitch) to the syllables in direct proportion to the height of their asterisk column in the metrical grid.

F&H also show how languages may differ minimally in the rules which form metrical grids, essentially in the choices of 'directionality' indicated by 'L' and 'R' in reference to the edge, the position of the head, and the edge from which construction of a gridline proceeds, as well as the starting position of asterisk-insertion and the length of the interval between insertions (see their (31)). But the central idea of a recursive formal grouping remains throughout.

Concerning metrical verse, F&H's central claim is that 'verse is composed of lines'. Lines, on the one hand, are restricted in length, and, on the other, show restrictions on the positions of stress- or rhyme-bearing syllables. The length restriction is captured by a principle along the lines of (4) (F&H's (22)):

```
(4) The last-to-be-generated gridline in a well-formed metrical grid
must contain a single asterisk.
```

The rhythmic quality of poetic metre can be captured by a condition like (5) (their (23)):

```
(5) A stressed syllable must project to gridline 1, and a gridline 1
asterisk must  project from a stressed syllable.
```

(In fact, F&H show that the more complex notion 'maximum' is required, in order to capture the slightly aperiodic nature of metre in languages such as English, but I will not go into this here). In these terms, the rules for iambic pentameter are as follows (F&H's (27)):

```
(6) Rules for iambic pentametre
  (a) Gridline 0: starting (just at the edge OR one asterisk in) at the
  R edge, insert a R parenthesis, form binary groups, heads R.
  (b) Gridline 1: starting just at the R edge, insert a R parenthesis,
  form ternary groups, heads R.
  (c) Gridline 2: starting just at the L edge, insert a L parenthesis,
  form binary groups, heads L.
```

This, with the proviso that the leftmost group must be incomplete, gives:

```
(7) Shall I compare thee to a summer's day?    (Shakespeare, Sonnet 18)
      *  )*   *   )*  *   )* *  )* *     )*    gridline 0
           *      )*       *     *)       *    gridline 1
                  (*                      *    gridline 2
                   *                           gridline 3
```

The condition that the last-generated gridline must contain a single asterisk effectively restricts the number of syllables the line can have, without introducing any kind of counting device into the system.

Stress rules and metrical rules differ in two respects: stress rules, but not metrical rules, may affect the phonetic make-up of the material they apply to, in virtue quite simply of assigning stress. Metrical rules, on the other hand, do not alter phonetic form. However, as we have seen, metrical rules function so as to limit length; stress rules, on the other hand, are completely insensitive to length. As F&H underline, the metrical concept of line is not a linguistic concept, while stress is part of the linguistic system (both points hold by definition: linguistic structure is never 'bounded' by a concept like line-length, while altering segmental phonetic form is inherently a linguistic matter). But in the present context the most important point is this: the grid applies in just the same way in both cases.

Finally, F&H turn to musical metre. Music, in almost all traditions, clearly has rhythm, measured conventionally by the beats in a bar. F&H's main point, *pace*

Lehrdal & Jackendoff (1983), is that musical beats are grouped, and indeed grouped by the very algorithm we have just seen in operation in stress and poetic metre. F&H demonstrate that certain impossible metrical structures in music, for which Lehrdal and Jackendoff (1983, p. 87) formulate a series of explicit Metrical Well-Formedness Rules (MWFRs), can be derived from the general grid. Consider, for example, (8), which corresponds to F&H's (33a):

```
(8) * * * * * * * * *   0
    *       *   *   *   1
        *           *   2
```

This structure is ruled out because there is an asterisk (in timeslot 3) on gridline 2 which is not there on gridline 1. F&H perform a similar demonstration for three other cases discussed by Lehrdal & Jackendoff (1983, see their discussion, pp. 14–16).

The grid applies in music in a different way from its application in stress or poetic-metre systems in that, in music, 'each note or pause has a fixed duration that is a multiple of some minimal duration (most commonly a 1/64th note)' (Lehrdal and Jackendoff 1983, p. 15). As in language, but unlike in poetry, the grid in its application to music is subject to no length restriction. All in all, though, we observe that the grid reveals 'a deep connection between music and language' (p. 18). The links between music, language and poetry may be culturally sanctioned through the adoption of specific conventions for musical structure (harmony, counterpoint, etc.) and the versification of poetry, but their roots arguably lie rather deep in the nature of human cognition. I will try to explore and clarify this last point in what follows.

The grid and the structure of language

In this section we briefly recapitulate what the basic properties of F&H's approach to the grid are, and then show that these hold across all the central areas of the structure of language: this observation of course strongly supports the general contention that the abstract similarities between music and language run rather deep.

F&H's grid relies on four principal notions. First, there is the idea that the linear sequence can be exhaustively divided into discrete structural elements. In the case of stress and poetic metre, these are syllables; in the case of music, they are timing units to which (part of) a note or pause may be mapped. Very importantly, as F&H point out '[m]etrical structure in all three cases is not a characteristic of the acoustic signal, but part of the mental representation of words or lines of verse, or sequences of music' (ibid). The cognitive system imposes a particular pattern on the linear signal.

Second, the grid makes use of a notion of head. That is, it is assumed that the discrete symbols are not arranged like beads on a string, but that rather there is a hierarchical structure of some kind: some elements in the string are singled out as more prominent than others.

Third, the grid makes use of a very simple grouping algorithm, which can refer to the distinction between heads and non-heads. It can therefore group together heads or non-heads. By grouping together heads, higher-order statements about the relations among elements in the string are made possible.

Fourth, and perhaps most important of all, the grouping algorithm is recursive, in the simple sense that it can reapply to its own output; a step of the procedure can be defined as the procedure itself. This has the consequence that grid-formation can take place over an unbounded domain (both linearly and hierarchically), although, as we saw above in the discussion of poetic metre, it is possible to impose an arbitrary bounding restriction. Imposing such a restriction can give the illusion that the system is able to 'count', when in fact it is simply obeying this restriction.

All four of these properties of the grid are pervasive in standard analyses of the structure of natural language. This is obvious for the case of phonology, as the grid serves to define stress-assignment domains (with the phonetic consequences that these may have, alluded to above). Concerning syntax, the four assumptions play a central role in the definition of constituent structure, as developed in the American structuralist tradition and formalized in generative grammar since Chomsky (1955). Thus, the linear string of morphosyntactic formatives is segmented into words and/or morphemes, certain of which are designated as heads. The 'grouping algorithm' is encoded in traditional phrase-structure rules, which generate phrase markers on which the standard notions of dominance and constituency can be defined; these are merely different ways of stating what is grouped. Phrase-structure rules are richer than F&H's grouping algorithm in that they typically also convey information as to the grammatical category of the elements whose combinations they encode, although the influential X-bar theory of phrase structure precisely does not directly specify this information in the structure-building (grouping) rules.[1] The minimalist conception of Merge, which recursively combines two syntactic units to form a third unit bearing the grammatical label of one of the two units combined (see Chomsky, 1995, pp. 241–49), is also rather clearly a grouping algorithm.

In semantics, the thesis of compositionality, usually attributed to Frege (1923–26), asserts that the meaning of a complex expression is a function of the meanings of its parts. In most contemporary theories of formal semantics (see, e.g. Chierchia & McConnell-Ginet, 1990; Heim & Kratzer, 1996; Larson & Segal, 1995), the structure which receives a compositional interpretation is generated by the syntax (by phrase-structure rules, possibly using the X-bar convention, or by Merge). In this way, the unbounded nature of the syntax, i.e. the fact that the syntax can produce an infinite number of well-formed structural descriptions of sentences, can be seen to underlie the fact that an infinite number of true propositions can be expressed. In fact, as has been recognized by Davidson (1967) and Higginbotham (1985), we can construct a recursive definition of truth of the kind envisaged by Tarski (1956) on the basis of the compositional interpretation of a set of well-formed syntactic structures. The validity of the Tarskian schema in (9) can be guaranteed by the interaction of an unbounded syntactic component and a fully compositional semantics:

(9) S is true iff *p*.

[1] Rewriting systems based on phrase-structure rules are also 'derivational'; that is, they contain information regarding the order of application of operations in deriving the structure. I will leave this very important point aside here, since it is not clear to me to what extent the grid is inherently derivational in this sense.

To put it rather simplistically, the nature of S is given by the syntax, and the nature of *p* by the compositional semantics.

So we observe that the four fundamental structural properties of F&H's grouping algorithm are common to other areas of the language faculty. We conclude from this that there is a significant structural common core between language and music.

Further commonalities between language and music

Of course, there are many other similarities between language and music. Here I will briefly review these, taking them—with the possible exception of the last one—to be largely uncontroversial.

First, both music and language are universal in human communities. Concerning music, Cross & Woodruff (2008, p. 3) point out that 'all cultures of which we have knowledge engage in something which, from a western perspective, seems to be music'. They also observe that 'the prevalence of music in native American and Australian societies in forms that are not directly relatable to recent Eurasian or African musics is a potent indicator that modern humans brought music with them out of Africa' (2008, p.16). Similarly, Hannon & Trehub (2005, p. 48) observe that '[a]ll cultures have sound patterns with repetitive temporal structures, which facilitate synchronous dancing, clapping, instrument playing, marching and chanting'. In their excellent and inspiring 'Introduction to evolutionary musicology', S. Brown, Merker, and Wallin (2000, p. 4) refer to music as 'A universal and multifunctional cultural behaviour', and go on to suggest three possible universals of music (p. 14). Mithen (2005, p. 1) says 'appreciation of music is a universal feature of humankind; music-making is found in all societies'. According to Mithen, Blacking (1976) was the first to suggest that music is found in all human cultures (see also Bernstein, 1976; Blacking, 1995).[2] Finally, Pinker (2002, pp. 435ff.) reproduces D. Brown's (1991) list of human universals. This features 'music; music, children's; music related in part to dance; music related in part to religious activity; music seen as art (creation); music, vocal; music, vocal, includes speech forms; musical redundancy; musical variation' (p. 437).

The same is true of language: no recognizably human group has been encountered which does not have language. This observation extends beyond the spoken-aural channel. It is now accepted that the signed languages (using the visual-gestural channel) of deaf communities are languages in every sense (Goldin-Meadow, (2005, pp. 201–2)). They differ from spoken languages only in the modality of transmission: gestural/visual as opposed to oral/aural. The signed languages which have been studied show all the structural features of spoken languages, including notably a syntax which has all the hallmarks of a generative system, being discrete, algorithmic, recursive, and

[2] Although Brown et al. (2000, p. 3) note that the pre-war Berlin school of comparative musicology investigated the question of musical universals and the evolution of music. Moreover, Darwin (1871) observes that 'the enjoyment [and] the capacity of producing musical notes' are present 'in men of all races'. He also points out that they are 'faculties of the least direct use to man in reference to his ordinary habits of life' and so 'must be ranked amongst the most mysterious with which he is endowed'.

purely formal. Signed languages also show duality of patterning, in that signs, which have a meaning, are made up of smaller units which themselves lack meaning, just as words (or morphemes) in spoken languages are made up of phonemes. Phonological processes such as assimilation have been observed, and phonological units such as the syllable proposed (see Sandler & Lillo-Martin, 2001, pp. 539–42) for a summary of the evidence for sign-language phonology). Finally, signed languages show the full range of semantic properties of spoken language. It is widely accepted, then, that wherever humans are found, complex language, with all its attributes, is found.

Second, both language and music are unique to humans. Regarding music, Cross et al. (n.d., pp. 7–8) conclude '[o]verall, current theory would suggest that the human capacities for musical, rhythmic, behaviour and entrainment may well be species-specific and apomorphic to the hominin clade, though . . . systematic observation of, and experiment on, non-human species' capacities remains to be undertaken.' They argue that entrainment (coordination of action around a commonly perceived, abstract pulse) is a uniquely human ability intimately related to music. Further, they point out that, although various species of great apes engage in drumming, they lack this form of group synchronization (p. 12).

Language is, of course, specific to humans. This is not to say that animals do not communicate; of course they do, and in a wide variety of ways (see Hauser, 1997 for an authoritative overview). However, no other species, primates included, appear to have the human capacity for mastery of a discrete, algorithmic system which pairs sounds and meanings over an infinite domain. As Hauser, Chomsky & Fitch (2002, p. 1570) put it: 'although bees dance, birds sing, and chimpanzees grunt, these systems of communication differ qualitatively from human language. In particular, animal communication systems lack the rich expressive and open-ended power of human language'. Famously, there have been numerous attempts to 'teach' language to various primates. These efforts have yielded interesting results, but they have not resulted in a non-human with truly human-like mastery of language; it seems that no other creature has the aptitude for language acquisition that every normal infant human has. Truswell (2008) looks closely at the syntactic abilities of the bonobo Kanzi, concluding that Kanzi's competence in English lacks constituent structure. It might be possible to interpret this as meaning that Kanzi lacks the narrow language faculty in the sense of Hauser, Chomsky, & Fitch (2002); see the next section.

Third, both language and music are readily acquired by children without explicit tuition. For the case of language, this is very well-known. The normal child's prodigious feat of attaining adult-like competence in its native language in the first few years of life is documented in the vast literature on developmental psycholinguistics, is familiar to any parent, and has led to the postulation of argument from the poverty of the stimulus, Chomsky's most important argument for an innate genetic underpinning to language. Regarding music, Hannon & Trainor (2007, p. 466) say 'just as children come to understand their spoken language, most individuals acquire basic musical competence through everyday exposure to music during development . . . Such implicit musical knowledge enables listeners, regardless of formal music training, to tap and dance to music, detect wrong notes, remember and reproduce familiar tunes and rhythms, and feel the emotions expressed through music'. Many cultures do not distinguish musicians from non-musicians: everyone participates in music (and dance). It may be a peculiarity of the Western tradition that one group of people silently—and motionlessly—watches another group of people make music (this anthropological oddity may have originated in nineteenth-century Vienna; see Ross (2008, p. 19) on Mahler's alleged role in this).[3]

Fourth, both music and language, although universal and rooted in human cognition, diversify across the human population into culture-specific and culturally-sanctioned instantiations: 'languages' and 'musical traditions/genres'. As Hannon & Trainor (2007, p. 466) say: 'Just as there are different languages, there are many different musical systems, each with unique scales, categories and grammatical rules'. Our everyday words for languages ('French', 'English', etc.) often designate socio-political entities: for example, we refer to the languages spoken on either side of the Dutch-German border as 'Dutch' and 'German', although the local dialects are slightly distinct varieties of Low German; conversely, the Swiss dialects of German are referred to as 'German', although they are as distinct from Standard German, by any reasonable measure, as Standard Dutch is. Musical genres, although generally less well-defined and less connected to political borders than differences among languages, are also cultural constructs. This is particularly clear in the case of highly conventionalized forms such as Western classical music, but it is equally true of a 'vernacular' form such as jazz (in all its geographical and historical varieties).

From the perspective of modern generative grammar, which sets itself the goal of developing a theory of the human language faculty, the differences among languages are relatively superficial. Instead the emphasis is on Universal Grammar (UG), the theory of the language faculty. The Principles and Parameters approach to UG underlines this: according to this approach the principles of UG specify the general, invariant structure of language but leave open a rather small number of choice points, parameters of variation; these parameters are responsible for many the differences among languages that we observe (alongside differences in vocabulary and phonetics). To give a

[3] Here I disagree with Pinker's (1997, p. 529) assertion that 'while everyone enjoys listening to music, many people cannot carry a tune, fewer can play an instrument, and those who can play need explicit training and extensive practice. Musical idioms vary greatly in complexity across time, cultures and subcultures.' Pinker's remarks on explicit training and extensive practice relate particularly to the Western classical tradition: one could equally point to the extensive training in reading and practice in writing of highly specific kinds (e.g. academic essays) that all Western children undergo in school, as well as to the complexity of the great works of Western literature, as indicative of the inherently greater complexity of Western languages in relation to languages with no literary tradition. But linguists know that this is confusing culture with cognition. Pinker seems to make that very mistake in the quoted remarks on music. Children develop self-expression through song and dance, and join in communal musical activities, through exposure to the prevalent cultural model, without explicit instruction. This happens in all cultures, including ours. There is also evidence that infants possess perfect pitch which, in the vast majority of individuals, is later lost (Saffran & Griepentrog, 2001). However that may be, only about 4–5% of the population are congenitally tone deaf (Johansson, 2008, p. 417).

simplified example, we can observe that in a simple transitive clause in English the verb precedes the object. In Japanese, on the other hand, the object precedes the verb:

```
(10)
  (a) The teacher scolded Taro.                        (English: V O)
  (b) Sensei-wa        Taro-o            sikata.       (Japanese: O V)
      teacher(Topic) Taro(Accusative) scolded
            'The teacher scolded Taro.'
```

We say, then, that English is a VO language and that Japanese is OV. In terms of Principles and Parameters, we could say that UG principles determine the nature of V (the universal theory of syntactic categories, i.e. nouns, verbs, etc., would do this), the nature of O (the universal theory of grammatical functions such as subject, direct object, indirect object, etc., would do this) and how they combine to form a VP (this is determined by the combinatorial system, some of whose properties we mentioned in the section 'The grid and the structure of language'). Universal principles dictate that a verb and its direct object combine to form a VP. The parametric option concerns the linear order of V and O—universal principles say nothing about this. Hence grammars may choose either of the two logical options: OV or VO. As we saw, Japanese takes the former option while English takes the latter. This account of the difference between English and Japanese implies an account of the acquisition of word order: since UG allows both OV and VO orders, the parameter must be 'open' in the initial state of language acquisition (at birth), and its value is set on the basis of experience. A child growing up in a Japanese-speaking family is exposed to OV orders, a child growing up in an English-speaking family is exposed to VO orders. Learning parametric systems, then, is a matter of selective learning (Lightfoot, 1991). New-born children are in principle equally able to acquire either kind of system, but exposure to one implies that the propensity to acquire the other atrophies. Many important parameters are set in the third year of life (Wexler, 1998; Guasti, 2002, pp. 148, 185, 242).

To my knowledge, the P&P approach to structural variation has not been applied to the comparative analysis of musical genres. The discussion of differences in perception and production of rhythmic patterns in Hannon & Trehub (2005) is, however, suggestive. First, they point out that Western rhythms tend to follow 'isochronous patterns at nested hierarchical levels that are related by simple integer ratios' (p. 49). On the other hand, 'music from Eastern Europe, South Asia, the Middle East, and Africa has an underlying pulse of alternating long and short durations in a 3:2 ratio . . . These complex metres, which are common in Bulgarian and Macedonian folk music, pose no problems for adult and child singers and dancers from those countries.' Further 'implicit knowledge of metrical structure . . . undoubtedly varies across cultures' (p. 49). These remarks are interesting, since rhythm can easily be seen as one of the most basic, and 'embodied,' aspects of music. One could think of a set of universal principles of rhythm, perhaps connected to the basic properties of the grid in something like F&H's sense, along with parameters relating to isochrony and duration ratios.

Hannon and Trehub present experimental evidence that North American adults were less able to recognize violations of the more complex rhythmic patterns in Balkan music, but able to recognize those in simple-metre patterns. Balkan adults were able to discriminate violations of the complex rhythmic patterns. But most interestingly, 6-month-old North American infants were able to make similar discriminations. Hannon and Trehub point out that their 'findings imply that the metrical biases of North American adults reflect enculturation processes rather than processing predispositions for simple metres' (p. 48) and conclude that '[a]bilities that are part of the initial state of auditory pattern processing are likely to undergo reorganization when young listeners discover which distinctions are common or meaningful in their culture' (p. 54). One could see this 'reorganization' in terms of parameter-setting on the basis of primary musical data. North Americans set the 'isochrony/duration parameters' to the isochrony, simple-ration values; part of this process entails losing the ability to process the more complex patterns. Other imaginable musical parameters concern the basic pitch interval (quarter-tone vs. semitone), the scale (diatonic, pentatonic, 'blue') and presumably many aspects of harmony and counterpoint.

For all the above reasons, then, we can see that language and music are remarkably alike. In the next section, I will make a simple conjecture as to why this is the case.

The narrow faculty of language and musical competence: a conjecture based on Hauser, Chomsky, and Fitch (2002)

My conjecture is the following:

(11) Language and music share a single cognitive computational system.

In other words, the relation between these two human cognitive capacities is not one of similarity or shared evolutionary origin but rather identity.

In order to see in more detail what (11) really amounts to, let us look at the conception of the language faculty put forward in Hauser, Chomsky, and Fitch (2002; henceforth HCF). HCF (pp. 1570–1) distinguish the *Faculty of Language—Broad Sense* (FLB) from the *Faculty of Language—Narrow Sense* (FLN). FLB includes FLN 'combined with at least two other organism-internal systems, which we call 'sensory-motor' and 'conceptual-intentional.' Despite debate on the precise nature of these systems, and about whether they are substantially shared with other vertebrates or uniquely adapted to the exigencies of language, we take as uncontroversial the existence of some biological capacity that allows us (and not, for example, chimpanzees) to readily master any human language without explicit instruction. FLB includes this capacity, but excludes other organism-internal systems that are necessary but not sufficient for language.' The conceptual-intentional system provides an interface between language and thought, and in particular can be seen as that part of the language faculty which deals with meaning: i.e. this is the semantic component of language. The sensory-motor system provides ways to 'externalize' the products of FLN. It can thus be seen as the interface with the organs of speech (where the oral/aural channel is used): this is the phonological/phonetic component of language. FLN, on the other hand, 'is the abstract linguistic computational system alone, independent of the other systems with which it interacts and interfaces. FLN is a component of FLB, and the mechanisms underlying it are some subset of those underlying FLB' (p. 1571). FLN contains a 'narrow syntax' which 'generates internal representations and maps them into the sensory-motor interface by the phonological system, and into the conceptual-intentional interface by the (formal) semantic system' (p. 1571).

In the light of HCF's distinction between FLN and FLB, (11) can be restated as follows:

(11') Language and music share FLN.

The postulation of (11') can immediately explain the very close similarities between language and music observed in the previous two sections. These similarities reflect a core cognitive identity between the two faculties: it is not possible for one to exist without the other. This hypothesis has the advantage of parsimony: we observe a range of similar properties, and attribute them to a single source. Hence we obey Occam's razor: we are not multiplying entities beyond necessity. The hypothesis also has the obvious merit of simplicity, and avoids the tricky question of which has phylogenetic or ontogenetic priority over the other. Language and music must evolve together, both in the species and in the individual. Further, HCF suggest that FLN contains 'only the core mechanisms of recursion as they appear in narrow syntax' (p. 1573). Essentially, this means little more than Merge (along with certain interface-sensitive apparatus such as the Agree relation (Chomsky, 2000, 2001)). So the claim is that both faculties share a minimal core of operations. These operations are of the general type postulated by F&H, being recursive grouping operations.

But of course there are differences. I propose that these are to be attributed to the fact that the single core computational system common to both relates to distinct interfaces in each case. Probably the most important single difference can be attributed to the fact that language interfaces, via semantics, with the 'thought systems': systems of knowledge, belief, and reasoning that we may take to be based on the formal semantic notions of truth and reference. Hence, FLB allows us to communicate beliefs, inferences, and propositional attitudes, owing to the interaction between FLN and the conceptual-intentional interface (concretely, many linguists hold that this happens through a compositional mapping of representations output by the narrow syntax FLN to a logical representation of some kind in such a way as to satisfy the Tarskian formula in (9) above). Music simply does not do this: it is pointless to ask what the entailments of a piece of music are, or what any kind of music—from a simple lullaby to the greatest works of the most sophisticated cultural traditions—contributes to our beliefs about the world. Or again: there is no sense at all in which a piece of music, of any kind, can be said to be true or false. As Pinker (1997, p. 529) observes 'Even a plot as simple as "boy meets girl, boy loses girl" cannot be narrated by a sequence of tones in any musical idiom'.[4] Putting the same point another way: music completely lacks any counterpart to basic logical notions such as negation, quantification, predication, etc.

[4] Stravinsky might have had the same idea in mind when he said 'I consider music, by its nature, incapable of expressing anything' (cited in Molino (2000, p. 174)), although this is not certain.

A natural reaction to a comment like Pinker's is to say that logical and semantic notions are irrelevant: the musical lexicon lacks a counterpart to simple words like *boy*, *meet* and *girl*. Music presumably has a lexicon: a static list of elementary elements which are input to the narrow syntax (which undergo Merge, in the terminology of current linguistic theory). But then why is its lexicon so limited? Again, the answer may lie in the fact that music, lacking semantic properties in the way described above, lacks a way to describe the world. Simple lexical items of language like *boy* contain a specification of what the word means (alongside its phonological properties—those relevant to the other linguistic interface—and its formal syntactic properties such as being a noun), and it has been observed since Saussure (1916) that the relationship between meaning and phonological form is arbitrary and hence varies unpredictably from language to language. The basic elements of the musical lexicon presumably have some formal properties and a characterization of their interface properties, but they lack a semantic specification because music does not interface with the thought systems. For the same reason, language has lexical items relating to logical concepts like negation, implication, and quantification.

Indeed, it may be that music lacks the duality of patterning of language for the same reason. Duality of patterning is really a very efficient way of relating the resources of the two interfaces together. The largest phoneme inventories known contain almost 150 phonemes (the Xhoisan language! Xũũ has 95 consonants and 46 vowels (F. Nolan, p.c.)); if each phoneme was a single meaning-bearing lexical item then the system would only allow that number of core concepts. But duality of patterning allows phonemes to combine to form many thousands of morphemes, each with its own core meaning. So it may be that duality of patterning follows from the nature of the conceptual-intentional interface.

So we can explain two major differences between language and music in terms of the simple idea that music lacks referential semantics. Of course, I do not mean that music is without 'meaning' in a more general sense: the claim is just that music lacks the kind of meaning which contributes to our beliefs about the world. Music clearly has 'affective' or 'connotative' meaning. Indeed, the extraordinary power of music in this regard, clearly a universal aspect of musical experience, suggests that music may interface with some facet of emotional psychology (since language also has the power to evoke emotion, there may be a linguistic interface to the emotions too).

The differences between music and language are perhaps less sharp when we consider the 'external' interfaces. Language is externalized through the sensory-motor interface, which, in the oral/aural channel, gives rise to the phonological and phonetic aspects of speech production and perception. Music may also be externalized in this way: this is song (in the sense of vocalization of music; singing lyrics is combining language and music). But music may have a further 'bodily' interface through dance. In general, as Cross et al.'s observations regarding entrainment show, music appears to be more of a 'whole-body' form of expression than language. Of course, gestures usually accompany language (and are subject to interesting intercultural variation), but it is worth observing that while no phonological system in the oral/aural channel has been reported which uses parts of the body other than the organs of speech, i.e. no system in which a handclap or stamp of the foot has phonemic or allophonic status, many cultures regard music and dance as a single activity, and have a single word to designate both (cf. the fact that, in lay language, 'language' and 'speech' or 'talking' are roughly synonymous).

The picture I am suggesting is schematized in the following diagram:

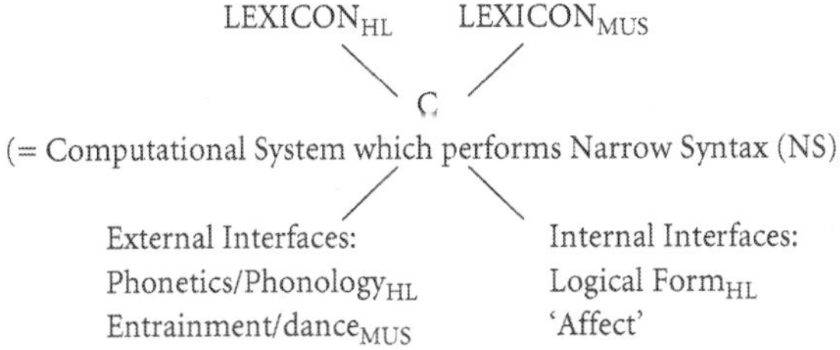

There is clearly much to add to this sketch. The main question concerns the mapping to the interfaces: it has often been proposed that the mapping to the external interfaces is achieved by an operation called Spell Out, which intervenes in the narrow syntactic sequence of operations (technically, the derivation) and strips away some parts of the structure generated up to that point. The internal interface is a mapping from the endpoint of the derivation. It is unclear how these notions would carry over to the musical derivation, but the alternative model developed since Chomsky (2000, 2001), which allows for interaction with both interfaces at designated points of the derivation, may be more promising. Unfortunately, space does not permit me to go into further detail in this point here.

To reiterate: my conjecture here, inspired by F&H, is that the computational system C, which, following HCF, may consist of little more than a recursive grouping algorithm, is the same for both music and language. The elements it manipulates are different, however, as determined by the respective lexica; presumably this also determines which interfaces are relevant. Finally, there appears to be some overlap between interfaces: speech uses pitch and rhythm (but not scales), language uses gesture (but this is not dance) and language has affect. The one case where there is no overlap appears to be LF: music simply lacks the properties relevant to this interface.

Conclusions

I have suggested a very simple hypothesis which can account for the core similarities between music and language, as well as taking care of the core differences between the two faculties. The proposal has clear implications for ontogeny (the interactions of music and language in the input to children, particularly very young babies, are discussed in Johannson (2008, pp. 414–15)) and phylogeny (Darwin (1871, p. 880) speculated that music may have preceded language as a form of courtship; see also Miller (2000), and S. Brown (2000) on 'musilanguage' in human evolution). A further implication, which I believe to be worth exploring independently of the specific claim about FLN entertained here, is that the Principles and Parameters approach could be fruitfully applied to the comparison of musical traditions.

HCF (p. 1571) observe that FLN gives rise to discrete infinity, a property shared with the natural numbers. If FLN underlies musical competence too, then we can see a new synthesis of our understanding the uniquely human capacities in language, music and mathematics (note that mathematics differs from both language and music in that it lacks an 'external' interface, and is like language, but unlike music, in interfacing with the thought systems).

A final point concerns the way we look at both music and language in evolutionary terms in the light of the above conjecture. It seems obvious that language has survival value, while music does not. But the account given above would suggest that referential semantics, not FLN itself, has survival value (although the way in which FLN gives rise to a compositional semantics capable of infinite expressivity may contribute to survival). What this account, like many others, does not tell us is what the evolutionary origins of FLN were, but the fact that FLN subserves music as well as language makes it perhaps less likely that FLN was an adaptation. Here again we see what HCF, in a different context, call 'the possibility that the structural details of FLN may result from . . . pre-existing constraints, rather than from direct shaping by natural selection targeted specifically at communication' (p. 1574). Further, HCF point out (p. 1573) that if FLN is restricted to a few simple recursive operations this has the consequence 'of nullifying the argument from design, and thus rendering the status of FLN as an adaptation open to question'. This observation fits well with the Pinker's (1997, p. 535) observation that music does not appear to be an adaptation (and see also Darwin's (1871) view, quoted in footnote 2 above).

Finally, I note that the view put forward here is compatible with HCF's closing speculation that 'the modular and highly domain-specific system of recursion may have become penetrable and domain-general' (p. 1578) during the course of evolution. If FLN is shared across two faculties, music and language, this idea of non-domain-specific recursion is sustained. If FLN is also implicated in mathematical knowledge, then the proposal made here may shed light on what Bickerton (2000, p. 161) refers to as 'hominization':

> The acquisition of . . . those traits that either have no equivalent in other species or that are developed to a degree unknown in other species.

References

Bernstein, L. (1976). *The Unanswered Question: six talks at Harvard.* Cambridge, MA: Harvard University Press.

Bickerton, D. (2000). Can biomusicology learn from language evolution studies? In N. Wallin, B. Merker, & S. Brown (Eds.), *The Origins of Music* (pp. 153–164). Cambridge, MA: MIT Press.

Blacking, J. (1976). *How Musical is Man?* London: Faber.

Blacking, J. (1995). *Music, Culture and Experience.* Chicago, IL: University of Chicago Press.

Brown, D. (1991). *Human Universals.* New York: McGraw-Hill.

Brown, S. (2000). The 'musilanguage' model of music evolution. In N. Wallin, B. Merker, & S. Brown (Eds.), *The Origins of Music* (pp. 271–300). Cambridge, MA: MIT Press.

Brown, S., Merker, B., & Wallin, N. (2000). An introduction to evolutionary musicology. In N. Wallin, B. Merker, & S. Brown (Eds.), *The Origins of Music* (pp. 3–24). Cambridge, MA: MIT Press.

Chierchia, G., & McConnell-Ginet, S. (1990). *Meaning and Grammar: An Introduction to Semantics*. Cambridge, MA: MIT Press.

Chomsky, N. (1955). *The Logical Structure of Linguistic Theory* [Published as N. Chomsky (1975). *The Logical Structure of Linguistic Theory*. New York: Plenum.]

Chomsky, N. (1995). *The Minimalist Program*. Cambridge, MA: MIT Press.

Chomsky, N. (2000). Minimalist Inquiries: The Framework. In R. Martin, D. Michaels, & J. Uriagereka (Eds.), *Step by Step: Essays on Minimalist Syntax in Honor of Howard Lasnik* (pp. 89–156). Cambridge, MA: MIT Press.

Chomsky, N. (2001). Derivation by Phase. In M. Kenstowicz (Ed.), *Ken Hale: A Life in Language* (pp. 1–52). Cambridge, MA: MIT Press.

Cross, I., & Woodruff, G. (2008). Music as a communicative medium. In R. Botha & C. Knight (Eds.), *The Prehistory of Language, Volume I* (pp. 113–44). Oxford: Oxford University Press.

Cross, I., J. Bisphan, Himberg, T., & Swaine, J. (n.d.). Evolution and musical rhythm. Ms, University of Cambridge.

Darwin, C. (1871). *The Descent of Man, and Selection in Relation to Sex*. London: Murray.

Davidson, D. (1967). Truth and Meaning. *Synthese, 17*, 304–23.

Frege, G. (1923–6). Logische Untersuchungen. Dritter Teil: Gedankengefüge. *Beiträge zur Philosophie des Deutchen Idealismus, 3*, 36–51.

Goldin-Meadow, S. (2005). What language creation in the manual modality tells us about the foundations of language. *The Linguistic Review, 22*, 199–226.

Guasti, M.-T. (2002). *Language Acquisition: The Growth of Grammar*. Cambridge, MA: MIT Press.

Hannon, E., & Trainor, L. (2007). Music acquisition: effects of enculturation and formal training on development. *Trends in Cognitive Sciences, 11*(11), 466–72.

Hannon, E., & Trehub, S. (2005). Metrical categories in infancy and adulthood. *Psychological Science, 16*(1), 48–55.

Hauser, M. (1997). *The Evolution of Communication*. Cambridge, MA: MIT Press.

Hauser, M., Chomsky, N., & Fitch, W. (2002). The Faculty of Language: What Is It, Who Has It, and How Did It Evolve? *Science, 298*, 1569–79.

Heim, I., & Kratzer, A. (1996). *Semantics in Generative Grammar*. Oxford: Blackwell.

Higginbotham, J. (1985). On semantics. *Linguistic Inquiry, 16*, 547–593.

Johansson, B. (2008). Language and music: What do they have in common and how do they differ? A neuroscientific approach. *European Review, 16*, 413–428.

Larson, R., & G. Segal (1995). *Knowledge of Meaning: An Introduction to Semantic Theory*. Cambridge, MA: MIT Press.

Lehrdal, F., & R. Jackendoff (1983). *A Generative Theory of Tonal Music*. Cambridge, MA: MIT Press.

Lightfoot, D. (1991). *How to set parameters: Degree-O learnability*. Cambridge, MA: Bradford Books.

Miller, G. (2000). Evolution of Human Music through Sexual Selection. In N. Wallin, B. Merker, & S. Brown (Eds.), *The Origins of Music* (pp. 329–360). Cambridge, MA: MIT Press.

Mithen, S. (2005). *The Singing Neanderthals*. London: Weidenfeld and Nicholson.

Molino, J. (2000). Toward an evolutionary theory of music and language. In N. Wallin, B. Merker, & S. Brown (Eds.), *The Origins of Music* (pp. 165–176). Cambridge, MA: MIT Press.

Pinker, S. (1997). *How the Mind Works*. London: Penguin.

Pinker, S. (2002). *The Blank Slate: The Modern Denial of Human Nature*. London: Penguin.

Ross, A. (2008). *The Rest is Noise: Listening to the Twentieth Century.* London: Picador.

Saffran, J., & Griepentrog, G. (2001). Absolute pitch in infant auditory learning: evidence for developmental reorganization. *Developmental Psychology, 37*, 74–85.

Sandler, W., & Lillo-Martin, D. (2001). Natural sign languages. In M. Aronoff, & J. Rees-Miller (Eds.), *The Handbook of Linguistics* (pp. 563–581). Oxford: Blackwell.

de Saussure, F. (1916). *Cours de linguistique générale*, publié par C. Bally et A. Sechehaye avec de A. Riedlinger. Lausanne: Payot.

Tarski, A. (1956). The concept of truth in formalized languages. In A. Tarski *Logic, Semantics, Metamathematics* (pp. 152–278). Oxford: Oxford University Press.

Truswell, R. (2008). Constituency a bonobo comprehension. Ms, University of Edinburgh.

Wallin, N., Merker, B., & Brown, S. (Eds.), *The Origins of Music.* Cambridge, MA: MIT Press.

Wexler, K. (1998). Very early parameter setting and the unique checking constraint: A new explanation of the optional infinitive stage. *Lingua, 106*, 23–79.

Chapter 7

Response to commentaries

Nigel Fabb and Morris Halle

We are grateful to the commentators for their remarks. Below we respond to two of the comments.

As explained in the paper, metrical grids are abstract structures assigned to linear sequences of elements, and metrical grids are crucial in three domains: the determination of rhythm in music, the assignment of stress contours to words and phrases, and in an account of the well-formedness of lines of metrical poetry. Metre and stress are (different) properties assigned to syllable sequences, whereas rhythm is a property of sequences composed of (musical) pitches and silences. In all three cases the elements are grouped into either pairs or triplets, and the grouping always results in the promotion of the first (or last) element in every group to the next gridline. The promoted elements are subject to a grouping operation of the same kind as the one just described, resulting in yet another gridline, and the elements promoted in this operation may be grouped one or several more times, where the additional groupings result in additional gridlines. The mechanism for grouping in all cases is an iterative rule that inserts junctures (parentheses) into (projections of) phoneme sequences. (To our knowledge, these are the only iterative rules in phonology.) Grids formed in this way are not notational variants of tree structures.

The demonstration that metre in poetry, stress in words, and rhythm in music are reflexes of grouping operations of the same kind leads to the further question as to the mechanisms that underlie our perception of rhythm in music, of metre in poetry, and of stress in words. This is a question for future research on human perception, and the simplest guess is that one and the same mechanism is involved in all three cases. This, however, is only a guess that may not even be close to what will actually be discovered by cognitive science in the years to come.

In their comment, Vaux and Myler bring up the metre of the well-known nursery rhyme 'Hickory, dickory, dock'. They point out that this metre, which involves syllable groups that strikingly differ in length (see (4) below) is beyond the capacity of the theory of metre presented in our paper. This is correct, but only because we limited our conference paper to metres of one kind, which in Chapter 2, this volume, we have called strict metres. As shown there, in addition to strict metres, there are also loose metres. The distinctive property of strict metres is that the iterative rules are the sole source of syllable grouping. In loose metres, by contrast, parentheses are introduced (and groups are formed) not only by iterative rules, but also by non-iterative rules that apply prior to the iterative rule. This has the consequence of disrupting the regular grouping process on gridline 0, freely generating groups with less than two (resp. three) syllables as well as allowing ungrouped syllables to intervene between groups. We have stated the rules for the nursery rhyme in (1), (2), and (3), and we have illustrated their effects in (4).

(1) On gridline 0 insert a right parenthesis (represented in (4) with a square bracket) to the right of an asterisk projecting from a syllable bearing the main stress in a polysyllabic word.

(2) On gridline 0 insert left parentheses iteratively from right to left at binary intervals, generating groups that are right-headed.

(3) On gridline 1 insert right parentheses iteratively from left to right at binary intervals, generating groups that are right-headed.

```
(4) Hickory, dickory, dock,
      *] *(*   *] *(*   *(        gridline 0
    )*         *)       *         gridline 1
               *                  gridline 2
    The mouse ran up the clock,
     (*  *    (*  *   (*   *(     gridline 0
        )*        *)       *      gridline 1
                  *               gridline 2
```

Referring to the parentheses in the metrical grid, such as those in (4), Dilley and McAuley write that 'it is not clear what these [two types of parenthesis] correspond to in terms of phonetic characteristics, perceptual or structural reality, etc.', and they criticize this as a shortcoming that undermines the validity of our theory. In response we note that the parentheses—as well as the asterisks and the metrical grids themselves—are parts of the abstract structure that we posit in order to account for the perception of musical rhythm, of poetic metre, and of the stress contours of words. The parentheses are similar in nature to the blank spaces between words in written (or printed) texts, and like the blank spaces separating the words, the parentheses lack unique phonetic stigmata. There is at present no mechanical procedure or device that correctly breaks up an acoustic signal of an utterance into the words that compose it. The lack of such a mechanical segmenter, however, does not undercut the psychological or linguistic reality of the words, for words are justified by facts of morphology, syntax, and other aspects of the utterance, in addition to phonetics. In a similar fashion, as we showed in our paper, the parentheses, the asterisks, and the metrical grids are formal objects needed to compute the correct rhythm of musical phrases, the stress contours of words, and the metrical form of lines in metrical poetry. Reference to such abstract objects is required in all accounts of the phonology and morphology of every known language.

Section 2

Evolution

Chapter 8

Introduction

Language and music have long been intertwined in considerations of the origins of communication, both in Western intellectual traditions (as Thomas, 1995, notes) and in those of many non-Western societies (see, e.g. Basso, 1985). In his contribution to this volume Tecumseh Fitch adopts an innovative perspective, focusing on the domain of rhythm as foregrounded in music and as an integral component of language. Rhythm is an apparently simple feature of music, so simple that it has remained under the radar of most contributors to debates on the evolution of music and language. Fitch shows it to be anything but simple, drawing on psychological, neuroscientific, and ethological evidence to reveal it as complex, multi-componential, and—as manifested not only in language but also in music—quite probably unique to modern humans. He uses his conceptualization of human rhythmic capacities—or rather, of the three-fold human capacity to carry out periodic motor behaviours, to abstract a beat from a complex series of events in time, and to *entrain* motor behaviour to the inferred beat—to support a neo-Darwinian hypothesis of the emergence of language (and music) from an earlier-developed communicative system with the attributes of a holistic protolanguage. This protolanguage subserved primarily social functions and manifested, in Fitch's view, features that can be linked to prosodic features of modern language and the aspects of contemporary musical structures and practices. Fitch puts forward a theory that he explicitly intends should generate hypotheses susceptible to empirical testing, and identifies areas where evidence is lacking; he particularly notes that exploration of the capacities of monkeys and apes to engage in rhythmic behaviour is at present severely neglected.

Simon Kirby largely agrees with Fitch's proposals, exploring in his contribution the extent to which the learnability of communicative systems informs the emergence of language- and music-like systems. In effect, Kirby conceives of language and music as culturally transmitted complex systems of which the development can be explored and evaluated in terms of the concept of fitness; this operationalization renders the exploration of language (and music) evolution computationally tractable and conditions Kirby's conclusions. Steve Mithen focuses his contribution on the efficacy of music in enhancing sociality. He suggests that Fitch's concern to frame a rigorous, ethologically comparative, set of hypothesis sets up a time frame that excludes consideration of the period of hominin evolution that archaeology is best suited to address, suggesting that more weight than Fitch allows should be accorded to the archaeological evidence.

Iain Morley presents a nuanced discussion that develops some of the ideas proposed, and the issues raised, by Fitch, stressing the interdependence of vocal gesture, facial expression, and corporeal gesture, and suggesting that this interdependence provides an appropriate locus for exploration of the commonalities between music and language. Elizabeth Tolbert takes issue with Fitch's characterization of music, noting that an ethnomusicological perspective offers a different sort of comparative framework for understanding music from the cross-specific comparisons that are proposed by Fitch; in effect, she suggests that a comparative ethnomusicological frame of reference must be prior in any consideration of music's relationship to evolutionary theory. The section concludes with Fitch's response to the commentaries.

References

Basso, E. (1985). *A musical view of the universe.* Philadelphia, PA: University of Pennsylvania Press.

Thomas, D. A. (1995). *Music and the origins of language: theories from the French Enlightenment.* Cambridge: Cambridge University Press.

Chapter 9

The biology and evolution of rhythm: unravelling a paradox

W. Tecumseh Fitch

Introduction: why can't dogs dance?

Periodicity is a ubiquitous feature of all living things, and coupled biological oscillators entrain to each other readily (Glass & Mackey, 1988; Strogatz, 1994, 2003). Despite this, humans are rare in our ability to entrain our musical motor output to that of others during singing, dancing, and playing in ensembles. This presents something of a paradox concerning human rhythmic entrainment and all that goes with it: why should a phenomenon seemingly so basic be so rare in nature? The paradox, put simply, is this: if periodicity and entrainment are ubiquitous features of all living organisms, why can't dogs dance? In this paper I will explore this paradox from multiple comparative viewpoints, exploring similarities and differences between humans and other animals, between different aspects of music (harmony and rhythm), and between music and spoken language. Although my approach will entail asking many more questions than we can, at present, answer, my overall goal is to help focus interest on a number of phenomena that can, at least in principle, yield to empirical investigation of several sorts. Because of the wide range of disciplines involved, my style will be synoptic rather than prolix, and the references are intended as entry points into the literature rather than being exhaustive.

I will suggest that the 'paradox of rhythm' can be resolved by recognizing that human rhythmic behaviour comprises several different components, each with their own biological basis and evolutionary history. Thinking of rhythm as a unitary, monolithic cognitive entity would be misleading and unproductive, while a 'divide-and-conquer' strategy provides a fruitful way forward (Fitch, 2006a; Patel, 2006). I suggest at least three separable components underlying the human capacity for rhythmic behaviour. These include periodic motor pattern generation itself (an ancient and ubiquitous phenomenon), pulse (or 'beat') extraction from complex patterns (a form of perceptual cognition that is shared with speech, at least), and entrainment of one's own motor output to this inferred 'beat' (which may be the most biologically unusual feature of human rhythmic behaviour). After reviewing the comparative evidence suggesting that these features are separable, and that the pattern perception component is shared between music and speech, I suggest that 'rhythm' incorporates both basic, primitive, biological elements and highly unusual (apomorphic) elements, probably recently evolved. Isochronicity, I suggest, is not a fundamental component of musical rhythm.

Rather, it is a probable (but not inevitable) interaction of the pattern extraction and entrainment components of the 'rhythm faculty', driven by a desire for group coherence and predictability. From the viewpoint advocated here, the mosaic pattern of shared and unique features characterizing rhythm, like that of speech, music, and language more generally, is consistent with Darwin's model of language evolution via a 'musical protolanguage': an intermediate communication system that was more like music than language.

Defining 'rhythm'

The Greek word 'rhythmos' derives from *rhein* 'to flow', and the English word 'rhythm' is used so frequently, and in so many ways, as to sometimes actually impede communication by causing misunderstanding (Sachs, 1952). In lay terms, we talk about the rhythm of the seasons or the rhythm of our heartbeat, which are simply examples of periodic behaviour. Thus, repetition at some relatively steady interval—quasi-periodicity—is one of the most basic connotations of the word 'rhythm' as normally used. However, for musicologists, rhythm means more than mere periodicity, and is intertwined with notions of a 'beat' (quasiperiodic tactus), metre, and stress, when a pattern of recurring events is structured into hierarchical chunks (phrases, or measures) that follow certain rules of number, subdivision, and accent. Not only are such structured patterns produced intentionally by a performer, but the extraction of such patterns from a 'raw' stimulus by the listener is a crucial part of musical rhythm perception, which allows a listener to tap their foot, dance to the beat, or play along with the pattern. Thus, the connotations of 'rhythm' in a musical context are far more complex and specific than simple periodicity. Finally, for linguists (specifically metrical phonologists) and poets 'speech rhythm' has connotations that only partially overlap with those of musicologists. In particular, the periodicity of speech is limited (thus one does not 'play along with,' or dance to, speech rhythms), but the hierarchical pattern-processing aspects of speech and musical rhythm appear to be largely shared.

Based on these and other considerations I will not try to define rhythm per se but rather to specify three separable components typical of musical rhythmic behaviour, and then explore the degree to which these components are just different sides of the same thing (as suggested by Sachs, 1952), or whether they are better thought of as separate components that rely on distinct cognitive/neural mechanisms. The musical context I have in mind is a ubiquitous one in human behaviour, typifying virtually any musical happening. Such situations, in the Western concert hall, include tapping one's foot or swaying back and forth to the beat. In Indian classical music venues, concert-goers often 'dance' along with the performers using fluid hand motions. Far more typical of the world's music is dancing, which involves extracting the beat from a patterned auditory stimulus, and then moving one's entire body to this inferred beat (alone, or in concert with one or more others). Finally, any sort of ensemble playing involves the processes engaged in such examples, but with the additional feature that the motor output produced is itself musically structured and produces audible output, allowing *mutual* entrainment between the members of the ensemble. I will use this last example—ensemble playing—as my example context. Furthermore, to abstract away from many complex questions of pitch extraction, playing in tune, and generating harmony, the ensemble I have in mind is purely percussive: all the instruments (bells, shakers, drums, sticks, hand claps) either lack defined pitch, or produce a fixed, unchangeable pitch. Such an ensemble can produce extremely complex musical patterns, presenting considerable cognitive challenges both for listeners and performers, but 'playing out of tune' or 'out of key' is impossible.

To be concrete, let us use the example of a West African drumming ensemble playing a complex polyrhythmic pattern, such as *agbekor* (a popular traditional rhythm in Ghana and neighbouring lands (Agawu, 1987; Zabana, 1997)). Similar social and cognitive principles typify a huge range of musical performance styles throughout Africa and the New World (Jones, 1954; Locke, 1987; Merriam, 1959; Pressing, 2002; von Hornbostel, 1928).

Three components of rhythmic behaviour

I hypothesize three components as necessary for ensemble playing and dancing: pulse extraction, beat entrainment, and motor pattern generation. The first involves auditory processing only, the second cross-modal (auditory to motor) integration, and the last sensorily-guided motor behaviour. First, I illustrate these for clarity, in the concrete context of an agbekor drumming ensemble. Then I will turn to an exploration of the biological and evolutionary roots of these hypothesized mechanisms.

In agbekor, a central role is played by a bell pattern, played on a 'gakogui' double bell, shown in Figure 9.1 (Toussaint, 2003; Zabana, 1997). Partly because bells are loud, and also because the patterns they play tend to be highly repetitive, with limited scope for improvisation, they provide the basic rhythmic pattern to which the other instruments and players respond and entrain. The bell player(s) can also, of course, entrain to other instruments, and in many cases a leader (e.g. the master drummer, or in other contexts the lead singers or master dancer) might provide the pulse. Nonetheless, we can simplify the situation in a natural way by assuming that the bell player 'leads' and the other instruments follow. Thus, for example, the master drummer may set the tempo and start the ensemble off by drumming the bell pattern.

Crucially, the bell pattern does not directly provide a 'beat' (a colloquial term I will use here to evoke both the Western musicological term 'tactus,' and the 'pulse' of ethnomusicologists (Arom, 1991)). This bell pattern is syncopated, and related in a quite complex fashion to the underlying pulse(s) inferred by other participants. The beat can be seen most directly by the footfalls of dancers responding to the music (and often of the players as well), but *none* of the instruments in the ensemble play a simple pulse on their instrument. Thus, there is nothing like the steady 'four on the floor' drumbeat pattern so typical of much Western dance music. Instead, every participant in such a rhythmic ensemble must *infer* a beat that *is not actually directly present* in the acoustic signal. Thus, the first and most basic cognitive activity is one of **pulse extraction:** the inference of a pulse or 'beat', given a patterned and repetitive acoustic stimulus (in European music, following (Lerdahl & Jackendoff, 1983), this process might be termed *tactus extraction*). This first cognitive requirement is as crucial for dancing as for playing along, and indeed even a passive listener cannot be said to understand the music if they cannot accomplish this first non-trivial step.

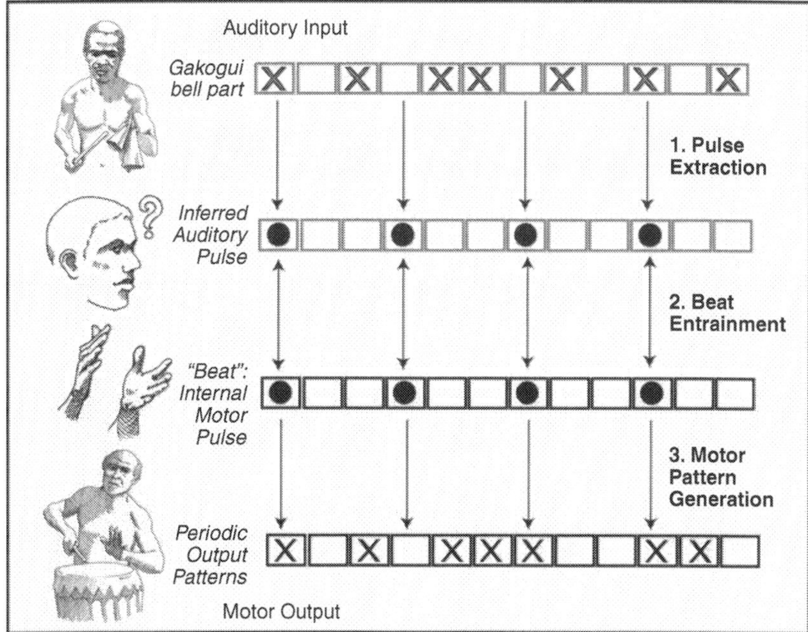

Fig. 9.1 A schematic view of the three cognitive processes hypothesized to underlie ensemble playing and/or dancing, using a West African 'agbekor' bell pattern and drumming ensemble as an example. Grey boxes represent auditory components, black boxes motor components. Xs indicate the onsets of externally observable events, while circles indicate the timing of mental events. Although the diagram represents a simplified, one-way movement of information from the bell pattern to a periodic motor output, in reality information can flow in both directions. In particular, the bell player may respond to the playing of the master drummer, constituting 'mutual entrainment'.

Pulse extraction is made more complex in much African drumming music by the fact that it is polyrhythmic: there are multiple ways to parse the musical surface into an underlying metre and pulse. This rhythmic ambiguity allows such music to be extremely cognitively complex, despite a strictly-kept time, the relative simplicity of the patterns played, and specific rules regarding variation. The formal structure of the agbekor bell pattern mirrors that of the diatonic scale (and indeed provides a rich range of rhythmic possibilities, comparable to that exploited in diatonic harmony in Western classical music, see below). Thus, there is a considerable range of complexity covered by the notion of 'pulse extraction', and the simple notion of tapping your foot to an insistent bass drum pulse does not even begin to do it justice (Arom, 1991). We will return to these issues below, but for now let us assume that the participant has inferred at least one possible pulse from the acoustic pattern, enough to potentially dance along with.

The next step is to entrain one's own motor output to the extracted pulse. If one's motor output is simply tapping one's foot, this could be as basic as periodically tensing a single leg muscle 'to the beat': this would represent what I will call **beat entrainment** and illustrates entrainment in its simplest form. More typically, for the musicians or dancers, entrainment involves using the pulse extracted from a complex auditory stimulus to drive one's own *complex* motor output. Such entrained **motor pattern generation** is a perfect example of complex cross-modal integration. Information from one cortical domain (auditory cortex, centred in the temporal lobe) must be coherently propagated to another (motor cortex, in the frontal cortex just anterior to the central sulcus). It involves both an entrainment of one's own internally-generated pulse to that extracted from the acoustic stimulus, and the use of this to generate a (potentially highly complex) motor output. This output is not simply a slavish reaction to, or acoustic mirror of, that extracted beat. Thus, the phenomenon of entrainment can be cloven into a synchronization component (where the listener's motor pulse is brought into alignment with that inferred from an acoustic signal) and a pattern output component, where the internal pulse is used to drive motor output. Note that the motor output can be simple or complex, and that in the case of complex output there are typically many different possibilities that are all, equally correctly, spoken of as 'entrained'. One can be able to play one drum part and not others (or a dancer may be unable to produce any of the instrumental parts, but produce various complex dances), but all of these performances may be equally 'entrained'. Thus, while the output of the pulse extraction and beat entrainment stages may converge on the same output for all participants (*the* pulse), the pattern output stage may be wonderfully divergent.

Summarizing, an ensemble player (or dancer) in an agbekor session must listen to the bell pattern (top row, Figure 9.1), extract the underlying pulse from this pattern (step 1, Figure 9.1), and then synchronize their own internal cognitive pulse to this (step 2, Figure 9.1). While this alone would be enough to constitute 'entrainment', most musical behaviour involves a final step, where this internal pulse is used to drive a complex motor output, a 'motor score', that could be implemented either via dancing, clapping or singing to this internalized beat, or by producing a different musical output (as symbolized in Figure 9.1, bottom row, with a notation of a master drum part).

As already noted, each of these steps might be, in some sense, just a different manifestation of a single 'rhythmic ability', which you either have or you don't (Sachs, 1952). Indeed to accomplished aficionados of a given musical style, the process just described certainly feels unitary. One does not, consciously, go through separate steps of pulse extraction, beat synchronization, and pattern generation. However, there is good reason to suspect that this subjective unity is misleading, and that neurally and biologically, rhythm is a composite system. Certainly, the perceptual and motor aspects can be separated, in the sense that one can hear the beat, internally, without manifesting it via any body movements of one's own. More crucially, one can infer a beat, and attempt to produce motor output entrained with it, but fail (e.g. because the ensemble is playing too fast, or because the part is too complex and has not yet been fully automatized). However, this last distinction I have made, between simple beat entrainment and complex pattern entrainment, may seem less motivated until we delve into the question from a biological viewpoint.

Coupled oscillators and entrainment in nature: the 'paradox of rhythm'

Oscillators are everywhere in nature, both in the physical world and the biological. At the physical level planetary motion gives us an important set of periodic phenomena (years, days, tides, seasons, . . .), and biology is rife with periodic functions including the familiar heartbeat and breathing cycles, but also including a set of biological clocks, tracking days and seasons, that are entrained to the physical timekeepers just mentioned. Such 'biological clocks' are present in the simplest forms of life, such as bacteria, algae, yeast, and other single-celled organisms. Thus both periodicity, and entrainment of biological clocks to external, physical timekeepers, are ubiquitous in biological systems.

It has also become clear with advances in our understanding of nonlinear dynamics that any form of coupling between nonlinear oscillators can easily lead to phase locking and mutual entrainment (e.g. between heartbeat and respiration, or two vocal folds: Fitch, Neubauer, & Herzel, 2002; Glass & Mackey, 1988). This leads to an apparent paradox: one that we might term the '**paradox of rhythm**'. Periodicity and entrainment seem to be among the most basic features of living things, yet the human ability (and proclivity) to entrain our motor output to auditory stimuli appears to be very rare: there is no credible evidence of even simple beat entrainment among other primates or mammals (Merker, 1999, 2000). Among *all* living organisms, mutual entrainment remains rare in its simplest forms (Greenfield, 1994, Patel et al., 2009, Schachner et al., 2009), and it is perhaps unique to our species in even the mildly complex forms observed in a musical ensemble playing a simple piece. The paradox, put simply, is this: if periodicity and entrainment are ubiquitous features of all living organisms, why can't dogs or most other animals keep a beat, or dance? Of course, one answer to this question is to note that absence of evidence does not provide strong evidence of absence. Perhaps dogs *can* dance, and we just can't *tell* that they're dancing. More pertinently, there remains much to be learned about rhythmic behaviour in great apes, and it is certainly too early to state firmly that they are incapable of entrainment (cf. Fitch, 2006a). A wide variety of bird species show duetting and various bodily movements suggestive of entrainment, but have not been thoroughly investigated from a musicological viewpoint. Nonetheless, it is safe to say that among primates, particularly the well-studied chimpanzees, evidence of entrainment is very sparse, and no published experimental data suggests entrainment. Thus I will cautiously proceed from the assumption that humans are unusual in our proclivity for mutual entrainment of complex patterns, and that this represents a quite marked difference from our nearest living relatives, even if the difference is not absolute, but rather a (large) quantitative difference.

It is interesting to note that cross-modal integration, in any form, was believed to be unique to humans, until the late 1960s, and this was seen as a crucial advance in cognitive organization between chimpanzees and humans (Cole, Chorover, & Ettlinger, 1961; Geschwind, 1970). However, numerous studies have now shown cross-modal transfer between sensory modalities in apes and monkeys (Davenport & Rogers, 1970; Ettlinger & Blakemore, 1969; Ghazanfar & Logothetis, 2003; Savage-Rumbaugh,

Sevcik, & Hopkins, 1988). The degree to which this is flexible and general, or tied to specific modalities (e.g. face/voice perception) remains unclear. Note that there is good evidence in both humans and other mammals for cross-sensory flexibility in vision, touch, and audition: humans born blind use their occipital cortex for Braille reading (Cohen, et al., 1997), and ferrets whose brains are 'rewired' *in utero*, so that visual information is directed to temporal cortex (which contains primary auditory cortex in normal mammals) develop a working visual cortex in the temporal lobe (Sur, Pallas, & Roe, 1990; von Melchner, Pallas, & Sur, 2000). These data suggest that sensory cortices are in some sense interchangeable during ontogeny. This may be because the structure of sensory cortices is relatively consistent across modalities, which all have a well-developed granular input layer (in layer IV of neocortex). This similarity may ease the computational burden of cross-modal transfer between sensory domains.

In contrast, cross-modal sensory/motor integration may provide a greater neurocomputational challenge. The cytoarchitectonic layout of primary sensory areas is very different from that of the motor cortex, which is agranular and includes a special 'output' cell type, the giant Betz cells in layer V that are a cytoarchitectonic indicator of mammalian motor cortex (for discussion see Shipp, 2005). In addition to this neural evidence, research in robotics has demonstrated sensory-guided motor behaviour to be one of the most challenging aspects of developing machines that behave with a modicum of intelligence. Although any living vertebrate out-performs current robots, this is almost certainly due to a half-billion years of intense selection, which has built up a large collection of neural tricks and shortcuts (hard-coded 'looming detectors' and the like), rather than a general solution to the sensory-motor integration problem (Brooks, 1989). Because the entire purpose of sensory systems is to guide adaptive behaviour, it is not surprising that brains are good at using this information. But since natural selection has no foresight, we expect (and find) partial, domain-specific 'Good Tricks' (Dennett, 1995) to the problem of sensory-guided action, and a palimpsestic inheritance and re-use of such tricks during vertebrate evolution. What would be surprising is the discovery of a general-purpose transform capable of transforming *any* complex sensory input into a complex motor output. But this is precisely what humans appear to have evolved (though see Patel, Iversen, Chen, & Repp, 2005).

Summarizing, the generation of a complex patterned motor output entrained to an *acoustic* pattern is not in any sense assured by the ubiquity of periodicity, or a capacity for cross-modal sensory transfer. Furthermore, even extraction of a beat, and entrainment to that beat in a pure motor fashion (for example, in dancing), does not assure the ability to *musically* entrain, for one can be a dancer (motor → motor) but not an instrumentalist (motor → acoustic). This is due to the fact that playing an instrument is a motor act, but a crucial aspect of this act is a careful attention to the instrument's acoustic output. Part of learning to play an instrument is the gradual (and difficult) process of closing the motor/auditory loop by playing, directly analogous to babbling in the vocal domain. Playing involves an additional level of complexity over the (already challenging) dancing problem.

Thus, the 'paradox of rhythm' already seems less paradoxical if we subdivide the cognitive capacities underlying rhythmic performance into different subcomponents. I will now turn to a consideration of the animal comparative data, in an effort to ascertain which (if any) of these sub-components was present before the emergence of humans.

Rhythm in our nearest cousins: the African great apes

Questions about the evolutionary timing of mechanisms underlying rhythm can be recast in phylogenetic terms as follows. Humans and chimpanzees (our nearest living cousins) shared a most-recent common ancestor ('last common ancestor' or LCA) between five to seven million years ago (Chen & Li, 2001). This species was neither a chimpanzee nor a human, but shared many characteristics with both (Carroll, 2003). We can use the comparative method, examining the behaviour of living humans, chimpanzees, and other apes, to reconstruct this LCA. From this reconstruction, we can determine which (if any) rhythmic capacities it possessed.

A striking fact, as soon as we search for rhythmic acoustic generation in other animals, is that both chimpanzees (a term I will use to denote both chimpanzees *Pan troglodytes* and bonobos *Pan paniscus*) and gorillas (*Gorilla gorilla*) generate periodic acoustic behaviour. These African great apes frequently create sounds by pounding with their limbs (most typically hands, but also often with their feet) on resonant objects. This behaviour is termed 'drumming' by ape researchers (e.g. Arcadi, Robert, & Mugurusi, 2004; de Waal, 1988; Schaller, 1963). This is strikingly similar, in many ways, to human hand drumming (found in virtually all human cultures). Ape drumming thus seems a plausible homologue of human drumming (Fitch, 2006a). Ape drumming appears throughout wild and captive chimpanzee populations (Arcadi, Robert, & Boesch, 1998; Arcadi, et al., 2004), and appears in gorillas who have never seen others perform the behaviour (Schaller, 1963), and thus appears to represent a genetically-based species-typical characteristic of African apes. Drumming functions both in playful behaviour among young animals and in display behaviour by adult males. While gorillas typically drum on their own (or sometimes others') bodies, chimpanzees tend to drum on external objects. Chimpanzee individuals seek out hollow or resonant objects with particular acoustic properties, and return to those objects repeatedly to drum, a behaviour clearly indicating a linkage between the auditory and motor systems (Kirschner, Call, & Fitch, in preparation). Drumming behaviour is found in these species, and in humans, but not in orangutans, suggesting that the underlying mechanisms represent an African great ape homology, present in the common ancestor of humans, chimpanzees, and gorillas, but not before (it thus evolved around ten million years ago). Although detailed studies of the similarities and differences in drumming behaviour between humans, chimpanzees and gorillas are underway (Kirschner, et al., in preparation), it is safe to say that this fascinating example of a potentially homology has gone little appreciated and remains poorly studied and understood; this is made more surprising by the fact that examples of such drumming are very rare outside of our particular primate lineage (cf. Fitch, 2006b). In the three-way distinction I have sketched above, I see ape drumming behaviour as providing clear evidence that the last performance stage—mapping a quasiperiodic motor pulse into an auditorily-monitored acoustic motor behaviour—was already present long before the emergence of humans as a separate lineage.

In contrast, there is currently little evidence of entrainment in ape drumming: 'Free rhythm . . . is doubtless the earlier quality. Strictness comes with man' (Sachs, 1953, pp. 20–21). Despite such statements, this area of animal cognition remains poorly explored. In general, chimpanzees perform their drumming displays alone (it is often a dominant male who produces the drumming at the climax of a display including a loud, stereotyped vocal component as well as vigorous motor activity), so there would be little opportunity for, and thus evidence of, social entrainment. While young gorillas sometimes exchange drumming bouts during play, often as a prelude to play chasing or other playful interaction, we have no observations of synchronized drumming and none are reported in the literature (e.g. Schaller, 1963). There is better evidence for mutual entrainment in vocalizations, for example, the 'staccato hooting' of bonobos (de Waal, 1988), or the elaborate interlocking duets of male and female gibbons and siamangs (Geissmann, 2000), suggesting that at least some degree of vocal synchronization may be possible in these species, but at present there is no definitive evidence of clear, periodic entrainment in ape drumming. Thus the safest assumption at present appears to be that beat entrainment either emerged, or underwent strong positive selection, sometime after the split between chimpanzees and humans around six million years ago. However, experimental data on chimpanzee entrainment is sorely needed to test this supposition.

Finally, what of pulse extraction (inference of a 'beat' from a complex acoustic pattern)? Here we know even less about animals. Part of the problem is methodological—the clearest way to ascertain if pulse extraction has occurred is to have the subject tap along to a complex rhythmic pattern and examine their pattern of abilities and errors (e.g. Fitch & Rosenfeld, 2007). But this obviously requires subjects who both have beat entrainment and can produce at least a simple motor output, in addition to the auditory perceptual abilities underlying pulse extraction. Although there is a long history of experimentation with animal timekeeping, in the sense of rats learning to press a bar with a certain periodicity (e.g. Collyer & Church, 1998), this ability concerns maintenance of a motor pulse, not entrainment of that pulse to an auditory stimulus. The clearest experiment, for an animal, is to do tempo matching, where complex patterns at the same or different tempos are presented, and the animal must respond appropriately whether the tempos are the same or different (Patel et al., 2009). Given the difficulties training macaques on a far simpler auditory 'same/different' task (see Brosch, Selezneva, Bucks, & Scheich, 2004) such an experiment would be very challenging to perform, and it is perhaps not surprising that results of such experiments have not, to my knowledge, been published. More promising species for such an operant task would be birds. Songbirds can be readily trained in auditory operant tasks (e.g. Gentner, Fenn, Margoliash, & Nusbaum, 2006) (though note that pigeons apparently fail to master even visual same/different tasks (e.g. Huber, 2001)). Thus, excepting parrots (see Chp 14), no broad comparative pronouncements can be made about pulse extraction at present. My guess is that animals such as parrots and songbirds can extract a pulse from a complex acoustic pattern, but this is speculative, and the situation is far less obvious for nonhuman mammals, such as rats or chimpanzees. However, another important source of 'comparative' data for pulse extraction from acoustic patterns must come from a comparison, within humans, of language and music, to which I will now turn.

In summary, there is good preliminary evidence for rhythmic motor output in great apes, and it supports the distinction I have made between beat entrainment and pattern generation. The comparative data suggest that what is missing in chimpanzees is the beat entrainment component, allowing a tentative hypothesis that this is the last of the three components to appear in human evolution.

Within-human comparisons in music and language

A long-running debate in human psychology concerns the 'modularity', or lack thereof, in the cognitive mechanisms underlying language (Bates, 1994; Fodor, 1983). Do language and music rely on domain-specific, or general purpose, cognitive and computational mechanisms (Patel, 1998, 2008; Peretz, 2006; Peretz & Morais, 1989)? Again we must recognize that 'language' has many components, and that the answer to this question may vary from one to the other. While long-term memory and fast learning mechanisms (e.g. for word meanings) may rely on precisely the same cognitive mechanisms as memorizing other facts about the world (e.g. Markson & Bloom, 1997), syntax might rely on dedicated mechanisms unique to the syntactic domain (Chomsky, 1986; Crain, 1991). There is no contradiction here, and the starting point for any reasonable discussion of modularity in language and music is thus a clear delineation of the specific cognitive abilities under discussion (as advocated in Fitch, Hauser, & Chomsky, 2005; Hauser, Chomsky, & Fitch, 2002; Patel, 2006). Here I compare the cognitive mechanisms underlying rhythmic musical performance discussed above with those involved in harmony and in speech, particularly in the domain of metrical phonology (cf. Goldsmith, 1990). I wish to draw particular attention to the abilities involved in acoustic pattern perception, which I will argue have an important shared, or general, component.

A major challenge confronting comparisons between language and other cognitive domains is that we know so much about language, at a detailed formal level, compared to other domains of human cognition. In the case of musical rhythm, however, our understanding seems to me adequate to attempt such a comparison in a relatively balanced fashion (e.g. Longuet-Higgins & Lee, 1984). But before this, it is worth asking whether there may be even more general pattern-perception capabilities, typical of all perceptual domains. This, of course, was the basic claim of the gestalt psychologists, starting with Wilhelm Wundt (1908), and continuing to the present day (e.g. in Bregman, 1990; Lerdahl & Jackendoff, 1983). While I think it is reasonable to assume, along with gestalt theorists, that certain aspects of perception are universal, this does not exclude the possibility of quite specific perceptual processes that apply to audition and not to, say, vision, touch or smell. The auditory system has its own rather specific problems to deal with, and hard-wired solutions to low-level problems like source-localization have no equivalent in the visual or tactile domains (Masterton & Imig, 1984; McAlpine & Grothe, 2003). Thus it seems reasonable to proceed on the assumption that pattern-extraction capabilities specific to the auditory domain *could* exist (e.g. Patel, et al., 2005), and let the data tell us if we're incorrect.

Comparisons within music: pitch and rhythm

A nice example of a domain in which gestalt principles and more general mathematical (group-theoretic) constraints might govern auditory perception is provided by a fascinating similarity across the rhythmic and tonal domains (Pressing, 1983; Schloss, 1985). This potential example of a pan-musical perceptual principle is nicely illustrated by the isomorphism between the agbekor bell pattern already discussed and the ubiquitous diatonic scale of Western music. As Figure 9.2 shows, the pattern of alternating large and small pitch intervals in the diatonic scale is identical to the pattern of durational intervals in the agbekor pattern. This isomorphism seems very unlikely to result from chance (cf. Toussaint, 2003). As Toussaint points out, the agbekor bell pattern (which he refers to by the Cuban name of the rhythm, 'bembé') is one of the most popular and widespread of all such patterns, found widely throughout sub-Saharan Africa and diverse musical cultures in the New World. We thus have an extremely popular and successful rhythmic pattern with the same structure as the diatonic system which is probably the most widespread scale on Earth today. Both rely upon an underlying division of a cycle (either the rhythmic period, or the octave) into 12 equal divisions; both use either one or two of these intervals as the spacing between events/notes; and both distribute these intervals in a directly isomorphic fashion. This suggests, perhaps surprisingly, that similar pattern-extraction mechanisms may apply in the domains of rhythm and tonality, despite gross differences in the musical surface analysed, providing support for the idea of broad cognitive/aesthetic principles applicable across musical domains.

What is the cause of this similarity, an isomorphism linking two very different musical domains (tonality and rhythm) and musical cultures (European and West African)? Both the rhythmic and tonal examples have received quite extensive mathematical treatment, and there are multiple ways of characterizing them mathematically, probably all valid to some degree (for an introduction to this literature see Cassirer, 1944; Pressing, 1983; Toussaint, 2003; Zweifel, 1996). Of course, mathematical similarity does not necessarily indicate any fundamental causal similarity: there are a huge variety of natural phenomena well-modelled by normal curves or power laws (distribution of star sizes, human heights, word frequency, personal incomes, or neuron interconnectivity) bearing no fundamental relationship at the level of the causal forces that generate these different phenomena (e.g. Keller, 2005). While these isomorphisms therefore render plausible the suggestion that fundamental neural, cognitive, or perceptual

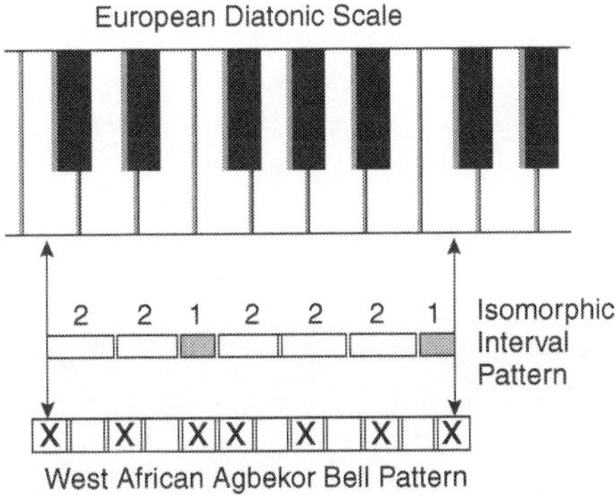

Fig. 9.2 Isomorphism between the (logarithmically-spaced) pitch intervals of the diatonic scale with the temporal intervals of the widespread 'agbekor' bell pattern.

constraints generate both the diatonic scale and the bell pattern, they by no means guarantee this conclusion (cf. London, 2002). It is quite possible that there is some fundamental constraint at the level of neural circuitry (perhaps a developmental constraint on how nerve networks are epigenetically wired together), but that the actual networks involved employ quite different neurons in different areas of the brain. Thus, we cannot expect brain imaging to necessarily resolve this question. Note further that if these similarities result from truly *perceptual* constraints, as opposed to musical or auditory constraints, we should expect similar isomorphisms in the domain of visual patterns in art (e.g. quilts, textiles, mosaics, pottery patterns, and similar plane patterns). But, despite some detailed mathematical analyses of such patterns (e.g. Washburn & Crowe, 1998, 2004) and a long history of suggestive allusions (e.g. Gombrich, 1984), I know of no evidence that this is the case.

Thus, the existence of isomorphisms in the rhythmic and tonal domains raises fascinating questions about the nature of human perception and aesthetic cognition that cannot be answered at present. Although this discovery certainly suggests that there are deeper commonalities in musical cognition than a modularist account might suggest (e.g. Peretz & Morais, 1989; Peretz & Zatorre, 2005) shared mechanisms have not been demonstrated. Nor can we conclude from such findings that there are 'general gestalt principles' that govern such phenomena, given the lack of evidence for similar phenomena in non-auditory perceptual domains. Indeed such phenomena might arise from *cultural* evolutionary processes, only broadly constrained by biological proclivities or limitations (cf. Merker, 2006). Although the within-music isomorphism itself is a fact, its causal basis remains a fascinating mystery, a mystery whose resolution may yield deep insights into (at least) musical cognition if explored experimentally at the perceptual, cognitive, and neural levels.

Hierarchy in speech and rhythm

I now turn to a comparison between 'rhythm' in spoken language and in music, a cross-domain similarity that appears to me to represent another fascinating isomorphism between two superficially very different domains (cf. Patel, 2008). Linguists use the term 'rhythm' in a rather different fashion from musicologists. For them, the term connotes an alternating system of accents combined with patterns of grouping, of the sort typical in poetry. Thus, for example, we describe the prosodic rhythm of Shakespeare's sonnets as 'iambic pentameter' because the syllables are arranged in pairs ('feet') with accents distributed in a weak-STRONG fashion (termed 'iambs'), and organized into lines of five iambs (hence 'penta-'). For example:

> When I / do COUNT / the CLOCK / that TELLS / the TIME, . . . (Sonnet 12)
> or
> Sha l I/ com PARE / thee TO / a SUM/mer's DAY? . . . (Sonnet 18)

Although the feet (separated above by '/') and the accented syllables will occur at roughly equal intervals, there is no suggestion that they should fall precisely on some isochronic beat. Indeed, if read in strict musical time, the output would seem somewhat forced and mechanical. Although human perceivers often *think* that syllables or stresses are evenly spaced or isochronous, which has led to the distinction between 'stress-timed' and 'syllable-timed' languages, repeated acoustic analyses have shown that neither type of speech in fact exhibits isochrony (Dauer, 1983; Ramus, Nespor, & Mehler, 1999; Roach, 1982).

Thus, a clear distinction between musical rhythm and poetic rhythm is the degree to which they connote (or require, in many forms of music) a strict, metronomic 'beat' governing the occurrence of events. Nonetheless, there are other fundamental similarities to consider, particularly if we compare spoken poetry with musical rhythm. Both have a metre (a rule or rules determining the size of the sets into which events are perceptually grouped). Both have a notion of 'accent' (also called 'stress' or 'prominence'), and rules about how such accents should be distributed. Furthermore, both have larger units into which these groups are arranged (e.g. phrases in music, lines or sentences in speech), and further rules governing relations among these phrases (e.g. phrases can be marked by phrase-final lengthening; non-adjacent phrases may be required to rhyme, etc.). Finally, all of these 'rules' are actually defeasible; they can be overridden for aesthetic or semantic purposes. Thus they are better thought of as constraints that provide some underlying conceptual structure and predictability, but not as rules strictly determining the structures actually produced. Together, these formal regularities comprise the **hierarchical structure** of speech prosody and music, and seem to represent one of the clearest examples of overlap between these domains. Recent neuroimaging data support the notion of shared processing of this aspect of speech and music rhythm (Geiser, Zaehle, Jancke, & Meyer, 2008).

Social origins of isochrony?

If the rhythm of speech, as studied by metrical phonologists, shows that isochronicity is dispensable, why then is it so ubiquitous in the music of the world? I think the *exceptions* to regularity in music help to understand the rule, for there are actually numerous forms of music in the world that lack isochrony. Most of these are *solo* forms. After the most comprehensive review of 'free rhythm' (musical styles lacking a pulse or metre) I know of, Clayton concludes that such music 'is unlikely to be performed by an ensemble (at least not in a manner demanding strict synchronization), or to be danced to' (Clayton, 1996, p. 330). This suggests that isochronicity is actually a by-product of a more fundamental need for synchronized interactions *between different individuals*. When an individual is speaking, producing music or dancing alone, there is no need for such synchronization: 'As long as singers stand alone . . . the urge for strictness in rhythm and tempo is very weak' (Sachs, 1953, p. 35). Indeed, in a solo situation, a far freer approach to tempo and metre is possible. This broadens expressive potential, allowing text meaning to dominate (as in many ritualistic/religious 'songs' in Jewish, Islamic, and Persian traditions (Frigyesi, 1993)), or allowing a freer approach to melodic improvisation, as in the unmetrical *alap* introduction typical of North Indian classical performance (Clayton, 1996).

But as soon as multiple individuals attempt to blend together, either producing separate events synchronously, with some syncopation, or even anti-synchronizing in call-and-response fashion, some predictable tempo becomes invaluable (cf. McNeill, 1995;

Merker, 1999). Anyone who has witnessed the cacophony of a room full of young children given drums for the first time, or attempted to dance to a beginners' drum circle keeping irregular time, will understand intuitively what I mean. Stating this "social convergence" hypothesis more formally, if the goal of an ensemble is to cooperatively generate temporally coherent patterns between multiple periodic events, produced by multiple individuals, the simplest way to achieve this is to chose a single base frequency (a 'tempo') for all patterns. By either following some timekeeper (a leader, or a metronome) or mutually entraining to one another, ensembles sharing such an underlying frequency can easily achieve phase locking even for quite complex, interlocking parts. Although it is formally possible to achieve phase coherence among different phases at different frequencies (e.g. in 'cross time' such as 2 against 3, or more complex polyrhythms), even in this case the frequencies should be small integer multiples of one another, and thus they connote a shared base frequency. This provides another reason to separate beat entrainment from complex, entrained pattern generation.

Furthermore, the fundamentally social nature of the drive I hypothesize underlying such (in principle rather simple) entrainment returns us to questions about the biology and evolution of such a capacity. Chimpanzees are highly-skilled at many complex motor actions. They exhibit sophisticated tool use, and their own drumming behaviour reveals their ability to generate patterns based on a quasiperiodic pulse. However, chimpanzees show little evidence, relative to humans, of a strong cooperative urge underlying complex group activities (e.g. Hare & Tomasello, 2004; Melis, Hare, & Tomasello, 2006). Even 'cooperative hunting' in chimpanzees (Boesch & Boesch, 1989; Boesch & Boesch-Achermann, 2000), which provides the best example of ape group action, can be seen as the self-organizing activity of multiple independent individuals, who share a common goal ('catch the monkey') but no shared plan for achieving this goal (Busse, 1978). In contrast, human rhythmic behaviour may represent just one expression of a more general 'cooperative urge'—a motivation to share experience, activities, and emotions with others—that is so typical of our species, and so unusual in the natural world (Cross, 2003; Dissanayake, 2000; Tomasello, Carpenter, Call, Behne, & Moll, 2005). This, I suggest, provides a ready explanation for our ability, and proclivity, to entrain to an isochronic beat. Recent data (Kirschner & Tomasello, 2009) suggest that a capacity to entrain body movements to an isochronic beat is already present in 2.5-year-old children, though in young children it depends on an adequate social context (a human drummer) to be reliable. These data suggest, again, that it is the capacity for entrainment to a *strict periodic pulse* that came latest in human evolution, but that this capacity might reflect some more general social, cooperative urge, rather than any specifically perceptual or musical mechanism.

This hypothesis has implications for discussions of the adaptive value of music. While many authors have noted the value of a componential approach to the *mechanisms* underlying music (Fitch, 2006a; Justus & Hutsler, 2005; McDermott & Hauser, 2005; Patel, 2006), it is not as frequently recognized that this applies just as well to the *selective functions* that they serve(d) (whether full-fledged adaptations or not). We cannot assume that behaviours of some extinct hominid which served as precursors to modern human music were themselves 'music'. Thus, when we (e.g. McDermott &

Hauser, 2005; Patel, 2006) pose questions about adaptive functions of specific mechanisms like pitch or rhythm perception in terms of 'natural selection for music' (or alternatively 'for language'), we implicitly downplay the possibility that the selective value of such mechanisms may have been unrelated to either. In this vein, the 'social convergence' hypothesis proposed above is not wedded in any specific way to music: musical synchronization might be just one of a host of different types of behaviours that are enabled by a general-purpose ability to predict and synchronize with the movements of others. Isochrony, rather then being an adaptation for music, may simply be a culturally discovered aid to synchronization.

While this hypothesis remains speculative given the dearth of data on mutual entrainment in other animals (cf. Merker, 1999), it is consistent with the available evidence and (more importantly) testable with new data that could be readily gathered. Two contrasting sets of predictions can be generated. First, noting the crucial role of cross-modal, audiomotor, integration in synchronization, Patel (2006) suggested that synchronization may be an offshoot of vocal learning—what he termed the 'vocal learning and rhythmic synchronization' hypothesis. This is a plausible hypothesis, and makes the strong prediction that synchronization will *not* be observed in chimpanzees, gorillas, or other 'drumming' mammals (e.g. kangaroo rats), where vocal learning is lacking. It also suggests that synchronization *will* be found in birds, seals, or cetaceans who possess well-developed vocal learning capabilities (cf. Chapter 14). In contrast, the 'social convergence' hypothesis predicts synchronization abilities should be best in group-living species, particularly those who engage in cooperative group behaviour (e.g. social canids, elephants, white pelicans), and perhaps in chimpanzees as well (accepting at face value the characterization of their hunting as 'cooperative' Boesch & Boesch, 1989; Boesch & Boesch-Achermann, 2000).

The biological basis of music/language similarities: Darwin's theory of language evolution

I end by discussing the phylogenetic trajectory that might have led to the mosaic of shared and dissimilar rhythmic components discussed in this paper. I will focus on the comparison between music and language, but many similar questions could be raised for the relationship between rhythm and tonality in human music, or indeed between human music and the complex, learned vocalizations called 'song' in other species (cf. Fitch, 2006a).

One place to start is with a consideration of the multiple 'design features' of language and music (Fitch, 2006a; Hockett, 1960). Spoken language and song share all the design features intrinsic to the audio/vocal modality, along with the features of being complex and being learned. As we have seen above, speech and musical rhythm also share a quite specific form of prosodic hierarchical structure. More generally, although both music and language primarily rely on the audiovocal channel, each can potentially be expressed via other channels (e.g. dance for music, and gesture or signed language for linguistic communication). Probably as result, both music and language can be written as well. Both are thus "supramodal" systems. Finally, both systems are culturally transmitted and thus subject to local diversification into dialects or styles, and these styles can themselves become 'badges' of one's provenance, and thus potential indicators of an individual's kinship or group affiliations. All of these factors, combined with the existence of complex, learned songs in songbirds, led Darwin to suggest that the first stage of the evolution of language involved something closer to music: a 'musical protolanguage' (Darwin, 1871, Fitch, 2010). A strange quirk of recent scholarship in the evolution of language and music is that Darwin's model has been almost universally overlooked (and indeed repeatedly reinvented, e.g. Brown, 2000; Livingstone, 1973). This oversight is all the more surprising given that *The Descent of Man and Selection in Relation to Sex* is hardly an obscure work, and more importantly by the fact that (at least in my view), it provides one of the strongest available models for language evolution.

Darwin's model, slightly updated in light of contemporary research, posits that, during an initial stage of human evolution since our deviation from chimps, proto-humans developed the capacity for complex vocal learning which underlies both speech and song. This system, akin to bird- or whale-song, was not meaningful in any propositional or denotational sense—and thus more like song than spoken language. However, neither was it identical to modern music: there is no reason to suppose that it used discrete pitches or isochrony. The uses of this vocal communication system may have been various (cf. Mithen, 2005; Morley, 2002; Roederer, 1984), including sexual (courtship and territorial advertisement), as proposed by Darwin, parent–offspring communication (Dissanayake, 2000; Falk, 2004; Trainor, 1996; Trehub & Trainor, 1998), or perhaps group bonding (Brown, 2000; Hagen & Bryant, 2003) or advertisement (Merker, 1999, 2000). Although none of these functions need be exclusive, the best data currently available support the parent–offspring, and specifically mother–infant, function at present (for a review see Fitch, 2006a). Only the group advertisement hypotheses (Merker, 1999) entail isochrony at this first stage. Thus, in essence, Darwin's hypothesis posits that the first stage of language evolution was 'bare' phonology: phonology without meaning. The crucial mechanisms here are vocal learning (shared by speech and song, representing a crucial difference between humans and chimpanzees), and hierarchical parsing (as shared by spoken language and musical rhythm). The properties shared by phonology and syntax (e.g. generativity, infinite use of finite means) would already be present at this stage, but complex syntax would not be.

A non-intuitive aspect of Darwin's model is that it suggests a two-stage evolution of complex syntax. In the first 'musical' stage, we would have only hierarchical structure, in the specific sense discussed above, including notions of grouping, metre, stress/accent, and phrasal prosody. An additional non-intuitive assumption of this model would be that meaning in protolanguage, to the extent that it existed, would have been quite general and probably context-dependent: although there might have been love songs, hunting songs and lullabies, there would have been no word for 'love', 'hunt' or 'sleep'. This 'holistic' aspect of meaning in the hypothesized protolanguage, as specified in (Arbib, 2005; Jespersen, 1922; Kirby, 2000; Wray, 1998), is the one that has attracted the most criticism (see Tallerman, 2007), and it certainly contrasts with the intuitive notion of cavemen grunting out monosyllables signifying meat, fire, spear, and the like (as posited in the more popular 'lexical protolanguage' model of Bickerton, 1990). By the Jespersen/Wray hypothesis, true words would appear only in the last stage of language evolution, by a slow cultural process of 'fractionation' of complex holistic phrases into more compositional subunits (cf. Fitch 2010). By hypothesis, this would be driven by the underlying, pre-existing compositionality of thought, via an accumulation of 'mistakes' where children perceive a compositional structure in adult speech that is not (from the speaker's viewpoint) really there. As non-intuitive as this proposition may seem at first blush, the existence of such fractionation processes can be empirically observed both in child language acquisition and historical linguistics (Jespersen, 1922; Mithen, 2005; Wray, 1998), and a simple and elegant computer simulation by Kirby demonstrates that a combination of phonological complexity (ala Darwin's musical protolanguage) and semantic/conceptual compositionality is all that is required for such a process to proceed (Kirby, 2000). The end product yields most of the complex features that differentiate modern syntax from phonology—long-distance dependencies, case-marking, 'movement' phenomena, etc.—with most of the complexities of such phenomena 'inherited' from the interface to the conceptual system.

Most of the data reviewed in this paper concerning rhythm are consistent with Darwin's hypothesis. Far more important, most of the open questions touched upon can serve as tests of the 'musical protolanguage' model of language evolution: as we learn more about entrainment, hierarchical pattern parsing and so on, and begin to understand the neural and ultimately genetic bases of such capacities, Darwin's hypothesis makes clear predictions about what we should find. In particular, our ability to crudely date the 'selective sweep' that drove particular alleles involved in particular cognitive capacities (as in Enard, et al., 2002) will allow us to order their times of occurrence during hominid evolution. If Darwin is correct, we should find that phonological and musical skills tend to co-occur in modern humans, share neural and genetic mechanisms, and that these mechanisms (both vocal learning and hierarchical parsing) were selected earlier than those involved in word learning, pragmatics, or skill at propositional expression. The lexical protolanguage hypothesis predicts, in contrast, a very early fixation of word-learning capacities, with hierarchical processing selected last. Although the day when such data are available may seem far off, the extraordinary progress in molecular biology and comparative genomics in the past decade suggests that it should be within most readers' lifetimes. Thus Darwin's hypothesis does what any good evolutionary scenario should do: makes testable predictions, and points to sources of empirical data that would otherwise remain unexplored.

Conclusion

I have suggested in this essay that by analysing human 'rhythm' into component mechanisms (pulse extraction, beat entrainment, and motor pattern generation), we can resolve an apparent paradox about its limited distribution among animals. Darwin's model resolves a similar, but broader, puzzle about the relation between music and language, because it is simultaneously a model of language evolution and of the evolution of music (and specifically song). By this model, music and song represent, in a sense, 'living fossils' of an earlier communicative stage of humanity. This supposition neatly solves a core puzzle about music: why should something so apparently useless as music be so ubiquitous in human cultures, attract so much of our time and interest, and seem to have such deep and powerful effects on our emotions? Why should these 'powers' of music seem to transcend cultural boundaries so much more readily that spoken language (which serves, quite effectively, to isolate human cultures from one another)?. While I do not endorse the naïve view that music is a 'universal language of emotion', both the emotional power and relative transcendency of music are among its most obvious features. By positing music as the vestige of a once-central communication system, ousted when language became our 'main' system, Darwin provides a coherent resolution to this puzzle.

Although one may dislike the connotations of the idea that music is a 'living fossil', as a musician I find the notion of musical protolanguage a profoundly attractive one. If this model is correct, the 'sidelining' of music by language has given our species a rich, unfettered playground for creative expression. Freed from any necessary adaptive, communicative functionality, the emancipated musical faculty, in myriad strands of human musical culture, has been allowed to explore vast aesthetic domains of profound intellectual interest and emotional depth. The diversity and greatness of the cultural achievements thus produced requires no utilitarian or adaptive function to justify the respect and admiration, as well as the devotion and passion, that music so widely evokes in humans around the globe.

Acknowledgements

I gratefully acknowledge the insightful comments of Tom Fritz, Sebastian Kirschner, Bjorn Merker, Daniel Mietchen, Ani Patel, Patrick Rebuschat, and W. Andrew Schloss on earlier versions of this manuscript.

References

Agawu, V. K. (1987). The rhythmic structure of West African music. *Journal of Musicology*, *5*(3), 400–18.

Arbib, M. A. (2005). From monkey-like action recognition to human language: An evolutionary framework for neurolinguistics. *Behavioral and Brain Sciences*, *28*(2), 105–67.

Arcadi, A. C., Robert, D., & Boesch, C. (1998). Buttress drumming by wild chimpanzees: temporal patterning, phrase integration into loud calls, and preliminary evidence for individual distinctiveness. *Primates*, *39*, 505–18.

Arcadi, A. C., Robert, D., & Mugurusi, F. (2004). A comparison of buttress drumming by male chimpanzees from two populations. *Primates*, *45*, 135–39.

Arom, S. (1991). *African polyphony and polyrhythm: Musical Structure and Methodology* (M. Thom, Trans.). Cambridge: Cambridge University Press.

Bates, E. (1994). Modularity, domain specificity and the development of language. *Discussions in Neuroscience*, *10*, 136–49.

Bickerton, D. (1990). *Language and Species*. Chicago, IL: Chicago University Press.

Boesch, C., & Boesch, H. (1989). Hunting behavior of wild chimpanzees in the Taï National Park. *American Journal of Physical Anthropology*, *78*(4), 547–73.

Boesch, C., & Boesch-Achermann, H. (2000). *The chimpanzees of the Taï forest*. Oxford: Oxford University Press.

Bregman, A. S. (1990). *Auditory Scene Analysis. The Perceptual Organization of Sound.* Cambridge, MA: MIT Press/Bradford Books.

Brooks, R. A. (1989). A robot that walks: Emergent behaviors from a carefully evolved network. *Neural Computation, 1*, 253–62.

Brosch, M., Selezneva, E., Bucks, C., & Scheich, H. (2004). Macaque monkeys discriminate pitch relationships. *Cognition, 91*(3), 259–72.

Brown, S. (2000). The 'Musilanguage' model of music evolution. In N. L. Wallin, B. Merker, & S. Brown (Eds.), *The Origins of Music* (pp. 271–300). Cambridge, MA: MIT Press.

Busse, C. D. (1978). Do chimpanzees hunt cooperatively? *American Naturalist, 112*(986), 767–70.

Carroll, S. B. (2003). Genetics and the making of *Homo sapiens. Nature, 422*(6934), 849–57.

Cassirer, E. (1944). The concept of group and the theory of perception. *Philosophy and Phenomenological Research, 5*(1), 1–36.

Chen, F.-C., & Li, W.-H. (2001). Genomic divergences between humans and other hominoids and the effective population size of the common ancestor of humans and chimpanzees. *American Journal of Human Genetics, 68*(2), 444–56.

Chomsky, N. (1986). *Knowledge of language: Its nature, origin, and use.* Westport, CT: Praeger.

Clayton, M. R. L. (1996). Free rhythm: ethnomusicology and the study of music without metre. *Bulletin of the School of Oriental and African Studies, University of London, 59*(2), 323–32.

Cohen, L. G., Celnik, P., Pascual-Leone, A., Corwell, B., Falz, L., Dambrosia, J., *et al.* (1997). Functional relevance of cross-modal plasticity in blind humans. *Nature, 389*(6647), 180–83.

Cole, M., Chorover, S. L., & Ettlinger, G. (1961). Cross-modal transfer in man. *Nature, 191*, 1225–26.

Collyer, C. E., & Church, R. M. (1998). Interresponse intervals in continuation tapping. In D. A. Rosenbaum & C. E. Collyer (Eds.), *Timing of Behaviour: Neural, Psychological and Computational Perspectives* (pp. 63–87). Cambridge, MA: MIT Press.

Crain, S. (1991). Language acquisition in the absence of experience. *Behavioral and Brain Sciences, 14*, 597–650.

Cross, I. (2003). Music, cognition, culture and evolution. In I. Peretz & R. J. Zatorre (Eds.), *The Cognitive Neuroscience of Music* (pp. 42–56). Oxford: Oxford University Press.

Darwin, C. (1871). *The Descent of Man and Selection in Relation to Sex* (First edn.). London: John Murray.

Dauer, R. M. (1983). Stress-timing and syllable-timing reanalyzed. *Journal of Phonetics, 11*(1), 51–62.

Davenport, R. K., & Rogers, C. M. (1970). Intermodal equivalence of stimuli in apes. *Science, 168*(3928), 279–80.

de Waal, F. B. M. (1988). The communicative repertoire of captive bonobos (*Pan paniscus*), compared to that of chimpanzees. *Behaviour, 106*, 183–251.

Dennett, D. C. (1995). *Darwin's Dangerous Idea.* New York: Simon & Schuster.

Dissanayake, E. (2000). Antecedents of the temporal arts in early mother-infant interaction. In N. L. Wallin, B. Merker & S. Brown (Eds.), *The Origins of Music* (pp. 389–410). Cambridge, MA.: MIT Press.

Enard, W., Przeworski, M., Fisher, S. E., Lai, C. S. L., Wiebe, V., Kitano, T., *et al.* (2002). Molecular evolution of FOXP2, a gene involved in speech and language. *Nature, 418*, 869–72.

Ettlinger, G., & Blakemore, C. B. (1969). Cross-modal transfer set in the monkey. *Neuropsychologia, 7*, 41–47.

Falk, D. (2004). Prelinguistic evolution in early hominins: Whence motherese? *Behavioral and Brain Sciences, 27*, 491–50.

Fitch, W. T. (2006a). The biology and evolution of music: A comparative perspective. *Cognition, 100*(1), 173–215.

Fitch, W. T. (2006b). On the biology and evolution of music. *Music Perception, 24*(1), 85–88.

Fitch, W. T., Hauser, M. D., & Chomsky, N. (2005). The evolution of the language faculty: Clarifications and implications. *Cognition, 97*(2), 179–210.

Fitch, W. T., Neubauer, J., & Herzel, H. (2002). Calls out of chaos: The adaptive significance of nonlinear phenomena in mammalian vocal production. *Animal Behaviour, 63*, 407–418.

Fitch, W. T., & Rosenfeld, A. J. (2007). Perception and production of syncopated rhythms. *Music Perception, 25*(1), 43–58.

Fitch, W. T. (2010). The Evolution of Language. Cambridge: Cambridge University Press.

Fodor, J. A. (1983). *The Modularity of Mind.* Cambridge, MA: MIT Press.

Frigyesi, J. (1993). Preliminary thoughts toward the study of music without clear beat: The example of 'flowing rhythm' in Jewish 'Nusah'. *Asian Music, 24*(2), 59–88.

Geiser, E., Zaehle, T., Jancke, L., & Meyer, M. (2008). The neural correlate of speech rhythm as evidenced by metrical speech processing. *Journal of Cognitive Neuroscience, 20*(3), 541–52.

Geissmann, T. (2000). Gibbon song and human music from an evolutionary perspective. In N. L. Wallin, B. Merker & S. Brown (Eds.), *The Origins of Music* (pp. 103–23). Cambridge, MA: MIT Press.

Gentner, T. Q., Fenn, K. M., Margoliash, D., & Nusbaum, H. C. (2006). Recursive syntactic pattern learning by songbirds. *Nature, 440*, 1204–1207.

Geschwind, N. (1970). The organization of language and the brain. *Science, 170*, 940–44.

Ghazanfar, A. A., & Logothetis, N. K. (2003). Facial expressions linked to monkey calls. *Nature, 423*, 937–38.

Glass, L., & Mackey, M. C. (1988). *From clocks to chaos: the rhythms of life.* Princeton, NJ: Princeton University Press.

Goldsmith, J. A. (1990). *Autosegmental and metrical phonology.* Oxford: Blackwell.

Gombrich, E. H. (1984). *The Sense of Order: a Study in the Psychology of Decorative Art* (2nd ed.). London: Phaidon.

Greenfield, M. D. (1994). Cooperation and conflict in the evolution of signal interactions. *Annual Review of Ecology and Systematics, 25*, 97–126.

Hagen, E. H., & Bryant, G. A. (2003). Music and dance as a coalition signaling system. *Human Nature, 14*(1), 21–51.

Hare, B., & Tomasello, M. (2004). Chimpanzees are more skillful in competitive than cooperative cognitive tasks. *Animal Behaviour, 68*, 571–81.

Hauser, M., Chomsky, N., & Fitch, W. T. (2002). The language faculty: What is it, who has it, and how did it evolve? *Science, 298*, 1569–79.

Hockett, C. F. (1960). Logical considerations in the study of animal communication. In W. E. Lanyon & W. N. Tavolga (Eds.), *Animal Sounds and Communication* (pp. 392–430). Washington, DC: American Institute of Biological Sciences.

Huber, L. (2001). Visual categorization in pigeons. In R. Cook (Ed.), *Avian Visual Cognition.* Medford, MA: Comparative Cognition Press.

Jespersen, O. (1922). *Language: Its Nature, Development and Origin.* New York: W. W. Norton & Co.

Jones, A. M. (1954). African Rhythm. *Africa: Journal of the International African Institute, 24*(1), 26–47.

Justus, T. C., & Hutsler, J. J. (2005). Fundamental issues in the evolutionary psychology of music: Assessing innateness and Domain specificity. *Music Perception, 23*(1), 1–27.

Keller, E. F. (2005). Revisiting 'scale-free' networks. *BioEssays, 27*, 1060–68.

Kirby, S. (2000). Syntax without natural selection: How compositionality emerges from vocabulary in a population of learners. In C. Knight, M. Studdert-Kennedy & J. R. Hurford (Eds.), *The Evolutionary Emergence of Language: Social function and the origins of linguistic form* (pp. 303–23). Cambridge: Cambridge University Press.

Kirschner, S., Call, J., & Fitch, W. T. (in preparation). Drumming behaviour in African Apes.

Kirschner, S., & Tomasello, M. (2009). Joint drumming: Social context facilitates synchronization in preschool children. *Journal of Experimental Child Psychology, 102*(3), 299–314.

Lerdahl, F., & Jackendoff, R. (1983). *A generative theory of tonal music*. Cambridge, MA: MIT Press.

Livingstone, F. B. (1973). Did the Australopithecines sing? *Current Anthropology, 14*(1–2), 25–29.

Locke, D. (1987). *Drum Gahu: The rhythms of West African drumming*. New York: Talman.

London, J. (2002). Some non-isopmorphisms between pitch and time. *Journal of Music Theory, 46*(12), 127–51.

Longuet-Higgins, H. C., & Lee, C. S. (1984). The rhythmic interpretation of monophonic music. *Music Perception, 1*(4), 424–41.

Markson, L., & Bloom, P. (1997). Evidence against a dedicated system for word learning in children. *Nature, 385*, 813–15.

Masterton, R. B., & Imig, T. J. (1984). Neural mechanisms for sound localization. *Annual Review of Physiology, 46*, 275–87.

McAlpine, D., & Grothe, B. (2003). Sound localization and delay lines—do mammals fit the model? *Trends in Neuroscience, 26*(7), 347–50.

McDermott, J., & Hauser, M. D. (2005). The origins of music: Innateness, uniqueness, and evolution. *Music Perception, 23*(1), 29–59.

McNeill, W. H. (1995). *Keeping together in time: Dance and drill in human history*. Cambridge, MA: Harvard University Press.

Melis, A. P., Hare, B., & Tomasello, M. (2006). Engineering cooperation in chimpanzees: tolerance constraints on cooperation. *Animal Behaviour, 72*(2), 275–86.

Merker, B. (1999). Synchronous chorusing and the origins of music. *Musicae Scientiae, Special Issue 1999–2000*, 59–74.

Merker, B. (2000). Synchronous chorusing and human origins. In N. L. Wallin, B. Merker & S. Brown (Eds.), *The Origins of Music* (pp. 315–27). Cambridge, MA: MIT Press.

Merker, B. (2006). The uneven interface between culture and biology in human music. *Music Perception, 24*, 95–98.

Merriam, A. P. (1959). Characteristics of African music. *Journal of the International Folk Music Council, 11*, 13–19.

Mithen, S. (2005). *The Singing Neanderthals: The Origins of Music, Language, Mind, and Body*. London: Weidenfeld & Nicolson.

Morley, I. (2002). Evolution of the physiological and neurological capacities for music. *Cambridge Archaeological Journal, 12*(2), 195–216.

Patel, A. D. (1998). Syntactic processing in language and music: Different cognitive operations, similar neural resources? *Musical Perception, 16*, 27–42.

Patel, A. D. (2006). Musical rhythm, linguistic rhythm, and human evolution. *Music Perception, 24*(1), 99–104.

Patel, A. D. (2008). *Music, Language, and the Brain.* New York: Oxford University Press.

Patel, A. D., Iversen, J. R., Chen, Y., & Repp, B. H. (2005). The influence of metricality and modality on synchronization with a beat. *Experimental Brain Research, 163*, 226–38.

Patel, A. D., Iversen, J. R., Bregman, M. R., & Schulz, I. (2009). Experimental evidence for synchronization to a musical beat in a nonhuman animal. *Current Biology, 19*(10), 827–30.

Peretz, I. (2006). The nature of music from a biological perspective. *Cognition, 100*, 1–32.

Peretz, I., & Morais, J. (1989). Music and modularity. *Contemporary Music Review, 4*, 279–93.

Peretz, I., & Zatorre, R. J. (2005). Brain organization for music processing. *Annual Review of Psychology, 56*, 89–114.

Pressing, J. (1983). Cognitive isomorphisms between pitch and rhythm in world musics: West Africa, the Balkans and Western tonality. *Studies in Music, 17*, 38–61.

Pressing, J. (2002). Black Atlantic rhythm: Its computational and transcultural foundations. *Music Perception, 19*(3), 285–310.

Ramus, F., Nespor, M., & Mehler, J. (1999). Correlates of linguistic rhythm in the speech signal. *Cognition, 73*, 265–92.

Roach, P. (1982). On the distinction between 'stress-timed' and 'syllable-timed' languages. In D. Crystal (Ed.), *Linguistic Controversies* (pp. 73–79). London: Arnold.

Roederer, J. G. (1984). The search for a survival value for music. *Music Perception, 1*, 350–56.

Sachs, C. (1952). Rhythm and tempo: An introduction. *Musical Quarterly, 38*(3), 384–98.

Sachs, C. (1953). *Rhythm and Tempo: A Study in Music History.* New York: Norton.

Savage-Rumbaugh, E. S., Sevcik, R. A., & Hopkins, W. D. (1988). Symbolic cross-modal transfer in two species of chimpanzees. *Child Development, 59*(3), 617–25.

Schachner, A., Brady, T. F., Pepperberg, I. M., & Hauser, M. D. (2009). Spontaneous motor entrainment to music in multiple vocal mimicking species. *Current Biology, 19*(10), 831–36.

Schaller, G. B. (1963). *The Mountain Gorilla.* Chicago, IL: University of Chicago Press.

Schloss, W. A. (1985). *On the Automatic Transcription of Percussive Music: From Acoustic Signal to High-level Analysis.* Stanford, CA: Stanford University.

Shipp, S. (2005). The importance of being agranular: a comparative account of visual and motor cortex. *Philosophical Transactions of the Royal Society of London, 360*(1456), 797–814.

Strogatz, S. H. (1994). *Nonlinear Dynamics and Chaos.* Cambridge, MA: Perseus.

Strogatz, S. H. (2003). *Sync: The emerging science of spontaneous order.* New York: Hyperion.

Sur, M., Pallas, S. L., & Roe, A. W. (1990). Cross-modal plasticity in cortical development: differentiation and specification of sensory neocortex. *Trends in Neuroscience, 13*(6), 227–33.

Tallerman, M. (2007). Did our ancestors speak a holistic protolanguage? *Lingua, 117*, 579–604.

Tomasello, M., Carpenter, M., Call, J., Behne, T., & Moll, H. (2005). Understanding and sharing intentions: The origins of cultural cognition. *Behavioral & Brain Sciences, 28*, 675–735.

Toussaint, G. (2003). *Classification and phyogenetic analysis of African ternary rhythm timelines.* Paper presented at the BRIDGES: Mathematical Connections in Art, Music and Science, Granada, Spain, July 2003.

Trainor, L. J. (1996). Infant preferences for infant-directed versus noninfant-directed playsongs and lullabies. *Infant Behaviour and Development, 19*, 83–92.

Trehub, S. E., & Trainor, L. J. (1998). Singing to infants: Lullabies and play songs. *Advances in Infant Research, 12*, 43–77.

von Hornbostel, E. M. (1928). African Negro music. *Africa: Journal of the International African Institute, 1*(1), 30–62.

von Melchner, L., Pallas, S. L., & Sur, M. (2000). Visual behaviour mediated by retinal projections directed to the auditory pathway. *Nature, 404*(6780), 871–76.

Washburn, D. K., & Crowe, D. W. (1998). *Symmetries of Culture: Theory and Practice of Plane Pattern Analysis*. Seattle, WA: University of Washington Press.

Washburn, D. K., & Crowe, D. W. (2004). *Symmetry Comes of Age: The Role of Pattern in Culture*. Seattle, WA: University of Washington Press.

Wray, A. (1998). Protolanguage as a holistic system for social interaction. *Language & Communication, 18*(1), 47–67.

Wundt, W. M. (1908). *Grundzüge der physiologischen Psychologie*. Leipzig: Wilhelm Engelmann.

Zabana, K. (1997). *African Drum Music: Slow Agbekor*. Accra, Ghana: Afram Publications.

Zweifel, P. F. (1996). Generalized diatonic and pentatonic scales: A group-theoretic approach. *Perspectives of New Music, 34*(1), 140–61.

Chapter 10

Darwin's musical protolanguage: an increasingly compelling picture

Simon Kirby

Introduction

The target article puts forward a very convincing account of the evolution of language and music, echoing Darwin's (1871) original and forward-thinking ideas that our ancestors developed a capacity for protomusic, an analogy to song behaviour in other species, and this formed the basis for the later evolution of language. In particular, Fitch for the first time shows how a wealth of evidence and analysis of the similarities and differences between rhythm in music, in language, and in other species supports the broadly Darwinian picture.

As such, I find that there is very little to disagree with in the target article, and instead I'd like to expand on some of the points that Fitch touches on. In particular, I think it is worth speculating, in the light of some recent theoretical models, on the difference in possible functional pressures operating in the pre-linguistic 'musical' stage, in modern language, and in other species that produce learned song. Much of this will hinge on the notion of *learnability* of systems and the different role this has to play in music and language—an issue that is at the core of understanding why we would have a musical protolanguage in the first place and how we get from there to a structured linguistic system.

Much of this discussion will be rather speculative, but I hope that it may highlight possible directions for future research. As Fitch correctly points out, good evolutionary scenarios make testable predictions and suggest novel sources for empirical data. Accordingly, I will make some tentative suggestions about the kinds of experimental data that might be useful.

The importance of learning

In an earlier paper, Fitch (2006) examines the famous design features of human language proposed by Hockett (1960) from the perspective of music. One of the central features that is shared by both language and music is *cultural transmission*. Musical behaviour, like language, is inherited culturally. Individuals acquire particular musical and linguistic competence through immersion in an environment where others are making use of that competence themselves. Active members of a musical or linguistic culture (in the latter case this includes virtually everyone) will go on to shape the music or language of future generations. Note that this is also true of the transmission of song in vocal learning species, such as songbirds, cetaceans, and so on.

Another shared feature, which I will argue is tied up with cultural transmission, is *complexity*. It is, of course, notoriously difficult to define what we mean by this term. We can operationalize it in various ways, but importantly these definitions may not always line up in the same way. For example, we might think of complexity in terms of the effort required to produce or perceive a behaviour; or we might consider the amount of information that can be carried by a behaviour; or finally, linking up with cultural transmission, we could couch complexity in terms of the time taken to learn the behaviour.

What I want to suggest is that there are different pressures acting on language, music, and learned song in other species that arise from the fact that these systems are culturally transmitted. These differing pressures relate to the various aspects of complexity mentioned above in interesting ways.

More specifically, an ongoing research effort into understanding the effects of cultural transmission of systems such as language (see, e.g. Brighton, Smith, & Kirby, 2005, for review) highlights the fact that cultural transmission will tend to automatically lead to an increase in learnability. As a language (or equivalently any cultural system acquired in a similar way) is repeatedly acquired and produced by generation after generation of individuals it passes through a transmission 'bottleneck'. A complete system of behaviour must be accurately inferred from only the observed instances of that behaviour available to the learner. What we have shown a number of times in various computational (Kirby, 2001), mathematical (Kirby, Dowman, & Griffiths 2007), and recently experimental (Kirby, Cornish, & Smith, 2008) models is that this leads to the evolution of increasingly learnable systems—systems that can more readily squeeze through the learning bottleneck.

If we pick our definition of complexity as being the effort involved in learning, this means that cultural evolution tends towards *simplicity* (see, Brighton, 2003, for extensive discussion of this, and a formal account in terms of compression). This appears to leave us with a paradox: why are music and language both complex and both culturally transmitted? I will explore the answer to this puzzle for the remainder of this commentary, and show how it highlights a difference between language on the one hand and music/animal song on the other.

Complex cultural behaviour as a reliable fitness indicator

Vocal learning species such as songbirds pass on their song behaviour culturally. If the models of cultural evolution mentioned above are correct, why isn't all bird song maximally simple? There must be something acting as a brake on simplicity in species that transmit song culturally in this way. Ritchie, Kirby, and Hawkey (2008) set out a formal model of bird song that shows how particular types of song can be culturally stable even though (and in fact, *because*) they are hard to learn. Their model is based on the 'Developmental Stress Hypothesis' proposed by Nowicki, Peters, and Podos (1998).[1]

[1] This was originally referred to as the 'nutritional stress hypothesis', but now the more general terminology is used.

This hypothesis rests on the observation that male chicks who suffer some environmental assault during early development in the nest (e.g. parasitism, or lack of nutrition) produce atypical song as adults. Furthermore, the difference between normal male song and the song of males who suffered developmental stress can be detected by females, who are more sexually receptive to the normal males. The ability to learn a culturally transmitted song can therefore be used as an unfakeable indicator of fitness (assuming that developmental stress can impact on the quality of a mate). Birdsong can be a reliable window on the early life of a bird.

This can only work, however, in the particular case where the song being transmitted culturally is in some way hard to learn—in other words, where acquisition is challenging for the developmentally stressed chick, but not for the normal one. What Ritchie, Kirby, and Hawkey (2008) show is that, in the case where birds are assessing fitness on the basis of song, cultural transmission maintains song types which distinguish between developmentally stressed and unstressed individuals.

If this approach is right for bird song, then could it also be relevant for the evolution of music? Could it be involved in the emergence of the Darwinian musical protolanguage? Darwin's (1871) own idea was that the early musical protolanguage evolved for sexual display: 'it appears that the progenitors of man, either the males or females or both sexes, before acquiring the power of expressing their mutual love in articulate language, endeavoured to charm each other with musical notes and rhythm' (p. 571). A generalized variant of the developmental stress hypothesis might give us insight into why music should charm[2] in this way: because it is a culturally transmitted system that is complex enough to take non-trivial investment to acquire. If a musical culture affords differing levels of musical ability, all the better. This will allow for more graded assessment of fitness. Of course, the differing levels of ability are not likely to reflect things such as poor nutrition or parasitic assault during childhood, but rather spare capacity (cognitive, economic, etc.) to spend time acquiring a musical skill. Rather than focusing on developmental stress, we might refer to this generalized version as the 'Investment in Learning Hypothesis'.

Although, at this stage, this idea is rather speculative, it fits in with an asymmetry that Fitch notes between producers and perceivers of musical rhythm, and suggests an explanation for why musical rhythm goes beyond what is required for minimal group entrainment—i.e. a simple pulse. To see why, it is worth considering what we might expect rhythmic structure to be like if it were to be used as a reliable fitness indicator in this way:

- It must be hard to learn to produce.
- It need not be hard to learn to perceive. It might actually make sense for the complexity of production learning to be as easy as possible to detect.

2 In fact, it is reasonable to suppose in a social species such as humans, any means to accurately determine individual fitness will be useful, whether or not it is between potential mates (or competitors). For example, in forming coalitions for joint activity, accurate assessment of others' abilities may be invaluable.

- It should exhibit some degree of cultural variation. There cannot be a single ideal system because then the population would be susceptible to invasion by cheaters who had that system innately coded. Remember, the logic of the argument is that difficulty in *learning* to produce is a better fitness indicator than just difficulty in production.

This seems to fit with what rhythmic structure looks like. Fitch notes in particular the asymmetry between rhythmic production and perception. It is relatively easy for humans to carry out beat inference and, I would submit, to detect the complexity of that inference task, which could presumably work as an indicator of the complexity of the rhythm.[3] However, it is much harder to produce a beat *without extensive learning* that would elicit a judgement of complexity in a perceiver. Also, despite similarities across cultures, there are undoubtedly differences in musical cultures that must be acquired.

More intuitively, this idea fits well with the common experience of being naturally drawn to behaviours in others that appear to reflect an investment on their part in acquiring the skill underlying that behaviour. Consider, for example, the following scenario. While walking down the street you hear a busker apparently playing a complex rhythm on a set of hand drums. Reaching into your wallet, you prepare to spend some time listening to the performance. As you walk closer you notice that she is miming along to a tape. You put your wallet away and walk swiftly on. Our level of change in interest and engagement with exactly the same stimulus reflects something about what we are really attending to in such a situation.

To move beyond these speculations, we really need some experiments. For example, we might imagine constructing a variety of rhythmic systems and get perceivers to judge them aesthetically. Can we find a trade-off between inferability of beat, complexity of production, and fit to culture in participants' assessment of value? Also, will participants rate rhythms produced by machine lower than *the same* rhythms apparently produced by a human (as expected by the busker scenario sketched above)?

Of course, the Investment in Learning Hypothesis cannot be the whole story. Firstly, it is focused firmly on the idea of rhythmic complexity resulting from an individual's performance. There are likely to be quite separate mechanisms that could generate complexity from ensemble performance. Note, however, that our preference for complexity as perceivers arising from an adaptation to detect fitness indicators may itself help encourage and reinforce complex behaviour even when that behaviour is not specifically signalling fitness. Secondly, it does not provide an answer to the key observation that Fitch makes about the striking presence of isochrony in music. Here, I think that Fitch is absolutely right in suggesting that selection pressures relating to group behaviours are the only ones that entail isochrony. In fact, this complements the Investment in Learning Hypothesis well.

Together, they explain why rhythmic structures are both isochronous *and* complex (e.g. hierarchically structured rather than consisting of simply a regular pulse). The isochrony is required for the group function, and the complexity of structure a result

---

[3] This is not to say that beat inference is a trivial task, or that we necessarily even have good models for how it is achieved, but rather that variation in individual ability in perception may be lower than variation in ability in production.

of, or perhaps scaffold for, the need for systems that are rich enough to pose a learning challenge for fitness-indicating purposes.

So, what about language?

The Investment in Learning Hypothesis gives us one possible reason why cultural transmission doesn't lead to the simplest possible musical systems, but is this the same explanation for the maintenance of complexity in language? I would argue not. Although there are theories relating to sexual selection and language (e.g. Miller, 2000), it seems to me less plausible that the complexity of modern language is itself primarily a fitness indicator. For example, the display of linguistic complexity does not appear to increase dramatically at puberty.

It may well be the case that language is used for sexual display, but this is not the same as suggesting the complex structural properties of language that are transmitted culturally serve that function in themselves by virtue of their being transmitted culturally. A much more straightforward explanation is that the function of language is very different from both animal song and music: it carries semantic information.

The models of cultural transmission of language I referred to earlier demonstrate that this fact is enough to save language from a collapse into highly learnable simplicity. In fact, the cultural process alone can find optimal trade-off between learnability and expressivity,[4] and these trade-off systems look very like natural language. For example, a recent experiment (Kirby, Cornish, & Smith, 2008) shows that a signalling system transmitted culturally through 'generations' of experimental participants will become increasingly simple and inexpressive unless constraints are placed on the transmission process that encourage differentiation of meanings. When these are in place, simple compositional syntax spontaneously emerges out of an original 'holistic' language where signals have no internal structure.[5]

The evolutionary scenario

In summary, we can sketch out the following evolutionary scenario as a slight elaboration of Fitch's proposal:

- In humans, a system for group bonding/coordination arose based on very simple isochronous signalling. This may have been driven by a unique motivation (among primates at least) for group cooperation.
- This system was appropriated as a vehicle for honest signalling of fitness and ramped up in complexity. This may have been the result of a kind of self-domestication. Okanoya

[4] By 'expressivity' here, I mean specifically the extent to which a system can carry semantic information, i.e. the ability of a system to distinguish meanings.

[5] Like the theory of a musical protolanguage, this idea has a long intellectual history that stretches back to 18th- and 19th-century philosophers like Jeremy Bentham. Stam (1976 , p.42) notes Bentham believed that 'single primitive utterances were equivalent to whole sentences. . . . Linguistic progress . . . came with analysis, the breaking down of primitive one-word sentences into their component parts'. This view has its clearest modern exposition in the work of Alison Wray (e.g. Wray 1998). See Smith (2008) for review.

(2002) notes that the complexity of song of a domesticated species of Bengalese finch is remarkably higher than its wild progenitor, proposing that domestication results in a reduction in other selection pressures that might bear down on rich culturally transmitted behaviours (e.g. predator evasion, species identification).

- The result was a rich, structured substrate that could in turn be appropriated for communication of complex meanings. Note that this could in principle have happened to any song-learning species. In practice, however, it requires both an ability to infer complex communicative intentions in others, and the motivation to engage in such communication. It may simply be that we are the only song-learning species to have these traits.
- This new protolinguistic system (existing alongside the previous protomusical one) lost the requirement for isochrony, and for fitness signalling, but gained a pressure to maintain expressivity, simply as a result of its change in function.
- Finally, a purely cultural process then took language off in a different direction to music. Adaptation by cultural transmission optimized the competing pressures of learnability and expressivity, creating syntactic structure as a reflection of the semantic structures being conveyed.

On this final point, it is worth speculating about the role of syntactic complexity, an oft-cited defining characteristic of language. Fitch notes that complex syntax would not be present in musical protolanguage. Why might we assume this? What do we mean by complex syntax anyway? We can learn something here from birdsong. There is no clear evidence that birdsong goes beyond finite state. However, recent experiments (Gentner, Fenn, Margoliash, & Nusbaum, 2006) suggest European starlings appear to be able to learn to discriminate songs that can be characterized as context free. A reasonable hypothesis is that the *capacity* for going beyond finite state is present in our musical protolanguage ancestor, but there is simply no need for this kind of structure to act as a fitness indicator. It only really becomes relevant when language is used to convey meanings.

If this is correct, it suggests that a change in our syntactic capacity is not a major part of the story of language emergence. Instead, what we see is a change in the use to which we put pre-existing capacities—a change which has profound consequences by virtue of the way it influences cultural evolution.

References

Brighton, H. (2003). *Simplicity as a driving force in linguistic evolution.* PhD thesis, Theoretical and Applied Linguistics, The University of Edinburgh.

Brighton, H., Smith, K., and Kirby, S. (2005). Language as an evolutionary system. *Physics of Life Reviews, 2*, 177–226.

Darwin, C. (1871). *The descent of man and selection in relation to sex.* London: John Murray.

Fitch, W. T. (2006). The biology and evolution of music: A comparative perspective. *Cognition, 100*, 173–215.

Gentner, T., Fenn, K., Margoliash, D., & Nusbaum, H. (2006). Recursive syntactic pattern learning by songbirds. *Nature, 440*, 1204–07.

Hockett, C. (1960). The origin of speech. *Scientific American, 203*, 88–96.

Kirby, S. (2001). Spontaneous evolution of linguistic structure: an iterated learning model of the emergence of regularity and irregularity. *IEEE Transactions on Evolutionary Computation*, *5*(2), 102–10.

Kirby, S., Cornish, H., & Smith, K. (2008). Cumulative cultural evolution in the laboratory: an experimental approach to the origins of structure in human language. *Proceedings of the National Academy of Sciences*, *101*(31), 10681–86.

Kirby, S., Dowman, M., & Griffiths, T. (2007). Innateness and culture in the evolution of language. *Proceedings of the National Academy of Sciences*, *104*(12), 5241–45.

Miller, G. (2000). *The mating mind*. London: Vintage.

Nowicki, S., Peters, S., & Podos, J. (1998). Song learning, early nutrition and sexual selection in songbirds. *American Zoologist*, *38*, 179–90.

Okanoya, K. (2002). Sexual display as a syntactical vehicle: the evolution of syntax in birdsong and human language through sexual selection. In A. Wray (Ed.), *The Transition to Language* (pp. 46–63). Oxford: Oxford University Press.

Ritchie, G., Kirby, S., & Hawkey, D. (2008). Song learning as an indicator mechanism: Modelling the developmental stress hypothesis. *Journal of Theoretical Biology*, *251*, 570–83.

Smith, A. D. M. (2008). Protolanguage reconstructed. *Interaction Studies*, *9*(1), 100–16.

Stam, J. (1976). *Inquiries into the origin of language: the fate of a question*. New York: Harper and Row.

Wray, A. (1998). Protolanguage as a holistic system for social interaction. *Language and Communication*, *18*(1), 47–67.

Chapter 11

The significance of stones and bones: understanding the biology and evolution of rhythm requires attention to the archaeological and fossil record

Steven Mithen

Fitch applies what I suspect is a unique blend of knowledge about music, language, biology, and neuroscience to provide an insightful consideration of the evolution of rhythm. Although not explicitly referred to, I felt that his own experience of performing and participating in music pervades his text, giving it an enhanced level of authority. Fitch addresses a range of complex issues with clarity, showing how they are intimately connected and that music and language are indeed closely related. That said, I would have preferred not to have come across the phrase 'coupled nonlinear oscillators' in the very first sentence.

Deconstructing rhythm

I admire the manner in which Fitch breaks down 'rhythm' into three component parts and then seeks to explore their independent evolutionary histories. There is, of course, a risk in doing so as each of those components could be further broken down, and so on ad infinitum. As he himself acknowledges, the human experience of rhythm is one of seamless unity rather than a succession of component parts. Fitch suggests this feeling is merely superficial, but I disagree. If we are ever to understand human musicality, we must pay equal attention to how, and when, its individual components became integrated to create the whole: biological reductionism alone imposes severe limits to understanding. This is made particularly evident by the example of agbekor that Fitch provides. This perfectly illustrates the remarkably complex and fully integrated character of human rhythmical understanding and entrainment. The whole is considerably more than merely the sum of its parts.

The use of comparative studies of living humans, chimpanzees, and other apes to establish which, if any, of Fitch's three component parts may have been present in the last common ancestor is the correct way to proceed. Fitch does a valiant job by reviewing what evidence exists, but he is ultimately stymied by the shortage of data. It would be an interesting study in the history of science to discover quite why drumming by gorillas and chimpanzees, so pervasive in the public mind from Tarzan films and so forth, appears never to have been subject to scientific study until the mid 1990s in the work of Arcadi and his colleagues, as cited by Fitch. It appears that Fitch, Call, and Kirschner have their own study underway, which I am sure will provide fascinating new insights. It is a pity he could not have given us a preview in this current paper. Equally surprising is that there has not been any study to formally demonstrate that chimpanzees cannot entrain to a rhythm, as is widely assumed to be the case. This would, surely, be a simple experiment to undertake and would make a significant contribution to current discussion.

My impression from the existing evidence is that comparative studies of humans and apes will ultimately make only a limited contribution to understanding the evolution of human musical ability, as well as that of language. That of song birds and cetaceans, while fascinating in themselves, have even less to offer as their communication systems have evolved along entirely independent trajectories to that of humans. There may be some common features arising from convergent evolution, but these will contribute little towards our understanding of human language and music.

The significance of sociality

I don't suppose anyone will doubt that Fitch is correct to argue that the synchronization that emerges via either mutual entrainment or by following a timekeeper when people sing, dance, or play instruments together derives from the peculiarly high levels of sociality found within humans as opposed to apes. I wasn't quite sure, however, about what precisely Fitch is suggesting. Is it simply that there is an underlying propensity to engage in cooperation—which Fitch describes as 'some general, social cooperative urge'—that results in this capacity, if not compulsion, for synchronization? This seems to be implied by Fitch's argument in his final paragraph that music is 'freed from any necessary adaptive, communicative functionality'. An alternative is that synchronization within group music making and other human activities plays an active role in facilitating such cooperation. This is surely what military bands, choirs, and such like are doing, perhaps by developing an enhanced level of trust between the individuals involved (Mithen, 2005). So I wonder whether we should be putting the cultural activity of music making and other synchronizing activities into the driving seat of human sociality rather than citing the latter as some pre-existing biological given. This is precisely what Cross (2001) seems to be doing with his critically important notion of 'floating intentionality'. I worry that Fitch may be relying on a rather outdated distinction between biological capacity and cultural activity.

The impact of bipedalism

I was disappointed that Fitch's discussion of the 'phylogenetic trajectory' that might have led to the modern human capacity for rhythm was so limited. His starting place, a consideration of the multiple 'design features' of music and language, was not unreasonable. But why then avoid any consideration of human phylogeny other than the gross statements about the 'initial stages of human evolution' and the 'last stage of human evolution'? When does Fitch think that these occurred? By 'initial stages' is he referring to the last common ancestor with the chimpanzee at seven to six million years ago, or does he include the first members of the *Homo* genus within this initial stage, or perhaps even the later big-brained hominins after *c*.600 000 years ago? Or is he referring to the earliest primates of 65 million years ago?

By avoiding any consideration of evolution within the *Australopithecus* genus and the *Homo* genus, Fitch avoids addressing the impact that the changes in human anatomy, and especially bipedalism, may have had on human musical capacities in general and rhythm in particular. As I have suggested elsewhere (Mithen, 2005, chapter 10), these are likely to have been immense. Bipedalism appears to have evolved in two rather distinct stages, the first leading to the partial bipedalism of the australopithecines by 3.5 million years ago, as evident from *Australopithecus afarensis* ('Lucy') and the second to the fully modern bipedalism of *Homo ergaster* by 1.5 million years ago, as evident from the WT15000 specimen, the 'Nariokotome boy'. The selective pressures for bipedalism, ranging from standing for fruit picking for the first stage (Hunt, 1994) to avoidance of heat stress and water loss for the second stage (Wheeler, 1984, 1991, 1992), need not concern us here, as our interest is on the musical implications of the changes in anatomy.

Aiello (1996) suggested that *Homo eragster*'s larger brain compared to that of australopithecines, not just in absolute but also in relative terms, could be explained by the new demands on sensorimotor control that bipedalism both required and enabled. Standing or walking on two legs requires that the centre of gravity is constantly monitored and small groups of muscles frequently recruited to correct its position; the movement of legs has to be integrated with that of arms, hands, and trunk to maintain a dynamic balance. As such, the evolution of a mental mechanism to maintain the rhythmic coordination of muscle groups is likely to have been essential.

The significance of such mental mechanisms becomes apparent from people who have either lost these because of cognitive pathologies or who have suffered mental disability from birth and always struggled to achieve fluid physical movements. When their lack of an internal rhythm mechanism is compensated for by provision of an external rhythm, marked improvements in walking and other physical movements occur.

The music therapist Dorita S. Berger (2002, p. 113) gives a striking example in her account of Alonzo, an eight-year-old autistic non-verbal boy:

> [Alonzo] ran around the music therapy classroom aimlessly while the piano played and I sang a song describing and reflecting his behaviour back to him. Alonzo remained at the far end of the large classroom and did not approach the piano. Occasionally, he would stop and cast glances across the room toward the piano, but his physical behaviour remained chaotic, distant, out of control.
>
> Abandoning the piano and song, I opted instead for the simplicity of pure rhythm played on the congo drum. No singing; no melody; nothing but rhythm. In an instant, Alonzo's running halted, his body and mind frozen in a state of attention. He looked across the room at me and the drum. As suddenly as he had stopped he began moving in an organized, rhythmic, stepping demenour, toward the sound. His steps accented the pulse of the congo's beat as he neared the drum.

While such anecdotal accounts are provocative, their scientific value is questionable as they rely on a subjective interpretation of events. Fortunately we have more than a decade of meticulously conducted scientific studies exploring the relationship between rhythm and movement conducted by the neuroscientist Michael Thaut, himself a very accomplished musician (Hurt, Rice, McIntosh, & Thaut, 1998; Thaut, McIntosh, McIntosh, & Hoemberg, 2001; Thaut, McIntosh, & Wright, 1997).

One of Thaut's key studies has been with people who suffer from Parkinson's disease. This is an impairment of the basal ganglia of the brain, which, among other effects, disturbs the temporal aspect of motor control. Thaut found that he could generate significant improvements in walking by providing Parkinson's sufferers with an externally generated rhythm from a metronome. The video recordings of Thaut's patients show that the improvements in gait are striking: a shift from cumbersome shuffling movements to a quite unexpected degree of muscle control and fluid movement, all from no more than the patient hearing a regular beat.

Thaut's studies, along with accounts of the impact of rhythm on children such as Alonzo, suggest that efficient bipedalism requires a brain that is able to supply temporal control to the complex coordination of muscle groups—just as Aiello (1996) had argued. The loss of this cognitive ability can be partly compensated for by use of an external beat, which may also instinctively incite further muscle movements in those who lack any such impairment. The key point is that as our ancestors evolved into bipedal humans, so too would their inherent rhythmical abilities evolve. One can easily imagine an evolutionary snowball occurring as the selection of cognitive mechanisms for timekeeping improved bipedalism, which led to the ability to engage in further physical activities that in turn required timekeeping for their efficient execution. Key among these would have been the use of hands, now freed from their locomotory function. They would have been used for hammering: bones to crack them open for the marrow inside, nuts to extract the kernels, and stone nodules to detach flakes.

Such critical developments in the evolution of rhythmic capacities are only recognized by examining the fossil and archaeological remains from human evolution. Comparative studies of the type relied upon by Fitch will only ever provide a partial understanding of how not only rhythm evolved, but also other aspects of musicality.

What about the Neanderthals?

Fitch's avoidance of human phylogeny leaves me unclear where in the course of human evolution he was positing the 'last stage of language evolution' to have occurred. Some argue that this was with the emergence of *Homo sapiens*, probably at 200 000 years ago, while others point to the first explicit appearance of symbolic behaviour at 70 000 years ago, which interestingly coincides with the dispersal of *Homo sapiens* out of Africa. But such arguments leave a massive question about the communicative systems of the big brained hominins such as *Homo heidelbergensis* and *Homo neanderthalensis*. I would like to have read Fitch's views on such issues as they are central to the question he is addressing. Did the Neanderthals have rhythm? Did *Homo erectus* or *Australopithecus afarensis*? An even more challenging question is whether the Neanderthals had compositional language, as defined by the use of words and a set of grammatical rules?

The Neanderthals, evolving in Europe between 500 000 and 150 000 years ago, provide us with seemingly contradictory lines of evidence (for reviews of Neanderthal archaeological and fossil record see Mellars, 1996; Stringer & Gamble, 1993). On the one hand, their vocal tracts are essentially the same as that of modern humans, as is their range of brain sizes—indeed the latter exceeds that of *Homo sapiens*. They made complex stone artefacts and survived through challenging and changing environmental conditions. What would those vocal tracts and large brains have been used for other than for compositional language not dissimilar to that which we possess today? How could the Neanderthals have been so ecological successful without the capacity for compositional language?

On the other hand, two lines of evidence argue strongly against the presence of compositional language. First there is the absence of symbolic artefacts: after more than a century of research there are no unambiguous examples of figurines or art objects of any kind made by Neanderthals or earlier hominins. Various claims have been put forward, such as the Berekhat figurine (Marshack, 1997) and incised bones from Bilzingsleben (Mania & Mania, 1988), but none of these are persuasive (Mithen, 2005). I find it inconceivable that if Neanderthals had been using audible symbols, as in words, that they would not have also been using visual symbols. Second, we must consider the immense cultural stability of the Neanderthals: the tools they made and their way of life at 250 000 years ago were effectively no different from those current at the moment of their extinction at 30 000 years ago. Compositional language is a force of change; it forms the basis for creativity and complex thought (Mithen, 1996). If Neanderthals had been using language to talk about their tools could they have remained so similar over such long periods of time? It is not as if the Neanderthals would not have benefited from some cultural innovation: the evidence for their demography (Trinkaus, 1995) suggests they were always teetering on extinction. If ever there was a population that needed to invent bows and arrows, the means for storing food, needles, and thread, and so forth, it was the Neanderthals. The absence of any such innovation is a compelling argument that they lacked compositional language.

My own way of resolving these apparently contradictory lines of evidence is to suggest that the Neanderthals had an advanced form of communication that made extensive use of variations in pitch, rhythm, and timbre, but did not use words or grammatical rules (Mithen, 2005). As such, it was a form of holistic communication of a type that has no analogy in the modern world. It was only with the emergence of modern humans in Africa after 200 000 years ago, that compositional language evolved, this ultimately being responsible for the appearance of visual symbols, global dispersal, and extinction of other types of human by competitive exclusion. Without examining the fossil and especially the archaeological evidence, it would be quite impossible to make this distinction between the communicative systems of the Neanderthals and of modern humans, and hence to understand when language and music evolved.

Unfortunate neglect

It is for this reason that I was disappointed that Fitch seems entirely uninterested in the potential of the archaeological and fossil records to help resolve how and why the human musical and linguistic capacities evolved, especially after he had made such welcome references to the need for empirical investigation rather than mere theorizing. He puts considerable faith in molecular biology and comparative genomics, seemingly to believe that unravelling the genetic basis of music and language is sufficient. This is, of course, essential but so, too, is seeking to find direct evidence for the manner in which human ancestors and relatives behaved and thought in the past—the same genetic constitution might have quite different expression in different ecological, economic, and social contexts. So without knowledge of those contexts, whatever information we have about the genetic and neurological basis of music and language is of limited value.

I was amused—or was it bemused—by Fitch's claim that 'a strange quirk of recent scholarship in the evolution of language and music is that Darwin's model has been almost universally overlooked'. This was the inaccurate assertion he made against my 2005 book, *The Singing Neanderthals: The Origins of Music, Language, Body and Mind* in an otherwise balanced review (Fitch, 2005). My book had, in fact, described, discussed, and evaluated Darwin's model at length and it was an inaccurate claim to suggest otherwise. Others have also drawn extensively on Darwin's views when discussing the evolution of language and music. Most notable is Geoff Miller (2000a, 2000b) in his detailed consideration of the role of sexual selection in human biological and cultural evolution.

References

Aiello, L. (1996). Terrestriality, bipedalism and the origin of language. In W.G. Runciman, J. Maynard-Smith, & R.I.M. Dunbar (eds.), *Evolution of Social behaviour Patterns in Primates and Man* (pp. 269–90). Oxford: Oxford University Press.

Berger, D. (2002). *Music Therapy, Sensory Integration and the Autistic Child.* London: Jessica Kingsley Publishers.

Bramble, D.M. & Lieberman, D.E. (2004). Endurance running and the evolution of *Homo. Nature, 432*, 345–52.

Cross, I. (2001). Music, mind and evolution. *Psychology of Music, 29*, 95–102.

Fitch, T. (2005). Dancing to Darwin's tune. Review of Mithen 2005. *Nature, 438*, 288.

Hunt, K.D. (1994). The evolution of human bipedality: ecology and functional morphology. *Journal of Human Evolution, 26*, 183–202.

Hurt, C.P., Rice, R.R., McIntosh, G.C., & Thaut, M.H. (1998). Rhythmic auditory stimulation in gait training for patients with traumatic brain injury. *Journal of Music Therapy XXXV*, 228–41.

Mania, D. & Mania, U. (1988). Deliberate engravings on bone artefacts of Homo erectus. *Rock Art Research, 5*, 91–107.

Marshack, A. (1997). The Berekhat Ram figurine: a late Acheulian carving from the Middle East. *Antiquity, 71*, 327–37.

Mellars, P. (1996). *The Neanderthal Legacy.* Princeton, NJ: Princeton University Press.

Miller, G. (2000a). Evolution of human music through sexual selection. In N.L. Wallin, B. Merker, & S. Brown (Eds.), *The Origins of Music* (pp. 329–60). Cambridge, MA: MIT Press.

Miller, G. (2000b). *The Mating Mind: How Sexual Choice Shaped the Evolution of Human Nature.* London: Heinemann.

Mithen, S.J. (1996). *The Prehistory of the Mind: A Search for the Origin of Art, Science and Religion*. London: Thames & Hudson.

Mithen, S.J. (2005). *The Singing Neanderthals: The Origins of Music, Language, Mind and Body*. London: Orion.

Stringer, C.B. & Gamble, C. (1993). *In Search of the Neanderthals*. London: Thames & Hudson.

Thaut, M.H., McIntosh, G.C., & Rice, R.R. (1997). Rhythmic facilitation of gait training in hemiparetic stroke rehabilitation. *Journal of Neurological Sciences*, *151*, 207–12.

Thaut, M.H., McIntosh, K.W., McIntosh, G.C. & Hoemberg, V. (2001). Auditory rhythmicity enhances movement and speech motor control in patients' with Parkinson's disease. *Functional Neurology*, *16*, 163–72.

Trinkaus, E. (1995). Neanderthal mortality patterns. *Journal of Archaeological Science*, *22*, 121–42.

Wheeler, P. (1984). The evolution of bipedality and the loss of functional body hair in hominids. *Journal of Human Evolution*, *13*, 91–8.

Wheeler, P. (1991). The influence of bipedalism on the energy and water budgets of early hominids. *Journal of Human Evolution*, *21*, 107–36.

Wheeler, P. (1992). The influence of the loss of functional body hair on hominid energy and water budgets. *Journal of Human Evolution*, *23*, 379–88.

Chapter 12

A grand gesture: vocal and corporeal control in melody, rhythm, and emotion

Iain Morley

Fitch's paper represents a timely enquiry into the rhythmic dimension of music origins, an aspect which has to date received far less attention than the tonal elements of musical behaviours. In particular, investigations into the relationships between musical and linguistic capabilities have often focused most on those elements which share the trait of vocal production—meaning, in the case of music, the production and perception of pitch and contour, and the structures within them. The research cited by Fitch in this paper and his own related ideas represent welcome additions to such investigations. It is increasingly evident that the rhythmic, gestural, expressive, and tonal production and perception systems are intimately related and interdependent, and any future considerations of music origins that do not consider all of these dimensions as integral to the emergence of the capacity will be incomplete.

There is far more of importance in Fitch's paper than it is possible to comment on here, so I must be selective and draw out just a few aspects to which I can immediately respond and which, in my opinion, raise particular queries for further elaboration. I then will respond in detail to one key point of interest raised in Fitch's paper—the relationship(s) between rhythm, melody, and corporeal motor control.

Fitch's division of 'rhythmic capability' into three components and discussion of the evidence for their presence in other higher primates is important, and the suggestion that it is the capacity for entrainment that is particular to humans is very interesting, and points to a key direction for future research. Fitch makes a distinction between **beat entrainment** (e.g. tapping one's foot to a beat) and **pattern generation** (*complex* motor output such as dancing or instrumental playing), with pattern generation relying on complex cross-modal integration, with information from the auditory cortex having to be successfully propagated to the motor cortex. Whilst there is clearly a distinction in complexity, surely this is a quantitative rather than qualitative difference between 'beat entrainment' and 'pattern generation', i.e. a difference in the number of different modes over which the entrainment is occurring?

When it comes to the separation of entrainment into two component activities, a 'synchronization component' and a 'pattern output component', it would seem to be worth also exploring the extent to which these components would need to have a two-way relationship. In other words the motor output must surely provide proprioceptive and auditory cues which then form both a part of the acoustic signal and a cue by which to tailor the relationship between the exterior stimulus, the listener's internal pulse and their motor pulse.

Fitch makes the important point that whilst the forms of the pattern output can be greatly divergent, the actual requirement of entraining one's motor control to an extracted pulse is equivalent whether for the purposes of playing another rhythm-producing instrument, clapping, or dancing (and the human body is in both latter cases itself a rhythm-producing instrument).

I wonder, however, whether he over-stresses the distinction between instrumental playing and dance, in the discussion of the generation of complex motor output. He says that 'extraction of a beat, and entrainment to that beat in a pure motor fashion (for example, in dancing) does not assure the ability to *musically* entrain, for one can be a dancer (motor → motor) but not an instrumentalist (motor → acoustic)'.

He highlights the necessity in instrumental playing of paying careful attention to the instrument's acoustic output and of '. . . closing the motor/auditory loop . . . adding an additional level of complexity over the (already challenging) dancing problem'. But surely dancing also involves some auditory feedback in moderating the motor act? Dancing must involve profound proprioceptive and other sensory feedback in moderating and maintaining it, as does instrumental activity. Admittedly this is not tonal but it is multi-modal nevertheless and may not be demonstrably less complex. Perhaps a distinction could be drawn between the use/role of the auditory loop in the two circumstances, rather than the implication that it is not used at all in the dance act.

Fitch makes the point that we can separate the perceptual and motor aspects of the process of 'rhythmic ability' because we can 'hear the beat, internally, without manifesting it via any body movements of one's own'. It will be very interesting to see in future research into the possible roles of mirror neuron activity in rhythmic and musical perception whether one actually *can* genuinely 'hear the beat internally' without the brain generating neurological activity which is equivalent to manifesting it via body movements. In a sense, 'hearing the beat internally' would thus rely on inducing the neurological corollary of its manifestation via actual body movements. I wouldn't be in the slightest bit surprised if it transpires that the brain can only extract rhythms to be heard internally through the generation of neurological activity that replicates its physical manifestation, in much the same way as has been evidenced to occur in mirror neurons for various other complex motor skills.

One aspect of auditory processing that is of particular interest in Fitch's paper is the apparent similarity between the structure of rhythmic and harmonic information processing, which 'suggests, perhaps surprisingly, that similar pattern-extraction mechanisms may apply in the domains of rhythm and harmony, despite gross differences in the musical surface analysed, providing support for the idea of broad cognitive/aesthetic principles applicable across musical domains'. He goes on to say that 'the discovery of isomorphisms in the rhythmic and harmonic domains raises fascinating questions about the nature of human perception and aesthetic cognition that cannot be answered at present. . . . Although the isomorphism is a fact, its causal basis remains a fascinating mystery, a mystery whose resolution may yield deep insights into (at least) musical cognition if explored experimentally at the perceptual, cognitive, and neural levels'.

It is possible that the following discussion, of research relating to relationships between vocal, corporeal, and rhythmic control, may shed some light on this isomorphism. Although more concerned with the production than the perception of vocalization and rhythm, it becomes evident that the production and perception are themselves intimately related.

The inter-relationship of vocal control and corporeal control in melody, rhythm, and emotion

Manual movement—and broader *corporeal gesture*—is a fundamental component of much musical behaviour and of vocal behaviour; it is also a key element of expression of emotion. Gesture and vocalization appear to be, in some respects, if not entirely, contiguous and interdependent systems, with neurological associations apparently existing between the fine control of orofacial and laryngeal musculature, and that of manual gesture. Further, investigation of the relationship between manual control and vocalization may help to shed light on the apparent strong association between rhythmic and melodic behaviours in music, and the structural parallel that Fitch highlights.

The involvement, often involuntarily, of manual gestures in vocal expression will be familiar to most people. This situation has led to a body of research examining the interrelationship of these functions (e.g. McNeill, 1992, 2000), and hypotheses that manual gesture and vocal control are functionally linked and share important neurological and/or evolutionary foundations. Some authors have suggested that manual gesture formed the foundation for syntactic elements of language (e.g. Hewes, 1973, 1992; Corballis, 1992; Armstrong, Stokoe, & Wilcox, 1994; Stokoe, 2000), whilst others have carried out experimental observation of interrelationships between manual and vocal control (e.g. Petitto & Marentette, 1991; Locke, Bekken, McMinn-Larson, & Wein, 1995; Feyereisen, 1997; Mayberry & Jaques, 2000; Locke, 2000).

Vocal content and manual gesture

Research by Mayberry and Jaques (2000) regarding gesture in normal speech and stuttered speech casts considerable light on the interrelationship between vocalization and gesture. They found that when disfluency occurs in stuttered speech it is accompanied by fewer gestures than fluent speech—in fact, at the time of stuttering, gesture ceases entirely. This is in contrast to disfluency in normal speech, in which case at a pause gesturing tends to increase along with vocalizations like 'uhm' and 'uhr'. These vocalizations actually maintain the elements of prosody in normal speech disfluencies, and gesture, likewise, is unaffected. In stuttering, on the other hand, the whole of speech prosody and rhythm cease, as does gesture.

So, in normal speech disfluency there is no disruption of the *motor* and *prosodic* elements of speech—these are maintained in ums and ahs, non-lexical vocalizations—the disfluency originates in a lexically-induced pause as one seeks the correct word or phrase, which does not affect gesture. This is not the case in stuttered disfluency. In the words of Mayberry and Jaques (2000, p.208):

> . . . gesture and speech are an integrated system in language production. When speech stumbles and stops as a result of stuttering, the hand always waits for speech so that the

> meanings being expressed by the hand in gesture always coincide with the meanings being expressed by the mouth in speech, even when the gesture must wait for a very long time. Gesture and speech are clearly not autonomous.

Mayberry and Jaques (2000, p. 209) observe that:

> the fact that the temporal concordance between gesture and speech execution is always maintained throughout stuttered and fluent speech suggests that the complex neuromotor patterns of gesture and speech are coordinated and integrated prior to their production in extemporaneous expression.

In fact, the concordance between speech and gesture does not appear to be instigated by the *lexical* components of the speech, but by *cyclical motor control.* Franz, Zelaznik, and Smith (1992) found that when subjects were required to produce repetitive movements with the finger, forearm, and jaw, and the repetition of a syllable, there was significant correlation within subjects of the cycle duration of each task; i.e. each subject reached a 'default' timing cycle for the repetitive muscular action, irrespective of which task was being performed. Franz et al. conclude that common timing processes are involved not only in movements of the limbs, but also in speech and non-speech movements of oral structures, and suggest this indicates a governing cognitive 'muscular timing module' responsible for instigating *all rhythmic cyclical muscular activity.*

This accords well with the findings of Alcock, Passingham, and Vargha-Khadem (2000) that the capacity to perform rhythms, both manually and verbally, forms an important foundation of oral/praxic ability—it seems that the capacity to perform planned sequences of complex muscular movements of rhythmic behaviour, both orally and manually, predate oral praxic abilities. Franz et al. (1992) also found that simultaneously produced finger, arm and oral movements concur whilst carrying out repetitive non-linguistic motor repetition, which Mayberry and Jaques (2000) suggest could be the mechanism by which gesture–speech coexpression occurs. The concordance of gesture and speech control appears to be instigated on a motor-control basis rather than a lexical basis (although the content of an utterance can clearly have some influence on the nature of the gesture). As Mayberry and Jaques observe, the harmonized complex motor patterns of the gesture and speech system must ultimately—in speech, at least—subsequently be integrated with the output of the conceptual linguistic systems.

The question still remains of what cycles in vocal control are being integrated with the gestural cycles. Mayberry and Jaques suggest from their research, and from that of McClave (1994) and Nobe (1996) that it is the prosodic patterns of speech that contain the oscillatory cycles of muscular control. McClave found that it is with the nuclei of tone groups that gesture co-occurs, rather than with syllable stress as was commonly thought, and Mayberry and Jaques' (2000) observations of the onset of gesture and vocalization in normal speakers and stutterers accord with those of McClave. The evidence suggests that the interrelationship between manual gesture and vocalization is a deep one, pre-linguistic, and relates complex rhythmic motor production with complexity in tone.

Developmental findings confirm a deep association

From the earliest stage, infants' babbling and gesture seem to be interrelated (Masataka, 2000; Mayberry and Jaques, 2000). Locke et al. (1995) observed a strong association between the onset of babbling behaviour in infants and their exhibiting of lateralization of motor control.

Trevarthen (1999) found that even congenitally blind infants make manual gestures in time with the rhythm of parental vocalizations (which, incidentally, are predominantly tonal with no linguistic meaning to the infant). It seems the perception, as well as production, of vocalization can be linked with gesture. The earliest gestures made by babbling infants are not iconic; they are rhythmic and emotionally determined (Trevarthen, 1999; Falk, 2004a, 2004b) movements that accompany the vocalizations, but do not add meaning or symbolism to them.

The implication of all this research is that the cross-modal coordination of gesture and vocalization doesn't require a central representation or linguistic input initially; such integration occurs whether utterances are linguistic or non-linguistic. This relationship is innate, and relates not only to the production but also the perception of vocalization. It seems that there is a cognitive rhythmic motor coordinator which instigates such muscular sequences irrespective of the musculature (corporeal or orofacial) that is used, and that the complex patterns of gesture (finger, hand, arm, shoulder and joint musculature) and vocalization (orofacial, laryngeal, and respiratory musculature) are coordinated (Mayberry & Jaques, 2000). The cycles of vocalization that are integrated with the gestural cycles are prosodic, tonal ones; in the case of speech, as opposed to non-linguistic vocalization, linguistic meaning and narrative sentence structure are integrated into the gesture–speech system subsequently, before their physical manifestation.

Rhythm, corporeal movement, and emotion

So how does this bear on a relationship between rhythm, melody, and emotion? Whilst rhythm and melody are apparently processed in neurologically specialized areas of the brain which are somewhat independent of each other (for discussion of this see, for example, Morley, 2002, 2003; Peretz & Morais, 1989; Peretz & Zatorre, 2005), there is also clearly some important integration of these systems, especially in the case of the interrelationship of rhythmic physiological movement, vocalization, and emotional state. The expression and perception of emotion clearly happens over multiple media, in particular tonal contour in vocalization (vocal gesture) and posture, gesture, and 'body-language' (corporeal gesture). The evidence discussed above for the integration of vocal control and corporeal control provides several clues as to reasons for the interrelation of vocal-melodic, rhythmic, and corporeal activity; but the relationship between the instigation of vocalization, corporeal muscular control, and emotional expression extends beyond manual gesture accompanying vocalization.

Not only is the production of tonal vocalization related to rhythmic-motor coordination, but also to facial expression and the communication of emotion. Orofacial musculature has a fundamental role in shaping the upper vocal tract and modulating the output of the vocal chords, in all vocalization, linguistic or otherwise. It is also responsible for the control of facial expression. It is thus perhaps unsurprising (though highly significant) that there is a correlation between given facial expressions and characteristics of vocalizations made at the same time. Facial expressions of disgust, happiness, sadness, and anger are not learned and culturally determined, and the capacity to produce and recognize them seems to be innate and universal (e.g. Ekman & Friesen, 1971; Ekman, 1980; Carlson, 1994). In humans, Tartter (1980) showed that vocalizations made whilst smiling were of a higher mean frequency than those made with neutral expression due to the effect of smiling on altering the shape of the upper vocal tract; smiling increases second formant frequency (Tartter & Braun, 1994). Tartter and Braun also showed that vocalizations made whilst frowning had lower formant frequency and longer vowel duration than speech with a neutral expression; listeners were able to discriminate speech made whilst frowning, smiling, and with neutral expression from each other with no visual input. Furthermore, they were able to do so in both vocalized and whispered speech, suggesting that the same effects of facial expression on elements of affect of vocalization would be applicable to vocalizations even in the absence great vocal chord versatility (which accords well with Morton's (1977) findings regarding vocalizations in other animals). Given the universality of certain fundamental facial expressions and the correspondence between these and characteristics of vocalizations, we can also expect characteristics of particular emotional vocalizations to be universal and innate too.

This correlation between facial expression and vocal quality also apparently has an ancient provenance, being shared by our nearest evolutionary relatives. Chimpanzees also frequently couple particular vocalizations with particular emotional facial expressions, the vocalizations being moderated by alterations of the size and shape of the mouth, and thus the resonating upper vocal tract (Falk, 2004a, 2004b). Amongst bonobos, utterances always occur along with facial expressions, gestures, and tactile communication (Bermejo and Omedes, 1999; Falk, 2004a, 2004b), which is true for human infant-directed speech too (Falk, 2004a, 2004b). Humans also use facial affect and vocal affect to inform judgement about the affective content of each other; they seem to be interdependent systems in both production and perception (DeGelder and Vroomen, 2000), with the former having had a significant impact on the development of the nature of affective communication in the latter.

So facial expression and emotional content of vocalization are closely related, with particular orofacial musculature configurations resulting in particular vocal qualities, and the production of certain vocal tones and contours being dependent upon the instigation of certain facial expressions. Furthermore, core emotional facial expressions seem to be human universals (e.g. Ekman and Friesen, 1971; Ekman, 1980).

What is especially interesting is that feedback from facial expression actually *affects* our emotional state. Levenson, Ekman, and Friesen (1990) found that asking subjects to carry out various facial movements to create the expressions of fear, anger, surprise, disgust, happiness, and sadness caused distinct changes to the activity of the autonomic nervous system, such as changes in heart rate, galvanic skin response (skin conductivity due to perspiration), and temperature. The subjects were not informed as to the facial expression being replicated, they were simply told to carry out a sequence of muscular movements which resulted in the formation of a given expression, for example, to raise their eyebrows, then pull them together, whilst tightening the skin under their eyes and stretching their lips horizontally (producing an expression of fear). This particular expression resulted in increased heart rate and reduced skin temperature, whilst a facial expression of anger increased both heart rate and skin temperature, and a happy expression decreased heart rate whilst leaving skin temperature unaffected (Carlson, 1994).

Furthermore, humans have an innate tendency to imitate the facial expression of others with whom they are interacting. Even at the age of 36 hours, infants tend to imitate facial expressions that they see (Field et al., 1982); clearly this is an innate, and not a socially conditioned, tendency, and results in some 'contagion' of the emotion being expressed. Wild, Erb, and Bartels (2001) found that even when exposed to images of another's facial expression (showing sadness, disgust, happiness, anger, surprise, fear, or pleasure) for as little as 500 m/s, subjects reported corresponding changes in emotional state. Carlson (1994, p. 351) suggests that:

> . . . imitation provides one of the channels by which organisms communicate their emotions. For example, if we see someone looking sad, we tend to assume a sad expression ourselves. The feedback from our own expression helps put us in the other person's place and makes us more likely to respond with solace or assistance.

Kraut and Johnston (1979) found that people in situations that were likely to make them smile were more likely to do so in the company of other people than when they were on their own, and the considerable implications for selective advantages of the ability to empathize with conspecifics have also been elaborated (Schmidt and Cohn, 2001; Sloboda and Juslin, 2001).

The implications of all of this for the present discussion are threefold:

> First, the production of particular vocal tones normally relies upon adopting certain facial expressions, and certain facial expressions correlate with certain emotional states.
>
> Secondly, the production of a particular facial expression whilst producing a particular vocalization will result in some degree of feedback which actually affects emotional state.
>
> Thirdly, there is a natural inclination to mimic such expressions and to feel such associated emotions; i.e. such physiological-emotional feedback may occur not only during production, but also during *perception* of such a stimulus.

But the non-verbal corporeal communication of affective state is not limited to facial expression, but incorporates the *whole body and posture*; i.e. vocal gesture, facial expression, and corporeal gesture (posture and body language) are all interdependent. The work of authors such as Trevarthen (1999) indicates that these above findings of feedback and 'contagion' of emotion, and their implications, also apply equally to whole-body expressions of affective state. This may go a considerable way towards explaining physical and emotional response to rhythmic and dance stimuli, both proprioceptively and visually.

As Mitchell and Gallaher (2001) observe, music and dance are historically interdependent developments, with many common features: they are both temporally organized, and described in terms of rhythm, tempo, beat, pace, movement, choppiness, or fluidity, for example. In fact, one rarely exists without some form of the other. Each of these properties can be observed and experienced across numerous modalities, in vision, audition, and kinaesthesis (the proprioceptive feedback associated with voluntary body-movement).

Particular pieces of music can elicit consistent emotional responses in listeners, and movements that often occur in response to music, which are kinaesthetically experienced, can also be a part of emotional experience.

Body posture and emotional state are strongly inter-related; our posture and movements can express a great deal about our emotional state, intentionally and unintentionally, and others' body-posture and movements thus provide important cues as to their emotional state. As well as being able to observe such cues, we can empathically experience something of their emotional state in mirroring them with our own bodies.

Musicality and rhythmic movement, Trevarthen (1999) points out, involve deliberate control and sequencing of this system. This can result in a self-directed feedback from movement into emotional state and, importantly, feedback and interaction between individuals, in terms of synchrony of movement and of emotional state.

Trevarthen (1999) has explored a functional system comprising the brain stem, basal ganglia and the limbic structures of the emotional motor system, which he calls the intrinsic motor formation (IMF). This is responsible for integrating functions of attention, learning, and physiological expression of emotion, including the synchronization and coordination of sequences of movements; it seems to be the case that *there is a close interrelationship between the emotional-controlling elements of the limbic system and the areas responsible for the co-ordination of motor sequences and posture.* This system is active automatically in all types of interpersonal interaction, but deliberate use of it is made in musical activities.

Other research that points in this direction, with specific reference to music and dance, has also been carried out. Krumhansl and Schenck (1997) found that subjects who listened to a piece of music and different subjects who observed a dance to that piece of music, showed great concordance both within and between the two conditions as to their interpretation of the timing of tension and emotion in each, and the emotion that they experienced at given points. That the dancer interpreted the music in such a way that crescendos in the music corresponded with high movements, high notes with leaps and staccato and legato sequences with matching physical movements perhaps renders that congruence in interpretation between the two less surprising, given the literality, or *iconicity*, of the interpretation; it nevertheless remains interesting that such physical movements are the (apparently) obvious way of physically representing such auditory phenomena, and that interpretation of them as such occurs. The main implication of the findings relevant to the current discussion is that both media equally represent tension, release and particular emotions, underlining the cross-modality of such affective expression and interpretation. The affective content is apparently interpreted equivalently in visual, auditory, and kinaesthetic media.

As with facial expression, this is not restricted to perception, but is also a two-way process. Mitchell and Gallagher (2001) review a considerable body of research which illustrates that 'music prompts kinesthetic (motor) responses in both children and adults that often match some aspect of the music' (Mitchell and Gallaher, 2001, p. 66), and that 'kinaesthetically experienced movements that sometimes occur in response to music can also be a normal part of emotions' (ibid. p. 66/67). This is a phenomenon with which most people are familiar already, of course, which is not to diminish the value of such research, but to add to it. That this coordination of emotional communication and of rhythmic behaviour is innate is evidenced by the aforementioned studies showing that very young infants can accompany emotive-tonal prosodic infant-directed speech, or in other circumstances singing, with rhythmic body movements which coordinate with the rhythm of the vocalization (Trevarthen, 1999). This is an innate capacity, as it can occur even in congenitally blind infants, who cannot possibly be imitating the movement of the parent.

Summary

- Orofacial expression of emotion (orofacial gesture) and corporeal expression of emotion (corporeal gesture/body language) are related and interdependent.
- The production of vocal sounds relies on the creation of orofacial expressions which correlate with emotional facial expressions; these can induce emotional response in both the vocalizer and perceivers, through voluntary or involuntary imitation and kinaesthetic feedback.
- There is an interdependence between complex orofacial vocal control and rhythmic corporeal gesture control—the production of complex sequences of vocal sounds relies on the same rhythmic-motor coordinating system as does complex manual/upper body gesture and the two frequently occur together.
- The production and perception of music (melody, rhythm, and dance) makes use of all of these systems—indeed, it *has* to.

Clearly the above conclusions are derived from a diverse and disparate body of research, and there is plentiful scope for further research specifically relating to the interrelationships above as they manifest themselves in musical production and perception. But it is possible that the connections highlighted go some way to elaborating some of the relationships that have previously been considered intriguing but mysterious.

It is clear that we are in a very exciting time regarding progress in our understanding of the relationships between the apparently great diversity of capabilities that comprise musical activity. It is increasingly evident that whilst diverse, these capabilities are also interdependent across a number of dimensions, and their congruence in musical activities may not be due to a convergence in their use but to genuine contiguity—interdependencies in their evolutionary heritage. Papers such as Fitch's presented in this volume are making important contributions to crystallizing our understanding and formulating how we might progress in furthering our understanding of this fascinating and fundamental human behaviour.

References

Alcock, K. J., Passingham, R. E., Watkins, K., & Vargha-Khadem, F. (2000). Pitch and timing abilities in inherited speech and language impairment. *Brain and Language*, *75*, 34–46.

Armstrong, D. F., Stokoe, W. C., & Wilcox, S. E. (1994). Signs of the origins of syntax. *Current Anthropology*, *35*, 349–68.

Bermejo, M., & Omedes, A. (1999). Preliminary vocal repertoire and vocal communication of wild bonobos (*Pan paniscus*) at Lilungo (Democratic Republic of Congo). *Folio Primatologica, 70*, 328–57.

Carlson, N. R. (1994). *The Physiology of Behavior.* Massachusetts: Allyn and Bacon.

Corballis, M. C. (1992). On the evolution of language and generativity. *Cognition, 44*, 197–226.

DeGelder, B., & Vroomen, J. (2000). The perception of emotions by ear and by eye. *Cognition and Emotion, 14*, 289–311.

Ekman, P., & Friesen, W. V. (1971). Constants across cultures in the face and emotion. *Journal of Personality and Social Psychology, 17*, 124–29.

Ekman, P. (1980). *The Face of Man: Expressions of Universal emotions in a New Guinea Village.* New York: Garland SPTM Press.

Falk, D. (2004a). Prelinguistic evolution in hominin mothers and babies: For cryin' out loud! *Behavioural and Brain Sciences, 27*, 461–62.

Falk, D. (2004b). Prelinguistic evolution in early hominins: Whence motherese? *Behavioral and Brain Sciences, 27*, 491–503.

Feyereisen, P. (1997). The competition between gesture and speech production in dual-task paradigms. *Journal of Memory and Language, 36*, 13–33.

Field, T., Woodson, R., Greenberg, R., & Cohen, D. (1982). Discrimination and imitation of facial expression in neonates. *Science, 218*, 179–81.

Franz E. A., Zelaznik, H. N., & Smith, A. (1992). Evidence of common timing processes in the control of manual, orofacial, and speech movements. *Journal of Motor Behavior, 24*, 281–87.

Hewes, G. W. (1973). Primate communication and the gestural origin of language. *Current Anthropology, 14*, 5–24.

Hewes, G. W. (1992). Primate communication and the gestural origin of language. *Current Anthropology, 33*, 65–84.

Kraut, R. E., & Johnston, R. (1979). Social and emotional messages of smiling: an ethological approach. *Journal of Personality and Social Psychology, 37*, 1539–53.

Krumhansl C. L., & Schenk, D.L. (1997). Can dance reflect the structural and expressive qualities of music? A perceptual experiment on Balanchine's choreography of Mozart's Divertimento No. 15. *Musicae Scientiae, 1*, 63–85.

Levenson, R. W., Ekman, P., & Friesen, V. W. (1990). Voluntary facial action generates emotion-specific autonomic nervous system activity. *Psychophysiology, 27*, 363–84.

Locke, J. L., Bekken, K. E., McMinn-Larson, L., & Wein, D. (1995). Emergent control of manual and vocal motor activity in relation to the development of speech. *Brain and Language, 51*, 498–508.

Locke, J. L. (2000). Movement patterns in spoken language. *Science, 288*, 449–51.

Masataka, N. (2000). The role of modality and input in the earliest stages of language acquisition: studies of Japanese sign language. In C. Chamberlain, J. Morford, & R. I. Mayberry (Eds.), *Language Acquisition by Eye* (pp. 3–24). Mahwah, NJ: Erlbaum.

Mayberry, R. I., & Jaques, J. (2000). Gesture production during stuttered speech: insights into the nature of gesture-speech integration. In D. McNeill (Ed.), *Language and Gesture* (pp. 199–214). Cambridge: Cambridge University Press.

McClave, E. (1994). Gestural beats: the rhythm hypothesis. *Journal of Psycholinguistic Research, 23*, 45–66.

McNeill, D. (1992). *Hand and Mind: What Gestures Reveal About Thought.* London: University of Chicago Press.

McNeill, D. (2000). *Language and Gesture.* Cambridge: Cambridge University Press.

Michell, R. W., & Gallaher, M. C. (2001). Embodying music: matching music and dance in memory. *Music Perception, 19,* 65–85.

Morley, I. (2002). Evolution of the physiological and neurological capacities for music. *Cambridge Archaeological Journal, 12,* 195–216.

Morley, I. (2003). *The Evolutionary Origins and Archaeology of Music: An Investigation into the Prehistory of the Human Musical Capacities and Behaviours.* Ph.D. thesis, Cambridge University, Cambridge. Available online at http://www.dar.cam.ac.uk/dcrr.

Morton, E. S. (1977). On the occurrence and significance of motivation-structural rules in some bird and mammal sounds. *American Naturalist, 111,* 855–69.

Nobe, S. (1996). *Cognitive rhythms, gestures, and acoustic aspects of speech.* Ph.D. thesis, University of Chicago. [Cited in Mayberry and Jaques, 2000.]

Peretz, I., & Morais, J. (1989). Music and modularity. *Contemporary Music Review, 4,* 279–93.

Peretz, I., & Zatorre, R. (2005). Brain organization for music processing. *Annual Review of Psychology, 56,* 89–114.

Petitto, L. A., & Marentette, P. F. (1991). Babbling in the manual mode–evidence for the ontogeny of language. *Science, 251,* 1493–96.

Schmidt, K. L., & Cohn, J. F. (2001). Human facial expressions as adaptations: evolutionary questions in facial expression research. *Yearbook of Physical Anthropology, 44,* 3–24.

Sloboda, J. A., & Juslin, P. N. (2001). Psychological perspectives on music and emotion. In P. N. Juslin, & J. A. Sloboda (Eds.), *Music and Emotion: Theory and Research* (pp. 71–104). Oxford: Oxford University Press.

Stokoe, W. C. (2000). Gesture to sign (language). In D. McNeill (Ed.), *Language and Gesture* (pp. 388–99). Cambridge: Cambridge University Press.

Tartter, V. C. (1980). Happy talk: perceptual and acoustic effects of smiling on speech. *Perception and Psychophysics, 27,* 24–27.

Tartter, V. C., & Braun, D. (1994). Hearing smiles and frowns in normal and whisper registers. *Journal of the Acoustical Society of America, 96,* 2101–07.

Trevarthen, C. (1999). Musicality and the intrinsic motive pulse: evidence from human psychobiology and infant communication. *Musicae Scientiae, Special Issue,* 155–215.

Wild, B., Erb, M., & Bartels, M. (2001). Are emotions contagious? Evoked emotions while viewing emotionally expressive faces: quality, quantity, time course and gender differences. *Psychiatry Research, 102,* 109–24.

Chapter 13

An ethnomusicological perspective on animal 'music' and human music: the paradox of 'the paradox of rhythm'

Elizabeth Tolbert

In Chapter 9, 'The biology and evolution of rhythm: unravelling a paradox', Fitch describes the emerging consensus (e.g. Bispham, 2003, 2006; Cross, Bispham, Himberg, & Swaine, in press) that musical rhythm consists of separable components with their own evolutionary histories, and that 'it is the capacity for entrainment to a strict periodic pulse that came latest in human evolution, [and] that this capacity might reflect some more general social, cooperative urge'. Fitch proposes the following components of the 'rhythm faculty': pulse extraction (a form of pattern extraction in the auditory domain more generally, and which is shared with speech), beat entrainment (or motor synchronization to the extracted pulse, which requires auditory to motor cross-modal integration), and periodic motor-pattern generation (which requires cross-modal sensory/motor integration). In order to demonstrate that these components are structurally separable, and to suggest new avenues for empirical research, Fitch reviews studies on grouping and timing mechanisms in music, language, and animal communication, and offers hypotheses about their underlying mechanisms and neural substrates. Fitch suggests that the ability to keep an isochronous beat is not specific to music, but that it emerges from the interface between internal biological oscillators and controlled motor output more generally. In particular, isochrony results from the 'interaction of the pattern extraction and entrainment components of the "rhythm faculty", driven by a desire for group coherence and predictability'. Fitch frames his characterization of the 'rhythm faculty' as consistent with Darwin's original protolanguage hypothesis, concluding that music is a 'living fossil' of this earlier stage of human communication.

In its broad outlines, this story is well accepted in the recent literature, a literature to which Fitch himself has made original and significant contributions (see Fitch, 2006; Hauser, Chomsky, & Fitch, 2002). Points of general agreement include the mosaic nature of musical rhythm, the status of entrainment as seemingly unique to humans, the separation of pulse extraction from entrained motor output, the interface between internal oscillators and temporally structured motor behaviour, and the cross-modal and social bases of entrainment. For example, Bispham (2006, p. 125) suggests that 'musical rhythmic behavior' consists of an evolutionary mosaic of subskills that 'share overlapping internal oscillatory mechanisms,' and include 'general timing abilities, smooth and ballistic movement (periodic and non-periodic), perception of pulse, [and] a coupling of action and perception', in addition to 'error correction mechanisms'. Drawing on Jones (1976) and Repp (2004), Bispham further proposes that entrainment is a uniquely human skill for coordinating social action, one characterized by 'reference to an external timekeeper and/or to an internally created and volitionally controlled attentional pulse' (p. 126), and is likely an 'entailment of the ability to make period corrections' (pp. 130–31). Cross et al. (in press) also emphasize the social bases of entrainment, stipulating that '[e]ntrainment in modern humans involves mutually-adaptive periodic sound-producing behavior, is grounded in cooperative interaction with others, and is multi-modal, involving regular temporal patterning not only of sound but also action' (p. 20; see also Cross, 2009).

Although Bispham and Cross et al. bring up many of the same points as Fitch, their strong emphases on the social underpinnings of entrainment lead them to take issue with some of Fitch's interpretations of the animal communication literature (which are reiterated in Fitch's contribution to this volume), in particular, Fitch's claim that differences between animal 'music' and human music are more quantitative than qualitative in domains such as 'song' or 'drumming' behaviours (Bispham 2003, 2006; Cross et al., in press). These concerns mirror my own, although I approach them from a slightly different perspective.

As an ethnomusicologist, my major disagreement with Fitch centres on the nature of music and its relationship to nonhuman animal communication. As do most Western music theorists and musicologists, Fitch seeks to understand music by analysing its sound structures, which he then compares with similar analyses of 'design features' in language and animal communication; however, from an ethnomusicological perspective, this understanding of music is highly ethnocentric, in that it assumes that sound patterns are perceived and interpreted in a similar manner (and are subserved by similar neural mechanisms) not only across human cultures, but also across species. This leads to the assumption that it is possible to identify shared mechanisms and make evolutionary hypotheses linking animal 'music' and human music simply by analysing these surface sound patterns. Fitch would probably agree with the notion that bird 'songs' sound like songs to us because humans can and do ascribe human-like meaning to them; however, contra Fitch, I would claim that such anthropocentric understandings cannot provide direct evidence concerning the status of bird song as a homologue or analogue to human music. Even though it is unquestionably the case that humans share common perceptual and cognitive abilities with other animals, such continuities (and discontinuities) need to be empirically established rather than assumed.

As a stalwart empiricist, Fitch's larger aim is indeed to 'generate testable hypotheses', and he comes up with many original interpretations of available data and intriguing suggestions for future research. However, despite his commendable efforts along these lines, I believe that Fitch's tendency to ascribe similar underlying mechanisms to superficially similar sound patterns sometimes leads him to overinterpret data that is too reduced to address his questions. This, in turn, sometimes leads Fitch astray when he formulates hypotheses. Although I agree for the most part with Fitch's general characterizations of the 'rhythm faculty', and find his synthesis both stimulating and provocative, I have several quibbles with the details, which I will discuss in more detail below.

Contra Fitch, I believe that the available evidence, particularly when considering music's social function to coordinate group action or regulate group emotion, supports the idea that musical rhythm is a *symbolic* behaviour, and therefore differs substantially from other animal communication in regards to at least some of its underlying mechanisms. Donald (1991) proposed almost two decades ago that the story of the evolution of language (and I would argue, music, or any other human semiotic system) is essentially the story of the evolution of symbolic representation, i.e. the evolution of *meaning* (see Cross & Tolbert, 2009). As I have argued for musical behaviour more generally (Tolbert, 2001, 2002), I consider musical rhythmic behaviour to be an example of what Donald terms *mimesis*, i.e. the capacity to abstract movement from its original context and refine it through conscious rehearsal for symbolic purposes. If mimesis is indeed applicable here, then there are several implications for Fitch's proposals. For example, beat extraction would not only involve auditory perception, but would also require an abstracted and implementable motor image of its production in order to refine it for semiotic means. My guess is that the pattern abstraction and manipulation that underlie mimesis, and by extension, beat extraction, is not on the same level and is not likely to be subserved by the same mechanisms as pattern abstraction in perception, although perceptual processes certainly constrain these higher level cognitive skills. Moreover, I am not convinced that the data Fitch brings to the table are likely to shed light on this question one way or the other.

For example, Fitch, following Pressing (1983), makes an analogy between the grouping of two's and three's in both the diatonic major scale and the West African agbekor bell pattern, hypothesizing that they represent a 'perceptual gestalt' in the auditory domain, and thus point to the underlying mechanism for beat extraction and its status as a separable component of the faculty of rhythm. However, the fact that it is possible to create an analogy between these pitch and rhythm patterns does not address the question of their underlying perceptual and cognitive mechanisms. Although there are certainly grouping and timing mechanisms that subserve pitch and rhythm perception, I question whether Fitch's examples illustrate a perceptual gestalt, as they do not seem to be comparable phenomena; the bell pattern is played during an entire performance of agbekor, whereas the diatonic scale is already an abstraction, i.e. an ordering of pitches, and is not necessarily performed as such. Yet even if we assume that they *are* examples of a perceptual gestalt, it does not necessarily follow that they inform beat extraction, as they do not provide evidence to establish beat extraction as a perceptual gestalt. But most importantly, I question whether the mechanisms underlying perceptual gestalts are sufficient to explain the conscious and volitional ability to abstract a beat in such a way that one could entrain to it, or if they are rather more similar to the capacities underlying edge detection in vision, which is an unconscious and automatic process. If beat extraction requires the flexible manipulation of an internal representation of the beat, then I would guess that it is more than a perceptual gestalt. Similarly, Fitch's positing of common grouping mechanisms in language and music does not address the question of whether beat extraction relies on such mechanisms. Again, it seems that the relevant issue concerns the underlying perceptual and/or cognitive mechanisms for beat extraction; if Fitch is trying to establish that beat extraction is a perceptual process, i.e. that beat extraction is *identical* to beat perception, then the data he cites neither confirm nor refute this point.

In a similar vein, Fitch states that 'the generation of a complex patterned motor output entrained to an acoustic pattern is not in any sense assured by the ubiquity of periodicity, or a capacity for cross-modal sensory transfer', an assertion that few would oppose; indeed, Fitch's 'paradox of rhythm', i.e. the pervasiveness of biological oscillators vis-à-vis the rarity of entrainment, is largely a straw man. But more to the point, Fitch attempts to support the case for the separability of biological oscillators, entrainment, and periodic motor output (and the cross-modal sensory and sensory-motor integration that underlie it) in reference to data that are either somewhat tangential and/or too reduced to address his claims. For example, if I understand him correctly, Fitch references the following in order to assert that cross-modal sensory-motor behaviour can occur without entrainment: Sur, Pallas, and Roe's (1990) work on the interchangeability of sensory cortex in mammalian ontogenetic development; the difference in the cytoarchitectonics of motor and sensory cortex as evidence of the presumed greater neurocomputational load for cross-modal sensory-motor integration as opposed to cross-modal sensory transfer; and the difficulty of building robots that emulate sensorily-guided motor behaviour (Brooks, 1989), posited as further evidence for the presumed greater neurocomputational load mentioned above. As for the independence of cross-modal sensory-motor behaviour and entrainment, this is not surprising, given that even lower vertebrates (thanks to their cerebellums) have been manoeuvring around in their environments for tens of millions of years. I am not entirely sure of Fitch's purpose here, but if he wants to point out the neural substrates for cross-modal sensory-motor integration, what are the implications for musical rhythm? In particular, if he wants to separate cross-modal sensory-motor integration from entrainment and beat extraction, how do the neural data support this point specifically?

As mentioned above, my major disagreements with Fitch stem from his claim that the differences between animal 'music' and human music are largely quantitative, not qualitative. As Bispham (2003, 2006) and Cross et al. (2008) have argued, bird song and chimp drumming are qualitatively different than human music, in that they rely on stereotypical forms, contexts, and non-decomposable motor behaviours, and/or are the result of the biomechanics of movement rather than the conscious control over movement in order to create intentional sound patterns. Fitch argues that chimp drumming is evidence of 'mapping a quasiperiodic motor pulse into an auditorily-monitored acoustic motor behaviour', and thus evidence of the separability of the last component of the rhythm faculty, i.e. 'periodic motor output', from entrainment. However, it seems that Fitch is equating disparate phenomena under the umbrella of 'periodic motor output', namely, chest beating and/or 'drumming,' and the ability to voluntarily create a steady motoric pulse. I would argue that periodicity is exactly what is missing in chimp drumming. Although chimp drumming might sound like it has a pulse to us, at least sometimes, and hence is 'quasi-periodic', there does not seem to be any evidence that chimps are intentionally producing such a pulse, or that it results from anything other than the biomechanics of pendular movement. Yet the fact that chimps are able to acoustically monitor their 'drumming' behaviour for social ends is a fascinating finding, and is certainly relevant to larger questions about the social bases of rhythm. However, since humans are the only animals presently known both to intentionally produce a steady motoric pulse and to entrain, the evidence from chimp drumming does not seem relevant to Fitch's hypothesis that they are subserved by *different* underlying mechanisms.

Regardless, Fitch is right to underscore the paucity of data in this area—we simply do not have enough information to understand what chimp 'drumming' has to tell us. Given that Snowball the cockatoo is apparently able to 'dance' and sometimes synchronize to the beat of a Backstreet Boys song played at varying tempos (Patel, Iversen, Bregman, Schulz, & Schulz, 2008), beat extraction and entrainment may themselves consist of several subskills that have yet to be identified.

When Fitch turns to the social bases of rhythm, his proposals are less controversial, and indeed, are compatible with much current thinking. From an ethnomusicological perspective, the social, and perhaps not specifically musical, origins of isochrony seem quite likely; the ethnographic record is rife with examples of social activity that involve the coordination of collective action around a beat, such as performative ritual or working in a group. As discussed earlier, the idea that rhythm, and in particular, entrainment, provides a focus for social engagement is generally accepted in the recent literature (e.g. see discussion in Clayton, Sager, & Will, 2005; Cross, 2005, 2009).

On the other hand, Fitch's assertion that his characterization of the rhythm faculty is consistent with Darwinian protolanguage is puzzling, as it does not seem to be in line with his stated goal of producing 'testable hypotheses'. Although Fitch claims that 'most of the open questions touched upon' in his paper 'can serve at tests of the "musical protolanguage" model of language evolution', it seems that Fitch is looking for data to support a hypothesis to which he is already committed, i.e. Darwin's *original* protolanguage hypothesis. Perhaps Darwin's characterization of protolanguage is attractive to Fitch for the very reasons it has been partially revised by others, i.e. because it assumes that there is no significant difference between animal 'music' and human music. In any case, the relevance of Darwinian protolanguage for Fitch's proposals concerning rhythm is unclear. I am guessing that Fitch is drawing on Patel's (2006) 'vocal learning and rhythmic synchronization' hypothesis to posit vocal learning as a benchmark for skills that are necessary, if not sufficient, for entrainment; thus, elucidation of the neural substrates for vocal learning might help establish a timeline for the relative emergence of vocal rhythm vis-à-vis entrainment and other components of the rhythm faculty. Needless to say, more work is needed to ascertain whether these assumptions are warranted. In any case, it would be helpful to this reader if Fitch were to clarify how aspects of a 'musical protolanguage' could be tested in reference to his conceptualizations of beat extraction, entrainment, and periodic motor output.

On another note, it is mystifying that Fitch would claim that 'Darwin's model has been almost universally overlooked (and indeed repeatedly reinvented).' Contra Fitch, an updated version of Darwinian protolanguage is widely accepted in the recent literature on both the evolution of language and evolution of music, despite disagreements over its nature, and is even the centrepiece of Mithen's argument in *The Singing Neanderthals* (2005). Furthermore, in writings about music, at least, protolanguage is considered to be predecessor of both music and language (e.g. Brown, 2000; Tolbert, 2001, 2002). Incidentally, and as I have argued elsewhere (Tolbert, 2002), if both music *and* language emerged from protolanguage, it does not seem justified to privilege music as a 'living fossil', when language is equally so.

Finally, I am grateful that Fitch has offered specific proposals and specific data for discussion; it has certainly forced me to focus my comments and thus to clarify my own thinking about fundamental issues. This exercise has also renewed my commitment to cross-disciplinary dialogue; bridging theoretical and methodological gaps between the sciences, social sciences, and the humanities demands not only good will, but immense effort, and underscores the need for careful and ongoing syntheses of a vast interdisciplinary literature. Since no one can have a command of all the disciplines involved, more of us need to present syntheses from our various disciplinary perspectives, as Fitch has done so admirably here.

References

Bispham, J. (2003). *An evolutionary perceptive on the human skill of interpersonal musical entrainment.* Unpublished M Phil dissertation, University of Cambridge.

Bispham, J. (2006). Rhythm in music: What is it? Who has it? and Why? *Music Perception*, *24*(2), 125–34.

Brooks, R. A. (1989). A robot that walks: Emergent behaviors from a carefully evolved Network. *Neural Computation*, *1*, 253–62.

Brown, S. (2000). The 'musilanguage' model of music evolution. In N. L. Wallin, B. Merker, & S. Brown (Eds.), *The Origins of Music* (pp. 271–300). Cambridge, MA: MIT Press.

Clayton, M., Sager, R., & Will, U. (2005). In time with the music: The concept of entrainment and its significance for ethnomusicology. *ESEM counterpoint*, *1*, 1–45.

Cross, I. (2005). Music and meaning, ambiguity and evolution. In D. Miell, R. MacDonald, & D. Hargreaves (Eds.), *Musical Communication* (pp. 27–43). Oxford: Oxford University Press.

Cross, I. (2009). The nature of music and its evolution. In S. Hallam, I. Cross, & M. Thaut (Eds.), *Oxford Handbook of Music Psychology* (pp. 3–13). Oxford: Oxford University Press.

Cross, I., & Tolbert, E. (2009). Music and meaning. In S. Hallam, I. Cross, & M. Thaut (Eds.), *Oxford Handbook of Music Psychology* (pp. 24–34). Oxford: Oxford University Press.

Cross, I., Bispham, J., Himberg, T., & Swaine, J. (in press). The evolution of musical rhythm. *Evolutionary Psychology*.

Donald, M. (1991). *Origins of the Modern Mind.* Cambridge, MA: Harvard University Press.

Fitch, W. T. (2006). The biology and evolution of music: a comparative perspective. *Cognition*, *100*(1), 173–215.

Hauser, M., Chomsky, N., & Fitch, W. T. (2002). The language faculty: What is it, who has it, and how did it evolve? *Science*, *298*, 1569–79.

Jones, M. (1976). Time, our lost dimension: Toward a new theory of perception, attention, and memory. *Psychological Review*, *83*, 325–35.

Mithen, S. (2005). *The singing Neanderthals: the origins of music, language, mind and body.* London: Weidenfeld & Nicholson.

Patel, A. D. (2006). Musical rhythm, linguistic rhythm, and human evolution. *Music Perception, 24*, 99–104.

Patel, A.D., Iversen, J.R., Bregman, M.R., Schulz, I., & Schulz, C. (2008). Investigating the human-specificity of synchronization to music. In K. Miyazaki, Y. Hiraga, M. Adachi, Y. Nakajima, & M. Tsuzaki, et al. (Eds.), *Proceedings of the 10th International Conference on Music Perception & Cognition (ICMPC10), August 2008, Sapporo, Japan* (pp. 100–04). Adelaide: Causal Productions.

Pressing, J. (1983). Cognitive isomorphisms between pitch and rhythm in world musics: West Africa, the Balkans and Western tonality. *Studies in Music, 17*, 38–61.

Repp, B. (2004). Comments on 'Rapid motor adaptations to subliminal frequency shifts during syncopated rhythmic sensorimotor synchronization' by M. Thaut & G. Kenyon. *Human Movement Science, 21*, 61–78.

Sur, M., Pallas, S. L., and Roe, A. W. (1990). Cross-modal plasticity in cortical development: differentiation and specification of sensory neocortex. *Trends in Neuroscience, 13*, 227–33.

Tolbert, E. (2001). Music and meaning: An evolutionary story. *Psychology of Music, 29*, 89–94.

Tolbert, E. (2002). Untying the music/language knot. In L. Austern (Ed.), *Music, Sensation and Sensuality* (pp. 77–95). New York: Routledge Press.

Chapter 14

Reweaving the strands: welcoming diverse perspectives on the biology of music

W. Tecumseh Fitch

It was gratifying to receive such a diverse range of comments on my target paper, integrating phenomena from stuttering to bipedalism and perspectives from evolution to ethnomusicology. I welcome the opportunity to clarify a number of misunderstandings, but space does not permit a full exploration of the many interesting issues raised.

I completely agree with Simon Kirby that we must be prepared to envisage different selective forces acting at different stages in the evolution of hominid communication (whether musical or linguistic), and I find his arguments about the relevance of the developmental stress hypothesis to the evolution of music compelling. We need to explain why human listeners find musical complexity fascinating and attractive, and I think he has outlined a plausible scenario, based on solid comparative evidence. It would be nice to explore this hypothesis further in mammals with complex, learned song, such as whales, seals, or bats (Knörnschild, Nagy, Metz, Mayer, & von Helversen, 2010).

Kirby and I agree that Darwin's 'musical protolanguage' hypothesis provides an increasingly compelling framework for understanding language evolution. We part ways only in that I think syntax played an important role in the evolution of meaningful propositional language. In the context of Darwin's model, I would separate 'syntax' into two basic components. The phrasal component combines small units into larger wholes in a hierarchical fashion, and then applies intonation contours and stress to these structures. This component seems to be shared between music and language, and by hypothesis originated before propositional language. The second component, which I termed 'complex syntax', includes such phenomena as case, anaphora, recursive embedding of phrases, subjacency, and restrictions on binding (Carnie, 2002; Jackendoff, 2002). Such complexities are not tied to the formal distinction between context-free and finite-state languages that Kirby mentions. Rather, they reflect the complex mapping between propositional *meaning* and syntactic phrase structure, a topic beyond formal language theory. Since, by Darwin's hypothesis, this mapping was acquired after the basic phrasal syntax of musical protolanguage was already well established, I suspect that there has been specific, independent selection for such complex aspects of syntax.

Steven Mithen requested several clarifications and elaborations. To clarify, I do not suggest that isochrony reflects only some vague general tendency towards group cooperation.

Rather I hypothesize that isochrony is a specific, mechanistic solution to the problem of entrainment by groups of interacting musicians/dancers, and that this specific ability is one facet of a more general drive towards cooperative interaction in our species. Regarding 'biological reductionism', recognizing the value of analysis does not deny the necessity for synthesis. I attempted to discuss both the forest and the trees in my decomposition of the mechanisms underlying rhythm. As a musician I fully appreciate the seamless whole that any successful musical performance seems to be, but as a scientist I also recognize that this whole involves multiple component mechanisms. Although my specific analysis might be inadequate, I am certain that some analysis along these lines is a prerequisite for an insightful future synthesis.

By 'human evolution' I meant the time period of roughly the last six million years, starting with our divergence from chimpanzees and ending with modern *Homo sapiens*. I am not uninterested in the fossil record (see Fitch, 2009, 2010) but I am skeptical whether fossils will resolve the big questions about exactly when music and language evolved. Neither language nor music fossilize, and the inferences that we can derive from stones and bones are always tenuous: they are not really 'direct evidence' concerning behaviour. The long-running debate about the Neanderthal 'flute' found at Divje Baba is an excellent illustration of the fact that, however solid an object might be, interpretation is always controversial (D'Errico, Villa, Llona, & Idarraga, 1998; Kunej & Turk, 2000; Turk, 1997). Of course we should incorporate palaeontological data, when available, in our models, as Mithen has done. In the phylogenetic scenario I find plausible, following the arguments of Merlin Donald (1991), *Homo erectus* was probably the first 'mimetic' species, and may have used a musical protolanguage. However, I do not share Mithen's conviction that such questions deserve the central place in understanding the biology and evolution of music, given the many difficulties involved in testing them.

Instead, I stress the value of work done on living animals, investigating the neural and genetic mechanisms underlying cognition, motor control and auditory perception generally, and music perception in particular. Such animal work may, in many cases, be directly relevant to human music (same genes, same brain areas). The value of data from living species applies even to convergently evolved traits (like vocal learning), because the same genes may govern analogous traits in widely-separated species (like humans and birds) (Scharff & Haesler, 2005). I stress this approach because this source of data remains relatively unexploited, in comparison to the now-abundant evolutionary speculation about origins (Fitch, 2006). An obvious example of missing data, of central importance in understanding the evolution of music, is the still-outstanding question of entrainment capabilities in chimpanzees or other primates.

Regarding scholarship and citations, I stand by my assertion that Darwin's central contribution in proposing the musical protolanguage hypothesis has been broadly overlooked. While Mithen's (2005) book does indeed cite Darwin, it is only in the context of sexual selection, and like several others Mithen credits Steven Brown (2000) with the basic hypothesis of a music-like precursor to language. Brown, in his long discussion of 'musilanguage', does not cite Darwin at all. My goal in reviewing this literature has been to re-assert Darwin's priority regarding these ideas, ensuring that newcomers to the field are not misled, rather than to deny the contributions of others.

But I apologize for failing to cite Mithen's useful and wide-ranging book more frequently in my target paper.

Iain Morley's commentary was admirably rich in the breadth of evidence adduced, and I strongly agree with his general point that discussions of music evolution need to integrate dance more closely. However, I do not share his conviction that dance and musical rhythmic behaviour necessarily make use of identical mechanisms. I know numerous excellent musicians who are not good dancers, and vice versa, suggesting considerable divergence is possible in the underlying mechanisms. I also did not mean to imply that dancers never use 'the auditory loop': auditory feedback is certainly a key component of certain types of dance (e.g. tap dancing), and I would be happy to agree with Morley that tap dancing is a form of drumming. But sound is not always involved in dance (e.g. waltz or ballet are mostly silent). At a general level, similar neural mechanisms are involved in virtually *all* forms of motor behaviour (e.g. basal ganglia, cerebellum, corticothalamic loops), but many animals have complex coordinated movement without having music or dance. Thus I suspect that different mechanisms, and/or changes in these broadly-shared mechanisms, underlie some aspects of music and dance.

I certainly agree that the complex of connections between facial display, motor control, gesture, speech, and song have important implications for the evolution of music, but I am not yet convinced that together they explain the specific isomorphism I highlighted between hierarchical structure in the rhythmic (agbekor) and harmonic (diatonic) realms. I suspect that a more detailed cognitive approach to auditory perception is required to resolve this puzzle. This is another area where detailed research on animals could potentially be very revealing, but does not currently exist.

In response to Elizabeth Tolbert's critique I would like to correct a number of apparent misconceptions concerning the assumptions underlying my approach. I certainly do not assume that we can simply extrapolate from surface auditory signals to homologous mechanisms; in contrast the empirical focus in my work has always been on specific, underlying cognitive mechanisms and their neural and genetic basis. Far from being 'highly ethnocentric', my opinions are based on a long familiarity with non-European musical traditions including West African and Afro-Caribbean percussion and song styles. My basic assumption is that there is a universal, shared 'music faculty' that is essentially equivalent, at birth, in all existing human populations, worldwide (cf. Hauser & McDermott, 2003; Jackendoff & Lerdahl, 2006). Finally, my central example is West African. How this all-embracing perspective can be seen as 'ethnocentric' baffles me.

I have furthermore nowhere advanced the claim of 'no significant difference between animal "music" and human music', nor do I think Darwin would ascribe to this view. Music requires a suite of mechanisms, some shared and others probably unique, and attempting to describe whole complex systems as either 'qualitatively' or 'quantitatively' different seems inevitably Procrustean to me. Similarly, I do not believe that the distinction Tolbert repeatedly draws between conscious/intentional/volitional on the one hand and perceptual/automatic/unconscious on the other is a profitable dichotomy. We have no objective way of knowing whether a chimpanzee's drumming or a bird's singing is 'consciously' or 'intentionally' produced, and a priori assumptions in either direction are unjustified. Even in humans, a key goal of musical practice is to turn initially conscious, intentional movement patterns into automatic, unconscious ones, and some of the most expressive performances are those where most of the basic motoric activity is fully automatized (cf. Sudnow, 1993). Attempting to draw conscious *versus* automatic distinctions in such contexts is positively misleading.

Regarding the analogy between diatonic scale patterns and those of agbekor and similar drumming styles, I absolutely agree that recognizing such an isomorphism is only the start of a serious analysis. The proper comparisons, however, are between either a played diatonic scale and the bell pattern, *or* between a free melody and a master drummer's improvised agbekor solo. To compare the repeated bell part with a free melody is to cross two different levels of abstraction. Again, learning to play or parse the agbekor bell pattern is initially a difficult, consciously-monitored task, but with experience becomes easy and automatized. Only then can the abstraction of a drum solo that fits within (or sometimes contradicts) the bell ostinato be fully understood, or performed. In much of Afro-Caribbean music (e.g. salsa or guaguanco), there is a 'clave' part, similar to the agbekor bell part, which practiced listeners know and recognize. Although this part may be played explicitly, it is often left implicit: everyone familiar with the music recognizes or infers the appropriate clave, without needing it to be played out, just as European musicians infer the scale and key when presented with a Western melody.

An important clarification is needed regarding what, precisely, I consider the 'paradox' of rhythm. The paradox results not from 'the pervasiveness of biological oscillators', as Tolbert suggests, but rather from the pervasiveness of *coupling* between oscillators and the resultingly ubiquitous possibility of entrainment. Such entrainment is very common in biological systems, from the coupling of sleep and sexual behaviour with the sun and moon, the coupling between heart and breathing rates in physiology, the coupling between neural oscillators in the brain, or the coupling of flashing in a tree-full of fireflies (Buzsaki, 2006; Glass & Mackey, 1988; Gleick, 1987; S. Strogatz, 2003; S. H. Strogatz, 1994). I intended to connote this ubiquity with the first sentence of the target paper, but I can see from Tolbert and Mithen's comments that I was not explicit enough.

Since Huygen's original experiments with pendulum-based clocks, where two clocks on the same wall become synchronized regardless of their starting phase, it has been recognized that coupling between nonlinear oscillators easily leads to synchronization (Bennett, Schatz, Rockwood, & Wiesenfeld, 2002). Biological systems, often, evolve in such a way as to exploit this physical fact. I presume, as Tolbert correctly recognizes, that human rhythmic entrainment also exploits this ubiquitous capacity. The paradox is not that we do so, but that so many other species do not (with the currently known exceptions including fireflies and some other insect species, a few chorusing amphibians, and now parrots (Greenfield, 1994; Merker, 2000; Patel, Iversen, Bregman, & Schulz, 2009; Schachner, Brady, Pepperberg, & Hauser, 2009)). Given the existence of sensorily-driven entrainment in fireflies and toads, we certainly cannot explain its broad absence in most birds or mammals in terms of consciousness, culture, or other high-order cognitive phenomena.

Finally, to return to Darwin's musical protolanguage, I am not 'already committed' to this hypothesis. Rather I am intrigued by Darwin's hypothesis, and am committed to understanding, updating, and testing it in the light of modern knowledge, and to ensuring that Darwin is cited appropriately. There are many ways in which the hypothesis can be tested (cf. Fitch, 2006). Within humans, we can look for correlations between musical and phonological behaviour (Patel & Daniele, 2003), examine overlap between brain regions involved in different linguistic and musical capacities (Grahn & Brett, 2007; Koelsch, et al., 2002; Patel, 2008; Peretz & Zatorre, 2003), and ultimately look at genes involved in music and language (Alcock, Passingham, Watkins, & Vargha-Khadem, 2000; Peretz, 2008; Peretz, et al., 2002), and determine whether they share functions in both cognitive domains.

Exploring cases of 'analogy', where shared abilities have evolved convergently, also allows us to test adaptive hypotheses about the evolution of specific aspects of music. For example, since the original target paper was written, it has become clear that parrots, but apparently not other birds, have a capacity for entrainment (cf. Fitch, 2009; Patel, et al., 2009; Schachner, et al., 2009). Delving deeper into the mechanistic basis of parrots' ability will allow us to investigate whether the same types of neural computations are involved in bird and human entrainment, or between avian vocal learning and entrainment (cf. Patel, 2006). More detailed ethological information will help test hypotheses about the adaptive role, if any, of such entrainment (e.g. for pair or group synchronization).

Thus I see no shortage of hypotheses or testable predictions regarding the biology and evolution of music, and rhythm in particular, but rather a significant shortage of scientists engaged in empirically evaluating these hypotheses. My goal in writing the target paper was to spur further empirical research along these lines. Such research will be necessary to either confirm or reject my tentative breakdown of rhythmic mechanisms, to seek homologous or analogous mechanisms in other species, and to help dissect the underlying neural and genetic bases for such cognitive mechanisms in humans and other animals. If the past few years are any guide, we can expect rapid and exciting empirical progress on many of these topics in the coming decade. However, given the current state of the art in 'biomusicology', we would be foolish to exclude any potentially-relevant data from consideration, and thus I whole-heartedly endorse the various extensions and new directions that the commentators have suggested. There's a lot left to learn, and many stones remain unturned.

References

Alcock, K. J., Passingham, R. E., Watkins, K. E., & Vargha-Khadem, F. (2000). Pitch and timing abilities in inherited speech and language impairment. *Brain and Language, 75*, 34–46.

Bennett, M., Schatz, M. F., Rockwood, H., & Wiesenfeld, K. (2002). Huygens's clocks. *Proceedings of the Royal Society of London A, 458*, 563–79.

Brown, S. (2000). The 'Musilanguage' model of music evolution. In N. L. Wallin, B. Merker & S. Brown (Eds.), *The Origins of Music* (pp. 271–300). Cambridge, MA: MIT Press.

Buzsaki, G. (2006). *Rhythms of the Brain*. New York: Oxford University Press.

Carnie, A. (2002). *Syntax: A Generative Introduction*. Oxford: Blackwell.

D'Errico, F., Villa, P., Llona, A. C. P., & Idarraga, R. R. (1998). A Middle Palaeolithic origin of music? Using cave-bear bone accumulations to assess the Divje Babe I bone 'flute'. *Antiquity, 72*, 65–76.

Donald, M. (1991). *Origins of the Modern Mind*. Cambridge, MA: Harvard University Press.

Fitch, W. T. (2006). The biology and evolution of music: A comparative perspective. *Cognition, 100*(1), 173–215.

Fitch, W. T. (2009). Biology of music: Another one bites the dust. *Current Biology, 19*(10), R403–404.

Fitch, W. T. (2009). Fossil cues to the evolution of speech. In R. P. Botha & C. Knight (Eds.), *The Cradle of Language* (pp. 112–34). Oxford: Oxford University Press.

Fitch, W. T. (2010). *The Evolution of Language*. Cambridge: Cambridge University Press.

Glass, L., & Mackey, M. C. (1988). *From clocks to chaos: the rhythms of life*. Princeton, NJ: Princeton University Press.

Gleick, J. (1987). *Chaos: Making a new science*. New York: Viking Penguin.

Grahn, J. A., & Brett, M. (2007). Rhythm and beat perception in motor areas of the brain. *Journal of Cognitive Neuroscience, 19*(5), 893–906.

Greenfield, M. D. (1994). Cooperation and conflict in the evolution of signal interactions. *Annual Review of Ecology and Systematics, 25*, 97–126.

Hauser, M. D., & McDermott, J. (2003). The evolution of the music faculty: A comparative perspective. *Nature Neuroscience, 6*, 663–68.

Jackendoff, R. (2002). *Foundations of Language*. New York: Oxford University Press.

Jackendoff, R., & Lerdahl, F. (2006). The capacity for music: what is it, and what's special about it? *Cognition, 100*(1), 33–72.

Knörnschild, M., Nagy, M., Metz, M., Mayer, F., & von Helversen, O. (2010). Complex vocal imitation during ontogeny in a bat. *Biology Letters, 6*, 156–59.

Koelsch, S., Gunter, T. C., Cramon, D. Y. v., Zysset, S., Lohmann, G., & Friederici, A. D. (2002). Bach Speaks: A Cortical 'Language-Network' Serves the Processing of Music. *NeuroImage, 17*, 956–66.

Kunej, D., & Turk, I. (2000). New perspectives on the beginnings of music: Archaeological and musicological analysis of a middle Paleolithic bone 'flute'. In N. L. Wallin, B. Merker, & S. Brown (Eds.), *The Origins of Music* (pp. 235–68). Cambridge, MA: MIT Press.

Merker, B. (2000). Synchronous chorusing and human origins. In N. L. Wallin, B. Merker & S. Brown (Eds.), *The Origins of Music* (pp. 315–27). Cambridge, MA: MIT Press.

Mithen, S. (2005). *The Singing Neanderthals: The Origins of Music, Language, Mind, and Body.* London: Weidenfeld & Nicolson.

Patel, A. D. (2006). Musical rhythm, linguistic rhythm, and human evolution. *Music Perception, 24*(1), 99–104.

Patel, A. D. (2008). *Music, Language, and the Brain*. New York: Oxford University Press.

Patel, A. D., & Daniele, J. R. (2003). An empirical comparison of rhythm in language and music *Cognition, 87*, B35–45.

Patel, A. D., Iversen, J. R., Bregman, M. R., & Schulz, I. (2009). Experimental evidence for synchronization to a musical beat in a nonhuman animal. *Current Biology, 19*(10), 827–30.

Peretz, I. (2008). Musical disorders: from behavior to genes. *Current Directions in Psychological Science, 17*(5), 329–33.

Peretz, I., Ayotte, J., Zatorre, R. J., Mehler, J., Ahad, P., Penhune, V. B., *et al.* (2002). Congenital amusia: A disorder of fine-grained pitch discrimination. *Neuron, 33*, 185–91.

Peretz, I., & Zatorre, R. J. (Eds.). (2003). *The Cognitive Neuroscience of Music*. Oxford: Oxford University Press.

Schachner, A., Brady, T. F., Pepperberg, I. M., & Hauser, M. D. (2009). Spontaneous motor entrainment to music in multiple vocal mimicking species. *Current Biology, 19*(10), 831–36.

Scharff, C., & Haesler, S. (2005). An evolutionary perspective on FoxP2: strictly for the birds? *Current Opinion in Neurobiology, 15*, 694–703.

Strogatz, S. (2003). *Sync: The emerging science of spontaneous order*. New York: Hyperion.

Strogatz, S. H. (1994). *Nonlinear Dynamics and Chaos*. Cambridge, MA: Perseus.

Sudnow, D. (1993). *Ways of the Hand: the organization of improvised conduct*. Cambridge, MA: MIT Press.

Turk, I. (Ed.). (1997). *Mousterian Bone Flute & Other Finds from Divje Babe I Cave Site in Slovenia*. Ljubljana: Institut za Arhaeologijo (Znanstvenoraziskovalni Center Sazu).

Section 3

Learning and processing

Chapter 15

Introduction

The third section of the volume focuses on how we acquire and process language and music, a question that has been addressed extensively over the past 15 years (see, e.g. Aslin, Saffran, & Newport, 1999; McMullen & Saffran, 2004; Tillmann & Bigand, 2002; and the contributions in Hallam, Cross, & Thaut, 2009, and Rohrmeier & Rebuschat, forthcoming). In their target article, Jamshed Bharucha, Meagan Curtis, and Kaivon Paroo frame musical communication as alignment of brain states. They argue that music and language differ in the sense that language serves primarily as a code to communicate meaning (in terms of propositions and propositional attitudes) whereas music communicates structure, affect, and motion and affords synchronization across individuals. The authors then present a formal model of alignment based on the representation of brain state vectors and discuss a connectionist approach to modelling tonal vectors in music, based on Bharucha's (1987a, 1987b) MUSACT model. Bharucha, Curtis, and Paroo show that the model predicts some experimental findings about Western music cognition with respect to harmonic priming, tonal short-term memory, or cross-cultural communicative misalignment with respect to North Indian modal music.

In their commentary to the target article, Zoltán Dienes, Gustav Kuhn, Xiuyan Guo, and Catherine Jones review a range of experimental studies on the implicit learning of complex musical structures and movement patterns. They show that participants can learn specific complex musical structures, such as symmetries or inversions, without becoming aware of the knowledge they have acquired. Cognitive modelling of behavioural data demonstrates that simple recurrent networks or buffer models predict human behavioural characteristics in ways that exceed the modelling approach followed by Bharucha, Curtis, and Paroo. In his commentary, Geraint Wiggins provides a detailed account of the theoretical underpinnings of computational modelling of cognitive processes. Wiggins is critical of the modelling approach followed by the target authors, especially with respect to its hand-crafted representation, musical presumptions, and its generality. He suggests that unsupervised, domain-general learning models are more informative and offer greater explanatory potential for cognitive modelling of music processing. Finally, the commentary by John Williams provides a nuanced reflection of the concept of alignment in music and language. Williams discusses the framework proposed by Pickering and Garrod (2004), in which alignment between communicating agents in dialogue is based on priming on syntactic and semantic levels, and suggests that repetition priming approaches would constitute appropriate, analogous methodologies to investigate alignment and representation in musical interaction. The learning and processing section concludes with Bharucha, Curtis, and Paroo's response to the commentaries.

References

Aslin, R. N., Saffran, J. R., & Newport, E. L. (1999). Statistical learning in linguistic and nonlinguistic domains. In B. MacWhinney (Ed.), *Emergence of Language* (pp. 359–80). Hillsdale, NJ: Lawrence Erlbaum Associates.

Bharucha, J.J. (1987a). MUSACT: A connectionist model of musical harmony. In *Proceedings of Ninth Annual Conference of the Cognitive Science Society* (pp. 508–17). Hillsdale, NJ: Lawrence Erlbaum.

Bharucha, J.J. (1987b). Music cognition and perceptual facilitation: A connectionist framework. *Music Perception*, *5*, 1–30.

Hallam, S., Cross, I., & Thaut, M. (Eds.) (2009). *Oxford Handbook of Music Psychology*. Oxford: Oxford University Press.

Jackendoff, R. (1991). Musical parsing and musical affect. *Music Perception*, *9*, 199–230.

McMullen, E., & Saffran, J. R. (2004). Music and language: A developmental comparison. *Music Perception*, *21*(3), 289–311.

Pickering, M. J., &Garrod, S. (2004). Toward a mechanistic psychology of dialogue. *Behavioral and Brain Sciences*, *26*, 169–226.

Rohrmeier, M. & Rebuschat, P. (Eds.) (forthcoming). Music cognition. *Topics in Cognitive Science* [Special issue].

Tillmann, B., & Bigand, E. (2002). A comparative review of priming effects in language and music. In P. McKevitt, S. O. Nuallain, & C. Mulvihill (Eds.), *Language, vision & music – Cognitive Science of Natural Language Processing*, CSNLP-8 (pp. 231–40). Amsterdam, PA: John Benjamins.

Chapter 16

Musical communication as alignment of brain states

Jamshed Bharucha, Meagan Curtis, and Kaivon Paroo

In this paper we sketch a framework for thinking about music as a communicative channel between brains. We argue that music serves to align peoples' brain states, but not necessarily for the purpose of communicating discernable meaning or emotion. Rather, the alignment of brain states enables a range of communicative objectives, including synchronization across individuals.

Both music and language are forms of communication. As such, both seek to align the brain states of others. Each has a range of communicative capacities, and these capacities overlap across the two domains. However, they diverge in critical ways that make each unique.

Among the capacities shared by music and language is the ability to communicate affect, of which emotion is a subset. Indeed, evoking emotion is typically cited as the objective of musical communication. However, eliciting affect is merely one of several communicative capacities of music. Music also communicates structure and a sense of motion (see Bharucha, Curtis, & Paroo, 2006).

What would be the purpose of communicating musical structure? The fundamental perspective offered in this paper is that music serves to align our brain states. The alignment can occur in any of several domains, including structure, affect, and motion. The underlying function of all these aspects of musical communication is not to communicate anything per se—be it structure, affect, or motion—but rather to align our brain states and thereby foster social cohesion. Thus alignment, and its derivative social gluing function, is the communicative goal. Sharing a structural representation can promote group identity, in much the same way as sharing an emotion or moving together in synchrony can.

By the same token, the affective experience communicated by music isn't just about getting across an emotion. Emotions evolved to serve certain functions (Cosmides & Tooby, 2000). However, music's capacity to communicate emotion is not restricted to these functions. The mere synchronization of emotion serves a social cohesive function that is independent of the emotions themselves.

Music can evoke feelings that are more nuanced than the standard emotions (see Raffman, 1993). What we feel as we listen to music can be so subtle as to not fall into clear emotional categories. And yet, by aligning their affective states, people can be united with a sense of group identity.

Not surprisingly, the spectra of affective experience communicated by language and music are not identical. Music can communicate affective experiences that are ineffable, i.e. difficult if not impossible to put into words. Thus while the affective spectra communicated by language and music overlap, each has bands that are unique. The musical spectrum is denser because it isn't bound by the constraint of verbalizability. For example, a musical gesture may evoke an affective experience that is too nuanced to describe easily.

In contrast to music, the most unique aspect of linguistic communication is the ability to communicate propositions. In propositional communication, syntax and phonology serve only as codes from which the receiver can retrieve propositional meaning; there is little communicative utility in just representing the grammatical structure other than as a means to retrieve meaning.

Of course, language can be used for purposes other than to get the receiver to understand propositional meaning. These non-propositional communicative functions may overlap with those of music, in that mere alignment—and the social integration it engenders—may be a goal. In such cases, music and language may have similar communicative objectives.

Alignment can be modelled formally if brain states are represented as vectors. We grant that there may be aspects of these states that may not lend themselves to vector representations. However, as we have shown in our earlier research, important aspects of musical structure do lend themselves to vector representations. If the functional aspects of a brain state can be characterized by the activation of a set of critical features, then an ordered set of activations of those features constitutes a vector. Brain states are aligned to the extent that these vectors are aligned.

Our prior work has focused on tonal structure. As such, in this paper we illustrate the potential for the alignment approach by drawing upon our work on the representation of tonal structure. For example, keys can be represented as vectors in chromatic space or chord space and modes as vectors in functional chromatic space. The correlation between vectors in a given space is a measure of their alignment.

Alignment enables individuals to be synchronized, thereby fostering a sense of group agency. We propose that synchronization can occur at several levels of abstraction. Literal synchronization across individuals would mean that they hear and attend to exactly the same pattern of sound, feeling exactly the same affect, or moving in exactly the same way.

In some instances, synchronization is possible even if it isn't literal. For example, different people attending to different melodic lines can produce synchronization as long as they are in the same key; here, a vector of activations across key units is aligned, even though the precise pitch-time sequences may differ. In the domain of rhythm, individuals can be synchronized by the underlying metre even though they are hearing or producing different temporal sequences or moving in different ways. Synchronization here is brought about by abstract representations such as keys, modes, or metres, which serve as vectors that provide coupling of states across brains.

Sometimes, we hear a piece of music and we seem to resonate to it affectively. We argue that this situation occurs when the affective brain state before listening is aligned with the state evoked by the music. In other words, the music seems to match the affective state one is already in.

We suggest that as the critical features that characterize domains of music other than tonality emerge from research, brain states in those domains can also be represented as vectors. Once we have a more cogent theory of the cognitive representation of motion, a particular movement pattern could perhaps be represented as a pattern of activation across a set of functional features. Likewise, as we have a better understanding of the critical features of emotional states, such that each state can be characterized as an ordered set of functional features, a formal structure that represents these features could enable measures of alignment.

The central thesis of this paper is that music serves to align brain states, be they structural, affective, or related to movement. The remainder of this article has three parts. First, we elaborate on the conceptual framework for understanding musical communication, as summarized above. Second, we propose a formalism of alignment in terms of vectors in features spaces. And third, we elaborate on one component of the framework—tonal vectors—the area in which we have done the most work.

Conceptual framework

Brain states

We use the term 'brain state' to stand for the neural instantiation of the experience induced by music at any given time. For our purposes, the term 'mental state' would be interchangeable, given that mental states are instantiated by brain states. Some philosophers (e.g. Fodor, 1975) have argued that 'mental state' is the more appropriate category for cognitive science, on the view that there may be a one-to-many mapping between mental states and underlying physical instantiations (e.g. brain tissue, electronic circuits, etc.). On this view, physical instantiations and the mental states they instantiate are *token identical* as opposed to *type identical*, i.e. some physical instantiation is necessary in order to have a mental state, but it needn't be neural; a computer could have functionally equivalent states. We don't take a position on this issue in this paper. Given that we are addressing human perception, we will use the term 'brain state'.

Brain states may be conscious or unconscious. The vast majority of cognitive processes are not accessible to consciousness. Conscious states thus represent just the tip of the processing iceberg. Conscious states are those in which attention is directed at selected subsets of active representations. In language, we are conscious primarily of meaning. If the prosody conforms to one's linguist subculture, we tend not to notice features of the sound. In fluent communication, meaning pops out, and we tend not to attend to the communicative code per se. When hearing an unfamiliar language, or a familiar language spoken in an unfamiliar way (with an 'accent'), the unfamiliar sound features pop into consciousness. In routine comprehension of speech, however, sound in language is processed automatically, unconsciously, and serves primarily as a code designed to communicate meaning, not to communicate the sound itself. Indeed, meaning in language can be communicated through other media.

In contrast, sound is intrinsic to music. Yet, although sound is the medium of communication for music, it isn't necessarily the object of communication.

We have argued (Bharucha, et al., 2006) that the brain states that music typically serves to align are of at least three types: those that represent musical structure over time, those that evoke affect, and those that trigger bodily motion. As a form of communication, language also serves to align brain states. Language has at least some capacity to communicate all three types of brain states that music can. For example, we use music-theoretic language to communicate aspects of musical structure; language has a rich capacity to evoke affect; and language surely can trigger bodily motion (e.g. the command 'Run!').

Propositional versus non-propositional states

Language has one specialized communicative function that music does not have, namely, the ability to communicate propositions. A proposition is either true or false, and assertions of truth and falsehood require propositional structure. Language is the only code we know that is able to communicate propositions. In its simplest form, communicating a proposition involves a speaker (or writer) aligning a listener's (or reader's) brain to represent a target proposition, P. Using language we can also communicate *propositional attitudes* (see Fodor, 1975) which include wishes, hopes, desires, feelings, promises whose objects are proposition, e.g. 'I wish that P', 'He promises that P', 'They hate the fact that P'.

In contrast, music communicates neither propositions nor propositional attitudes, but nevertheless is a form of communication. Music serves to elicit at least three broad categories of states: the experience of structure, affect, and motion. Music (and potentially other forms of non-verbal communication, such as communication using facial or other bodily gestures in a non-propositional context) can communicate a spectrum of brain states that may be difficult if not impossible to communicate using language.

The syntactic structure of language requires formal operations that require a symbolic representations system (Fodor & Pylyshyn, 1988; Pinker & Prince, 1988). Attempts to use vector representations in connectionist models have failed for language for this reason (Pinker & Prince, 1988). In contrast, there is no known reason why brain states and the operations they entail in the perception of music cannot be modelled in this way.

Propositional representations are not specific to a sense modality. Hence the brain-states that represent them are not auditory. Although sound (as used in speech) is the principal communicative vehicle for language, the pervasiveness of written and manual signed languages (as well as the use of touch in Braille) make clear that propositional communication is abstract. That is not to say that uniquely musical experiences are necessarily auditory in nature. Sound in music is merely a vehicle or code for the communication of certain conscious experiences or their underlying brain states. The brain states may instantiate experiences that are auditory (e.g. the characteristic timbre of an oboe), but they may also instantiate affect or motion (which are not intrinsically auditory). And some of the affective and motion states evoked by music may not be evocable by language.

Grammatical structure in language (whether syntactic, phonological, or morphological) is a formal code. It provides a code for communicating semantic content but is not itself the object of communication. In contrast, semantic structure is the object of communication, but cannot support a communicative code. In other words, for propositional communication to occur, syntax, phonology, and morphology exist only as communicative codes that serve to communicate meaning. They permit a structured transmission of information from one brain to another, which when parsed, activates meaning (which cannot be communicated directly).

The sound patterns of languages differ significantly. The mapping from sound onto meaning in language is thus arbitrary. Not surprisingly then, in language we remember the meaning of the underlying proposition better than the actual sentence used to convey the proposition (Jarvella, 1971). Memory for sentences is enhanced by the use of poetic structure: metre, rhythm, and rhyme (Rubin, 1995). Indeed, Rubin argues that before the use of writing, oral traditions employed poetic devices in order to preserve the precise language of epics and thus minimize the drift and distortion of meaning over time. Metre and rhythm constitute an important commonality between language and music (Lerdahl & Jackendoff, 1983). In both music and language, they serve as dimensions along which a code can be structured, yet yield different categories of brain states—different categories of communicative content—when employed in the two domains.

In language, arbitrarily different sound patterns (i.e. the same proposition uttered in different languages) can code for the same proposition. In contrast to language, the sound patterns of music do not map arbitrarily onto communicative content. Lerdahl and Jackendoff (1983) claim that the mapping of the musical sound surface onto more abstract levels of representation takes the form of a reduction. The time-span reduction gives the surface representation a structure that enables it to be perceived not just as a horizontal sequence of sounds, but rather as a sequence of sounds that can be heard and remembered at several levels of abstraction. Unlike language, there is little sense in which arbitrarily different sound patterns from different cultures can have the same communicative content in music. However, in both music and language, the same sound patterns can have different communicative content in different cultures by virtue of the cultural learning that influences the mapping from sound onto communicative content.

It might seem, then, that although no sensory modality is necessary for propositional communication in language, sound is essential to musical communication. However, we would not argue that sound is the essential communicative content of music. As with language, sound is only a communicative vehicle (albeit perhaps the only one) that supports systematic manipulation and provides the medium for a communicative code. The difference is that the medium of the code is entirely arbitrary for propositional language (although language can indeed utilize sound in modality-specific ways, albeit not for the communication of propositions); in contrast, the medium isn't entirely arbitrary for music.

A possible exception could be Mozart's famous comment about grasping a piece of music in its entirety by looking at the score, without having to play the entire piece in his mind (Anderson, 1985). The implications of this observation are much debated, but there is no reason to deny absolutely the ability of musical communication to remain intact without sound or auditory imagery for highly trained individuals.

Patterns of activation in the brain support the notion that, even for aspects of musical structure (such as harmony) that would seem to be intrinsic to sound are not represented as sound. For example, relationships between the 12 major and 12 minor keys seem to be represented in prefrontal cortex, not in auditory cortex (Janata et al., 2002). It is entirely plausible that musical relationships can be communicated by visual notation if the perceiver has the highly automated, learned capacity to map directly from visual representations onto the communicative content of music.

Although tonal relationships might seem to be more abstract than auditory, it is more difficult to make that case for timbre, which seems at first blush intrinsic to sound. The conscious experience of sound is certainly part of the repertoire of communicative content for music, even though it may not be a necessary condition.

Affect and ineffable experience

The average listener would nominate emotion as the principal object of musical communication. We would broaden that to include a range of conscious experiences that we more generally call *affect.* Under the rubric of 'affect' we would include the standard array of emotions, as well as conscious experiences of expectation, fulfilment, and violation (Meyer, 1956), and feelings of tension and relaxation (Lerdahl, 2001). We would also include what is commonly referred to as musical gesture. These include all experiences that can be reported as felt—what Raffman (1993) calls *feeling states.* There's nothing about our framework that requires that all these diverse conscious experiences be lumped into a category such as 'affect'; we do so only to contrast these experiences with two other broad categories of conscious musical experience: the experience of musical structure and the experience of motion.

Some musical experiences seem to be ineffable, in the sense that we cannot capture them in words. The issue of ineffability and the related issue of *qualia* are controversial in philosophy (see, for example, Raffman, 1993). Our framework doesn't rest on any particular position about ineffability or qualia. However, we would argue that the spectrum of musical experiences (and hence brain states evocable by music) is not identical with the spectrum of experiences evocable by language. There are regions of the musical spectrum that overlap with experiences evoked by other modes of communication, including the use of facial expressions and non-linguistic, non-musical gestures. While there certainly is overlap, there are regions of the musical spectrum that are evoked by music uniquely.

Communication as alignment

Music is a form of communication in which the composer or performer seeks to align the brain states of listeners. The listeners would typically include the performers themselves. Alignment can take two forms. First, the composer or performer may seek to align the listeners' brain state with his or her own. Second, the composer or performer may seek to align the listeners' brain state in a certain way, even though he or she may not be representing those states. (The listener can of course be oneself, as when you play music for yourself.) For example, I may want to elicit a certain brain state in the listener even though I'm not in that state myself.

The evolution of music and its precursors would have occurred while the voice and perhaps limited instruments were the means of communicating sound. The development of musical instruments has since expanded the range of brain states we can communicate. With electronic media, the scope of communicative activity broadens so that even non-musicians can seek to align the brain states of listeners, for example, by giving them a recording to listen to (hence the popularity of sharing digitized music with friends through the Internet).

Failed, ambiguous, or contradictory musical communication and communicative efficacy

Music is fraught with failed communication. For example, when musicians talk about their work, the listener often doesn't hear in it what is intended, and what is said underdetermines what is heard. Failed communication is caused in part by variability in the past experiences of the listeners, which results in the same pattern of sound eliciting different brain states. The more similar the cultural and subcultural backgrounds of the listeners, the greater is the alignment, all other factors being equal. Composers of *new music* have a unique challenge in aligning the experiences of their listeners.

Misalignment may also be caused by an inherent variability in one's brain state immediately prior to listening, even assuming similar cultural backgrounds. This variability in turn may be a result of several sources of variability, including the circumstantial and emotional state of the person at the time, and perhaps genetic variability as well. Misalignment can also occur because of differences in culturally induced neural representations, as we illustrate later.

Another source of misalignment may stem from differential attention across musical features. The relative salience of structure, affect, motion, and other factors vary across individuals and contexts. Some people are disproportionately focused on structure, others on affect, and yet others on motion. There also is variability in attention across structural parameters, such that tonality is most salient to some, rhythm or timbre to others. Finally, even among tonal factors, one may attend more to the horizontal line at one point in time and the vertical structure at another; or one may attend to one voice rather than another. The limited capacity of attention ensures variability in brain states across individuals and across listening episodes.

The flip side of misalignment is contradictory alignment of different vectors in their evocation of affect. For example, musical features may tend to evoke one emotion while the lyrics evoke another.

Communication failure, ambiguity, and contradiction also occur in language. However, propositional language can be checked because propositions are either true or false. If someone has misunderstood a proposition, the communication failure results in two contradictory meanings that can be clarified one way or another. Music is inherently ambiguous, and since musical expressions do not have truth values associated with them, the states evoked in people cannot easily be checked for conformity. Ambiguity of communication lends itself to the development of an art form. The ability to hear things that were not intended (or to fail to hear what was intended) is part of what makes art interesting, but the evolutionary precursors of musical communication (pre-linguistic auditory communication) may have been limited to less ambiguous codes.

The vector approach makes it straightforward to frame the issues of how efficacious communication is. Communicative efficacy can be thought of simply as the correlation between the intended and evoked brain states.

Resonance

When a listener's brain state happens to be close to alignment prior to listening, the listening experience produces a *resonance.* For example, the listener may already be in the target affective and motion states. (Indeed, the affective and motion states are themselves elicited by the structural vector—see Bharucha et al., 2006). In this case, only the structural vector needs to be aligned, and the listener has the feeling that the music captures perfectly what he or she is feeling.

Synchronization

A special case of alignment is synchronization. In a live performance, the performer is not just seeking to align the brain states of members of the audience, but is doing so in synchrony. Furthermore, the members of a performance ensemble are seeking to align the brain states of not just the audience but also of each other.

In addition to the experiences aligned by the music, the synchrony itself can produce powerful experiences, as anyone who has played in a string quartet or a band, or sung in a choir, can attest. Music promotes group cohesion. Brown et al. (2006) has mentioned the role music plays in supporting synchronization at the group level, but the mechanisms have not been clearly articulated.

We suggest that attribution theory in social psychology offers such a mechanism. As humans we have a strong and automatic tendency to attribute causes for what we observe. Such causal attributions are widespread in our perception of both the physical and social worlds. In the physical world, causal attributions take the form of naïve physics (our intuitions for which are often at odds with scientific physics), seeing patterns where none exist (as in illusions of probability), or the attribution of divine powers. Random dots moving on a computer screen lead to causal attributions if two dots happen to move in seemingly correlated ways (one appears to be pulling the other, or both appear to be moved by a common force). In the social domain, attribution theory has been used to account for how we infer—often unfairly—enduring personality traits from brief exposure to other peoples' behaviour. We also make causal attributions to explain our own behaviour and our own feelings. The impulse to attribute causality is hard to suppress. We therefore propose that precise synchronization of movement or affect leads to an attribution (not necessarily conscious) of group agency—of a cause that transcends the individuals and that is a property of the group as a whole. This attribution then can elicit a range of rewarding feelings that people describe as exhilaration, transcendence, synergy, an expansiveness beyond the oneself, and collective consciousness. This mechanism may be called *synchrony-induced group attribution.*

While strict alignment of motion vectors would be expected when a group is moving in tandem (e.g. marching), most ensemble playing requires the members of the ensemble to be moving in different ways and playing different parts. Components of their structural vectors (e.g. the features coding for metre and key) may be aligned, but the composite structural vectors will not be aligned, because members of the ensemble are playing different parts. Thus synchrony requires a more complex account of alignment.

There are two conditions for synchrony. First, there must be good alignment between the intended and actual vector for each member of the group, even though the intended vectors vary across members of the group. Second, there must be component vectors that are aligned across individuals, to enable them to play together in an orderly way. Typically, these will be component vectors coding for abstract features of timing, such as metre and tempo, and abstract features of tonality, such as key or mode. We call these coupling vectors. Thus, a component vector specifying exact pitch-time events would not be a coupling vector, whereas a component vector at a more abstract level of the tonal or event hierarchy would. Indeed, this may be a fundamental reason why invariant abstract representations are extracted from the surface; the abstract representations may be coupling vectors that allow synchrony in the face of surface variability.

In pop or rock-n-roll music, where the vocal line is highly syncopated, the coupling vector is elicited by the drums, which provide a steady beat. In a string quartet playing rhythmically complex music with no conductor, subtle acoustic and visual cues keep the musicians coupled in time, and careful attention to intonation keeps them coupled in pitch.

A formal framework for communication as alignment

The brain state that instantiates musical experience at any given time can be modelled as a set of vectors to which we attend selectively. In this section we sketch some of the component vectors that are communicated with music. The list is necessarily not exhaustive. While listening to music, multiple vectors are active, representing a variety of musical experiences. Attention may be focused on subsets of these vectors at any given time, thereby highlighting them in consciousness. For example, one might attend to the tone level at one point in time, to the chord level at another.

Earlier we suggested three fundamental types of musical experience: the experience musical structure, the experience of affect, and the experience of motion. Each can be represented as a vector of features. Thus, there are at least three domain-specific vectors, plus perhaps others.

If *s* is the vector representing structure, *a* is the vector of affective activation, *m* is the motion-related vector, and *o* is the vector of other extra-musical parameters, then the omnibus brain-state vector, *b*, is given by:

$$b = \alpha\,[s, a, m, o]$$

where α is a weighting function that specifies the allocation of attention, and other possible weighting factors, across vectors and elements of vectors.

Musical structure typically is defined by three components: tonality, rhythm, and timbre. The structure vector, s, is thus:

$$s = [t, r, x]$$

where *t* is a tonality vector, *r* is a rhythm vector, and *x* is a timbre vector.

The tonality vector, *t*, contains both schematic and veridical components (Bharucha & Todd, 1991). Schematic vectors indicate which musical elements typically follow a musical context, e.g. which tones or chords are most expected following a context in a familiar form of music. Veridical vectors represent the actual next event in a familiar piece of music, and thus constitute a memory for specific pieces (see Bharucha & Todd, 1991, for an account of how these two kinds of expectation are generated in a vector-driven neural net). Much of the time, schematic and veridical expectations (as represented by levels of activation of the corresponding vectors) converge. But expectancy violation is an important aspect of musical aesthetics. So these two forms of expectation sometimes do diverge. The brain has to keep track of what is typically expected but also what is actually expected in a particular piece with which one is familiar but that contains expectancy violations. Thus:

$$t = [\text{schematic, veridical}]$$

The schematic vector itself contains both absolute pitch and pitch-invariant (or relative pitch) representations (see Bharucha & Mencl, 1996). At any given time, our brains track the absolute pitch levels of the tones, chords, keys, and modes currently being played. But we also extract from the absolute code a pitch-invariant representation, in which pitches are heard in relation to a tonal centre or reference tone (Bharucha & Mencl, 1996). Thus:

$$\text{schematic} = [\text{pitch absolute, pitch invariant}].$$

Pitch-absolute vectors include component vectors for pitch, both spectral and virtual (Bharucha, under review). They also include component vectors representing pitch class, chord, and key (e.g. Bharucha, 1987a, 1987b; Tillmann, Bharucha, & Bigand, 2000):

$$\text{Pitch absolute} = [\text{spectral pitch, virtual pitch, pitch class, chord, key}].$$

Pitch-invariant vectors include tonal functions and modes:

$$\text{Pitch invariant} = [\text{tone function, mode}].$$

Veridical vectors in turn include features relating to surface structure, time-span reduction *a la* Lerdahl and Jackendoff (1983), in which vectors can represent different levels of abstraction of the surface, and anchoring relationships (Bharucha, 1996) that indicate how unstable tones want to resolve:

$$\text{veridical} = [\text{surface, anchoring, timespan}].$$

Communicative efficacy, the match between the target or intended brain state and the evoked one, κ, can be stated as:

$$\kappa = \mathbf{r}\,(b_t, b_e).$$

b_t is the target brain state, b_e is the brain state elicited or evoked by the music, and r is a correlation coefficient. Affective resonance, ρ_a, the match between the affective state before and after listening, can be stated as:

$$\rho_a = \mathbf{r}\ (a_0, a_e)$$

where a_0 is the state before listening occurs, a_e is the state elicited or evoked by the music, and r is the correlation coefficient.

Synchrony may occur at many levels. First-order synchrony is literal synchrony. In first-order synchrony, the coupling vectors are surface representations. In second-order synchrony, coupling occurs along one dimension, e.g. there may be different melodic lines or voices, but they are synchronized in time by a common rhythm vector. In third-order synchrony, the coupling vectors are abstract.

In our earlier work, we have modelled aspects of the processing of harmony by showing how vector representations of tonal patterns can map onto more abstract representations of chords and keys (see Bharucha, 1987, 1991, 1998; Bharucha & Todd, 1991; Tillmann, et al., 2000). Here we seek to extend the vector representation framework for the study of musical communication across individuals. Our central argument is that musical communication involves the attempted alignment of brain states across people. Brain states can be represented as vectors defined over activation patterns.

Future research will be required to define the precise nature of these vectors. Our earlier work has focused on tonal vectors. Considerable work has been done on specifying the elements of rhythm. The components of timbre have received some attention, suggesting how this may be specified. Recently, the determinants of emotion in music have received considerable attention (e.g. Juslin, 2001; Peretz, Gagnon, & Bouchard, 1998), potentially enabling the definition of an emotion vector. But as we have discussed above, the nameable emotions constitute only one band of the spectrum of musical affect. The affect vector would include measures of tension/relaxation, in order to capture important recent work (Lerdahl, 2001). It would include measures of expectation fulfilment and violation resulting from the processing of structure using structural vectors. It would include a potentially vast and dense spectrum of felt states that we experience from musical gestures, patterns, and timbres, many of which are ineffable. Finally, it would include extra-musical determinants of affect while listening to music; these could include factors such as characteristics of the performer or the cultural or performance context.

In computational neural terms, the objective of musical communication is to cause the listener to represent the omnibus brain-state vector as closely as possible. This could be because the composer or performer is representing this vector and seeks to 'share' the experience with the listener, or in the more indirect case because the composer or performer simply wants the listener to have the experiences associated with that brain state.

Tonal vectors

Whereas the above approach may not be suited to language, because of the unique structure of syntax, we would argue it is suited to many aspects of music. The approach to musical communication sketched above is supported in the domain of tonality by a range of psychological experiments, as reported by Tillmann et al. (2000).

The representation of schematic knowledge and expectation in vector terms was first described in a model called MUSACT (Bharucha, 1987a, 1987b). In this model, units tuned to pitch classes are linked to units tuned to chords, which are linked to units tuned to keys. In the early version of the model the connections were hand-wired. But a functionally equivalent connectivity is learned by neural self-organization (Bharucha, 1991a, 1987b, 1992, 1998; Tillmann, et al., 2000). The assumptions built into the model are parsimonious, and do not include any specific knowledge of harmony, unlike rule-based or symbolic models of harmony, which specify explicitly the relationships they yield. The assumptions of the self-organizing model include: 1) the existence of pitch-tuned units at the input level, 2) the validity of self-organizing algorithms, which are predicated essentially on Hebbian learning, and 3) the pervasiveness of regular patterns with which tones are combined simultaneously to form chords and keys in the Western environment. The chord units emerge from learning, as do the key units, and are not assumed by the model. The network organizes itself to internalize the hierarchical structure of tones in the Western musical environment, in which tones the clustering of tones as major and minor chords and keys dominates our musical environment.

Following learning, the network represents schematic knowledge of harmonic regularities in the weights of its connections. While hearing music, the model represents the current tonal experience of the listener via the levels of activation of the units. The model in effect consists of three vector representations of schematic expectation (tones, chords, and keys), and operates upon those vectors by multiplying them by the matrices of connection weights. A listener can attend to the various components to varying degrees, but under the surface of conscious awareness there is a robust and multifaceted representation of both long term musical schematic knowledge as well as current perception.

After learning, when the network hears a set of tones (either simultaneously or integrated over a window of time), the corresponding tone units are activated. They in turn activate the chords units, which in turn activate the key units. Activation also spreads top down, implementing the effect of prior schematic knowledge on current perception. When the network settles, it represents the listener's tonal experience as driven by the tones heard as well as the tones, chords and keys implied through the spread of activation.

The network makes predictions that have been tested in a series of psychological experiments. The most critical prediction is as follows. After hearing the three tones C, E, and G, activation spreads up to the chord layer, resulting in the activation of chords that contain at least one of the sounded tones. This reflects only bottom-up processing. At this point, the E major chord unit is more active than the D major chord unit, because the E major chord contains the tone E (which was sounded), whereas the D major chord contains none of the sounded tones. However, after activation has had a chance to reverberate through the network, bottom-up and top-down until the network settles, the relative activations of the E major chord and the D major chord are reversed. Top-down activation pushes the D major chord's activation so that it exceeds that of the

E major chord. At this point, the pattern of activation across the chord units mirrors the circle of fifths: the C major chord unit is of course the most active (because all three of its component tones were sounded), and D major is more active than E major, mirroring their relative distance from C major around the circle of fifths.

This prediction was tested by Tekman and Bharucha (1998) using priming. The prediction was that immediately following a C major chord, people would process an E major chord more quickly than a D major chord, because of the relative activations of these units. However, after the network has had a chance to reverberate, the relative reaction times would be reversed. This is indeed what Tekman and Bharucha (1998) found. When presented roughly 50 milliseconds following the C major chord, the E major chords was processed more quickly than the D major chord. But within 200 milliseconds, the E major chord was processed more slowly than the D major chord. This is an example of a non-obvious prediction that is not made by any other known model in the literature.

The Tekman and Bharucha (1998) result is a critical test that supports the vector activation approach over rule-based models of harmony, which lack the appropriate dynamic properties. The model also replicates nicely the data from a range of other experiments in the literature, in simulations reported by Tillmann et al. (2000). For example, the probe tone results of Krumhansl (1990) are replicated by reading off the activations of the tone units that correspond to the probe: following the context, the activation of the probe tone unit drives the ratings given by subjects. The probe tone serves to direct attention to the corresponding unit; its activation is then reported as the rating judgement. Through top-down activation, tones that were not sounded but belong to highly activated keys become indirectly activated.

The model also accounts for data from short-term memory experiments involving sequences of tones or chords. In a classic experiment, Dowling (1978) presented subjects with a sequence of tones followed by a second sequence that was either identical or had one tone changed. Subjects judged whether the sequences were the same or different. For each tone in the second sequence, the model reads off the activation of that tone as it occurred in (was remembered from) the first sequence. When a diatonic tone is replaced by a non-diatonic tone, the model says 'different' with a higher level of confidence than if a diatonic tone is replaced by another diatonic tone, because all diatonic tones receive top-down activation. Similar results were obtained for sequences of chords (Bharucha & Krumhansl, 1983), and the model accounts for them in an analogous way. Bharucha and Krumhansl (1983) also found an asymmetry in the memory judgements, such that a diatonic chord replaced by a non-diatonic chord was more easily detected than the reverse. The model accounts for this result because a diatonic tone that has not occurred has more activation than a non-diatonic tone that has not occurred.

This model alone represents only a small piece of tonal perception. We have expanded the scope of this effort to a few other tonal vector components described in the previous section. MUSACT uses absolute pitch. Elsewhere we have shown how a pitch-invariant vector can be extracted from an absolute-pitch vector, using key activations to map from one to the other (Bharucha & Mencl, 1996, Bharucha, in preparation). The process is shown in Figure 16.1.

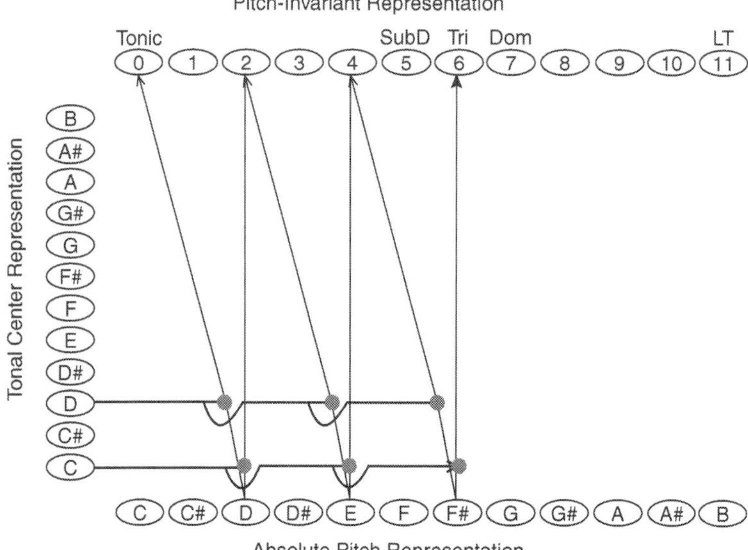

Fig. 16.1 A network that maps tones into a pitch-invariant format that corresponds to a tonic-based harmonic function. The key units (on the left) are from the MUSACT network. They gate the tones (or chords) from the same network (bottom) into the pitch-invariant format (top) via sigma-pi units. An absolute pitch gates into a pitch-invariant pitch slot depending upon how active the corresponding tonic is.

The tone units from MUSACT are projected onto the absolute pitch vector at the bottom of the structure shown in Figure 16.1, and the key units are projected onto the tonal centre vector on the left side. When the key of C major is most active, it gates activation from the C tone into the tonic unit shown at the top. The gating is achieved by sigma-pi units that multiply activation from the two sources. When the tonal centre is C, tone C activates the tonic (labelled '0') and tone D activates the supertonic (labelled '2'). When the tonal centre is D, tone D activates the tonic, and so on. As the key changes, so does the activation pattern across the tonal centre units, resulting in a different mapping of absolute pitches into the pitch-invariant vector.

We have also explored the acquisition of schematic musical knowledge of other cultures. Indian music is based on modes rather than keys. The modes can be learned through self-organization, with pitch-invariant units in the input layer. These simulations enable a demonstration of misalignment of vectors in cross-cultural communication.

Cross-cultural misalignment can occur for any of a number of reasons. Here we illustrate how it can occur because of a divergence in the mapping of the same sound pattern onto abstract representational structures that have been learned. Consider a self-organizing network with 12 input units tuned to the twelve chromatic functions: Do, Re–, Re, Me–, Me, Fa, Fa+, So, La–, La, Ti–, Ti. In Indian music this would be Sa,

Re−, Re, Ga−, Ga, Ma, Ma+, Pa, Dha−, Dha, Ni−, Ni. At the next level are units available to learn modal patterns.

Consider three cultures distinguished by the modes that are prevalent: the major and minor modes in the West today; ten modes (thaat's) from India; and ancient Greek modes. For each culture, a simulation was run. Each simulation consisted of presenting the network repeatedly with each of the modes of that culture until the units at the second level became specialized to respond to those modes. In order to examine how a listener from one culture would hear the music of another, we presented the acculturated networks with an ambiguous subset of the tones from the mode of one culture.

Take, for example, the Indian mode Bhairav, which consists of: Do, Re−, Me, Fa, So, La−, Ti. In one test, we omitted Re− and presented the remainder of Bhairav to each of the three networks. After the mode units were activated, we allowed activation to spread back in a top-down fashion to the tone units, representing the cultural implication of tones that belong to a familiar mode regardless of whether they were heard. If we look at the top-down activations of tone units, we see that for the Indian network, the Re− unit is activated to some degree, because it is expected even though it's missing. For the Western network, Re− is not activated at all, because none of the Western modes employ the flatted second. What's interesting is that the ancient Greek network does show some activation of Re−, because of familiarity with this scale degree from the Phrygian (Do, Re−, Me−, Fa, Pa, La−, Ti−) and Locrian (Do, Re−, Me−, Fa, Fa+, La−, Ti−) modes.

There are other parts of the tone vector that show interesting evidence of top-down implication. The Indian network correctly implies La− rather than La. One might think this unsurprising, because La− was actually presented. However, the Western network shows equal implied activation for La− and La, even though La− was played and La wasn't. That's because the presence of Me causes it to activate the major mode unit, thereby activating La. Similarly, the presence of La− causes it to activate the minor mode unit, thereby activating Me−. Thus Me− and Me are equally activated as well: the network hears the impoverished Bhairav ambiguously as major and minor, but certainly not as Bhairav. If we correlate the implied vectors across the three cultures, we see that Indian music is the most likely to align the structural brain vectors of Indian listeners.

Conclusion

While both music and language are forms of communication that serve to align brain states, the communicative functions can be quite different. The essential function of musical communication is not to impart meaning or a message, but rather to align brain states so as to foster social cohesion. In other words, simply getting the listener to have a certain brain state—even if it doesn't mean anything or evoke a clear emotion—is sufficient to achieve this objective. Affective, motion-related, and even structural alignment can serve this purpose.

Whereas language involves propositional communication that cannot easily be modelled in associationist terms as patterns of activation across vectors of features, important aspects of music can be modelled in this way. Our own work on tonality enables us to extend the framework from processing within a brain to communication across brains. It is our hope that future work in other structural domains, as well as affect and emotion, could build on this perspective.

References

Anderson, E. (1985). *The letters of Mozart and his family.* New York: Norton.

Bharucha, J.J. (1987a). MUSACT: A connectionist model of musical harmony. In *Proceedings of Ninth Annual Conference of the Cognitive Science Society* (pp. 508–17). Hillsdale, NJ: Lawrence Erlbaum.

Bharucha, J.J. (1987). Music cognition and perceptual facilitation: A connectionist framework. *Music Perception, 5,* 1–30.

Bharucha, J.J. (1991a). Pitch, harmony, and neural nets: A psychological perspective. In P. Todd & G. Loy (Eds.), *Music and Connectionism.* Cambridge, MA: MIT Press.

Bharucha, J.J. (1991b). Cognitive and brain mechanisms in perceptual learning. In J. Sundberg, L. Nord & R. Carlson (Eds.), *Music, Language, Speech and Brain.* London: Macmillan.

Bharucha, J.J. (1992). Tonality and learnability. In M.R. Jones & S. Holleran (Eds.), *Cognitive bases of musical communication* (pp. 213–23). Washington, DC: American Psychological Association.

Bharucha, J.J. (1998). Neural nets, temporal composites and tonality. In D. Deutsch (Ed.), *The Psychology of Music* (2nd Ed.) (pp. 413–41). New York: Academic Press. [Reprinted in Levitin, D. L. (Ed.) (2002). *Foundations of Cognitive Psychology.* Cambridge, MA: MIT Press.]

Bharucha, J.J. (under review). Modeling aspects of pitch and harmony.

Bharucha, J.J., & Krumhansl, C.L. (1983). The representation of harmonic structure in music: Hierarchies of stability as a function of context. *Cognition, 13,* 63–102.

Bharucha, J.J. & Mencl, W.E. (1996). Two issues in auditory cognition: Self-organization of categories and pitch-invariant pattern recognition. *Psychological Science, 7,* 142–49.

Bharucha, J.J., & Todd, P. (1991). Modeling the perception of tonal structure with neural nets. *Computer Music Journal, 13,* 44–53. [Reprinted in P. Todd & G. Loy (Eds.), *Music and Connectionism* (pp. 128–37). Cambridge: MIT Press.]

Bharucha, J.J., Curtis, M., & Paroo K. (2006). Varieties of musical experience. *Cognition, 100,* 131–72.

Brown, S., Martinez, M.J., & Parsons, L.M. (2006). The neural basis of human dance. *Cerebral Cortex, 16,* 1157–1167.

Cosmides, L., & Tooby, J. (2000). Evolutionary psychology and the emotion. In M. Lewis & J.M. Haviland-Jones (Eds.), *Handbook of Emotions* (2nd ed.). New York: Guilford.

Dowling, W.J. (1978). Scale and contour: Two components of a theory of memory for melodies. *Psychological Review, 85,* 341–54.

Fodor, J.A. (1975). *The language of thought.* Cambridge, MA: MIT Press.

Fodor, J.A. & Pylyshyn, Z.W. (1988). Connectionism and cognitive architecture: A critical analysis. *Cognition, 28,* 3–72.

Janata, P., Birk, J., Van Horn, J., Leman, M., Tillmann, B., & Bharucha, J.J. (2002). The cortical topography of tonal structures underlying Western music. *Science, 298,* 2167–70.

Jarvella, R.J. (1971). Syntactic processing of connected speech. *Journal of Verbal Learning and Verbal Behavior, 10,* 235–36.

Juslin, P.N. (2001). Communicating emotion in music performance: A review and a theoretical framework. In P. Juslin & J. Sloboda (Eds.), *Music and emotion: Theory and research* (pp. 309–37). New York: Oxford University Press.

Krumhansl, C.L. (1990). *The cognitive foundations of musical pitch.* Oxford: Oxford University Press.

Lerdahl, F. (2001). *Tonal pitch space.* New York: Oxford University Press.

Lerdahl, F. & Jackendoff, R. (1983). *A Generative Theory of Tonal Music.* Cambridge, MA: MIT Press.

Meyer, L. (1956). *Emotion and meaning in music.* Chicago, IL: University of Chicago Press.

Peretz, I., Gagnon, L., & Bouchard, B. (1998). Music and emotion: Perceptual determinants, immediacy, and isolation after brain damage. *Cognition, 68,* 111–41.

Pinker, S. & Prince, A. (1988). On language and connectionism: Analysis of a parallel distributed processing system of language acquisition. *Cognition, 28,* 73–194.

Raffman, D. (1993). *Language, music, and mind.* Cambridge, MA: MIT Press.

Rubin, D. C. (1995). *Memory in oral tradition: The cognitive psychology of epic, ballads, and counting-out rhymes.* New York: Oxford University Press.

Tekman, H.G. & Bharucha, J.J. (1998). Implicit knowledge versus psychoacoustic similarity in priming of chords. *Journal of Experimental Psychology: Human Perception & Performance, 24,* 252–60.

Tillmann, B, Bharucha, J.J. & Bigand, E. (2000). Implicit learning of tonality: A self-organizing approach. *Psychological Review, 107,* 885–913.

Chapter 17

Communicating structure, affect, and movement

Zoltán Dienes, Gustav Kuhn, Xiuyan Guo, and Catherine Jones

In Chapter 16, Bharucha, Curtis, and Paroo propose that music serves to communicate affect, the experience of motion, and an inducement to a particular structural interpretation. We will take the meaning of 'communicate' to be broad and not necessarily implying all the pragmatic constraints that successful communication often entails. For example, we will take a structure to be successfully communicated even if the recipient is not consciously aware of what the structure as such really is. Commonly people appreciate musical structure, and have the experiences intended by the composer, yet are not consciously aware of what the structure is. Indeed, this commentary will focus on the case where a structure put into music by us is detected by listeners without them being able to say what it is exactly they have detected. We show how some musical structures are analogous to certain linguistic structures in virtue of exhibiting mirror symmetries. We argue that people can come to implicitly learn to detect symmetries, musical inversions in particular (Dienes & Kuhn, forthcoming). Such implicit learning leads to greater liking of the structures learnt. Then we will show that just as music may communicate affect, structure, and movement, so can movement communicate structure and affect. Just as melody is a type of movement in tonal space, so can physical movement embody the same symmetry patterns of our melodies. Likewise, we present evidence that people can implicitly learn symmetries in movement. Finally we will discuss computational models of acquiring sensitivity to these structures in music and movement. First we will start with a brief introduction to implicit learning.

Implicit learning

The term 'implicit learning' was coined by Reber in 1967 to refer to the process by which we acquire unconscious knowledge of the structure of our environment. A key example that inspired Reber was natural language: Young children acquire knowledge of their native syntax in a way that does not allow them to verbalize what has been learned, even though they may have learned it very well indeed. Reber sought to investigate such learning in the lab using artificial grammars with adults. Whether or not there is a general purpose implicit learning process that applies in the same way to any structured domain, as Reber thought, he nonetheless could observe implicit learning—the acquisition of unconscious knowledge—using artificial grammars in the lab. He used an artificial finite state grammar to specify allowable strings of letters, such that the letter strings were structured but on casual inspection did not appear to be so. People were asked to memorize such strings of grammatical letters without being told there was a grammar. After a few minutes of exposure to the training strings, people were then informed that there was a complex set of rules determining the order of letters within strings. People were asked to classify new strings as being either grammatical or not. Reber found people could classify above chance (e.g. 65%) even though they had poor ability to verbalize relevant rules and often reported they were sorry to have messed up the experiment. On the face of it, people had acquired unconscious knowledge of the finite state grammar. Reber's work was ignored for a couple of decades but then triggered an extensive literature, debating what exactly it is that people learn in the artificial grammar learning paradigm (e.g. Pothos, 2007) and whether or not it is unconscious (e.g. Shanks, 2005). In terms of the latter issue, simply asking people to describe the rules, as Reber had originally done, may be an insensitive measure of conscious knowledge. Research subsequent to Reber's original papers has used more sensitive measures. The evidence for unconscious knowledge depends on which theoretical framework is used for defining consciousness (see Seth, Dienes, Cleeremans, Overgaard, & Pessoa, 2008, for discussion). If knowledge is conscious when one is conscious of having the knowledge, then there is good evidence that people do indeed acquire unconscious knowledge in Reber's artificial grammar learning paradigm (Dienes, 2008; cf. Shanks, 2005).

In terms of what is learned, Reber's original claim was that people had learned abstract knowledge of the finite state grammar. This was a good first guess because people could generalize from the training strings to novel strings generated by the grammar. Brooks (1978) made the first and most radical challenge to Reber's claim. Brooks pointed out that people could simply memorize whole training strings and classify a test string on the basis of its similarity to one or more training strings: no abstract knowledge need be induced in training at all. In general, according to this approach, conceptual knowledge could be based on storing all encountered exemplars of a concept, with no further attempt at abstraction. Computational versions of such exemplar models (also called 'case-based reasoning' in other contexts) have been tested in artificial grammar learning (e.g. Dienes, 1992; Jamieson and Mewhort, 2009) and can fit a range of findings, though not all (e.g. Pothos & Bailley, 2000). It is unlikely people implicitly learn about musical structure through memorizing whole musical pieces, but rather, if exemplar learning is involved, of fragments. Fragments of what size? In artificial grammar learning, people appear to implicitly learn fragments of two, three, and sometimes four letters (e.g. Servan-Schreiber & Anderson, 1990; Perruchet & Pacteau, 1990), and Wiggins (see commentary, Chapter 18, this volume) has modelled the learning of musical structure with similar sized fragments of musical notes.

As people can implicitly learn more than fragments, as we will discuss later, another approach to modelling the implicit learning of structure is to use connectionist networks, which can flexibly learn a range of structures. Connectionist networks can learn allowable fragments yet also produce representations which lie somewhere on a continuum of abstractness from exemplar models to rules of a grammar per se (Cleeremans, 1993; Dienes, 1992). Cleereman's used a simple recurrent network (SRN) and showed that it learned not only the conditional probabilities of successors to sequences of increasing length (i.e. fragment information) but also organized its internal representations in a way similar to the structure of a finite state grammar. The SRN was also adapted to learning the constraints in musical compositions by Mozer (1994). We will consider a specific abstract structure, mirror symmetry in music, and its learnability by the SRN below.

Bharucha et al. used a connectionist network to model musical knowledge consisting of nodes coding notes connected to nodes coding chords connected to nodes coding keys. One version of the model self-organized into the required hierarchical structure. Self-organizing maps have yet to be systematically explored in implicit learning generally, and this is a promising line of research. However, as we will see, Bharcha's model will need augmenting to deal with the symmetry structures we will consider in this paper.

Music communicates affect and structure

Zizak and Reber (2004) proposed that implicit learning of the structure of a domain can lead to greater preference for items having that structure: a structural mere exposure effect. They reviewed and presented new evidence that implicit learning of visual sequences obeying a finite-state grammar could lead to enhanced liking of novel sequences obeying the same grammar. That is, the communication of structure is the means by which affect is itself communicated. In the finite-state grammars used by Zizak and Reber, most of the structure in the grammar is accounted for by the ability of sequence elements to predict their immediate successors, i.e. by commonly occurring chunks of two or three sequence elements. Such chunking is an important part of learning music as well as language, but it does not account for all the structure that people can learn in either. The grammars above finite-state in the Chomskian hierarchy allow recursion and hence different types of symmetries. Figure 17.1 shows such two types of symmetry.

Consider a sequence of four elements, which we will arbitrarily call 'k l m n'. The letters of the alphabet are used simply to indicate the temporal order of the element (k comes before l etc.), but the identities of the elements are free to vary. Each element could, for example, be a tone, and the sequence a melody. We will label the notes of a particular melody: k1 l1 m1 n1. On the right hand side of Figure 17.1, this melody is indicated schematically. In the top it is reflected through a horizontal mirror. This creates a musical inversion. The diagram on the left indicates the mapping relation between notes (or intervals): the first note in the melody predicts the first note in the inversion; the second note in the melody predicts the second in the inversion and so on. The case of an inversion is illustrated in Figure 17.2 as well, showing that the mapping of intervals involves going to their opposite: if the melody initially descends three steps, the inversion initially ascends three steps and so on. Now consider the symmetry in the bottom part of Figure 17.1. Now the melody is reflected in a vertical mirror and a retrograde results. The mapping relation is shown on the left.

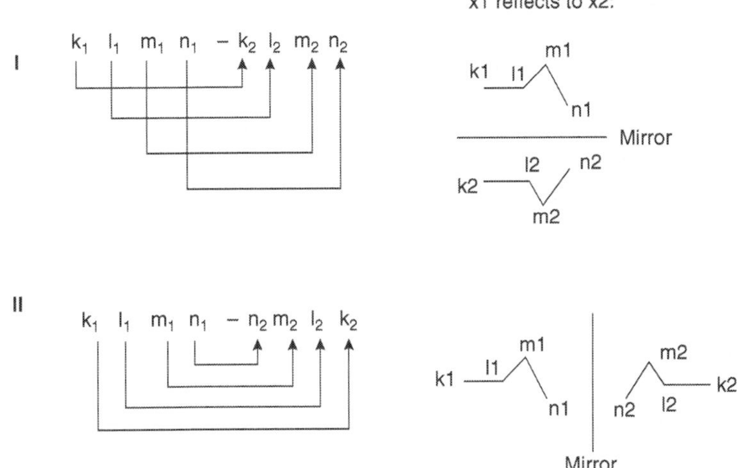

Fig. 17.1 Two types of symmetry.

The first mapping relation in Figure 17.1 corresponds to inversions and transposes, and also to certain linguistic structures. The 'respectively' construction has the same structure, for example: 'Tenzin, Trinley, and Tumpo wore yellow, black, and red hats, respectively', in which the first name goes with the first colour, the second with the second, and so on. The same structure is seen in cross serial dependencies in Dutch and Swiss German. Such dependencies require a grammar more powerful than context free. The second mapping relation in Figure 17.1 corresponds to musical retrogrades, and also to nesting structures in language like centre embedding: 'The bamboo the panda ate was fresh'. The first noun goes with the last verb and the last noun with the first verb. Such dependencies can be produced by context free grammars.

Most models of implicit learning were designed to account for the way people can implicitly learn chunks (for a review see e.g. Pothos, 2007); but no amount of chunk learning can make one sensitive to symmetries per se. A different sort of computational model is needed for detecting symmetries than forming chunks. Yet symmetries in an abstract way are part of language and a part of music, and also of movement: Most movements we can do, we can also do backwards to get back to where we started;

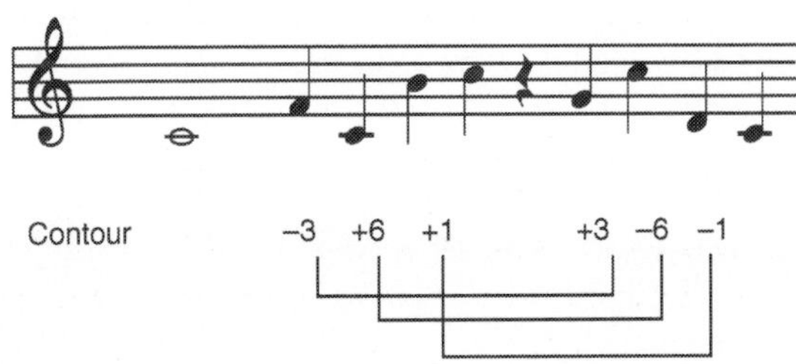

Fig. 17.2 A musical inversion.

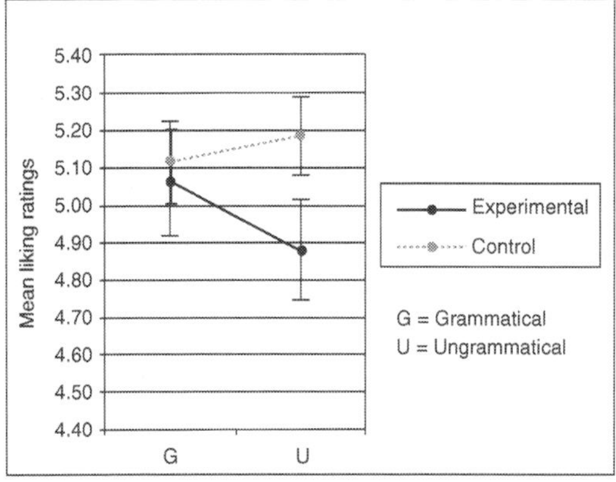

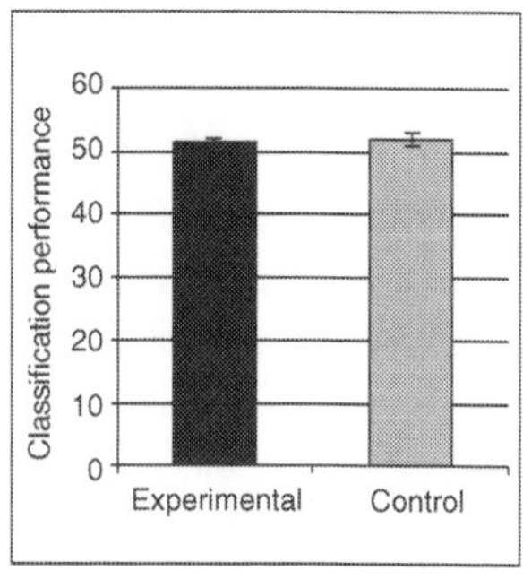

Fig. 17.3 Learning inversions. Reproduced from Kuhn, G, & Dienes, Z. (2005). Implicit learning of non-local musical rules, *Journal of Experimental Psychology: Learning, Memory & Cognition*, 31, pp. 1417–32.

and movements we do with the left hand we can do mirror reflected with the right, while appreciating they are in some sense the same. It would make evolutionary sense for perceptual systems to learn to detect symmetries, if only because detecting symmetries allows shorter length encodings of stimuli and hence easier storage. Are mirror symmetries indeed the sort of structures that we can implicitly learn and that can thus influence our affect?

Kuhn and Dienes (2005) asked participants to listen to 120 tunes, each tune consisting of eight notes. The last four notes were always an inversion of the first four, though participants were not informed of this relation, nor indeed that there were any structural invariants in the melodies: participants just tried to detect for each melody whether it had occurred before, a cover task which served simply to keep them concentrating on each tune as a whole. Then subjects either rated how much they liked a set of new strings or classified them. The new test strings were composed of novel pairings of tunes and of intervals, so the chunks of which they were constructed had never occurred in the training phase. Half the new tunes had the same inversion structure as the training tunes, and half did not. For the classification task subjects were told that the strings they had been listening to were generated by a rule and they were about to hear some new strings, half of which followed the rule. They were asked to classify half of the tunes as following the rule and half as not. We also ran a control group that had no training but just completed the test phase. As shown in Figure 17.3, while the control subjects preferred the non-inversions to the inversions, the trained subjects preferred inversions. Exposure to inversions led to a relative liking of inversions. Knowledge that the rule in question was inversion appears to be unconscious: trained subjects could not classify the strings as rule following or not at above chance levels. Melody communicated structure and affect (see also Dienes & Kuhn, submitted).

Dienes and Longuet-Higgins (2004) used more complex sequences that followed the constraints of serialist music, i.e. each sequence was a 'tone-row' (i.e. 12 notes long and each note A to G occurred once and only once). People were asked to assess whether the 'reply' (second half of the tone row) went with the 'theme' (first half). The

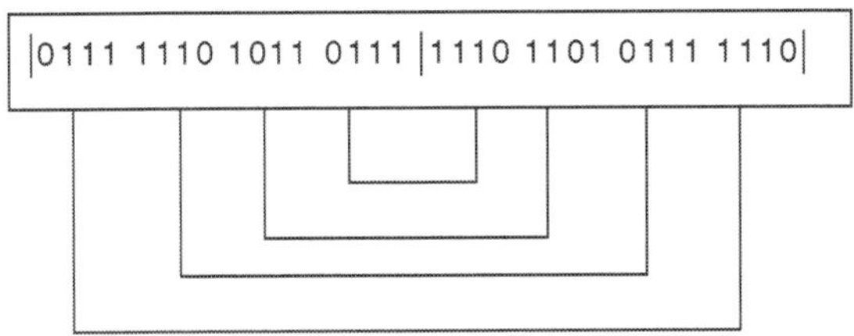

Fig. 17.4 An example of a rhythmic retrograde.

tone rows could instantiate serialist transposes, inverses, retrogrades, or inverse retrogrades. Highly experienced aficionados of serialist music could discriminate each of these from tone rows not exhibiting such symmetries—even when they believed they were literally guessing.

As Bharucha et al. indicate, melody is not the only aspect of music that can communicate structure. We have been investigating implicit learning of the rhythm of drum beats. In a training phase subjects listened to rhythms that instantiated a retrograde structure: The last half of each sequence was rhythmically the first half played backwards. Figure 17.4 shows an example: a '1' stands for a hit and a '0' for a rest. In a subsequent test phase using sequences constructed of novel chunks, when people said they were using intuition or just guessing, they reliably picked new retrogrades as being like the old ones: Figure 17.5 shows 95% confidence intervals for people's ability to discriminate the retrogrades from the non-retrogrades (d'). When trained subjects thought they were guessing or using intuition, they discriminated retrogrades from non-retrogrades (whereas untrained subjects did not).

Often the musical communication of structure involves feelings (for example, liking, intuition) that indicate the presence of structure that has been consciously discerned as existing, though not what that structure is (compare Norman, Price, & Duff, 2006). And sometimes people are not even aware they have discerned structure at all: this is

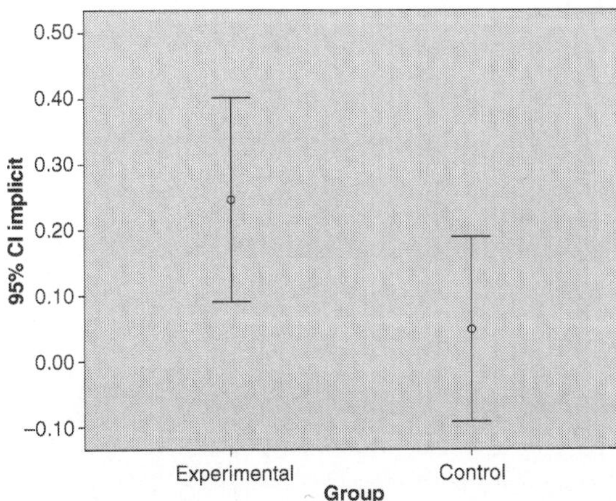

Fig. 17.5 Ability to discriminate rhythmic retrogrades from non-retrogrades when people thought they were guessing or just using intuition.

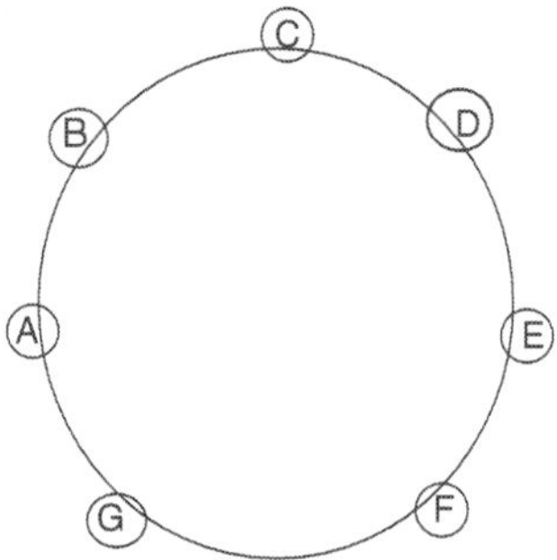

Fig. 17.6 Clock face structure of C major.

implicit learning, which underlies but does not yet fully constitute successful communication. Nonetheless, we had, as Bharucha et al. put it, induced an alignment of our subjects' brain states coding structure with those states we had intended.

Movement communicates affect and structure

Music and movement are similar. Melodies are movement in a pitch space (and also movement in a richer tonal space, e.g. Longuet-Higgins, 1976). Figure 17.6 shows the modulo representation of the tones of C major. A person physically moving around the clock face would produce movements structurally isomorphic with corresponding melodies. Like movement in tonal space, physical movements have natural opposites: moving two steps anti-clockwise is the opposite to moving two steps clockwise. A series of the opposites of a sequence of movements constitutes its inverse. We are currently exploring the implicit learning of symmetries in movement. We had people walk around a circle on the ground, walking out inverses (unbeknownst to them), under the cover story of practising moving meditation. This procedure is fairly time-consuming, so despite some initial encouraging results, we streamlined it by asking subjects to trace their fingers around a circle, as shown in Figure 17.7. Figure 17.7 shows two separate screen displays as seen by subjects. The subject first sees the left display and places their finger on the highlighted character. When the next display comes up (the one on the right), the subject moves their finger in the direction of the arrow to reach the next highlighted character. And so on until a sequence has been

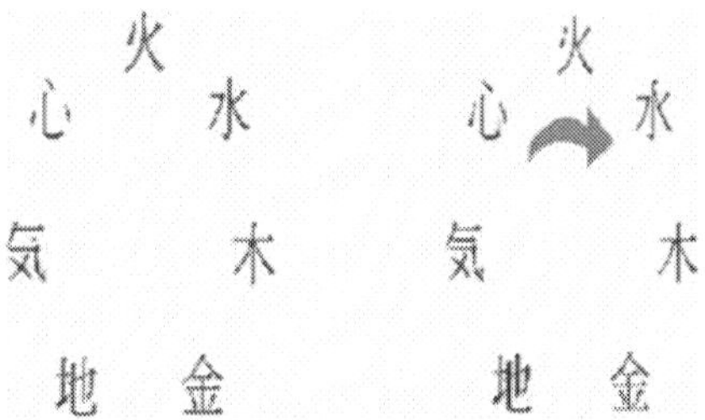

Fig. 17.7 Two successive screen displays seen by people tracing out inversions.

traced out. None of our subjects knew Chinese characters; thus, the material was difficult to verbalize. We used a subset of the very same materials used in Kuhn and Dienes (2005). The melodies in the latter were all contained within the interval from middle C to the C above. To make the structure slightly harder to discern and the mapping onto music non-obvious, for our initial finger movement study, these two Cs were represented by different characters. To encourage processing the movements as a theme followed by a reply, after each half sequence had been traced, subjects tried to re-trace it unaided in one flow, then after the second half judged for the sequence as a whole whether it had occurred before. In the test phase, subjects classified the new sequences as rule following or not and then indicated the basis of their decision: guessing, intuition, rules or recollection (Dienes & Scott, 2005). As can be seen in Figure 17.8, when people thought they were guessing or using intuition, they picked out the inverses over the non-inverses, suggesting they had implicitly learned to detect inverses. Movement can communicate structure and hence feelings of intuitive rightness.

The methodology of our music and movement studies allows a novel test of the claim that 'music communicates movement'. Does listening to musical inverses induce a person to classify or like movement inverses over non-inverses? (Compare Altmann, Dienes & Goode, 1995, who used finite state grammars and obtained transfer between music and visual symbols.) To what extent is this true for other symmetries? Conversely, does following movement inverses prime one to like musical inverses? These remain questions for future research. They are related to the role of 'embodiment' in understanding language (e.g. Zwaan & Taylor, 2006). According to theories of embodied cognition, one understands the concept of an action or object by activating the motor patterns that are involved in engaging with that action or object. Is there in addition an embodied component to understanding syntax? We have shown that people can learn movement patterns instantiating grammars of complexity greater than context-free (namely, inverses and also retrograde inverses). Does understanding the inversion structure of music entail in any way activation of movement inversions? Is understanding centre embedding in language facilitated by performing movement retrogrades—or hearing musical retrogrades—or conversely harmed by performing movement inverses? These also remain for the time being unanswered questions.

Computational models of learning symmetries in music and movement

Learning inversions and retrogrades go beyond the computational models considered by Bharucha et al. The latter's models were designed to learn the co-occurrence relationships that occur in tonal music. However, inversions can occur in atonal music (as, for example, investigated by Dienes & Longuet-Higgins, 2004) and do not depend on any particular co-occurrence of tones or intervals. Similarly, learning inverses go beyond chunking models in the implicit learning field, because our test melodies were made of chunks not heard in the training phase (see Cleeremans & Dienes, 2008, for a review of computational models of implicit learning). What sort of model could learn the inversions we used? An inversion (or a retrograde) is a type of long distance dependency.

So any model that just learned to predict one tone (or interval) from the preceding one would fail. The model needs some kind of buffer or memory store. A computational model that has a long history of use in implicit learning is Elman's simple recurrent network, or SRN, illustrated in Figure 17.9 (see Cleeremans, 1993), which has an elegant memory store. This model learns structure in sequences not by having a memory of past events of any particular length but by (fallibly) learning how far into the past it should remember. At time one, the input units code the first note played and attempt to predict the second note at the output units by flowing activation through the hidden layer. Errors in prediction are used to adjust weights by back propagation. At the next time step, the hidden unit activations are copied to the context units. The input units code the second note and attempt to predict the third. But now the third is predicted by not just the input layer but also the activation across the context units, which carry information about the first note from the previous time step. So predictions about the third note can in principle be sensitive to the identity of both the first and second notes. Because the hidden layer receives input from the context and input units it now contains information about both the first and second notes. At the next time step this pattern of activation on the hidden layer is copied to the context units. The input units code the third note. Both the context units and input units together try to predict the fourth note. So the fourth note can in principle be predicted based on the first, second and third notes. And so on. Of course, whether the network really develops hidden unit representations carrying useful information from a long way back in time is in practice for any given case an open question. In principle it can do it if the small appropriate changes in the weights results in error reduction for each time step.

Cleeremans (1993) showed that initially when exposed to a sequence structured by a finite state grammar, the SRN learns first order dependencies—what elements predict what other immediate successors. It then learns to use the preceding two elements to predict the next—and the preceding three elements and so on. That is, the SRN learns chunks of progressively higher order. But there is no reason to think the SRN is just a chunk learner. If the buffer can keep track of number of tones it may eventually be able to learn the ith tone predicts the (i+ 4)th tone, regardless of the intervening material. Kuhn and Dienes (2008) trained the SRN on the materials of Kuhn and Dienes (2005) to see if it could indeed learn the long-distance dependencies that the inversion entailed.

We also used another model applied to implicit sequence learning by Cleeremans (1993), the fixed buffer model, illustrated in Figure 17.7. This model stores what has happened for a fixed amount of time into the past, here for precisely four notes into the past. This would correspond to say a fixed length working memory slave system (Baddeley, 1986). This model can learn associations between any tone in the preceding four trials and the current tone; in fact the model predicts any of these associations would be just as easy to learn as any other.

Kuhn and Dienes (2005) did not only present subjects with a test set consisting of novel chunks (the 'abstract' set) as we have discussed above; we also presented subjects with a test set where the tunes that happened to be inverses could be distinguished from the non-inverses by the frequency with which the chunks had occurred in training. Thus we can see whether subjects or models are more sensitive to the inversion or to chunk statistics.

We trained the models on the same material as people for the same number of exposures and tested them on the same test sets. Figure 17.10 shows the ability of each

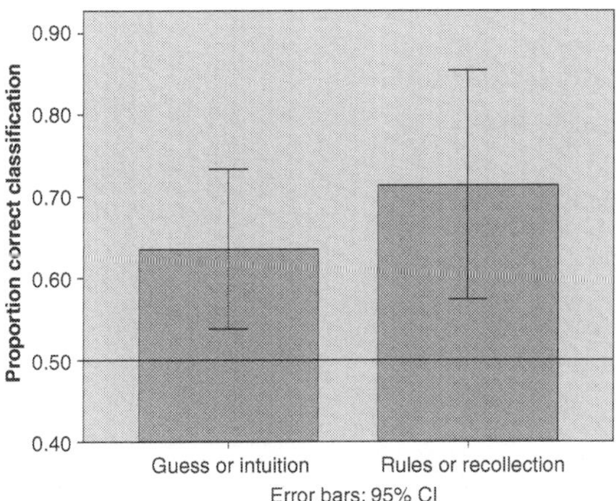

Fig. 17.8 Ability to discriminate movement inverses from non-inverses when people thought they were guessing or just using intuition. Bars are 95% confidence intervals.

model to discriminate inverses from non-inverses where each point corresponds to a certain combination of parameter values. There were a number of parameters free to vary as is typical for any computational model: the learning rate, the number of hidden units, and so on. Because different combinations of free parameter values can dramatically affect the results the model produces, how do we know when a model is a good explanation? If a model could predict all possible outcomes by adjusting free parameters it would hardly be an explanation of any outcome. To determine the explanatory power of each model we explored a full range of parameter space to determine to what extent model predictions concentrated in the region of human performance. We regard this as a superior methodology for evaluating models than simply fitting data.

The y-axis in Figure 17.10 shows performance on the test set where discrimination could be achieved by knowledge of chunks and the x-axis shows performance on the abstract set where all chunks were novel. The small squares are specific combinations of free parameter values for fixed buffer models and the crosses are for SRN models. It can be seen that the SRN models were very sensitive to chunks; the crosses rise steeply

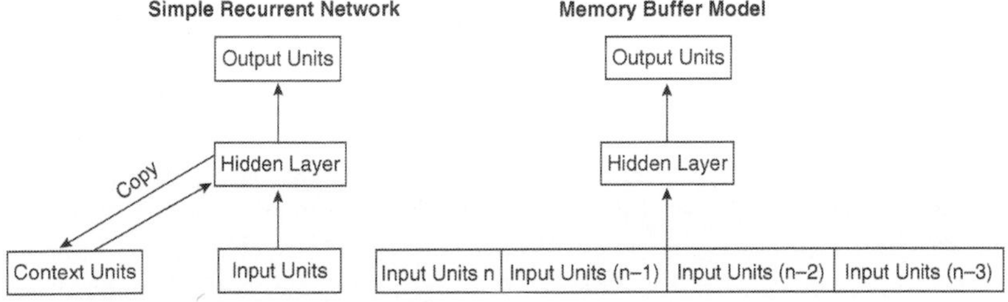

Fig. 17.9 The two computational models used by Kuhn and Dienes (2008). Reprinted from Cognition, 106(1), Gustav Kuhn and Zoltán Dienes, Learning non-local dependencies, pp. 184–206. Copyright (2008). With permission from Elsevier.

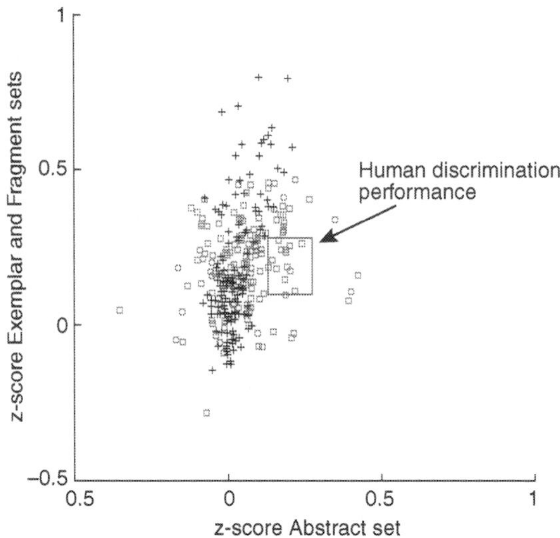

Fig. 17.10 Discrimination performance of models and people. The y-axis represents ability to discriminate inverses from non-inverses when chunk frequency can aid that discrimination. The x-axis represents discrimination performance when all chunks in the test phase were novel. Small squares represent fixed buffer models; crosses SRN models. The large square is the mean for people plus or minus one standard error.

in the figure. Conversely, the fixed buffer models are not sensitive to chunks in particular: As long as there are associations, they don't have to be between adjacent elements to be learned. The large square is the mean for human data plus or minus a standard error. Notice that while the SRN *can* learn the abstract set and the chunk sets as well as people for particular combinations of free parameters, what the SRN typically does is learn chunks. In consequence, while 12 out of 150 fixed buffer models are contained in the large square, zero out of 150 SRN models are. More fixed buffer models are concentrated around human data than SRN models are ($p < 0.0005$); characteristically, the buffer model behaves more like people than the SRN model does.

The models learned particular long distance associations. But this is different from learning inverses as such. To know that a C predicts an F four tones later is not to detect a mirror symmetry as such. We do not yet know what people have implicitly learned either—a set of specific associations or the 'operation over variables' (Marcus, 2001) that whatever interval was in ith position in the theme must be (−1) times that interval in the ith position in the inverse. The latter knowledge allows generalizations to C predicting tones other than specifically F where appropriate, and to spotting inverses of arbitrary length. Our models are models of learning the specific task we set subjects but not yet models of learning the full symmetry our materials instantiated. We look forward to future work determining what it is that people actually learn and what models can explain that ability. Finally, our models fail completely to be models of musical interpretation in general. What we need is a model that explains the tonal nature of our musical appreciation, as addressed by the model of Bharucha et al., as well as our ability to detect and appreciate symmetry in music, as we have taken first step to addressing with the models reported here.

References

Altmann, G., Dienes, Z., & Goode, A. (1995). On the modality independence of implicitly learned grammatical knowledge. *Journal of Experimental Psychology: Learning, Memory, & Cognition, 21*, 899–912.

Baddeley, A.D. (1986). *Working Memory*. Oxford: Clarendon Press.

Brooks, L. R. (1978). Non-analytic concept formation and memory for instances. In E. Rosch & B. Lloyd (Eds.), *Cognition and concepts*. Hillsdale, NJ: Erlbaum.

Cleeremans, A. (1993). *Connectionist models of sequence learning*. Cambridge, MA: MIT Press.

Cleeremans, A., & Dienes, Z. (2008). Computational models of implicit learning. In R. Sun (Ed.), *Cambridge Handbook of Computational Psychology*. Cambridge: Cambridge University Press

Dienes, Z. (1992). Connectionist and memory array models of artificial grammar learning. *Cognitive Science, 16*, 41–79.

Dienes, Z. (2008) Subjective measures of unconscious knowledge. *Progress in Brain Research, 168*, 49–64.

Dienes, Z., & Kuhn, G. (submitted). Implicitly learning to detect symmetries: Reply to Desmet et al. http://www.lifesci.sussex.ac.uk/home/Zoltan_Dienes/Dienes & Kuhn 2008.doc

Dienes, Z. & Longuet-Higgins, H. C. (2004). Can musical transformations be implicitly learned? *Cognitive Science, 28*, 531–58.

Dienes, Z., & Scott, R. (2005). Measuring unconscious knowledge: Distinguishing structural knowledge and judgment knowledge. *Psychological Research, 69*, 338–51.

Jamieson, R. K. & Mewhort, D. J. K. (2009). Applying an exemplar model to the artificial-grammar task: Inferring grammaticality from similarity. *Quarterly Journal of Experimental Psychology, 62*, 550–75.

Kuhn, G., & Dienes, Z. (2005). Implicit learning of non-local musical rules. *Journal of Experimental Psychology: Learning, Memory, & Cognition, 31*, 1417–32.

Kuhn, G., & Dienes, Z. (2008). Learning non-local dependencies. *Cognition, 106*, 184–206.

Longuet-Higgins, H. C. (1976). The perception of melodies. *Nature, 263*, 646–53.

Norman, E., Price, M.C., & Duff, S.C. (2006) Fringe consciousness in sequence learning: The influence of individual differences. *Consciousness and Cognition, 15*, 723–60.

Marcus, G. (2001). *The algebraic mind*. Cambridge, MA: MIT Press.

Mozer, M. C. (1994). Neural network music composition by prediction: Exploring the benefits of psychoacoustic constraints and multi-scale processing. *Connection Science, 6*, 247–80.

Perruchet, P., & Pacteau, C. (1990). Synthetic grammar learning: Implicit rule abstraction or explicit fragmentary knowledge? *Journal of Experimental Psychology: General, 119*(3), 264–75.

Pothos, E. M. (2007). Theories of artificial grammar learning. *Psychological Bulletin, 133*(2), 227–44.

Pothos, E. M. & Bailey, T. M. (2000). The importance of similarity in artificial grammar learning. *Journal of Experimental Psychology: Learning, Memory, and Cognition, 26*, 847–62.

Reber, A.S. (1967). Implicit learning of artificial grammars. *Journal of Verbal Learning and Verbal Behavior, 6*, 317–27.

Servan Schreiber, E., & Anderson, J. R. (1990). Learning artificial grammars with competitive chunking. *Journal of Experimental Psychology: Learning, Memory, and Cognition, 16*(4), 592–608.

Seth, A., Dienes, Z., Cleeremans, A., Overgaard, M., & Pessoa, L. (2008). Measuring consciousness: relating behavioural and neurophysiological approaches. *Trends in Cognitive Sciences, 12*, 314–21.

Shanks, D. R. (2005). Implicit learning. In K. Lamberts & R. Goldstone (Eds.), *Handbook of cognition* (pp. 202–20). London: Sage.

Zizak, D. M. & Reber, A. S. (2004). The structural mere exposure effect: The dual role of familiarity. *Consciousness and Cognition, 13*, 336–62.

Zwaan, R.A., & Taylor, L.J. (2006). Seeing, acting, understanding: motor resonance in language comprehension. *Journal of Experimental Psychology: General, 135*, 1–11.

Chapter 18

Computer models of (music) cognition

Geraint A. Wiggins

Introduction

This chapter presents some abstract thinking about computational modelling of cognition (or, more precisely, cognitive function). It is partly placed in a tradition of scientific philosophy, including the work of Popper (1934), Lakatos (1978), Marr (1982), Pylyshyn (1984) and McClamrock (1991a, 1991b), but is intended primarily to present a practical context for cognitive science research using computational modelling, rather than to carry the philosophy per se further.

The idea of cognitive modelling, qua description of cognitive process, has been current for longer than computers, and perhaps that has meant that the 'natural progression' from pen-and-paper models to computational ones has been taken for granted, as an obvious route. It is a good idea, in research, to step back and take stock of *what* one is actually doing—and *why*—once in a while, and that is the aim here, in the context of computational cognitive modelling. Many of the points made will be obvious to many readers, possibly so obvious that those readers would not consider making them explicit. But questioning what seems obvious is one of the functions of science, and therefore doing so in the context of what is, perhaps, taken for granted in methodology is occasionally worthwhile.

The argument is grounded in reference to the models reported and cited by Bharucha, Curtis, and Paroo (Chapter 16, this volume) and the work current in the Intelligent Sound and Music Systems group at Goldsmiths, University of London, using information dynamics to model music cognition (Pearce, Conkilin, & Wiggins, 2004; Pearce and Wiggins, 2004, 2006; Potter, Wiggins, & Pearce, 2007; Pearce, Müllensiefen, & Wiggins, 2008; Wiggins, Pearce, and Müllensiefen, 2009), taking these two as in some sense paradigmatic. It is appropriate to state in advance that any comparisons arising are not intended to be confrontational, but are meant as sources of important debate about how cognitive science may usefully progress through computational modelling.

Why model?

Motivations for cognitive modelling without computers seem quite easy to identify. In order to develop a science of cognition, researchers needed a method of describing their theories. A good way of beginning to do this is to write down rules of cause and effect, and/or maps of the relationships between functions, in some more or less formal, but in any case *well-defined*, language (which may, of course, be a graphical language). Having begun to do so, researchers can then engage in discussion about which (combination) of the languages in the literature is the best to use, and so terminology and notation is defined by consensus.

With the arrival of computers powerful enough to run programs which model cognition to anything like a realistic extent, and large enough to store the enormous quantities of data that biological nervous systems process without, literally, even noticing it, the motivations become more complicated, because models which are *operationalized*, in the sense that they are embodied as working computational processes, have the capacity to tell us not only about the thing or process being modelled, but also about the thing or process doing the modelling, and about the nature of the modelling process. It is methodologically important, therefore, to consider exactly where each piece of research is located in this multidimensional spectrum of potential discovery.

In artificial intelligence (AI), in particular, there is a very broad spectrum of activity ranging between what might be called 'pure engineering' and, in contrast, 'pure cognitive science', with different combinations and motivations along the way. At the engineering end, one motivation is to solve problems that are (sometimes provably) too difficult for more traditional analytical methods, but which can evidently be solved by humans: the hope is that solutions inspired by human cognition will therefore be successful. Another engineering motivation is to make computers more human-like, so as to render them easier to understand for people. At the cognitive end, the aim is purely to understand the workings of the mind and/or brain by means of successive approximation to functional replication, a distinctly Lakatosian framework (Lakatos, 1978). Somewhere in between is research that aims to understand the hard problems themselves, and the methods for solving them in human-like ways, at a level of abstraction probably quite remote from the reality of brains, but which nevertheless captures aspects of human reasoning: a paradigmatic example of this is the work of Bundy, Basin, Hutter, and Ireland (2005) in mathematical reasoning.

In cognitive science in general, there is a very good reason to move from non-computational models to computational ones: in the computational context, it is usually easier to test a theory to destruction, and this is a good way of providing supporting evidence that it may be correct, or testing hypotheses that might falsify it (Popper, 1934). There are several ways in which this is true. First, for a theory to be implemented as a program, it must be specified to an extreme level of detail and precision: the theorist is forced to make explicit, in advance, any implicit, tacit assumptions or decisions which he or she might previously have made in working with a pen-and-paper model. Secondly, once a theory has been specified to this level of mathematical detail and precision, and implemented, it may be thoroughly and objectively tested across the whole range of its possible input data, which was not previously possible because, firstly, it would take too long on paper, secondly, because people readily make errors in repetitive tasks, and, thirdly, because people are prone to interpret results as they go along, and be affected by that interpretation; computers alleviate all these problems. In these ways, operational versions of theories, which are implemented on a computer, enforce a particular and desirable kind of rigour on theorists. A clear, if negative, example of this effect is found in the various attempts in the literature to implement the Generative Theory of Tonal Music (Lerdahl and Jackendoff, 1983), nearly all of which have foundered (or maybe floundered) at the level of time-span reduction, because of the under-specification of the rules (e.g. Hamanaka, Hirata, & Tojo, 2005): a human (or what AI authors sometimes refer to as an 'oracle': a source of information extrinsic to the model) is needed to make certain crucial decisions. (In defence of Lerdahl and Jackendoff, their *magnum opus* makes no claims to being implementable, and forms probably the most important descriptive model—in terms elaborated below—in the history of the cognitive sciences of music, to date.)

There are other concomitant advantages of computational modelling, also relating to the scientific method. One is that the program is a detailed, unambiguous statement of the theory, which can be shared and studied without the need for subjective interpretation; likewise, computerized numerical data, given a common framework for representation, is constant, and can be shared very easily. Another is that, given a fault-free computer, a program that does not include an explicit source of randomness will reliably reproduce results; where there is such indeterminacy, it can be clearly located and its effects studied.

Computer models can help in both ethical and hypothetical situations too. We can require a computer program to undergo (simulated) conditions which would not be acceptable for live participants, and thus study the predictions made by theories in these circumstances. We can hypothesize alternatives to our theory, adapt the program in precise and controlled ways, and then run 'what if?' scenarios, enabling us to specify precise conjectures and thence sets of competing hypotheses, which can subsequently be tested empirically. These experiments can, in principle, falsify the theory, but they can also refine it, and, importantly, allow us to identify surprising possibilities which were not evident from a passive pen-and-paper model alone. Thus, a cognitive research programme based on computational methods can be more *progressive* than others, in the sense of Lakatos (1978), because they have more and quicker methods of refinement. Conversely, because it is easier to identify surprising possibilities which would render a theory invalid, a computational theory which is not supported can *degenerate* (in the same sense) more quickly, and then be appropriately abandoned. These modelling methods can also allow the study of empirically ineffable science, such as the processes guiding protohuman evolution, though of course the resulting hypotheses cannot be subject to subsequent empirical verification (Bown and Wiggins, 2009).

A clear advantage is conferred, therefore, by using computational methods for certain kinds of research, where a theory is being proposed to explain a mechanism. Too many researchers to list exhaustively here have built models of various different kinds of musical behaviour in the past (e.g. Ebcioğlu, 1988; Cope, 1991; Papadopoulos and Wiggins, 1999; Cambouropoulos, 2001; Widmer and Tobudic, 2003). However, because of the broad spectrum of motivations and approaches outlined above, there are many questions that can be asked about the activity of computational modelling that cannot be asked about its non-computational ancestor. It is incumbent on researchers in the field, therefore, to ask those questions of themselves and their work. In the case of MUSACT (Bharucha, 1987) and the subsequent work, the 'What are we doing?' question is particularly important, because there are several possible answers. The attempt as described is to model musical harmony perception using various kinds of neural network, ranging from a human-programmed perceptron net to a self-organizing map. The question, here, is not only 'What does modelling musical harmony with a neural network tell us?' but also 'What does it tell us about?'. In the 1987 work, it certainly does not tell us about *music*, because the musical information is explicitly *given* to the model by hand, and, in immediately subsequent versions, as supervised training data. In later versions (Tillmann, Bharucha, & Bigand, 2000), a different architecture is used—the self-organizing map (SOM)—which is capable of implicit, unsupervised learning from data, and where chord groupings are inferred without supervision by 'looking at' large amounts of data in the form of co-occurrent sets of pitches. However, again, the study is not telling us about music, since music theory is the criterion used to test for success. No claim to learn about music is made, either, so the reader must look elsewhere for a message.

More problematically, in terms of the claims being implied, it is difficult to argue that the 1987 work tells us anything more about *cognition* than the hand-programmed, rule-based systems that Bharucha contrasts it with: it is, in fact, a hand-programmed rule-based system itself, with its rules expressed in connections and weights, instead of predicate logic. In the later work, including the SOM-based studies, things are less clear-cut: we might say that these systems are modelling music cognition, at some level of abstraction, in as far as—and no further than—SOMs model cognition. However, this is not a strong claim: Teuvo Kohonen, inventor of the SOM, describes it merely as a visualization tool for high-dimensional data (Kohonen, 1995), and the best that can be said is that SOMs are *inspired* by neural activity. Perceptrons, too, are only a very approximate model of neuron behaviour, also, so there is a strict limit as to what can be inferred about brains from the operation of a perceptron network. As explained below, this need not invalidate using either network type to help understand cognition, but it does mean that careful thought is needed about the true implications of the modelling, before claims are made.

What the MUSACT experiments show most clearly is that tonal harmony, represented at this level of abstraction, can be programmed into or learned by these different networks. In a traditional perceptron net, this is unsurprising, since basic harmony and key identification from note occurrences is essentially a problem of counting and constraining note co-occurrences (trivial examples being that the occurrence of F♯ tells us we are not firmly in the tonic of C major, whereas a sharpened fourth probably does appear in a region of tonic-dominant modulation); the constraint satisfaction approach to musical harmony has been studied in its own right elsewhere (Ovans, 1992; Pachet and Roy, 1998). The hard part is discerning the boundaries between the regions so identified. It would be disappointing indeed if a multi-layer perceptron net, with sufficient nodes and supervised learning, could not reproduce the mapping from triads to chord names, and thence to key, which are familiar from well-behaved tonal music; but data is not given on the boundary detection problem. It is less obvious that a SOM would be capable of the necessary clustering to do the learning required here, but knowing that it can does not advance SOM theory very far—although there are many useful applications for such a computer program, mostly in visualization (e.g. Purwins,

Blanketz, & Obermayer, 2000); and again, the boundary detection issue is not really addressed.

The point at which computer models become clearly cognitively meaningful is when one of them is able to predict something unexpected, which can then be verified empirically (Honing, 2006). A good example of this is the work reported by Tekman and Bharucha (1998) and summarized by Bharucha et al. (Chapter 16, this volume). Here, a counterintuitive prediction of the model (that an initial harmonic expectation of E major is weakly evoked by a C major chord, but then almost immediately overridden by D major) is tested empirically in humans and found to hold; Bharucha explains it in plausible terms of 'bottom-up' effects of the immediate note combination and 'top-down' effects of learned musical 'grammar' based on the cycle of fifths, with the latter applying more slowly than the former. The suggestion, here, then, is that there is actually something mechanistic going on in the network that models brain activity at some level; it is not clear, though, how these top-down effects are learned by the network, and it would be useful to study this point in more detail. Nevertheless, the effect is exciting, because it emerges spontaneously from the dynamic operation of the network. Unfortunately, the conclusion drawn from this is the wrong one: it is not the case that this 'supports the activation approach over rule-based models' (Bharucha et al., Chapter 16, this volume), because, given the data, it would not be difficult to construct a rule-based model that did work in this way, and, further, this study gives no evidence that no already extant rule-based model can make this prediction. The erroneous conclusion obscures the much more important and positive one: that Bharucha's network model serendipitously predicted a human trait accurately, giving weight to its own validity, rather than competing with something not quite comparable. Having said this, in the context of the current paper, the 'activation approach' is significantly ill-defined as a term: it is not clear whether it is intended to mean 'activation of nodes in a neural network in exactly this way'—in which case we need to know *which* of Bharucha's ways is meant—or something more general, in which case it is not clear how the term relates the models to the brains and/or to the cognition. This issue is pursued further below.

The argument above leads back to the 'Why do we model?' question. There is very little to be gained by applying a particular computational technique in a particular context, other than knowledge about that technique in that context. This is the commonest criticism of work in musical applications of AI; whether the criticism holds true depends on the intent of the modelling work: if one is interested in pure engineering, then this is exactly what one needs to know, but the information is not very helpful if one aims to model brains veridically, unless there is a strong (if hypothetical) relationship between the modelling technique and the (aspects of) brains one is interested in. There is even less value in making claims that one technique is better than another at a particular task, when they are quite different and when they exhibit different virtues (e.g. learning techniques vs. user-programmed rules), unless the comparison is squarely based on the particular features of the techniques and the problem to which they are applied (cf. Wiggins, Papdopoulos, Phon-Amnuaisuk, & Tuson, 1999). What is needed, in order for these network models really to contribute to cognitive science, is a careful, detailed description of the level(s) of abstraction at which they operate, so that the claims being made can be subjected to thorough scrutiny, and exhaustive testing, across a very broad range of potential data, including outliers. Until this the case, they will remain disconnected from cognitive reality. These issues, too, are addressed in more depth below.

At this point, it is appropriate to introduce the Information Dynamics of Music (IDyOM) project, which will be used as a contrasting example in the rest of this chapter. IDyOM is a long-term research programme (in the Lakatosian sense), testing the validity of probabilistic and information-theoretic mathematical structures and processes as models of music cognition at a certain specific level of abstraction. Preliminary work focused on Markov models of tonal harmony (Ponsford, Wiggins, & Mellish, 1999) and melodic segmentation (Ferrand, Nelson, & Wiggins, 2002); later work developed a Markov-based probabilistic model of pitch expectation (Pearce and Wiggins, 2006) and, at the time of writing, is extending this into further models of musical structure (Potter et al., 2007, Pearce et al., 2008, Wiggins et al., 2009); and the whole programme is placed in a context of modelling and understanding human creative behaviour (Wiggins et al., 2009). The particular contrast of note here is between the testing of an overarching hypothesis that information theory is a good model of mind/brain activity (at a specific and useful level of abstraction), which motivates the whole of the IDyOM programme, and the application of particular technologies to particular cognitive problems.

What constitutes a model?

Minimal functional requirements

As already explained, one of the virtues of a computational model is the precision with which it must be specified, which forces theorists to make all the precise details of the model explicit. The starting points for a computational model are necessarily a *representation* and an *inference system*. Marr (1982) makes an important distinction between three different ways of looking at this; for the moment, the current discussion is restricted to the abstract level of *description of the problem and solution*, which Marr confusingly calls the 'computational' level—he means the level of specification of the computation, as opposed to the level(s) at which the computation is implemented. The representation is the notation in which data and results will be expressed and processed; the inference system is the encoding of the process being modelled in computational terms. These two components are, of course, intimately interlinked: the latter is what gives meaning to the former in context of the model. They are discussed in detail in the next two sections.

Representation

The choice of representation for a cognitive model is not a trivial matter. First, and obviously, it must be able to express and differentiate between all the possible states of the world which are relevant to the subject of the model, *including results which may be unexpected*. Secondly, it must do so in a way which is not ad hoc, so that a claim can be made that the results and the behaviour of the model in general are not dependent on any particular representation.

Consider the modelling of musical pitch. For many Western-musical purposes, pitch can be treated as a simple integer calculus, as in the MIDI real-time control system, for example (Rothstein, 1992). This calculus needs to allow subtraction (which gives rise to a representation of pitch interval), and the addition of such pitch intervals to pitches to give transposed pitches, and certain other operations (Wiggins, Harris, & Smaill, 1989). Importantly, for many operations, it does not matter whether we use, say, MIDI's 61 or C, or any other symbol combination, to represent that note, so long as the whole story fits together *consistently*. This calculus can represent any pitch system which uses 12 categories of pitch (like the chromatic scale) so long as that system tolerates identity between intervals in the appropriate way: in other words, every member of every interval category (major third, perfect fifth, etc.) generable in the scale must be considered identical to all others, even if, as in just intonation, for example, they are not all exactly the same. In this case, the modal or tonal functions of the intervals are abstracted out in the representation exactly as they are in score notation, and this is exactly why standard score notation works for tunings other than equal-temperament, so long as they use a 12-note scale.

Nevertheless, this representation is inadequate in several different cases. In quarter-tone music, 24 pitch categories are needed, with a correspondingly extended range of intervals. In the music of, for example, Xenakis, portamenti must be explicitly represented, and a portamento is perceptually very different from the scalic glissandi to which a discrete pitch representation is limited. In certain circumstances, amplitude can affect pitch perception, though this does not matter in most musical contexts, and it will not be considered further here. Choosing not to consider this effect, is an example of *abstraction*, which is the key to effective representation design: we *pull out* exactly those aspects of the world in which we are interested, and choose not to represent those which are not relevant for the current purpose. In doing so, it is important to justify information loss, so as to avoid lacking what is needed later, and, in the example above, the justification is made on practical musicological grounds.

The representation used in MUSACT (Bharucha, 1987, Tillmann et al., 2000) is in some senses like the above, but without the calculus that allows us to reason about pitch, and without the explicit notation. Nodes in the networks represent chroma categories, abstracting away octave information, which is assumed to be irrelevant to harmony. So rather than describing the pitch of a note, the network representation encodes in its a priori structure the notion that there are 12 pitch categories. Therefore, the model cannot account for alternative pitch systems, and, since it has no notion of interval, it cannot ever represent the subtle differences between functionally equivalent intervals in different parts of the just intoned Western scale, or the complex intonations of the Indian scales studied in the current chapter. One implication of this is that, for example, sharpened leading notes, a fundamental indication of key centre in performed tonal music, cannot be represented. Since equal-tempered instruments express music perfectly well without such subtle inflections, perhaps this does not matter in a model of *music as written in a score*. However, since the subtleties evidently can be perceived, and evidently do add to harmonic perception, the model, as a *cognitive* model, is necessarily limited in its veridicality, from the start. Methodologically, this may not ultimately matter: the model may merely be one level in a hierarchy of abstractions (an idea which is elaborated below), and therefore may take its place in a sequence of successive approximations to an 'actual' musical world.

It is easy to see how one could enrich the pitch representation of the model, by greatly increasing the number of nodes in the 'note' level of the network, and assigning each one a micro-tone, and it seems that this is what Bharucha intends. However, because the time taken to train the resulting networks increases superlinearly with the size of the network, and because more data is needed to train the network as that data becomes sparser, this solution cannot be glibly presupposed to be feasible in practice.

Perhaps more importantly, the 1987 MUSACT model is not amenable to adaptation by itself, nor by user intervention, without re-engineering or retraining (depending on which version) from the start, with the consequence it is very firmly situated in a pre-defined music-cognitive context, and it is immovable from that context. So it will never be a general model, and general models usually have greater explanatory power than specific ones, by virtue of that generality. One methodological consequence of this is that it is difficult to make small, formally conservative changes to the model, as one progresses in one's research programme, and this makes controlled progression difficult.

The issue here is that the early MUSACT model *presupposes* a fundamental aspect of the micro-world whose behaviour it is required to learn: that there are 12 pitch categories in the musical scales used. This, of course, makes it easier for the networks to learn how that world works.

Compare this with the representational presuppositions made in the IDyOM model (Pearce and Wiggins, 2006). IDyOM presupposes only three things: that there are musical events, which are describable in terms of explicit features; that the events form (possibly overlapping) sequences in time; and that the events are discrete. Note that a representation with discrete *events* does not rule out portamenti, as in the discrete *pitch* example above, because the pitch feature of an event may in principle use a continuous, time-functional representation. IDyOM, therefore, is not restricted to a particular pitch system, nor even to use pitch itself at all, and so, in the future, it may account for the more complicated effects generated by just-intoned performance, or by more complicated pitch systems, or by unpitched percussion. IDyOM is restricted in a different way, which, it is claimed, is more general: it is presented as a model of perception of events (of whatever kind) in time; sequence is the only thing built in to the representation. Within the framework of that representation, features are arbitrary.

It would reasonably be expected that a suitably trained SOM would be able to cluster representations of different tunings of notes together, based on inference from their usage in harmony. However, the large amounts of variation in this data would render it sparse, as mentioned above, and therefore, as above, much more training would probably be needed to achieve results comparable with those of the existing SOM network. This would be an interesting study, again primarily yielding insights about the capabilities of SOMs in this context.

In the current volume, Bharucha et al. (Chapter 16) describe a model inspired by the idea that sets (or 'vectors') of parameters determine the behaviour of a neural network, by controlling the same underspecified 'activation'; they suppose that there is a one-to-one correspondence between mind- and brain-state (Fodor, 1974),[1] and, thence, claim that, at some level, we can give lists of numbers which parameterize a notional neural network to represent a particular brain state, and that the purpose of music is to align the brain states of the listeners to the music with those of its producers.[2] However, the architecture of the supposed network is not given, and this leads back to a point mentioned above: a representation means precisely nothing without an interpretation, and, in computational terms, the only interpretation available here is the neural network, which is mentioned, but unspecified. In the absence of an interpretation mechanism, the 'vectors' of numbers listed here actually convey little meaning, except in that (human readers can see that) they are grouped together by music-cognitive function; and their meaning has to be explained informally. The model has degenerated, therefore, to a notation, or maybe something less, and is not amenable to empirical testing in itself. This seems dangerously close to what Lakatos (1978) calls 'pseudoscience'.

The lack of an inference system in this 'model' is highlighted by a more specific criticism, which relates to the self-organizing nature of the putative networks. There is an assumption implicit in this thought-experimental use of 'vectors' that the network constituting each brain will have a particular, common structure, and therefore the values in the vectors (weights) can be meaningfully transferred between them, or, put another way, that the mappings encoded in the networks can be compared meaningfully by means of mere weight-vector comparison. This *may* be the case, but it cannot be assumed, because there is an infinite number of neural networks that can compute each function, and when training an artificial network for its task, the unbiased approach is to begin with random weights. It is therefore likely that a pair of non-trivial self-organizing artificial networks trained on the same dataset will have different structures, and, furthermore, there is no reason in general why those structures should be topologically isomorphic. The same reasoning applies to local brain structure. It is clear that Bharucha et al. intend the 'alignment' of their vectors to be achieved indirectly, by means of musical stimulus—that is the whole point of the model. However, without well-defined common structure in the networks, it is not possible to specify the property of equality between the vectors in different brains, and so 'alignment' and 'resonance' cannot be reliably described or detected. So, when taken literally, the quasi-formal framework can predict nothing.

In fairness to Bharucha et al., the defence can reasonably be given that this presentation is merely analogical, and therefore it does not need complete elaboration. It is not clear, though, what is to be gained from such an analogy. If the formalism does not

1 McClamrock (1991b) argues against this position, on the grounds that context is all-important, but omits to note that the only context a mind has is that mediated by its nervous system, and that it is therefore a closed system in this respect, unless one appeals to mysticism.

2 To address this Romantically lavish claim would require another chapter in this volume. The current author is a composer whose existence refutes the stated hypothesis: inflicting one's own brain states on others certainly seems to be pushing the boundaries of ethics! The view is, though, much more convincing in the context of cooperative musical activity such as group performance and/or improvisation.

facilitate drawing of conclusions, it will probably serve little purpose, and may even obfuscate. Alternatively, the defence may be given that it is abstract, and not intended to represent exact brain details; however, this too is meaningless without a precise definition of what it *does* represent. Ultimately, then, the notational framework says nothing that words could not say.

Inference

To confer meaning upon a representation, and to allow expression of a process, an inference system is needed. Here, *inference* is used in a general sense of 'making explicit what was implicit': this can include statistical analysis, or the mathematical combination of two continuous values to give a third, for example, as well as the more obvious Boolean or other logical inference. It may also involve background information, such as that learned in Bharucha's networks, or compressed into the memory of the IDyOM model. In these terms, the training process of a neural network is one of inference: a perceptron net infers a function which approximately maps the input data on to the training data; a SOM infers clusters of data from co-occurrence, and represents them spatially in its output map. The subsequent production of an output from unseen (i.e. not training) input data is then inference of the corresponding pair in the network's input–output relation. Equally, the process of entropic optimization that IDyOM uses to choose its preferred model of what it has 'heard' may be viewed as inference (Pearce and Wiggins, 2006).

The important question, from the point of view of cognitive modelling, is the relationship between the inference process and the behaviour being modelled (assuming a representation which reasonably and appropriately represents the world in which the behaviour takes place). Given this, one must be wary of making strong claims about a model merely because it is capable of approximating the data for which it was constructed or on which it was trained. As described above, this point is embodied in the practice of reserving a test set from one's data when training a network; but all even this can do is add validity to the model *of the training data*: necessarily, it says nothing about data that happens not to be included in the training set. When we are modelling a process in the world, there is always new data to be found, and a very good way of proceeding is to run through the model's predictions, exhaustively, and look for unexpected ones, which can then be tested empirically. Only when the model has made predictions—the less obvious the better (Honing, 2006)—and when they have been supported by empirical verification, can we begin to argue that the model is a model of the *cognitive process* as opposed to merely a model of the *data gathered about the cognitive process*. The difference is in the unknowns: the latter model might be very good, as far as it goes, but it might not be a model of the cognitive process at all, *except where this particular data is concerned.*[3] The timing prediction referred to above is

[3] An illustrative, but apocryphal, anecdote from the early days of artificial neural network research involves training a network to detect tanks among trees. Photographs were used for the training, and the network was successful in discriminating the tankful photographs from the ones of empty forest. However, on further analysis, it proved that the two photographs had been taken in different weather conditions, and the network was actually discriminating

a good example of just such a back-verification in Bharucha's models, and the engaging study of activation in networks trained in different scales is another, which is rich in further possibilities for empirical validation. Tillmann et al. (2000) use data extant in the literature to verify a model in a similar way, and, while this is not as empirically strong as testing a previously unknown result predicted by the model, it is an effective technique, so long as the model was not trained on this data; the same approach was used in validating the IDyOM pitch prediction model (Pearce and Wiggins, 2006). A stronger means still of validating a model is to use it to predict different, but related phenomena, or to abstract out the representation and use the inference system for something different; these ideas are elaborated further in the next section. First, however, a framework is presented in which the ideas discussed here can be brought together.

What is a model of, and what, if anything, does it explain?

Levels of description

For computational models of cognition to be useful, a coherent framework is needed to fit them into a Lakatosian programme. It seems a good idea that this framework should be similar in shape to, if not the same shape as, the framework used in cognitive psychology in general: a carefully controlled piecemeal understanding of a very complex system, by means of black box[4] modelling at multiple levels of detail. A match between the computational and the empirical in this way allows the two domains to support each other. This description in the large of the research process leads back to the hierarchies that seem to be unavoidable in methodological discussions.

One possible view of a cognitive science research programme is as the construction of a hierarchy of processes, locally stratified by level of abstraction of representation, each layer below being more detailed than (or, conversely, each layer above being a synthesis of parts from) the current one. At the very top of this hierarchy would be 'cognition'; at the very bottom would be 'brain function'—the latter also being amenable to description of various different levels, right on into the biochemistry. This hierarchy will not be a skyscraper of constant width, but a pyramid, with components which multiply as we move downwards, because a process at a high level of abstraction is often composed of more than one component process at lower levels. While not forgetting the need to study contextual effects (and therefore not naïvely assuming that these components can simply be treated independently), we can say some useful things about the relationship between model components at different levels. If we

the colour of the sky, rather than the presence of military hardware. True or not, the story illustrates two points: learning systems do not necessarily learn what their users expect them to; and a model which does not explain itself—as most non-symbolic models do not—is open to misconstruction.

4 In engineering, *black box testing* involves testing the visible function of a module of a system, without considering what is going on inside. This is very like what cognitive psychologists do, except that engineers have the advantage of a specification of the system they are testing.

have a good idea of the component structure of the system we are modelling, a component at one level will never be a part of more than one component at a higher level: this is not to say that the same *mechanism* can not recur, but that each *expression* of a given mechanism is distinct *in the model*. When we are modelling cognition, this rule keeps our models clean and clear, and it is a constraint *on the expression of the model*, and *not* on the system being modelled (so it can admit, but it does not necessarily entail, a Fodorian modularization of mind). However, when we reach grounding in the biology, the strict hierarchy will break down: it is evident that most physical neural components, viewed at a certain gross level of detail (e.g. hypothalamus, hippocampus), take part in more than one activity at once, and this needs to be modelled, presumably with actual or notional sub-components of these physical structures. This breakdown is not a flaw in the approach, but a feature of the (at least apparent, to date) mapping between identifiable physical brain differentiation and mental function, which is not one-to-one; in the purely abstract part of the models, where *mind* function is the interest, there is no such problem. If the breakdown of hierarchical structure is intolerable to a theorist, he or she may represent models of brain *function* in a hierarchy similar to the cognitive-modelling one, and then identify correspondences one by one between the two distinct model hierarchies as knowledge develops.

This view seems uncontroversial: it is a means to an end, rather than a strong philosophical claim, because it is a framework for modelling; it does not constrain cognition *itself*, but only describes models of it. But a further question needs an answer before that framework can be used, however: how are the different levels connected, in practical terms? Is it enough to imagine a black box as merely composed of some other black boxes, and the movement from one level to another, lower one as a process of opening the relevant box and looking inside?

Wiggins (2007) introduces a distinction between cognitive models which are *descriptive* and those which are *explanatory*. A *descriptive* model is one which describes the relationship between a process' inputs and outputs, without making claims about how that relationship is achieved in the system being modelled. An *explanatory* model is one which claims to describe not only the input/output relationship but also the mechanism by which it is achieved *in the system being modelled at the relevant levels of abstraction*. The distinction is similar to that between Aristotle's *formal* and *efficient* explanations (Aristotle, 1998). The following is a helpful example of the two extremes it encompasses.

Consider modelling the weather. One method would be to take very many measurements of air pressure, wind speed, humidity, and so on, over a long period of time, and then compile a large book of tables to allow a user to look up what precipitation (for example) was associated, historically, with the current conditions. Up to a point, this may work well, especially if lots of data is gathered, and the ancient adage 'Red sky at night, shepherd's delight' is a real example of such a model generalized into a compact form. However, neither the book of tables, nor the folk-wisdom, is able to explain *why* it will rain when humidity is high and temperature drops, and, for this reason, neither is able to predict what will happen when a set of conditions arises which has not been previously encountered. This, then, is a *descriptive* model: it merely describes the outcome of a state of affairs, without any attempt to explain why that state of affairs arises.

Contrast this with the kind of model used in the modern business of weather prediction. Large supercomputers are used to build models using techniques such as finite-element analysis, theory about fluid physics, data from satellites and earth stations, and so on. The programs these vast machines run encode the sum of human knowledge about weather physics, directly, as equations applied to simulations, and are set up in such a way as to give quasi-statistical confidence levels in their predictions. They can be given data about the past week's (or year's) weather, and then be run forward into the future to consider a range of possible scenarios: the chaotic nature of weather and the inaccuracies introduced in the model (which can never be perfect because the information available to the forecasters is never complete) mean that confidence decreases with increasing projection into the future. But the key point here is that this model can, in practice, *explain why* the output data is the way it is. If rain is predicted in a particular place at a particular time, the source of the precipitation can be identified, and, in principle, traced back to whichever ocean the water originally evaporated from. This, then, is an *explanatory* model: it does not just predict the outcome, but encodes an explanation as to its *cause*.

Even so, there are levels at which this model is not explanatory. For example, a weather model based on the gas equations of classical physics, Boyle's law, etc., will not be able to account for the movement of individual molecules in the atmosphere which actually give rise to precipitation. Indeed, these 'laws' are themselves derived by what amounts to statistical generalization from observed data, and so, at *this* level, are descriptive but not explanatory models. And here is the connection between descriptive models and explanatory ones: a correct descriptive model can constrain the outputs of a developing explanatory one, and thus define a frame within which an explanatory model can be developed. So, for example, the behaviour of gas in different conditions of temperature and pressure may be explained at the molecular level, but any model produced must conform to the relevant macro-level descriptive equations, if it is to be valid. It is useful to build descriptive models before trying to build explanatory ones, because doing do allows theorists to focus on different aspects of the problem separately and precisely, thus improving the chances of success. So the distinction made here is as much about what the models are intended for, and what their authors claim, as it is about the relationship between them and what they are supposed to model.

A paradigmatic example of this relationship in psychology is the gestalt laws of perception, which are, as originally formulated, an entirely descriptive model, derived entirely from empirical observation and subsequent generalization. The gestalt laws can be encoded in models (e.g. Cambouropoulos, 2006), and used directly. However, doing so necessarily causes a gap in the explanatory power of the model, because a mechanism (that underlying the gestalt rules) is left unexplained. On the other hand, if another model is capable of explaining the same phenomena, *without* recourse to assumption of the gestalt laws, then it is a candidate for explaining how they arise, and this claim can be empirically tested—the current IDyOM model is one such (Pearce and Wiggins, 2006). Even discounting the presupposition of the gestalt laws, such a model may be more or less descriptive: its rules may work together in a way that actually models cognition at some level, or they may not, or they may fall in between the extremes.

But articulating which of these possibilities is the case is important, because doing do gives a signpost to possible next steps in the research programme.

It is evident from all this that the descriptive/explanatory distinction is a relative one; a model which is explanatory of a described process may serve only as an descriptive model at a different level of abstraction in the modelling hierarchy, and this is how the research programme may progress: by alternation of description and explanation. Of course, sometimes, it may be possible to cut directly to the explanatory chase, omitting the descriptive phase.

Although the description/explanation process is a means of progression for a Lakatosian research programme, it does not follow that successive description and explanation in this way necessarily draws ideas from the Lakatosian protective belt into the hard core, though it may be expected to generate auxiliary hypotheses. However, the more fully elaborated and justified layers we have in our model, the more evidence there is that it is a good model. So this is a framework in which the development of models and the collation of evidence may be managed, and which, in particular, gives a means of contextualizing Lakatosian auxiliary hypotheses. Again, it is important to remember that these ideas apply to *models* and *not* to the things or processes being modelled.

It is now possible to relate the descriptive/explanatory hierarchy to Marr's (1982) levels of description, a very well-known attempt to address the philosophy of machine modelling of perception. Marr, concisely summarized by McClamrock (1991a, §3), describes three levels on which a machine model of an information-processing task must be considered:

> 1. Computational theory: What is the goal of the computation, why is it appropriate, and what is the logic of the strategy by which it can be carried out?
> 2. Representation and algorithm: How can this computational theory be implemented? In particular, what is the representation for the input and output, and what is the algorithm for the transformation?
> 3. Hardware implementation: How can the representation and algorithm be realized physically?
>
> (Marr (1982, p. 25.)

There is a superficial similarity between the relationship between the first pair of these levels and the descriptive/explanatory distinction proposed here. The third of Marr's levels is outside the scope of the modelling framework: from the point of view of cognitive modelling, it is not important how the model is implemented in computer hardware, so long as the implementation is a true representation of the theory. The difference between what is proposed here and Marr's proposal is the relationship with what is being modelled—perhaps surprisingly, the phenomenon being studied is only implicit in Marr's notion of 'goal', in his Computational Theory level, as described above. Here, Marr's levels 1 and 2 are interpreted as standing in the same relationship as do a computer program specification and implementation: the Computational Theory level says what the program must do; the Representation and Algorithm level says how the program will actually do it. Crucially, Marr does not specify how much detail is given in his Computational Theory of how the program will do what it does, and here lies the difference. A Computational Theory may be either descriptive or explanatory: it may specify only an input/output relation, or it may specify exactly the mechanism by which the computation of that relation was to be carried out (or, indeed, it may do something in between). The resulting program (at the Representation and Algorithm level) embodies and operationalizes the Computational Theory, but, if necessary, must add detail if the Computational Theory does not give enough. In this way, the Computational Theory is giving meaning to the Representation and Algorithm by allowing its behaviour to be interpreted in context. However, there is nothing in Marr's specification to determine the relationship between the Computational Theory and the subject of the modelling activity. Therefore, that theory can be either descriptive or explanatory in the current terms, and that will determine how its Representation and Algorithm level counterpart models the process. Because of this, Marr's level 2, the implementation, does not necessarily have to be an explanatory construction, as might be supposed. Even though an algorithm must be given, that algorithm may have no bearing at all on the reality of what is being modelled, so the program may still be a descriptive model, if the level 1 description is not explanatory.

Marr's (1982) three levels of hierarchy are not different levels of description of the same thing, but in fact different *kinds* of thing: specification, software, and hardware; McClamrock (1991a) argues against Marr's levels, and asks for more. It is proposed here that, in fact, both are right, since it is easy to imagine a hierarchy of many levels, each of which is of one of Marr's types, describing different levels of detail in different ways—one could even say that the hierarchies under discussion are actually orthogonal. The descriptive/explanatory distinction presented here relates to the progress of a research programme through the model hierarchy, and is therefore more similar to McClamrock's multi-level view than to Marr's, though it is the same as neither.

What species is my model?

Necessarily, therefore, if one wishes to develop a progressive programme using this kind of structure, a key element is the progress from descriptive to explanatory, because that is the primary route by which understanding of the model and what is being modelled is reached. So, for example, if our theories are based entirely on the gestalt principles, and make no attempt to explain them, then at this level (but not necessarily at other levels) they are descriptive. Any model which makes the same assumptions can be used as a descriptive constraint on explanatory models of not just their own specific phenomena but also of the general gestalt rules themselves, as applied in context.

A good heuristic for identifying descriptive cognitive models (or, equivalently, models of phenomena whose operational aspects are still to be explained) can be expressed in terms of the nature of their data and operations, as follows. If (part of) the model's output is specified in terms purely of its representation, by means of condition-action rules, then (that part of) it is likely to be descriptive. An example of this might be a rule saying that a melodic segment boundary appears between notes separated by a large pitch interval. On the other hand, if (part of) the model's behaviour is determined by a process external to the semantics of the specific representation, then (that part of) it is likely to be explanatory. For example, the IDyOM model encodes a notion of sequence and requires a notion of equality to do its inference (Pearce and Wiggins, 2006). Since that equality is merely syntactic identity, it is independent of the music representation, as is the sequence mechanism (see above). Nevertheless, it is capable of predicting segment boundaries in melodies by appeal to information theory, independently of representation, and without reference to specific cases (Pearce et al., 2008). IDyOM therefore can claim to be an explanatory model because its inference process is not *dependent* on the semantics of its representation, but merely *uses* that semantics in a way which is defined *in*dependently.

Empirical support within the modelling hierarchy

Meta-models

Finally, the concept of *meta-model* (named from the Greek μετα, meaning *after* or *beyond*) is introduced. This refers to a model intended for and validated with respect to a particular (cognitive) phenomenon, which is then (directly or indirectly) able to predict the behaviour of another related but different phenomenon. It is useful to make this distinction because this capacity adds considerable weight to the argument that the model is in some sense a *good* model in general terms, both of its original target phenomenon, and possibly of some larger underlying process (Honing, 2006). As an example, consider the IDyOM model, which was developed to predict pitch expectation and validated against empirical work (Pearce and Wiggins, 2006), but which seems also to be capable of predicting human segmentation of melody (Pearce et al., 2008).

IDyOM applies the principles of information theory (Shannon, 1948) to a large body of learned melodic data. The full detail of the pitch-expectation model is beyond the scope of the current discussion, but is given by Pearce (2005). The data is encoded as n-grams (Ponsford et al., 1999) of arbitrary length, and a complex application of this uncomplicated idea is used to generate a statistical distribution representing the expectation of each note in a tonal-melodic sequence, given knowledge of what has gone before. The model accounts for up to 81% of the variance in empirical studies of human pitch expectation (Pearce and Wiggins, 2006).

But IDyOM can do more than this: the outputs of the very same pitch-prediction model can be used to predict melodic segmentation, with only a little further analysis, and, crucially, *without changing the pitch-prediction model.* By taking the Shannon entropy (that is, the negative logarithm of the probability in context) of each note, as it appears, and identifying peaks in the resulting time-variant signal, it is possible to predict expert segmentation results, to a precision/recall correlation (F1) of 0.58 (Pearce et al., 2008). Both this entropy (which is viewed in the IDyOM work as 'unexpectedness') and the entropy of the distribution (calculated as the expected value of this unexpectedness value across the whole distribution from which each note is drawn), which can be viewed as a measure of 'uncertainty', seem to have relationships with musicological features and points of interest in larger scale musical works (Potter et al., 2007).

Putting this latter more speculative work aside for the moment, it is useful to make the distinction between the segmentation process of IDyOM, which is here called a meta-model, from the original pitch expectation process from which it is derived, which is simply a model. The point of making this distinction, and introducing a term for it, is that the meta-model is not only a model of a particular behaviour in its own right, but that it adds evidence for the *original* model, and evidence which is of a different nature from that gleaned in the original validation. Evidently, meta-models are also economical, because they build on the outputs of existing models, and so require less trimming by Occam's razor than more arbitrary collections of less strongly interrelated models. In this way, the construction of a sequence of meta-models matches more closely with the idea of a Lakatosian programme than modelling based on independent, unrelated attempts to model cognitive (or other) phenomena.

In terms of the modelling hierarchy described above, meta-models give a way of reinforcing the connections between the different parts of a level, but also a rigorous way of relating levels together. In particular, the output of a black box explaining a phenomenon at one level is a meta-model based on one or more black box models at a more detailed level. So the idea of the meta-model is more than an epistemological flourish: it can, in fact, constitute the step from which the larger modelling framework, discussed above, is rigorously constructed.

Models in multiple domains

In the discussion of the model of Bharucha (1987), above, a distinction was drawn between what the model explains about the thing being modelled and what it explains about the modelling technique; both are important, but it is also important to consider which one is doing when drawing conclusions. Empirical support can be sought for a particular technique through another way of navigating the modelling hierarchy, which is different from the meta-model route, in terms of a different kind of abstraction. Instead of breaking up a process into sub-processes and abstracting just the relevant detail of each in isolation, the converse attempt is made to identify common mechanisms by abstracting the detail relevant to more than one sub-process, and discarding that which is specific. In this approach, differently from before, abstraction increases *down* the tree, rather than *up* it, because the detail of domains which are unified by moving up the black box hierarchy is discarded in the attempt to find processes which apply more than once *within* levels of the tree.

An example of this is the use, in IDyOM, of Shannon information theory. As explained above, the IDyOM model is independent of data representation, except in that it encodes sequence. In principle, then, exactly this model could be applied in other areas of music (such as harmony: Whorley, Wiggins, & Pearce, 2007) or in language research (indeed, it was partly motivated by cross-domain work such as that of Saffran, Johnson, Aslin, & Newport, 1990). It is improbable, due to the need to account for semantics, that a model designed for music would fully account for language, but the production of a model of language, whose process was based on exactly the same application of information theory to an appropriate representation would constitute a strong argument that Shannon's ideas do indeed model cognition at some level. If this is so, then Shannon information theory provides a strong descriptive model, to which other attempts at explanation should conform, thus constructively narrowing the scope of search for veridical models. If such a model of language proved to be a meta-model (as above) based on aspects of a model of music, this might be construed as circumstantial evidence about the evolution of both faculties, allowing us to generate new hypotheses. These issues constitute current work.

Conclusion: whither computational modelling?

The ideas presented here show how computational modelling can have a useful place in cognitive science, but also constitute a warning that it is not enough merely to model, no matter how accurately. To be ultimately useful, the modelling activity needs to be placed in every bit as careful a methodological framework as the empirical studies in which psychologists excel. In particular, for a research programme to be progressive, in the Lakatosian sense, there should ideally be a planned path from prior experiments through current ones into future ones, expressed in terms of a framework like the one described here; otherwise, it is hard to demonstrate that the programme is indeed progressive, even if it is so. This does not mean that a programme necessarily needs to follow one of the paths outlined above, from more to less abstraction, or up or down the hierarchy, or from models to meta-models; it means simply that there should be an explicit rationale for each modelling attempt and approach, in much the same way that there should be a rationale for empirical work.

The rigour offered by computational methods has a lot to offer cognitive science. But the relative youth of computer science does not excuse it from the need for methodological introspection, in whatever application. This paper has presented just one approach to this issue: many others are possible, and there is no doubt that the debate will proceed for some considerable time into the future.

Acknowledgements

I am grateful to my colleagues in the Intelligent Sound and Music Systems at Goldsmiths for the intellectual environment that shaped the thinking presented here, and particularly to Marcus Pearce, who has been a stalwart sceptic of the best kind, resolutely forcing me to say exactly what I mean. Grants GR/S82220/01 'Informaion Dynamics of Music' and EP/D038855/01 'Modelling Musical Memory and the Perception of Melodic Similarity' from EPSRC and 'MeTAMuSE: Methodologies and Technologies for Advanced Musical Score Encoding' from the Andrew W. Mellon Foundation supported the thinking reported here.

References

Aristotle (1998). *Metaphysics.* (H. Lawson-Tancred, Trans.) London: Penguin Books.

Bharucha, J. (1987). Music cognition and perceptual facilitation: a connectionist framework. *Music Perception*, 5, 1–30.

Bown, O., & Wiggins, G. A. (2009). From maladaptation to competition to cooperation in the evolution of musical behaviour. *Musicae Scientiae*, Special Issue, 2009/10, 'Music and Evolution', 387–411.

Bundy, A., Basin, D., Hutter, D., & Ireland, A. (2005). *Rippling: Meta-level guidance for Mathematical Reasoning.* Cambridge: Cambridge University Press.

Cambouropoulos, E. (2001). The Local Boundary Detection Model (LBDM) and its application in the study of expressive timing. In *Proceedings of the International Computer Music Conference (ICMC'2001)* (pp. 17–22), Havana, Cuba.

Cambouropoulos, E. (2006). Musical parallelism and melodic segmentation: A computational approach. *Music Perception, 23*(3), 249–69.

Cope, D. (1991). *Computers and Musical Style.* Oxford: Oxford University Press.

Ebcioğlu, K. (1988). An expert system for harmonizing four-part chorales. *Computer Music Journal, 12*(3), 43–51.

Ferrand, M., Nelson, P., & Wiggins, G. A. (2002). A probabilistic model for melody segmentation. In *Proceedings of ICMAI'02.* New York: Springer-Verlag.

Fodor, J. (1974). Special sciences: Or the disunity of science as a working hypothesis. *Synthese, 28*, 97–115.

Hamanaka, M., Hirata, K., & Tojo, S. (2005). ATTA: Automatic Time-span tree analyzer based on extended GTTM. In *Proceedings of ISMIR 2005, the Sixth International Conference on Music Information Retrieval* (pp. 358–65). London.

Honing, H. (2006). Computational modeling of music cognition: a case study on model selection. *Music Perception, 23*(5), 365–76.

Kohonen, T. (1995). *Self-Organizing Maps* (Series in Information Science Vol. 30). Heidelberg: Springer. [Second edition, 1997.]

Lakatos, I. (1978). *The Methodology of Scientific Research Programmes: Philosophical Papers* (J. Worrall and G. Currie, Eds.). Cambridge: Cambridge University Press.

Lerdahl, F., & Jackendoff, R. (1983). *A Generative Theory of Tonal Music.* Cambridge, MA: MIT Press.

Marr, D. (1982). *Vision: A Computational Approach.* San Francisco, CA: Freeman & Co.

McClamrock, R. (1991a). Marr's three levels: A re-evaluation. *Minds and Machines, 1*(2).

McClamrock, R. (1991b). Methodological individualism considered as a constitutive principle of scientific inquiry. *Philosophical Psychology, 4*(3).

Ovans, R. (1992). *Efficient music composition via consistency techniques. Technical Report CSS-IS TR 92–02.* Burnaby, B.C.: Centre for Systems Science, Simon Fraser University.

Pachet, F., & Roy, P. (1998). Reifying chords in automatic harmonization. In F. Pachet, & P. Codognet (Eds.), *Proceedings of the ECAI'98 Workshop on Constraints for Artistic Applications.*

Papadopoulos, G. and Wiggins, G. A. (1999). AI methods for algorithmic composition: A survey, a critical view and future prospects. In G. A. Wiggins (Ed.), *Proceedings of the AISB'99 Symposium on Musical Creativity* (pp. 110–17). Brighton: AISB.

Pearce, M., Conklin, D., and Wiggins, G. (2004). Methods for combining statistical models of music. In U. K. Wiil (Ed.), *Proceedings of the Conference on Music Modelling and Retrieval,* number 3310 in LNCS (pp. 295–312). New York: Springer-Verlag.

Pearce, M., & Wiggins, G. A. (2004). Improved methods for statistical modelling of monophonic music. *Journal of New Music Research, 33*(4), 367–85.

Pearce, M. T. (2005). *The Construction and Evaluation of Statistical Models of Melodic Structure in Music Perception and Composition* (PhD thesis). Department of Computing, City University, London.

Pearce, M. T., Müllensiefen, D., & Wiggins, G. A. (2008). Melodic segmentation: A new method and a framework for model comparison. In *Proceedings of ISMIR 2008.*

Pearce, M. T., & Wiggins, G. A. (2006). Expectation in melody: The influence of context and learning. *Music Perception, 23*(5), 377–406.

Ponsford, D., Wiggins, G. A., & Mellish, C. S. (1999). Statistical learning of harmonic movement. *Journal of New Music Research, 28*(2), 150–77.

Popper, K. (1934). *The Logic of Scientific Discovery.* London: Routledge.

Potter, K., Wiggins, G. A., & Pearce, M. T. (2007). Towards greater objectivity in music theory: Information-dynamic analysis of minimalist music. *Musicae Scientiae, 11*(2), 295–324.

Purwins, H., Blanketz, B., & Obermayer, K. (2000). Computing auditory perception. *Organised Sound, 5*(3), 159–71.

Pylyshyn, Z. (1984). *Computation and Cognition: Towards a Foundation for Cognitive Science.* Cambridge, MA: MIT Press.

Rothstein, J. (1992). *MIDI: a comprehensive introduction.* Oxford: Oxford University Press.

Saffran, J. R., Johnson, E. K., Aslin, R. N., & Newport, E. L. (1990). Statistical learning of tone sequences by human infants and adults. *Cognition, 70,* 27–52.

Shannon, C. (1948). A mathematical theory of communication. *Bell System Technical Journal, 27,* 379–423, 623–56.

Tekman, H. G., & Bharucha, J. J. (1998). Implicit knowledge versus psychoacoustic similarity in priming of chords. *Journal of Experimental Psychology: Human Perception and Performance, 24,* 252–60.

Tillmann, B., Bharucha, J., & Bigand, E. (2000). Implicit learning of tonality: A self-organizing approach. *Psychological Review, 107*(4), 885–913.

Whorley, R. P., Wiggins, G. A., & Pearce, M. T. (2007). Systematic evaluation and improvement of statistical models of harmony. In A. Cardoso and G. A. Wiggins (Eds.), *Proceedings of the 4th International Joint Workshop on Computational Creativity* (pp. 81–88). London.

Widmer, G. and Tobudic, A. (2003). Playing Mozart by analogy: Learning multi-level timing and dynamics strategies. *Journal of New Music Research, 32*(3), 259–68.

Wiggins, G. A. (2007). Models of musical similarity. *Musicae Scientiae, Discussion Forum 4a.*

Wiggins, G. A., Harris, M., & Smaill, A. (1989). Representing music for analysis and composition. In M. Balaban, K. Ebcio lu, O. Laske, C. Lischka, & L. Sorisio (Eds.), *Proceedings of the 2nd IJCAI AI/Music Workshop* (pp. 63–71). Detroit, Michigan. [Also from Edinburgh as DAI Research Paper No. 504.]

Wiggins, G. A., Papdopoulos, G., Phon-Amnuaisuk, S., & Tuson, A. (1999). Evolutionary methods for musical composition. *Journal of Computing Anticipatory Systems, 4.* [Also available as a Research Paper from the School of Informatics, University of Edinburgh.]

Wiggins, G. A., Pearce, M. T., & Müllensiefen, D. (2009). Computational modelling of music cognition and musical creativity. In R. Dean (Ed.), *Oxford Handbook of Computer Music* (pp. 383–420). New York: Oxford University Press.

Chapter 19

Alignment in language and music

John N. Williams

In this commentary I shall consider the similarities and differences between Bharucha, Curtis, and Paroo's notion of alignment in music (Chapter 16, this volume) and the notion of alignment in verbal communication that has been recently developed within psycholinguistics (Garrod & Pickering, 2004; Pickering & Garrod, 2004). Psycholinguistic research sheds light on underlying mechanisms of alignment that may also be applicable to music, at least in some contexts. It also suggests methodologies that could be adapted to empirically investigate musical alignment. First, though, I shall sketch out a psycholinguistic approach to communication and alignment.

The traditional view of verbal communication within psycholinguistics runs as follows. Suppose A and B are two people involved in a conversation. In A's and B's heads there are various levels of linguistic representation. We need make no commitment here to the specifics of these representations, but let us suppose that the idea that A wants to express is represented in the form of a 'situation model' (Kintsch, 1998) which then interfaces with a level of lexical semantic information in order to select abstract representations of relevant lexical items and associated syntactic information (Levelt, Roelofs, & Meyer, 1999). These activated representations then pass through a stage of syntactic structure building and onto a stage of phonological retrieval (Garrett, 1990). Finally the phonetic plans for words are retrieved, and sent to the articulators which then produce sound waves. B extracts the temporal and spectral information from the sound waves and maps this onto lexical representations (possibly via phonological representations, but not necessarily (Marslen-Wilson & Warren, 1994)). Semantic and syntactic information is retrieved, a syntactic representation constructed, and together the syntactic and semantic information guide the construction of a situation model. Although these levels of processing in production and comprehension can be simply described as following in a serial chain, many believe that in real-time processing both production and comprehension display a high degree of interaction between top-down and bottom-up processes. For example, knowledge of which words are possible in a language affects the perception of letters (Reicher, 1969) and phonemes (Ganong, 1980), and knowledge of which events are more probable in the world influences resolution of lexical (Seidenberg, Tanenhaus, Leiman, & Bienkowski, 1982) and syntactic (Taraban & McClelland, 1988) ambiguities. This has led to the idea of language processing as constraint satisfaction (MacDonald, Pearlmutter, & Seidenberg, 1994; Seidenberg & MacDonald, 1999).

Within the traditional view of language production and comprehension just outlined, successful communication consists in the transmission of ideas. Specifically, the situation model in A's mind that motivated the utterance comes to be represented in B's mind along with associated propositional attitudes (e.g. B believes that A believes that such and such is the case). But the correspondence, or 'alignment' between the representations in A's and B's heads presumably also extends to the phonological, lexical, semantic, and syntactic representations that are involved in deriving the situation model. That is, A's and B's representational states can be said to be 'aligned' to the extent that similar representations are formed at these various levels. However, misunderstandings can occur. Ambiguity is rife at both the lexical and syntactic levels, although in comprehension these ambiguities are often rapidly resolved through the constraint satisfaction process. More critically, the construction of the situation model involves making many kinds of inferences that are dependent on background knowledge and particular contextual assumptions (Kintsch, 1998). Whilst a cooperative speaker might tailor their utterance so as to make their intended meaning recoverable through a minimal number of inferences based on highly accessible information (Sperber & Wilson, 1995), the fact remains that complete alignment cannot be guaranteed.

All this seems very similar to Bharrucha et al.'s claims for music. Linguistic levels of representation can be substituted by their musical analogues (tones, chords, a theory of musical syntax, notions of musical meaning), and in the MUSACT model Bharucha et al. assume an interaction between bottom-up and top-down processing that is very similar to that found in psycholinguistic models of word recognition and sentence processing. Obviously, the goal of musical communication is not to convey propositions, but through alignment at the various levels of musical structure the performer can hope to induce similar affect and motion states, and in some cases succeed in communicating similar musical meanings. Clearly, though, a lower level of alignment is to be expected in music than in language. As Bharucha et al. point out, music is much more ambiguous, particularly at the level of meaning, and our musical experience is strongly affected by attention (whereas in the case of language attention is fixed more securely on meaning). Another factor is competence. Adult native speakers of the same language would be expected to have similar levels of linguistic competence—similar sized vocabulary and syntactic repertoire—making alignment in representational states feasible. But how often can we assume similar competence between musical performer and listener? Perhaps at the level of some core aspects of musical cognition we can, at least for popular music within our own culture. But when it comes to higher forms of music maybe we should think of the listener more as a learner of a language, either a child, or a second language learner attempting to understand a native speaker.

But we are missing something here. We are forgetting an important difference between linguistic and musical communication. In the case of language, communication often occurs in the context of dialogue. As Pickering & Garrod (2004) point out, traditional models of verbal communication are models of monologue. But in dialogue additional 'channels of alignment' are opened up, permitting a greater degree of alignment at the various levels of representation. This is essentially because dialogue involves imitation. The lexical, syntactic, semantic, and situation model representations that A uses become activated in B's mind, and then are likely to be used in B's production, thereby reactivating those representations in A's mind, and so on. This cyclic interaction provides a continual force towards alignment at different levels of representation. For Pickering & Garrod (2004) the communication mechanism that is involved in this kind of alignment is entirely unintentional and unconscious, and is in fact nothing more than the familiar mechanism of priming.

We know from studies of social interaction that people mimic each other's posture and gestures. This is known as the 'chameleon effect' (Chartrand & Bargh, 1999). A crosses his legs, B crosses hers, B scratches her ear, A scratches his. These are unconscious processes of imitation that lead to conscious feelings of rapport between the interlocutors. This behaviour presumably reflects the operation of mirror neurons—neurons that fire both when an action is observed and when it is imitated (Rizzolatti & Craighero, 2004). But imitation is also observed with respect to the language choices that interlocutors make. If A uses a word to refer to something, B is likely to use it too (even if there are other lexical choices available). Interlocutors converge on a common set of referring expressions, often with dialogue-specific senses, to refer to particular concepts in their discourse. The underlying mechanism for this is lexical priming. Interlocutors also imitate each others syntax (Branigan, Pickering, & Cleland, 2000). If A says 'Mary gave John a box of chocolates' (using a double object dative construction), B is likely to say 'and John gave Mary a bunch of flowers' (repeating the double object construction). B could have said 'John gave a bunch of flowers to Mary' (using the prepositional dative), but didn't. Research has shown that this is indeed due to priming of syntactic, rather than semantic or discourse, representations since it persists even when non-syntactic factors are controlled (Bock, Loebell, & Morey, 1992). Moreover, whilst the effect can be obtained in monologue situations due to the passive activation of syntactic representations in comprehension, it is particularly strong in dialogue suggesting that the effect is amplified by the drive towards alignment (Branigan, Pickering, McLean, & Cleland, 2007). Properties of the situation model may also converge through priming. For example, interlocutors are likely to adopt a common frame of reference for talking about spatial positions. Given a choice between egocentric ('turn left down Queens Road'), or allocentric ('head North along Queens Road') frames of reference, if one person adopts the egocentric perspective ('Turn left'), the other person will too ('and then is King's College on my right?'). There is interesting evidence that even a temporal reference frame can prime an analogous spatial reference frame (Boroditsky, 2000). However, according to Pickering & Garrod (2004) the major force towards alignment at the level of the situation model comes from priming of lower levels of lexical and syntactic representation. Given that interlocutors activate common lexical and syntactic resources, so their mental model representations also naturally converge. This follows from the interactive processing architecture assumed in their alignment model.

All of the above means that there is a much higher probability of alignment in dialogue than in monologue. But what are the advantages of alignment? Primed representations are more available, and so require less effort to retrieve. Lexical items, or indeed whole phrases, become routinized. Also, choices that have to be made at lexical, syntactic, and situation model levels are in some cases already made by one's interlocutor (whose utterances prime certain representations and not others). Both of these factors work to make dialogue easier than monologue (Garrod & Pickering, 2004; Pickering & Garrod, 2004).

But alignment could also drive acquisition (Dominey, 2004). If A is an adult and B a child, what is priming in the short term could, given sufficient repetition, be acquisition in the long term. The fact that there is also pressure on the adult to align with the child increases the probability that what A says is not too far beyond the child's ability to process it. So dialogue becomes central to acquisition, and over time, the child's competence converges with that of the adult speaker.

If musical performance is to be likened to verbal communication, then it is clearly more like communication in the sense of monologue than dialogue. Like monologue, musical performance will lead to relatively low levels of alignment, and the level of alignment in musical performance will be lower than that in verbal monologue for the reasons that Bharucha et al. outline. Of course there are also other situations in which musical communication can be more like verbal dialogue. For example, improvising jazz musicians in an ensemble presumably imitate each other to some extent, both melodically and rhythmically, and develop more aligned representations as a result (those who attended the final performance by The Ecosonic Ensemble at the Cambridge Language and Music as Cognitive Systems conference (2007) will have witnessed an excellent example of musical dialogue in spontaneous improvised music). Improvising with more competent players than oneself might accelerate one's musical development since the pressure to align could drive acquisition. Thus, it is possible to apply the framework for thinking about alignment in dialogue to alignment in musical communication, but only under special circumstances.

There may be a more general implication of research on verbal alignment. Probably the main reason for the recent surge of interest in imitative behaviour during verbal interactions is that it reveals priming phenomena, and in the history of cognitive psychology, priming has provided an essential tool for exploring the structure of mental representations. The specific kind of priming involved here is known as *repetition priming*, where the prime and target events are related by virtue of the repetition of some aspect of their structure (which is distinguished from *semantic priming*, where the events are related by virtue of their meanings). For example, repetition priming has been used to differentiate between different components of the lexicon involved in visual and spoken word recognition (Morton, 1969, 1979), and to explore the morphological structure of words (Marslen-Wilson, Tyler, Waksler, & Older, 1994). Structural repetition priming reveals a level of abstract syntactic representation that is distinct from form or meaning (for a review see Pickering & Ferreira, 2008). Subsequent work has used these techniques to further explore the nature of syntactic representation, for example, showing that bilinguals activate common underlying syntactic representations for aspects of grammar that are shared by the languages they know (Salamoura & Williams, 2007, 2008; Schoonbaert, Hartsuiker, & Pickering, 2007). Imitation within dialogue involves priming from comprehension to production (Branigan et al., 2000, 2007), thus revealing representations that are at such a level of abstraction that they are shared between comprehension and production processes. As Marslen-Wilson et al. (1994) argue, priming phenomena that span modalities reveal the abstract structure of linguistic representations.

Of course, priming has been extensively used within music research as well (e.g. Tekman & Bharucha, 1998; Tillman, Janata, & Bharucha, 2003), although this is normally more akin to semantic priming since it typically involves manipulating the harmonic relatedness of the prime and target events. But in order to investigate alignment it is presumably necessary to examine repetition priming as a mechanism for imitation, where aspects of musical structure that have been perceived subsequently resurface in performance. Jungers (2007) reports an initial attempt at this kind of work, providing evidence that imitation can shed light on the nature of musical representation (specifically, whereas metre was expressed through intensity in the music the subjects heard, it was expressed by articulation in their performance, suggesting an underlying abstract representation of metre). The methodological challenge in this kind of work will be to ensure that priming from perception to performance occurs unconsciously, as is assumed to be the case in verbal dialogue, and not as a result of a conscious intention to imitate, which may be more natural in music. Thus, investigations of repetition priming phenomena within musical monologue and dialogue situations may provide a methodology not only for empirically investigating alignment, but also for shedding light on the structure of musical representations.

References

Bock, K., Loebell, H., & Morey, R. (1992). From conceptual roles to syntactic relations: Bridging the syntactic cleft. *Psychological Review, 99*, 150–71.

Boroditsky, L. (2000). Metaphorical structuring: Understanding time through spatial metaphors. *Cognition, 75*, 1–28.

Branigan, H. P., Pickering, M. J., & Cleland, A. A. (2000). Syntactic co-ordination in dialogue. *Cognition, 75*, B13–25.

Branigan, H. P., Pickering, M. J., McLean, J. F., & Cleland, A. A. (2007). Syntactic alignment and participant role in dialogue. *Cognition, 104*, 163–97.

Chartrand, T. L., & Bargh, J. A. (1999). The chameleon effect: The perception-behavior link and social interaction. *Journal of Personality and Social Psychology, 76*, 893–910.

Dominey, P. F. (2004). Situation alignment and routinization in language acquisition. *Behavioral and Brain Sciences, 26*, 195.

Ganong, W. F. (1980). Phonetic categorization in auditory word perception. *Journal of Experimental Psychology: Human Perception and Performance, 6*, 110–25.

Garrett, M. F. (1990). Sentence processing. In D. H. Osherson & H. Lasnik (Eds.), *An invitation to cognitive science, Volume 1.* (pp. 133–75). Cambridge, MA: MIT Press.

Garrod, S., & Pickering, M. (2004). Why is conversation so easy? *Trends in Cognitive Sciences, 8*, 8–11.

Jungers, M. K. (2007). Performance priming in music. *Music Perception, 24*, 395–99.

Kintsch, W. (1998). *Comprehension: A Paradigm for Cognition.* New York: Cambridge University Press.

Levelt, W. J. M., Roelofs, A., & Meyer, A. S. (1999). A theory of lexical access in speech production. *Behavioural and Brain Sciences, 22*, 1–75.

MacDonald, M. C., Pearlmutter, N. J., & Seidenberg, M. S. (1994). Lexical nature of syntactic ambiguity resolution. *Psychological Review, 101*, 676–703.

Marslen-Wilson, W., Tyler, L. K., Waksler, R., & Older, L. (1994). Morphology and meaning in the English mental lexicon. *Psychological Review, 101*, 3–33.

Marslen-Wilson, W., & Warren, P. (1994). Levels of perceptual representation and process in lexical access: Words, phonemes, and features. *Psychological Review, 101*, 653–75.

Morton, J. (1969). The interaction of information in word recognition. *Psychological Review, 76*, 165–78.

Morton, J. (1979). Facilitation in word recognition: Experiments causing change in the logogen model. In P. A. Kolers & M. E. Wrolstad & H. Bouma (Eds.), *Processing of visible language* (Vol. 1, pp. 259–68). New York: Plenum.

Pickering, M. J., & Ferreira, V. S. (2008). Structural Priming: A Critical Review. *Psychological Bulletin, 134*, 427–59.

Pickering, M. J., & Garrod, S. (2004). Toward a mechanistic psychology of dialogue. *Behavioral and Brain Sciences, 26*, 169–226.

Reicher, G. M. (1969). Perceptual recognition as a function of meaningfulness of stimulus material. *Journal of Experimental Psychology, 81*, 275–80.

Rizzolatti, G., & Craighero, L. (2004). The mirror-neuron system. *Annual Review of Neuroscience, 27*, 169–92.

Salamoura, A., & Williams, J. N. (2007). Processing verb argument structure across languages: Evidence for shared representations in the bilingual lexicon. *Applied Psycholinguistics, 28*, 627–60.

Salamoura, A., & Williams, J. N. (2008). The representation of grammatical gender in the bilingual lexicon: Evidence from Greek and German. *Bilingualism: Language and Cognition, 10*, 257–75.

Schoonbaert, S., Hartsuiker, R. J., & Pickering, M. J. (2007). The representation of lexical and syntactic information in bilinguals: Evidence from syntactic priming. *Journal of Memory and Language, 56*, 153–71.

Seidenberg, M. S., & MacDonald, M. C. (1999). A probabilistic constraints approach to language acquisition and processing. *Cognitive Science, 23*, 569–88.

Seidenberg, M. S., Tanenhaus, M. K., Leiman, J. M., & Bienkowski, M. (1982). Automatic access of the meanings of ambiguous words in context: Some limitations on knowledge-based processing. *Cognitive Psychology, 14*, 489–532.

Sperber, D., & Wilson, D. (1995). *Relevance: communication and cognition*. Oxford: Blackwell.

Taraban, R., & McClelland, J. L. (1988). Constituent attachment and thematic role assignment in sentence processing: Influences of content-based expectation. *Journal of Memory and Language, 27*, 597–632.

Tekman, H. G., & Bharucha, J. J. (1998). Implicit knowledge versus psychoacoustic similarity in priming of chords. *Journal of Experimental Psychology: Human Perception & Performance, 24*, 252–60.

Tillman, B., Janata, P., & Bharucha, J. J. (2003). Activation of the inferior frontal cortex in musical priming. *Cognitive Brain Research, 16*, 145–61.

Chapter 20

Alignment of brain states: response to commentaries

Jamshed J. Bharucha, Kaivon Paroo, and Meagan Curtis

The commentaries by Williams and by Dienes, Kuhn, Guo, and Jones nicely complement our chapter entitled 'Musical communication as alignment of brain states'. Our response focuses on the commentary written by Wiggins, who provides a spirited critique of network models, and the MUSACT model (Bharucha, 1987) in particular—drawing extensively on the philosophy of science.

We agree with Wiggins that it would be desirable to develop a 'detailed description of the level(s) of abstraction at which [network models] operate', 'so that the claims being made can be subjected to thorough scrutiny, and exhaustive testing, across a very broad range of potential data, including outliers'. However, it certainly is a leap to argue that until a model satisfies all these criteria, it is 'disconnected from cognitive reality'. We know of no model of cognition, let alone of music cognition, that has achieved this stage of development—and certainly not in one fell swoop. Cognitive science has proceeded by a ratcheting process: a new result may inspire a new model that, in spite of its limited scope, inspires a new experiment, whose result itself becomes a constraint on new models. Cognitive science and cognitive neuroscience are still in their infancies, their domains are vast, and we are still scratching the surface.

In the case of the MUSACT model, it makes unanticipated, testable predications that few models of cognition have been able to make, for example, that expectations for chords have time courses: they are driven initially by spectral information but then over-ruled by implicitly learning cultural regularities that exert their influence in a top-down fashion (Tekman & Bharucha, 1992). Like all models in science, this one will be superseded. However, it is a significant step in thinking about harmony not as a set of rules—which we believe it is not—but as the fusing of elements into more abstract perceptual units (tones fused into chords, and over time, into keys), based on a small set of general assumptions about how the tuning of neural elements can be acquired through passive perceptual learning. Wiggins repeats some familiar criticisms levelled at network models. One is that the units (e.g. that respond to chords and keys) are pre-fixed, even though they emerge from self-organization. The other is that the model acquires its connectivity because of the statistics of the cultural environment, even though this is precisely the point!

In commenting on the Tekman and Bharucha (1992) finding, Wiggins observes, post hoc, that 'it would not be difficult to construct a rule-based model that did work in this way'. Yet no rule-based model that we are aware of in the literature has made this prediction and motivated its experimental testing. Wiggins ought to consider the reverse argument, namely, that a network of neurons can be constructed to work in the same way as a rule-based system; indeed, the brain is such a network if it represents rules at all. This portion of Wiggins's commentary boils down to the arbitrary but oft repeated assertion that if a cognitive process can be described by rules, it must be explained by rules. The ability to describe the lawfulness of psychological phenomena with rules doesn't imply that the rules drive the behaviour. Strong arguments have been made for the existence of rules in the area of syntax processing, but Wiggins has not mustered any proof that the regularities of musical harmony necessarily reflect an underlying system based on represented rules.

In any case, the explicit objective in our paper was not to advance a particular model of harmony, but rather to sketch a framework for thinking about musical communication as the alignment and synchronization of brain states. This framework is not wedded to any specific model of harmony or any other aspect of music. Rather, it is wedded to the notion that in each musical domain, there are features that characterize the state of mind of the listener or performer at any given time. Thinking of feature strengths (activations) concatenated as a vector provides a scalable way to represent the brain state in an abstract way. For example, at any given time, such-and-such pitch classes, chords, keys, modes, metres, timbres are present in perception. Our central point is that this framework potentially enables us to compute how similar are the musical states of two or more people, i.e. how synchronized they are.

In a footnote, Wiggins states that as a composer, he finds the notion of 'inflicting one's own brain states on others . . . to be pushing the boundaries of ethics!'. However, when we communicate with others, whether through language, non-verbal cues, or music, we influence their brain states, whether we like it or not. It strains neuroscientific credulity to imagine that a performance does not evoke a response from the brains of listeners, unless the listeners are asleep. And most performances, musical or otherwise, do indeed communicate emotion, whether intentionally or not—and whether successful or not. If influencing what's happening in other peoples' brains is an ethical violation, one would be obliged to refrain from ever speaking to anyone, because one's facial expressions and tone of voice are likely to 'inflict' emotional states on other peoples' brains. The evocations of emotion by speech and music are intertwined, as a surge of recent research suggests (e.g. Curtis & Bharucha, 2010). In these processes, the speaker aligns the brain state of the listener enough for the emotion to be recognized. And when the emotion of the speaker has been induced in the listener, the brain states are synchronized in this respect.

In conclusion, Wiggins is correct to assert that some aspects of the framework proposed in our article are more notational than explanatory. However, the purpose of our original paper was to float a proposal about synchronization and alignment of brain states as an objective of musical communication. A full-blown model of all aspects is a long-term programmatic effort. The neural net models are described in the paper only as examples of the way in which a feature approach (captured by vectors across musical dimensions) can form the basis for thinking about synchronization.

References

Bharucha, J.J. (1987). Music cognition and perceptual facilitation: A connectionist framework. *Music Perception*, 5, 1–30.

Curtis, M.E. & Bharucha, J.J. (2010). The minor third communicates sadness in speech, mirroring its use in music. *Emotion*, *10*, 335–48.

Tekman, H.G. & Bharucha, J.J. (1992). Time course of chord priming. *Perception & Psychophysics*, *51*, 33–39.

Section 4

Neuroscience

Chapter 21

Introduction

The fourth section of the volume focuses on the neuroscience of language and music, an area that has received considerable attention over the past 10 years (see, e.g. the contributions in Aventine, Faenza, & Minciacchi, 2003; Aventine, Lopez, & Koelsch, 2006; Dalla Bella et al., 2009; Peretz & Zatorre, 2003; Spiro, 2003; Zatorre & Peretz, 2001). The section contains two target articles and sets of comments. In the first target article, Aniruddh Patel presents his *resource-sharing framework* for the comparative study of language and music. Resource sharing is based on two principles: (1) language and music involve domain-specific representations, and (2) when similar cognitive processes are conducted on these representations, the brain shares neural resources between the two domains. As an example, Patel focuses on the processing of linguistic and musical syntax. The units involved in the processing of language and music are unique to their respective domains (hence, domain-specific)—language has words, while music has tones or chords. However, when these units are assembled to form longer sequences, both domains share the same neural networks. In his chapter, Patel discusses evidence for resource sharing in online syntactic comprehension and presents his *shared syntactic integration resource hypothesis* (SSIRH), which generates specific predictions about neural overlap in the processing of linguistic and musical syntax. The last part of Patel's chapter illustrates how the resource-sharing framework can be applied to developmental processes, i.e. to the acquisition of linguistic and musical systems.

In his commentary to Patel's target article, Stefan Koelsch largely agrees with Patel's notion of shared resource networks. However, as Koelsch points out, little research has analysed in detail which cognitive mechanisms are shared between the two domains. Koelsch describes some of the processes that are likely to be limited to the processing of musical syntax and suggests cognitive functions that are shared between the syntactic processing of language and music. In her commentary, Jessica Grahn discusses advances in neuroimaging techniques and implications for Patel's SSIRH. She focuses on the predictions made by Patel's SSIRH and on ways in which these can be tested by means of functional neuroimaging. She reviews a selection of novel techniques, including multivoxel pattern analysis (MVPA). She argues that tools such as MVPA might provide definite evidence for or against the SSIRH. The third commentary is sceptical of Patel's proposal. Justin London argues that the syntax of music and language are fundamentally different, and that music is not 'syntactic' in the way that language is. He then discusses the implications of this view for Patel's resource sharing framework. The first part of the neuroscience section concludes with Patel's response to the commentaries.

The second target article focuses on modularity in language and music. Isabelle Peretz suggests that an updated view of modularity can provide a useful framework within which to study cognitive systems (including language and music) and expands the modularity position to singing and speaking (hence, modularity *in action*). She first clarifies the concept of modularity and then reviews evidence for modularity in speaking and singing from four sources: neuropsychological dissociations, overlaps in neuroimaging, interference effects, and domain-transfer effects. Peretz concludes her target article by contrasting her position with the resource sharing framework proposed by Patel.

In their commentary to Peretz's target article, Erika Skoe and Nina Kraus point out that the modularity debate has centred on the cortex. Their commentary intends to widen the theoretical discussion of modularity by presenting research on the role of subcortical structures in auditory processing. They suggest that human subcortical auditory function can provide a new conceptual framework for studying modularity. In their commentary, Mireille Besson and Daniele Schön focus on four points, namely (1) genetics and the origins of music and speech, (2) the evolution of the concept of modularity, (3) the utility of comparing cognitive functions by means of different approaches, and (4) the inferential power of different methods (e.g. Bayesian inference). Besson and Schön agree that the notion of modularity provides a useful framework for empirical research. At the same time, however, they argue that brain and behaviour cannot easily be decomposed into independent modules or functions. In the third commentary, Usha Goswami reviews empirical data from developmental psychology and animal cognition that is relevant to the modularity debate. Goswami agrees with Peretz's view that developmental disorders can offer valuable insights into the discussion about modularity and illustrates this with regards to rhythmic processing, prosody and rhythmic entrainment in developmental dyslexia and specific language impairment. The last commentary, co-authored by Leigh VanHandel, Jennie Wakefield, and Wendy Wilkins, describes an experiment on the role of working memory in the processing of pitch in language and music. Working memory is a resource shared by both language and music, and their experiment focuses on tone perception in music and language. Their results suggest that specific types of working memory are a factor in pitch discrimination tasks for both language and music. The second part of the neuroscience section concludes with Peretz's response to her commentators.

References

Aventine, G., Faenza, C., & Minciacchi, D. (Eds.) (2003). The neurosciences and music [Special issue]. *Annals of the New York Academy of Sciences, 999.*

Aventine, G., Lopez, L., & Koelsch, S. (Eds.) (2006). The neurosciences and music II: From perception to performance [Special issue]. *Annals of the New York Academy of Sciences, 1060.*

Dalla Bella, S., Kraus, N., Overy, K., Pantev, C., Snyder, J. S., Tervaniemi, M., *et al.* (Eds.) (2009). The neurosciences and music III: Disorders and plasticity [Special issue]. *Annals of the New York Academy of Sciences, 1169.*

Peretz, I., & Zatorre, R. (Eds.) (2003). *The cognitive neuroscience of music.* Oxford: Oxford University Press.

Spiro, J. (Ed.) (2003). Music and the brain [Special issue]. *Nature Neuroscience, 6*(7).

Zatorre, R., & Peretz, I. (Eds.). (2001). The biological foundations of music [Special issue]. *Annals of the New York Academy of Sciences, 930.*

Chapter 22

Language, music, and the brain: a resource-sharing framework

Aniruddh D. Patel

Introduction

This paper discusses a theoretical framework for the cognitive study of music–language relations called resource sharing. Resource sharing makes a basic conceptual distinction between domain-specific knowledge and shared neural resources that operate upon this knowledge as part of cognitive processing. This framework was originally proposed as a way to reconcile contradictory evidence on music–language relations with respect to syntactic processing, since neuropsychology had pointed to independence and neuroimaging had pointed to overlap (Patel, 2003, 2008). This paper expands this framework, applying it to online processes of syntactic comprehension and to developmental processes involved in learning the phonemic structure of language. In both cases, resource sharing suggests that aspects of language and music which are very different in their structural organization can have deep connections in terms of cognitive processing.

The paper is organized as follows. The next two sections ('Neuropsychology: evidence for domain-specificity' and 'Neuroimaging: challenges to domain-specificity') provide a brief background on the neuropsychological and neuroimaging studies that gave rise to the resource sharing framework. The following section ('The resource-sharing framework') provides some details on the framework itself. The section entitled 'Syntax', which constitutes the body of the paper, discusses resource sharing with respect to musical syntax, while the 'Phonology' section shows how this framework can be applied to developmental processes. The final section provides concluding remarks.

Throughout the paper, the focus is on comparing mechanisms involved in the comprehension of instrumental music and of ordinary spoken language. This reflects the greater amount of research on perception than on production in both domains. Furthermore, the focus is on the Western European tonal tradition (which has received the greatest amount of theoretical and empirical research within music cognition), though the framework should apply to many other types of musical systems.

Neuropsychology: evidence for domain-specificity

Among the most exciting discoveries in music neuroscience have been cases of selective deficits of music cognition in normal individuals with focal brain damage ('acquired amusia'). While rare, such cases are significant because they imply that brain networks can be specialized for musical functions, without overlap with networks involved in language, environmental sound perception, etc. (Peretz & Coltheart, 2003). For example, Peretz and colleagues (Peretz, 1993; Peretz et al., 1994) studied a patient, G.L., who suffered an enduring loss of sensitivity to musical key structure after suffering bilateral temporal lobe damage due to strokes (those unfamiliar with the concept of a musical key may consult the later section entitled 'Some basics of musical key'). G.L.'s primary auditory cortex was spared, but there was damage to rostral superior temporal gyri, which encompasses several auditory association areas (cf. Tramo, Bharucha, & Musiek, 1990).

G.L. could discriminate changes between single pitches and was sensitive to differences in melodic contour in short melodies. However, he showed an absence of sensitivity to musical key. For example, G.L. was given a probe-tone task in which a few notes (which established a musical key) were followed by a target tone. The task was to rate the how well the target fit with the preceding context. Normal controls showed the standard effect, whereby tones from the key were rated higher than out-of-key tones. G.L., in contrast, showed no such effect, and tended to base his judgements on the pitch distance between the penultimate and final tone. He also failed to show an advantage for melodies that did versus did not adhere to a key (i.e. tonal vs. atonal melodies) in short-term memory tasks, in contrast to controls. Additional experiments showed that his problems could not be accounted for by a general auditory memory deficit. Importantly for the current purposes, G.L. scored in the normal range on standardized aphasia tests, showing that he had 'amusia without aphasia'.

While G.L.'s case concerns musical syntax (cf. section 'Some basics of musical key' below), other cases from neuropsychology demonstrate music–language dissociations at the phonological level. For example, individuals with 'pure word deafness' (typically associated with bilateral lesions to the posterior superior temporal lobe) can no longer understand spoken material but retain sensitivity to other sounds, including music (Poeppel, 2001). Since these patients can speak and can understand and/or produce language in other modalities (e.g. writing), this disorder appears to be a selective problem with auditory phonemic encoding.

Neuroimaging: challenges to domain-specificity

If we only had evidence from neuropsychology, it would be tempting to conclude that music and language are largely independent cognitive functions (Marin & Perry, 1999). Neuroimaging has challenged this view, however, by revealing significant overlap in certain aspects of musical and linguistic processing in normal individuals. For example, the processing of one aspect of musical grammar (the harmonic structure or chords and keys) appears to involve brain operations also involved in linguistic syntactic processing. This was first demonstrated in an event-related potential (ERP) study which embedded an out-of-key chord in the middle of a tonal chord sequence (Patel, Gibson, Ratner, Besson, & Holcomb, 1998a) This out-of-key chord elicited a P600, an ERP component known to be associated with linguistic syntactic processing (see Gouvea, Phillips, Kazanina, & Poeppel, 2010, for a recent discussion of the linguistic processes underlying the P600). In fact, the P600 to out-of-key chords was statistically indistinguishable from the P600 generated by linguistic syntactic incongruities in sentences heard by the same participants. On this basis, it was suggested that the P600 reflected processes of structural integration shared by language and music.

Subsequent neuroimaging work provided further evidence of overlap between music and language. Using magnetoencephalography (MEG), Maess, Koelsch, Gunter, & Friederici (2001) found that a different ERP component elicited by out-of-key chords, an early right anterior negativity (or ERAN), was generated in Broca's area and its right hemisphere homologue. Later research using fMRI (functional magnetic resonance imaging) and PET (positron emission tomography) converged with electrophysiological measures in suggesting overlap in a number of brain regions involved in processing linguistic and musical structure, including (but not limited to) Broca's area (Koelsch et al., 2002; Tillmann, Janata, & Bharucha, 2003; Schmithorst, 2005; Brown, Martinez, & Parsons, 2006).

Of course, it is possible to raise a number of questions about these findings. For example, the musical P600 was elicited in a study where participants were explicitly asked to attend to (and make decisions about) the harmonic structure of a sequence. In other studies using out-of-key chords in which the participants' attention is not drawn to harmonic structure via task instructions, a P600 is not always elicited by out-of-key chords. Instead, one often observes a different, negative-going ERP component (the N500), which is distinct from ERPs components elicited by language processing (e.g. Koelsch, 2005). In terms of the ERAN, while this component does appear to have a generator in left Broca's area, it also appears to have a stronger generator in the right hemisphere Broca's homologue, suggesting an opposite hemispheric bias for grammatical processing in music and language (cf. Tillmann et al., 2006). Finally, with regard to overlapping brain regions for music and language observed with fMRI and PET, it is possible that functionally separate networks are interdigitated within a common cortical region, and cannot be resolved given the spatial resolution of current neuroimaging techniques (Peretz & Zatorre, 2005).

The resource-sharing framework

The preceding sections show that neuropsychology and neuroimaging yield rather different perspectives on music–language relations in the brain, the former favouring domain-specificity and the latter challenging this view. While there are certainly open questions about existing neuroimaging findings (as outlined above), these data at least raise the possibility that there are aspects of music and language (e.g. syntax) that exhibit domain-specificity *and* neural overlap. If this is the case, then one needs a conceptual framework for reconciling this contradiction and for guiding future work. Resource sharing is one such a framework, and is based on two basic principles:

1. Language and music involve domain-specific representations—for example, knowledge of words and their syntactic properties involves a set of representations which are distinct from the representations of chords and their harmonic relations. The resource sharing framework posits that domain-specific representations are stored in long-term memory in distinct associative networks (cf. Tillmann, Bharucha, & Bigand, 2000). Hence these representations are susceptible to selective damage,

leading to dissociations between linguistic and musical cognition (e.g. the case of G.L.).

2. When similar cognitive operations are conducted on domain-specific representations, the brain shares neural resources between the two domains—principle 2 posits that representational specificity (as posited by principle 1) should be conceptually distinguished from processing specificity. That is, there are circumstances where similar cognitive operations are conducted on domain-specific knowledge, as part of building coherent percepts. In this case, principle 2 suggests that these operations share neural resources. Hence it is possible to observe similar brain signatures for certain aspects of linguistic and musical processing.

The remainder of this paper will focus on evidence for resource sharing in online syntactic comprehension ('Syntax' section), and in learning linguistic and musical sound systems ('Phonology' section). Before proceeding, it is worth commenting on the motivation for these choices. In terms of online comprehension, there are several areas (other than syntax) where one could explore resource sharing, such as the affective appraisal of auditory signals (Juslin & Laukka, 2003; Thompson, Schellenberg, & Husain, 2004) and the encoding of melodic contour patterns (Patel, Peretz, Tramo, & Labrecque, 1998b). Syntactic processing is chosen because it has been the locus of strong claims for domain-specificity in both language and music (e.g. Fodor, 1983; Jackendoff & Lerdahl, 2006). It is also arguably unique to humans, and cross-domain research may yield insights into basic mechanisms underlying this special aspect of human cognition. Finally, linguistic and musical syntax have been well studied both theoretically and empirically, making this area attractive for research.

In terms of the second topic, a focus on the learning of sound categories is motivated by growing evidence for a link between musical ability and linguistic phonemic abilities (e.g. Slevc & Miyake, 2006; Wong, Skoe, Russo, Dees, & Kraus, 2007). This finding has significant implications for educational and clinical issues, including the rehabilitation of certain language disorders (cf. Goswami, 2009). Understanding the nature of shared processing for sound category learning may thus have important practical consequences.

Syntax

Language is a syntactic system: it has discrete structural elements (e.g. words) which are combined in principled ways to form hierarchically organized sequences (e.g. sentences). These sequences have a rich relationship between their structure and the meaning they convey. For example, the sentence 'The girl who kissed the boy opened the door' contains the word string 'the boy opened the door', but a speaker of English knows that the boy did not do the opening, because the relative pronoun 'who' indicates an embedded relative clause that separates 'girl' and its dependent verb, 'opened' (Figure 22.1).

Like language, music also has discrete structural elements (e.g. tones or chords) which are combined in principled ways into hierarchically-structured sequences (Lerdahl & Jackendoff, 1983). The syntactic architecture of these sequences differs from linguistic syntax in a number of ways. For example, music does not have the

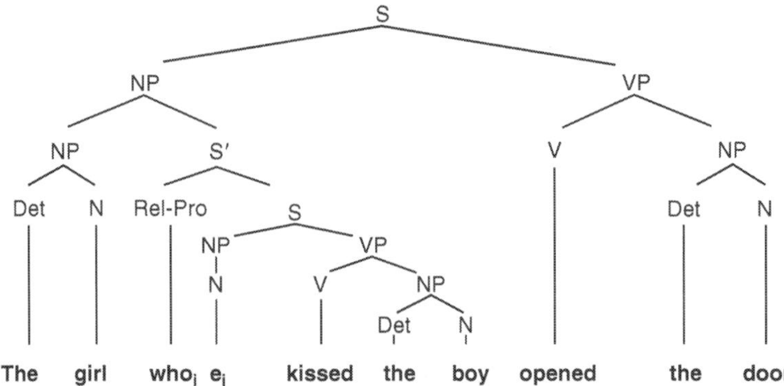

Fig. 22.1 A sentence of English, showing its hierarchical phrase structure. Note that although the words 'boy' and 'opened' are immediately adjacent, they belong to different syntactic phrases. (S, sentence; NP, noun phrase, VP, verb phrase, S', sentence modifier [relative clause]; N, noun; V, verb; Det, determiner; Rel-Pro, relative pronoun.) Within the clause the relative pronoun 'who' is referred to as a filler and is interpreted as the actor for the verb 'kissed'. This relationship is identified by the presence of a co-indexed empty element ei in the subject position of the relative clause. Reproduced from Patel, A.D., Music, Language, and the Brain, © 2008, Oxford University Press, with permission.

same kind of dependency structure as language, where an incoming element demands a cognitive connection with a specific distant prior structural element (as in the relation between 'opened' and 'girl' in the sentence in the previous paragraph). Instead, certain pitches in musical sequences are considered structurally more prominent than others, forming an 'event hierarchy' that defines the structural skeleton of a piece (Bharucha, 1984), as illustrated in Figure 22.2.

Before discussing evidence for resource sharing in the syntactic processing of language and music, it is worth reviewing some basic information about musical keys, since key structure is central to the experiments that follow.

Some basics of musical key

One important aspect of musical syntax concerns the notion of a musical 'key'. In Western tonal music, music within a given key selects a subset of seven out of 12 available pitches within the octave, which form a musical scale (such as the major scale). One of these pitches (the 'tonic', or 'do' in the do-re-mi system of labelling pitches) acts as the most stable pitch, often serving as a point of repose. Other pitches vary in their degree of structural stability: for example the seventh tone of the scale ('ti') is very unstable, and conveys a sense of restlessness that requires resolution. This 'tonal hierarchy', in combination with rhythmic factors, plays an important role in determining which pitches are perceived as structurally more prominent than others in musical sequences (the 'event hierarchy' mentioned earlier).

An interesting feature of the tonal hierarchy is the contrast between physical and psychological distances between tones in a key. When listeners are asked to rate the perceived relatedness of tones in a key context, a subset of three tones (do, mi, and so, or c, e, and g in the key of C-major) are rated as closely related each other. The remaining

Fig. 22.2 A time-span reduction of the first two phrases of the children's song 'Hush little baby' (tree notation from Lerdahl & Jackendoff, 1983). Shorter branches terminate on less important pitches, while longer branches terminate on more important pitches. The lower staves show the dominant events at successively higher levels of tree structure. [The oval shape in the right part of the tree is meant to indicate that the short motif that projects upward to it from the left (the first four notes of the second phrase, C-C-G-G) is subordinate to both branches touched by the oval, not just the left branch (cf. Lerdahl & Jackendoff, 1983, p. 138). This subtlety is not essential for the current discussion.] Reproduced from Edward W. Large, Caroline Palmer, and Jordan B Pollack, Reduced memory representations in music, cognitive Science, 19(1), pp. 53–96 ©1995 with permission from John Wiley and Sons.

scale tones are rated as less related to each other and to the tonic note, and out-of-key notes (e.g. c#) are rated as distantly related to notes within the key (in simple tonal melodies these out-of-key notes pop out as 'sour notes'). Using multidimensional scaling, these relatedness judgements can be represented spatially, with the degree of perceived relatedness corresponding to the distance between the tones on the graph (Figure 22.3). A notable feature of this figure is the large distance which separates tones which are adjacent in frequency, such as c and c#. This contrast between the physical and psychological proximity of pitches is likely to be part of what animates tonal music.

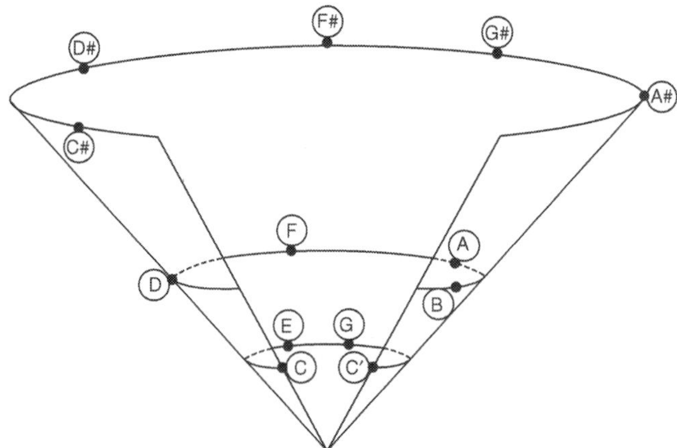

Fig. 22.3 Geometrical representation of perceived similarity between musical pitches in a tonal context. The data are oriented toward the C major scale, where C serves as the tonic. C′ is the pitch one octave above C. Reprinted from Cognitive Psychology, 11(3), Carol L. Krumhansl, The psychological representation of musical pitch in a tonal context, pp. 346–74, copyright (1979). With permission from Elsevier.

Tones from a musical key can be combined to form chords, which are then combined in sequences to form chord progressions. Both the 'vertical' and 'horizontal' organization of chords follows principles to which listeners are sensitive (Smith & Melara, 1990, Lhost & Ashley, 2006). At a higher level still, musical keys themselves are have a systematic organization with respect to each other. Keys sharing more tones and chords are perceived as more closely related to each other, forming a 'circle of fifths' (Figure 22.4) where increasing distance between two keys along the circle corresponds to a decrease in the perceived relatedness between these keys (Thompson & Cuddy, 1992).

In terms of relating structure and meaning in music, the key system has an important role to play. Composers use out-of-key notes and chords in systematic ways to create a sense of tension in musical pieces (Lerdahl & Krumhansl, 2007), and empirical studies indicate that the ebb and flow of tension is part of the emotional meaning of music (Meyer, 1956; Steinbeis, Koelsch, & Sloboda, 2006).

Structural integration in language and music

In comprehending language and music, the structural relationship of incoming elements (such as words or chords) to preceding events must be determined in order to make sense of the sequence. On the basis of neuroimaging data and cognitive theory, Patel (2003) suggested that some aspect of this structural integration process is shared by language and music. Specifically, it was proposed that structural integration involves the rapid and selective activation of items in associative networks, and that language and music share the neural resources that provide this activation to the networks where domains-specific representation reside. This idea, termed the 'shared syntactic integration resource hypothesis' (SSIRH) can be conceptually diagrammed as follows (Figure 22.5).

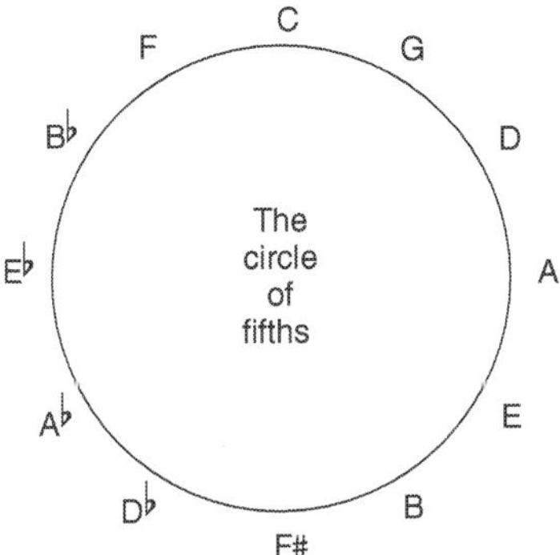

Fig. 22.4 The circle of fifths for major keys. Each key is represented by a letter standing for its tonic.

The diagram in Figure 22.5 represents the hypothesis that linguistic and musical syntactic representations are stored in distinct brain networks (and hence can be selectively damaged), whereas there is overlap in the networks which provide neural resources for the activation of stored syntactic representations. Arrows indicate functional connections between networks. Note that the circles do not necessarily imply highly focal brain areas. For example, linguistic and musical representation networks could extend across a number of brain regions, or exist as functionally segregated networks within the same brain regions.

How does this proposal map onto neural architecture? At the moment the answer to this question is not known. In its original formulation, the SSIRH combined the functional proposal outlined above with a rough localizationist proposal, namely that that neural resources reside in frontal brain regions, while syntactic representations reside in posterior regions. This was inspired in part by a view of the inferior frontal cortex as providing activation to posterior regions for the purpose of selecting between competing representations in those regions, both in language and in other domains (Thompson-Schill, 2006, cf. Hagoort, 2006). Patel (2003) noted that testing this

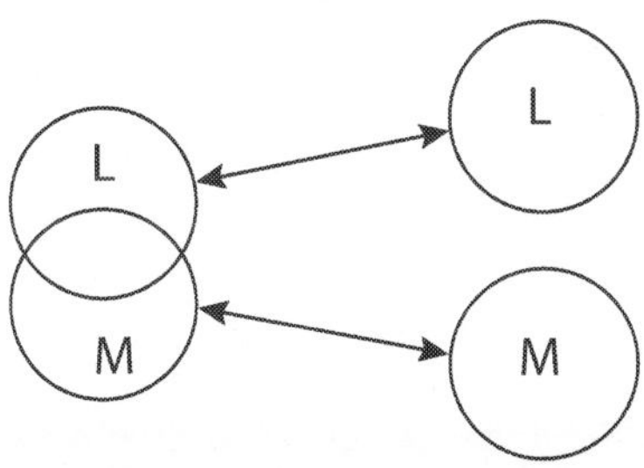

Fig. 22.5 Schematic diagram of the functional relationship between linguistic and musical syntactic processing. L, language; M, music.

proposal required localization techniques such as fMRI, applied to within-subjects comparisons of syntactic processing in language and music. Such work remains to be done. For the current purposes, the salient point is the functional and localization aspects of the SSIRH can be conceptually decoupled.

What sorts of predictions does this hypothesis make? One prediction, based on the idea of shared, limited resources for activation, is that simultaneous resource-intensive structural integrations in language and music should interfere with each other.

In language, resource-intensive structural integrations come in at least two forms. First, an incoming word can be distant from a prior word with which it shares a syntactic dependency. According to Dependency Locality Theory (Gibson, 1998, 2000), this integration is costly because it involves reactivating the representation of the prior dependent word, whose activation level has decayed since it was first encountered. This theory accounts for a number of language processing phenomena, including the difference in processing difficulty for sentences containing subject-relative versus object-relative clauses. For example, by a number of measures, sentence a) below is easier to process than sentence b) (King & Just, 1991).

a) The cop that met the spy wrote a report about the case.

b) The cop that the spy met wrote a report about the case.

In a) the subject-relative clause 'that met the spy' contains only local integrations, while in sentence b) the object relative clause 'that the spy met' requires a distant integration between 'met' and 'that'.

Another type of resource-intensive structural integration in language involves the violation of a syntactic expectancy. There is growing evidence that the human parser continuously predicts the syntactic category of upcoming words (Gibson, 2006; Lau, Stroud, Plesch, & Phillips, 2006), and that violations of these predictions cause processing difficulty. For example, according to 'constraint satisfaction' models, during incremental sentence processing different possible syntactic analyses of a sentence have different levels of activation, with the currently preferred analysis having the highest level of activation. An incoming word that is syntactically unexpected can force a re-ranking among the possible syntactic analyses, and this is costly because resources must be reallocated to boost the activation of a different structure (e.g. MacDonald, 1993, cf. Marslen-Wilson, 1975).

Expectancy effects can account for a range of processing phenomena in language (Levy, 2008), including the difficulty of 'garden path' sentences such as:

c) The man accepted the prize was not going to him.

In c), when a person first processes 'the prize', s/he tends to interpret it as the direct object of 'accepted', and does not expect a following verb. The appearance of 'was' violates this expectancy and forces a revision of the preferred syntactic structure (making 'the prize' the subject of a reduced sentence complement), leading to processing difficulty (Trueswell & Kim, 1998).

Turning to music, one can conceive of resource-intensive structural integrations as those involving incoming elements which are harmonically distant from the current tonal context, where distance is measured in terms of tonal pitch space (Lerdahl, 2001, cf. Figures 22.3 and 22.4). For example, when in the key of C, a D-flat major chord is harmonically quite distant (five steps away on the circle of fifths). Activating harmonically distant elements is costly because they have not been primed by spreading activation in associative networks that store knowledge of harmonic relations (Bhaurcha, 1984; Tillmann et al., 2000). Note that given the structural norms of tonal music, events that are harmonically distant from the current context (e.g. out-of-key notes and chords) are also unexpected (Huron, 2006). Hence manipulations of harmonic distance in music can also be thought of as manipulations of musical syntactic expectancy.

The foregoing discussion suggests that simultaneous resource-intensive structural integrations in language and music can be created by pairing resource-intensive sentences with resource-intensive musical sequences. More specifically, words that cause structural integration difficulty in sentences (due to distance or expectancy effects) can be aligned with out-of-key notes or chord in tonal music. According to the SSIRH, this should lead to interference between language and music processing (Patel, 2003). The following section describes three tests of this prediction, one using ERPs and two using behavioural methods.

Testing resource sharing with neural and behavioural methods

As background, it is worth noting that past studies combining language and music to study processing interactions have focused on the relationship between linguistic semantic processing and musical harmonic processing. For example, in an ERP study Besson, Faita, Peretz, and Bonnel (1998) used opera-like vocal melodies to combine semantic incongruities in language with out-of-key notes in music. The authors found that the semantic anomalies gave rise to a N400, while the out-of-key notes gave rise to a late positive component (resembling a P600), and that a simple additive model predicted the data for combined semantic/harmonic violations quite well. Using similar stimuli in a behavioural study, Bonnel, Faïta, Peretz, and Besson (2001) had listeners either perform a single task (judge the incongruity of final word or note) or a dual-task (judge the incongruity of both), and found that the dual task did not result in a decrease in performance compared to the single-task conditions. These findings have been taken as evidence for the cognitive independence of musical and linguistic processing.[1] In contrast to these studies, the studies reported here combine a linguistic *syntactic* manipulation with a musical harmonic manipulation, which from the foregoing discussion of the SSIRH, is predicted to lead to an interaction. Each study below takes a different approach, but all three provide converging evidence which supports this prediction.

Koelsch, Gunter, Wittforth, and Sammler (2005) conducted an ERP study in which short sentences were presented visually in a word-by-word format simultaneously with musical chords, with one chord per word. In some sentences, the final word created a grammatical violation via a gender disagreement (the sentences were in German, in which many nouns are marked for gender). An example of a gender violation used in

[1] A study by Poulin-Charronat, Bigand, Madurell, and Peereman (2005) combined semantic anomalies in language with a harmonic manipulation of chord sequence structure in music, and found an interaction between semantic and musical processing. However, subsequent research by Escoffier and Tillmann (2006) suggests that this is due to a non-specific effect of the musical manipulation on attention, rather than representing a specific cognitive link between semantic and harmonic processing.

this study was: Er trinkt den kühlen Bier, 'He drinks the$_{masculine}$ cool$_{masculine}$ beer$_{neuter}$. This final word violated a syntactic expectancy in language. The chord sequences were designed to strongly invoke a particular key, and the final chord could either be the tonic chord of that key or an unexpected out-of-key chord from a distant key (e.g. a D-flat major chord at the end of a C-major sequence). The participants (all non-musicians) were instructed to ignore the music and simply judge if the last word of the sentence was linguistically correct.

Koelsch et al. focused on early ERP negativities elicited by syntactically incongruous words and chords. Previous research on language or music alone had shown that the linguistic syntactic incongruities were associated with a left anterior negativity (LAN), while the musical incongruities were associated with an early right anterior negativity (ERAN) (Gunter, Friederici, & Schriefers, 2000; Koelsch, Gunter, Friederici, & Schröger, 2000; Friederici, 2002). For their combined language-music stimuli, Koelsch et al. found that when sentences ended grammatically but were accompanied by an out of key-chord, a normal ERAN was produced. Similarly, when chord sequences ended normally but were accompanied by a syntactically incongruous word, a normal LAN was produced. The question of interest was how these brain responses would interact when a sequence had simultaneous syntactic incongruities in language and music. The main finding was that the brain responses were not simply additive. Instead, there was an interaction: the LAN to syntactically incongruous words was significantly *smaller* when these words were accompanied by an out-of-key chord, as if the processes underlying the LAN and ERAN were competing for similar neural resources. In a control experiment, Koelsch et al. showed that this was not due to general attentional effects because the LAN was not influenced by a simple auditory oddball paradigm involving physically deviant tones on the last word in a sentence. Thus the study supported the prediction that tasks which combine linguistic and musical syntactic integration will show interference between the two processes.

Turning to recent behavioural research, Fedorenko, Patel, Casasanto, Winawer, and Gibson (2009) manipulated syntactic integration difficulty via the distance between dependent words, rather than via expectancy violations. These researchers used fully grammatical sentences of the type shown in a) and b) in the earlier section 'Structural integration in language and music', reproduced here:

a) The cop that met the *spy* wrote a report about the case.

b) The cop that the spy *met* wrote a report about the case.

The sentences were sung to melodies (one note per word) that did or did not contain an out-of-key note on the last word of the relative clause, *underlined* above. (Recall that this word is associated with a distant structural integration in b) but not in a)). A control condition was included for an attention-getting but non-harmonically deviant musical event: a 10-dB increase in volume on the last word of the relative clause. After each sentence, participants were asked a comprehension question, and accuracy was assumed to reflect processing difficulty.

The results revealed an interaction between musical and linguistic processing: comprehension accuracy was lower for sentences with distant versus local syntactic integrations (as expected), but crucially, this difference was larger when melodies contained an out-of-key note. The control condition (loud note) did not produce this effect: the difference between the two sentence types was of the same size as that in the conditions that did not contain an out-of-key note. These results suggest that some aspect of structural integration in language and music relies on shared processing resources.

The final study described here, by Slevc, Rosenberg, & Patel (2009), manipulated linguistic structural integration difficulty via syntactic expectancies, and also directly compared the influence of musical harmonic manipulations on linguistic syntactic vs. semantic processing (cf. Steinbeis & Koelsch, 2008). However, unlike the Koelsch et al. (2005) study, linguistic expectancy was manipulated via garden-path sentences rather than via grammatical incongruities.

In Slevc et al.'s study, participants read sentences phrase by phrase on a computer screen. They controlled the timing of phrases by pushing a button to get the next phrase. In such studies, the amount of time spent viewing a phrase is assumed to reflect the amount of processing difficulty associated with that phrase. This 'self-paced reading' paradigm has been used often in psycholinguistic research. The novel aspect of Slevc et al.'s study was that each phrase was accompanied by a chord so that the entire sentence made a coherent, chorale-style chord progression.

The sentences contained either a linguistic syntactic or semantic manipulation. In the syntactic manipulation, sentences like d) included either a full or reduced sentence complement clause, achieved by including or omitting the word 'that'. (Note: the vertical slashes below indicate the individual phrases used in the self-paced reading experiment):

d) The scientist | wearing | thick glasses | confirmed (that) | the hypothesis | *was* | being | studied | in his lab.

In such sentences, the omission of 'that' results in the reduced complement clause 'the hypothesis was being studied in his lab'. In this case, readers tend to interpret 'the hypothesis' as the direct object of 'confirmed', which causes syntactic integration difficulty when 'was' is encountered, as this signals that 'the hypothesis' is actually the subject of an embedded clause. In other words, the simple omission of 'that' leads to a downstream localized processing difficulty (on 'was') due to violation of a syntactic expectancy.

In the semantic manipulation, sentences like e) included either a semantically consistent or anomalous word, thereby confirming or violating a semantic expectancy.

e) The boss | warned | the mailman | to watch | for angry | *dogs / pigs* | when | delivering | the mail.

The chord played during the critical word (underlined) was either harmonically in-key or out-of-key. (Out-of-key chords were drawn from keys three to five steps away on the circle of fifths from the key of the phrase. For example, a chord progression in C major might have an E-major chord as the out-of-key chord, cf. Figure 22.4). Since out-of-key chords are harmonically unexpected, the experiment crossed syntactic or semantic expectancy in language with harmonic expectancy in music. The dependent variable of interest was the reading time for the critical word.

The main finding was a significant three-way interaction between linguistic manipulation type (syntactic or semantic), linguistic expectancy, and musical expectancy. That is, syntactically and semantically unexpected words were read more slowly than their expected counterparts, but a simultaneous out-of-key chord caused substantial additional slowdown for syntactically unexpected words, but not for semantically unexpected words. Thus, processing a harmonically unexpected chord interfered with the processing of syntactic, but not semantic, relations in language. (A control experiment showed that when a chord of unexpected timbre, which created an attention-getting psychoacoustic event, was aligned with the target word, it did not interfere with either type of linguistic processing.) Once again, these results support the claim that neural resources are shared between linguistic and musical structural integration.

The three studies described above provide converging evidence for interactions between musical and linguistic syntactic processing. Interestingly, there appears to be a specific interaction between musical harmonic processing and syntactic (versus semantic) processing in language, suggesting some level of separation between the brain systems that handle linguistic syntax versus semantics (cf. Osterhout et al., in press; Tyler & Marslen-Wilson, 2008). Furthermore, the work points to a specific point of convergence between linguistic and musical syntactic processing, namely, a sharing of neural resources for activating items in associative networks as part of a process of structural integration. This shows how linguistic and musical syntax can have an important point of contact despite many differences in the formal organization of syntactic structures in the two domains.

In terms of connections to broader issues, studies combining language and music could help refine our understanding of the brain mechanisms involved in generating syntactic expectations. It seems that in both language and music the brain continuously predicts the structural categories of upcoming events, perhaps because this leads to more efficient processing of predicted events (which constitute the majority of events). Expectation-based syntactic processing is an emerging research area in psycholinguistics (Levy, 2008), and can perhaps benefit from a conceptual synthesis with the study of expectation in music processing, a topic of active research with a long intellectual history (Meyer, 1956; Huron, 2006). Using music and language together could help identify the more abstract cognitive operations that are being computed by brain circuits involved in generating syntactic expectancies.

Phonology

The remainder of this paper briefly discusses evidence for shared resources involved in learning the sound systems of language and music. The focus is on the relationship between musical abilities and phonemic abilities in language. There is growing evidence that either pitch-related or rhythm-related musical skills are related to phonemic abilities in language, such as the segmentation, categorization, or discrimination of phonemes. However, as noted earlier in this paper, there is also evidence from neuropsychology that auditory phonemic encoding of sounds can be selectively disrupted by brain damage, leaving the perception of musical sounds intact (i.e. in pure word deafness). Hence the relationship between musical and phonemic skills fits nicely into a resource-sharing framework, under the assumption that the end *products* of phonemic development are unique, but that some of the *processes* that give rise to these representations are shared by music and language (cf. McMullen & Saffran, 2004). If this is the case, the key issue is to specify the nature of the shared neural resources linking music and language. This issue is addressed below, after describing evidence for a relationship between musical and phonemic abilities.

Evidence for a link between musical and phonemic skills

This section describes two studies which support a link between pitch-related musical abilities and linguistic phonemic abilities. For studies examining a link between musical rhythmic abilities and linguistic abilities, see Overy (2003) and Corriveau & Goswami (2009).

Anvari, Trainor, Woodside, and Levy (2002) studied the relation between early reading skills and musical development in a large sample of English-speaking four- and five-year-olds. Learning to read English requires mapping visual symbols onto phonemic contrasts, and thus taps into linguistic sound categorization skills. The children were given an extensive battery of tasks, which included tests of reading, phonemic awareness, vocabulary, auditory memory, and mathematics. (Phonemic awareness refers to the ability to identify the sound components of a word, and a large body of research indicates that children with greater phonemic awareness have advantages in learning to read.) On the musical side, both musical pitch and rhythm discrimination were tested. The pitch tasks included same/different discrimination of short melodies and chords, and the rhythm tasks involved same/different discrimination of short rhythmic patterns and reproduction of rhythms by singing. The most interesting findings concerned the five-year-olds. For this group, performance on musical pitch (but not rhythm) tasks predicted unique variance in reading abilities, even when phonemic awareness was controlled for. Furthermore, statistical analysis showed that this relation could not be accounted for via the indirect influence of other variables such as auditory memory.

Turning to research on adults, Slevc and Miyake (2006) examined the relationship between proficiency in a second language and musical ability. Several prior studies on this topic had not found any significant relationship between these variables. Crucially, however, these studies had always relied on participant's self reports of their own musical ability. Slevc and Miyake went beyond self-report and tested both linguistic and musical skills in a quantitative fashion. Working with a group of 50 Japanese adult learners of English living in the USA, they administered language tests which examined receptive and productive phonology, syntax, and lexical knowledge. (The tests of receptive phonology included identifying words which differed by a single phoneme, e.g. 'clown' vs. 'crown'.) The musical tests examined pitch pattern perception, e.g. via the detection of an altered note in a chord or in a short melody, as well as accuracy in singing back short melodies. In addition to these tests, the researchers also measured a number of variables known to be associated with second language proficiency, such as age of arrival in the foreign country, number of years spent living there, amount of time spent speaking the second language (L2), and phonological short-term memory in the native language. The question of interest was whether musical ability could account for variance in L2 ability beyond that accounted for by these other variables. As in Anvari et al. (2002), the authors used hierarchical regression to tease apart the influence of different variables. The results were clear: musical ability did in fact predict unique variance in

L2 skills. Most relevant for the current discussion, this predictive relationship was confined to L2 receptive and productive phonology, i.e. to phonemic skills.

What is the nature of the shared neural resources?

What neural mechanisms could mediate associations between musical abilities and phonemic skills? Overy (2003) has suggested that musical training improves temporal processing abilities, which are relevant to phonological segmentation skills (cf. Goswami, 2009). In an update of this idea, Tallal and Gaab (2006) suggested that musical training improves auditory rapid spectrotemporal processing, which is used in the processing of linguistic phonemic components. Both hypotheses suggest that musical experience improves sensory encoding of dynamically changing sounds, and that this improved sensory processing benefits the perception of speech. However, they do not specify at what level of the nervous system this 'sensory tuning' acts.

A recent study by Wong, Skoe, Russo, Dees, and Kraus (2007) provides intriguing evidence that such tuning occurs at a very early stage of brain processing. The study used scalp-recorded electroencephalography (EEG) to examine an oscillatory brainstem neural response to sound known as the frequency-following response (FFR), which is thought to be generated in the inferior colliculus and other brainstem regions. The FFR has been shown to have an interesting relationship to voice pitch, in that its oscillation contains considerable energy at the fundamental frequency (F0) of the voice, and can dynamically track linguistically-relevant F0 changes over short time scales (such as a single syllable, approximately 250 milliseconds in duration). Previous research had examined the FFR during perception of syllables of Mandarin Chinese. (Mandarin uses pitch to distinguish between words, so that a single syllable can have different lexical meanings depending on its pitch pattern.) Specifically, Krishnan, Xu, Gandour, and Cariani (2005) examined the FFR during perception of Mandarin monosyllables and found that the quality of F0 tracking was superior in native speakers of Mandarin than in native speakers of English. This suggested that auditory experience could tune subcortical sound processing mechanisms.

Wong et al. (2007) extended this work by examining F0 tracking of Mandarin monosyllables in musicians versus non-musicians, neither of whom had prior familiarity with Mandarin. Participants heard the syllable 'mi', spoken with different lexical tones, in the background as they watched a movie. Wong et al. found that that the quality of F0 tracking was superior in musicians, and found positive correlations between F0 tracking quality and amount of musical training, and between F0 tracking quality and performance on identification and discrimination tasks using Mandarin syllables. While prior evidence had indicated that musicians are more sensitive to subtle pitch variations in speech than non-musicians (as reflected in behavioural measures and cortical evoked potentials, e.g. Schön, Magne, & Besson, 2004; Magne, Schön, & Besson, 2006) Wong et al.'s findings were surprising because they suggest that musical experience influences speech processing at a very basic neural level. However, the correlational nature of the findings does raise questions about causality, as discussed in the next section (cf. Patel & Iversen, 2007).

Avenues for future research

The hypotheses of Overy (2003) and Tallal and Gaab (2006) suggest that musical training actively shapes brain mechanisms that impact linguistic ability. However, most of the behavioural and neural data supporting an association between musical skills and phonemic skills (including the study of Wong et al., 2007) are correlational in nature. Hence it is not clear if the neural resources for musical and phonemic processing are genuinely intertwined in the brain, or inborn differences in brain anatomy or physiology influence distinct neural resources involved in musical versus phonemic abilities. The only way to address this issue is via experimental studies where groups of individuals are matched at the outset in terms of neural and behavioural measures of musical ability, and then exposed to different amounts of musical training (cf. Norton, Winner, Cronin, Overy, Lee, & Schlaug, 2005). If musical training improves phonemic abilities, this would be strong evidence for shared neural resources, and a variety of neural techniques could then be brought to bear to study the nature of these resources (e.g. ERPs, fMRI, MEG, transcranial magnetic stimulation (TMS)).

Another important issue for future research concerns the acoustic features used in musical training versus phonemic testing. The study of Wong et al. (2007) focused on linguistic pitch processing, which was sensible since pitch is a highly structured aspect of music. However, it is of considerable interest to know whether musical training that focuses on one acoustic dimension (e.g. pitch) can benefit phonemic skills that rely on a different acoustic dimension (e.g. timbre). If this is the case, it would suggest that language and music share more abstract cognitive processes involved in sound categorization, possibly involving common cortical mechanisms.

Conclusion

This paper has presented a framework for music-language studies which draws a basic distinction between domain-specific representations and shared neural resources which act upon these representations, either in online processing or as part of cognitive development. Of course, language and music are unlikely to be unique in terms of resource sharing. When the two domains draw on common brain resources, they do so because these resources provide a particular processing function needed in both domains. If other mental faculties also require these resources, they will likely share them with both language and music.

While the resource-sharing framework is rooted in cognitive neuroscience, testing this framework requires an integrated approach involving cognitive theory and behavioural methods. The goal of such work is to generate hypothesis-driven research which will illuminate the shared cognitive foundations of linguistic and musical abilities.

Acknowledgements

I thank John Iversen and Bob Slevc for helpful comments. Supported by Neurosciences Research Foundation as part of its programme on music and the brain at The Neurosciences Institute, where ADP is the Esther J. Burnham Senior Fellow.

References

Anvari, S., Trainor, L. J., Woodside, J., & Levy, B. A. (2002). Relations among musical skills, phonological processing, and early reading ability in preschool children. *Journal of Experimental Child Psychology*, *83*, 111–30.

Besson, M., Faita, F., Peretz I., & Bonnel, A.J.R. (1998). Singing in the brain: independence of lyrics and tunes. *Psychological Science*, *9*, 494–98.

Bharucha, J.J. (1984). Event hierarchies, tonal hierarchies and assimilation: A reply to Deutsch and Dowling. *Journal of Experimental Psychology, General*, *113*, 421–25.

Bonnel, A.-M., Faïta, F., Peretz, I., & Besson, M. (2001). Divided attention between lyrics and tunes of operatic songs: Evidence for independent processing. *Perception and Psychophysics*, *63*, 1201–13.

Brown, S., Martinez, M.J., & Parsons, L.M. (2006). Music and language side by side in the brain: a PET study of the generation of melodies and sentences. *European Journal of Neuroscience*, *23*, 2791–803.

Corriveau, K.H., & Goswami, U. (2009). Rhythmic motor entrainment in children with speech and language impairments: Tapping to the beat. *Cortex*, *45*, 119–30.

Escoffier, N. & Tillmann, B. (2006). Tonal function modulates speed of visual processing. In M. Baroni, R. Addessi, R. Caterina, & M. Costa (Eds.) *Proceedings of the 9th International Conference on Music Perception & Cognition (ICMPC9)* (p. 18–78). Bologna: SMPC and ESCOM.

Fedorenko, E., Patel, A. D., Casasanto, D., Winawer, J., & Gibson. E. (2009). Structural integration in language and music: Evidence for a shared system. *Memory & Cognition*, *37*, 1–9.

Fodor, J. A. (1983). *Modularity of mind.* Cambridge, MA: MIT Press.

Friederici, A. D. (2002). Towards a neural basis of auditory sentence processing. *Trends in Cognitive Science*, *6*, 78–84.

Gibson, E. (1998). Linguistic complexity: Locality of syntactic dependencies. *Cognition*, *68*, 1–76.

Gibson, E. (2000). The dependency locality theory: A distance-based theory of linguistic complexity. In Y. Miyashita, A. Marantaz, & W. O'Neil (Eds.), *Image, Language, Brain* (pp. 95–126). Cambridge, MA: MIT Press.

Gibson, E. (2006). The interaction of top-down and bottom-up statistics in the resolution of syntactic category ambiguity. *Journal of Memory and Language*, *54*, 363–88.

Goswami, U. (2009). Mind, brain, and literacy. Biomarkers as usable knowledge for education. *Mind, Brain, and Education*, *3*, 176–84.

Gouvea, A., Phillips, C., Kazanina, N., & Poeppel, D. (2010). The linguistic processes underlying the P600. *Language and Cognitive Processes*, *25*, 149–88.

Gunter, T. C., Friederici, A. D., & Schriefers, H. (2000). Syntactic gender and semantic expectancy: ERPs reveal early autonomy and late interaction. *Journal of Cognitive Neuroscience*, *12*, 556–68.

Hagoort, P. (2006). On Broca, brain and binding. In Y. Grodzinsky & A. Amunts (Eds.), *Broca's Region* (pp. 242–53). New York: Oxford University Press.

Huron, D. (2006) *Sweet Anticipation: Music and the Psychology of Expectation.* Cambridge, MA: MIT Press.

Jackendoff, R., & Lerdahl, F. (2006). The capacity for music: What is it, and what's special about it? *Cognition*, *100*, 33–72.

Juslin, P., & Laukka, P. (2003). Communication of emotions in vocal expression and music performance: Different channels, same code? *Psychological Bulletin*, *129*, 770–814.

King, J. & Just, M. A. (1991). Individual differences in syntactic processing: The role of working memory. *Journal of Memory and Language*, *30*, 580–602.

Koelsch, S. (2005). Neural substrates of processing syntax and semantics in music. *Current Opinion in Neurobiology*, *15*, 207–12.

Koelsch, S., Gunter, T. C., Friederici, A. D., & Schröger, E. (2000). Brain indices of music processing: 'non-musicians' are musical. *Journal of Cognitive Neuroscience*, *12*, 520–41.

Koelsch S., Gunter T.C., von Cramon D.Y., Zysset S., Lohmann G., & Friederici A.D. (2002). Bach speaks: A cortical 'language-network' serves the processing of music. *Neuroimage*, *17*, 956–66.

Koelsch S., Gunter T.C., Wittforth, M., & Sammler, D. (2005). Interaction between syntax processing in language and music: An ERP study. *Journal of Cognitive Neuroscience*, *17*, 1565–77.

Krishnan, A., Xu, Y., Gandour, J., & Cariani, P. (2005). Encoding of pitch in the human brainstem is sensitive to language experience. *Cognitive Brain Research*, *25*, 161–68.

Krumhansl, C.L. (1979). The psychological representation of musical pitch in a tonal context. *Cognitive Psychology*, *11*, 346–74.

Large, E. W., Palmer, C., & Pollack, J. B. (1995). Reduced memory representations for music. *Cognitive Science*, *19*, 53–96.

Lau, E., Stroud, C., Plesch, S., & Phillips, C. (2006). The role of structural prediction in rapid syntactic analysis. *Brain & Language*, *98*, 74–88.

Lerdahl, F. (2001). *Tonal Pitch Space.* Oxford: Oxford University Press.

Lerdahl, F., & Jackendoff, R. (1983). *A Generative Theory of Tonal Music.* Cambridge, MA: MIT Press.

Lerdahl, F., & Krumhansl, C. (2007). Modeling tonal tension. *Music Perception*, *24*, 329–66.

Levy, R. (2008). Expectation-based syntactic comprehension. *Cognition*, *106*, 1126–77.

Lhost, E., & Ashley, R. (2006). Jazz, blues and the language of harmony: Flexibility in online harmonic processing. In M. Baroni, Addessi A. R., Caterina, R., & Costa, M. (Eds.) *Proceedings of the 9th International Conference on Music Perception & Cognition (ICMPC9)* (pp. 1282–88). Bologna: SMPC and ESCOM.

MacDonald, M. C. (1993). The interaction of lexical and syntactic ambiguity. *Journal of Memory and Language*, *32*, 692–715.

Maess, B., Koelsch, S., Gunter, T., & Friederici, A.D. (2001). Musical syntax is processed in Broca's area: an MEG study. *Nature Neuroscience*, *4*, 540–45.

Magne, C., Schön, M., & Besson, M. (2006). Musician children detect pitch violations in both music and language better than nonmusician children: Behavioral and electrophysiological approaches. *J. Cognitive Neuroscience*, *18*, 199–211.

Marin, O. S. M., & Perry, D.W. (1999). Neurological aspects of music perception and performance. In D. Deutsch (Ed.), *The Psychology of Music, 2nd Edition* (pp. 653–724). San Diego, CA: Academic Press.

Marslen-Wilson, W. D. (1975). Sentence perception as an interactive parallel process. *Science*, *189*, 226–28.

McMullen, E., & Saffran, J.R. (2004). Music and language: A developmental comparison. *Music Perception*, *21*, 289–311.

Meyer, L.B. (1956). *Emotion and Meaning in Music.* Chicago, IL: University of Chicago Press.

Norton, A., Winner, E., Cronin, K., Overy, K., Lee, D.J., & Schlaug, G. (2005) Are there neural, cognitive, or motoric markers for musical ability prior to instrumental training? *Brain and Cognition, 59,* 124–34.

Osterhout, L., Wright, R., & Allen, M. (in press). The psychology of linguistic form. In P. Hogan (Ed.), *The Cambridge Encyclopedia of the Language Sciences.* Cambridge: Cambridge University Press.

Overy K. (2003). Dyslexia and music: From timing deficits to musical intervention. *Annals of the New York Academy of Sciences, 999,* 497–505.

Patel, A.D. (2003). Language, music, syntax, and the brain. *Nature Neuroscience, 6,* 674–81.

Patel, A.D. (2008). *Music, Language, and the Brain.* New York: Oxford University Press.

Patel, A.D., Gibson, E., Ratner, J., Besson, M., & Holcomb, P. (1998). Processing syntactic relations in language and music: An event-related potential study. *Journal of Cognitive Neuroscience, 10,* 717–33.

Patel, A.D., & Iversen, J.R. (2007). The linguistic benefits of musical abilities. *Trends in Cognitive Sciences, 11,* 369–72.

Patel, A.D., Peretz, I., Tramo, M., & Labrecque, R. (1998b). Processing prosodic and musical patterns: a neuropsychological investigation. *Brain and Language, 61,* 123–44.

Peretz, I. (1993). Auditory atonalia for melodies. *Cognitive Neuropsychology, 10,* 21–56.

Peretz, I., & Coltheart, M. (2003) Modularity of music processing. *Nature Neuroscience, 6,* 688–91.

Peretz, I., Kolinsky, R., Tramo, M., Labrecque, R., Hublet, C., Demeurisse, G., & Belleville, S. (1994). Functional dissociations following bilateral lesions of auditory cortex. *Brain, 117,* 1283–302.

Peretz I., & Zatorre, R.J. (2005). Brain organization for music processing. *Annual Review of Psychology, 56,* 89–114.

Poeppel, D. (2001). Pure word deafness and the bilateral processing of the speech code. *Cognitive Science, 21,* 679–93.

Poulin-Charronnat, B., Bigand, E., Madurell, F., & Peereman, R. (2005). Musical structure modulates semantic priming in vocal music. *Cognition, 94,* B67–78.

Schmithorst, V.J. (2005). Separate cortical networks involved in music perception: Preliminary functional MRI evidence for modularity of music processing. *Neuroimage, 25,* 444–51.

Schön, D., Magne, C., & Besson, M. (2004). The music of speech: Electrophysiological study of pitch perception in language and music. *Psychophysiology, 41,* 341–49.

Slevc, L.R., & Miyake, A. (2006). Individual differences in second language proficiency: Does musical ability matter? *Psychological Science, 17,* 675–81.

Slevc, L.R., Rosenberg, J.C., & Patel, A.D. (2009). Making psycholinguistics musical: Self-paced reading time evidence for shared processing of linguistic and musical syntax. *Psychonomic Bulletin and Review, 16,* 374–81.

Smith, J.D., & Melara, R.J. (1990). Aesthetic preference and syntactic prototypicality in music: 'Tis the gift to be simple.' *Cognition, 34,* 279–98.

Steinbeis, N., Koelsch, S., & Sloboda, J.A. (2006). The role of harmonic expectancy violations in musical emotions: Evidence from subjective, physiological, and neural responses. *Journal of Cognitive Neuroscience, 18,* 1380–93.

Steinbeis, N., & Koelsch, S. (2008). Shared neural resources between music and language indicate semantic processing of musical tension-resolution patterns. *Cerebral Cortex, 18,* 1169–78.

Tallal, P., & Gaab, N. (2006). Dynamic auditory processing, musical experience and language development. *Trends in Neurosciences, 29*, 382–70.

Thompson, W.F., & Cuddy, L.L. (1992). Perceived key movement in four-voice harmony and single voices. *Music Perception, 9*, 427–38.

Thompson, W.F., Schellenberg, E.G., & Husain, G. (2004). Decoding speech prosody: Do music lessons help? *Emotion, 4*, 46–64.

Thompson-Schill, S. L. (2006). Dissecting the language organ: A new look at the role of Broca' area in language processing. In A. Cutler, (Ed.) *Twenty-First Century Psycholinguistics: Four Cornerstones* (pp. 173–89). Mahwah, NJ: Lawrence Erlbaum.

Tillmann, B., Bharucha, J.J., & Bigand, E. (2000). Implicit learning of tonality: a self-organizing approach. *Psychological Review, 107*, 885–913.

Tillmann, B., Janata, P., & Bharucha, J.J. (2003). Activation of the inferior frontal cortex in musical priming. *Cognitive Brain Research, 16*, 145–61.

Tillmann, B., Koelsch, S., Escoffier, N., Bigand, E., Lalitte, P., Friederici, A.D., & vonCramon, D.Y. (2006). Cognitive priming in sung and instrumental music: Activation of inferior frontal cortex. *NeuroImage, 31*, 1771–82.

Tramo, M.J., Bharucha, J.J., & Musiek, F.E. (1990) Music perception and cognition following bilateral lesions of auditory cortex. *Journal of Cognitive Neuroscience, 2*, 195–212.

Trueswell, J. C., & Kim, A. E. (1998). How to prune a garden path by nipping it in the bud: fast priming of verb argument structure. *Journal of Memory & Language, 39*, 102–23.

Tyler, L. K., & Marslen-Wilson, W. (2008). Fronto-temporal brain systems supporting spoken language comprehension. *Philosophical Transactions of the Royal Society, 363*, 1037–54.

Wong, P.C.M., Skoe, E., Russo, N.M., Dees, T., & Kraus, N. (2007). Musical experience shapes human brainstem encoding of linguistic pitch patterns. *Nature Neuroscience, 10*, 420–22.

Chapter 23

Response to target article 'Language, music, and the brain: a resource-sharing framework'

Stefan Koelsch

Based on a number of studies from the last decade it is now safe to say that language- and music-syntactic processing rely on at least partly overlapping cognitive and neural resources. The strongest evidence for shared neural resources is provided by electro-encephalographic (EEG) studies showing interactions between event-related potentials (ERPs) reflecting language- and music-syntactic processing (Koelsch, Gunter, Wittforth, & Sammler, 2005a; Steinbeis & Koelsch, 2008), and the strongest evidence for shared cognitive resources stems from behavioural studies showing interactions between language- and music-syntactic processing (but not between language-syntactic processing and auditory oddballs, Slevc, Rosenberg, & Patel, 2009; Fedorenko, Patel, Casasanto, Winawer, & Gibson 2009; see also target article by Patel). Moreover, functional imaging studies revealed that music-syntactic processing involves inferior frontolateral and anterior superior temporal cortex (Koelsch, 2009), analogous to language experiments which report involvement of these areas in language-syntactic processing (e.g. Friederici, Wang, Herrmann, Maess, & Oertel, 2000, Friederici, 2002).

Notably, the only functional neuroimaging study I am aware of in which music- and language-syntactic processing has been compared within-subjects is a study from Sammler et al. (2009) using electrocortical recordings. Sammler et al. measured perisylvian electrocortical potentials elicited in epileptic patients by syntactic errors in music (irregular chord functions) and in language (phrase structure violations). The localization of these potentials using source current density mapping showed that these potentials emerged from sources located within very similar temporo-frontolateral brain areas (however, she also observed stronger activations of the temporal than the frontal lobes in language, whereas in the music domain the frontal and the temporal lobes were equally involved). These results corroborate the notion that the processing of sequential musical and linguistic information recruits partly identical resources within the perisylvian region, although the language and music tasks used in that study led to a different recruitment of temporal and frontal brain structures.

Thus, the idea of shared 'resource networks' (that is, of neural resources that serve the processing of both musical and linguistic syntax) is highly plausible. However, so far practically no research has been carried out investigating which cognitive mechanisms are actually shared between language- and music-syntactic processing (and which are not). The processing of both musical and linguistic syntax relies at least partly on cognitive functions that are likely to serve not only one domain, but operate in a way that allows information from several domains to be processed. However, as depicted in the model of Patel's target article (Figure 22.5), there are also resources that are likely to be engaged only by music- or language-syntactic processing.

The following sections will first describe some of the processes that are likely to be engaged only for music-syntactic processing, and suggest cognitive functions that are shared between the syntactic processing of language and music (and perhaps also other domains). I will also illustrate where in the brain these functions are located.

Processes involved in music-syntactic processing

In major-minor tonal music (often simply referred to as 'Western' music), music-syntactic processing of chord functions (be they constituted by chords or by subsequent tones) comprises several sub-processes. These sub-processes are grouped in the following into several core aspects (see also Koelsch, 2009), with the ordering of these aspects not being intended to reflect a temporal order of music-syntactic processing (that is, the sub-processes may partly happen in parallel). Note that musical syntax also comprises other structural aspects, such as melodic (e.g. voice leading), rhythmic, metric, and timbral structure. Syntactic processing of such structural aspects has, however, to my knowledge not been investigated thus far.

(1) Extraction of a tonal centre. In major-minor tonal music, music-syntactic processing of chord functions (be they constituted of chords or melodies) relies on the extraction of a tonal centre, for example, *C* in the case of a passage in *C* major. The tonal centre corresponds to the root of a tonal key (and is perceived as the best representative of a tonal key, see Krumhansl & Kessler, 1982). In terms of harmonic function, the tonal centre is also the root of the tonic chord (see Chapter 22 for explanation of the term 'tonic'), and thus the reference point for the tonal hierarchy or chord functions (see also below).

The process of establishing a representation of a tonal centre is normally an iterative process (Krumhansl & Toivainen, 2001), and this process has to be engaged each time the tonal key changes. To extract a tonal centre, or to detect a shift in tonal key (and thus a shift of the tonal centre), listeners have to sequence musical information, abstract a tonal centre from the different tones of a musical passage, keep the representation of the tonal centre in short-term memory, and realize when the memory representation of a tonal centre differs from that of new musical information. A description of the cognitive representation of tonal keys is provided, e.g. in Krumhansl & Kessler (1982).

Previous studies have shown that listeners tend to interpret the first chord (or tone) of a sequence as the tonic (that is, as the tonal centre; Krumhansl & Kessler, 1982). In case the first chord is not the tonic, listeners have to modify their initial interpretation of the tonal centre during the perception of subsequent tones or chords (Krumhansl & Kessler, 1982; for a conception of key identification within the tonal idiom see the intervallic rivalry model from Brown, Butler, & Jones, 1994).

This sub-process of music-syntactic processing is presumably unique for music-syntactic processing, because language-syntactic processing does not rely on a tonal centre.

(2) Successive tones and chords are related to the tonal centre, as well as to each other, in terms of harmonic distance (presumably by neural resources located in inferior frontolateral cortical areas). E.g. in *C* major, a *G* major chord is more closely related to *C* major than a *G#* major chord. On a more abstract level, the establishment of relations between elements of sequences that are structured according to complex regularities, is required for both music- and language-syntactic processing (see also further below).

(3) Based on the harmonic relations between chords, a tonal order (or 'hierarchy', Bharucha & Krumhansl, 1983; see also Tillmann, Bharucha, & Bigand 2000; Tillmann, Janata, Birk, & Bharucha, 2008) is established, according to which the configuration of previously heard chord functions forms a tonal structure (or a structural context). For example, within the tonal 'hierarchy of stability' (Bharucha & Krumhansl, 1983) the tonic chord is the most 'stable' chord function, followed by the dominant and the subdominant, whereas chord functions such as the submediant and the supertonic represent less stable chord functions (ibid.).

Importantly, when individuals familiar with major-minor tonal music listen to such music, they transfer the sensual pitch information (that is, information about the pitches of the tones of melodies or chords) into a cognitive representation of the location of tones and chords within the tonal hierarchy of a key, as well as within the (major-minor) tonal key space. For example, within a *G* major context, the sensory percept of three simultaneously sounding tones with pitches forming a major triad (such as c', e', and g') is transformed into the location relative to the tonic as well as relative to the tonal centre (that is, relative to the tonal reference point). The term 'location relative to the tonal centre' refers to the place in the map of keys (or on the torus of keys; Krumhansl & Kessler, 1982) in relation to the tonic, and the term 'relative to the tonic' refers to the chord function (c-e-g is the subdominant in *G* major). In other words, when processing harmonic information, listeners relate new harmonic information to the previous harmonic context in terms of harmonic distance, and in terms of its functional-harmonic information. To illustrate this using the previous example: Within a *G* major context, it is highly likely that a *C* major chord (c, e, g) functions as the subdominant, but there is also a possibility that the *C* major chord turns out to be a tonic chord (e.g. if the key changes to *C* major, or if the larger harmonic context is actually *C* major). That is, harmonic information is not only represented in terms of its harmonic function, but also in terms of the probability of the tonal centre's stability. This is reminiscent to the process of ascribing a probability of syntactic function to phrases of a sentence (see example of the 'garden path' sentence 'The man accepted the prize was not going to him' in the target article).

Note that pitch height information is one-dimensional (ranging from low to high), whereas the cognitive representation of major-minor tonal space is at least two- (if not four-) dimensional (Krumhansl & Kessler, 1982, see ibid. for a description of the multi-dimensional cognitive representation of major-minor tonal space; see also

Krumhansl, Bharucha & Kessler, 1982). The distances between chord functions and keys in terms of music theory correlate with acoustic similarity (see Leman, 2000, who showed that the key profiles obtained by Krumhansl & Kessler, 1982, can largely be accounted for by measures of acoustic similarity). However, acoustic similarity of two chords is a one-dimensional measure, whereas the tonal space of chord functions and keys appears to be represented in listeners in more than one dimension (see above and Krumhansl & Kessler, 1982; Krumhansl et al., 1982). That is, when we listen to a musical piece (at least if we are familiar with major-minor tonal music), we do not only monitor chord transitions with regard to their acoustic similarity, but also with regard to both the tonal space of keys, and the hierarchy of stability (that is, with regard to their chord function). This difference in dimensionality is an important difference between 'acoustical' and 'musical' processing. Nevertheless, the fact that tonal hierarchies, and music-syntactic regularities of major-minor tonal music, are partly grounded on acoustic similarities (e.g. Leman, 2000) stays in contrast to language-syntactic regularities.

(4) Once a harmonic hierarchy is established, moving away from a tonal centre may be experienced as tensioning, and moving back as releasing (see also Lerdahl, 2001; Patel, 2003). This simple statement has several important implications: Firstly, moving through tonal space establishes hierarchical processing (for details see Lerdahl, 2001 and Patel, 2003). Secondly, the tension-resolution patterns emerging from moving through tonal space have emotional quality (Meyer, 1956; Steinbeis, Koelsch, & Sloboda, 2006; Koelsch, Kilches, Steinbeis, & Schelinksi, 2008). Thirdly, moving away, and back to a tonal centre also opens the possibility for recursion, because while moving away from a tonal centre (e.g. to the dominant, that is in *C* major: a *G* major chord), a change of key might take place (e.g. from *C* major to *G* major), and within the new key (now *G* major)—which now has a new tonal centre—the music might again move away from the tonal centre (e.g. to the dominant of *G* major), until it returns to the tonal centre of *G*, and then to the tonal centre of *C* major (for studies investigating neural correlates of the processing of changes in tonal key with electroencephalography or functional magnetic resonance imaging see Koelsch et al., 2002; Janata, Tillmann, & Bharucha, 2002; Koelsch, Gunter, Schröger, & Friederici, 2003; Koelsch, Fritz, Schulze, Alsop, & Schlaug, 2005b).

The hierarchical processing of music is likely to rely on neural resources that are also involved in the hierarchical processing of language-syntactic information.

(5) In addition, the succession of chord functions follows statistical regularities, that is, probabilities of chord transitions (Riemann, 1877; Rohrmeier, 2005). For example, in a statistical study by Rohrmeier (2005) on the frequencies of diatonic chord progressions in Bach chorales, the supertonic was five times more likely to follow the subdominant than to precede it. These statistical regularities are an important characteristic of musical syntax with regard to the harmonic aspects of major-minor tonal music (other characteristics pertain, e.g. the principles of voice-leading). The representations of such regularities are implicitly learned (in the sense that they are extracted without conscious effort by individuals), and

stored in long-term memory (see also Tillmann et al., 2000); that is, by its very nature it needs listening experience to extract the statistical properties of the probabilities for the transitions of chord functions. These representations of regularities are presumably stored in 'representation networks' (see target article) that are different from those storing language-syntactic regularities.

It is important to understand that, while listeners familiar with (Western) tonal music perceive a sequence of chords, they automatically make predictions of likely chord functions to follow. That is, listeners extrapolate expectancies for subsequent sounds of regular chords, based on representations of music-syntactic regularities; chords (or tones) that mismatch with the music-syntactic sound expectancy of a listener elicit processes that are electrically reflected in an ERAN (Koelsch et al., 2009). The mathematical principles from which the probabilities for chord transitions within a tonal key might have emerged are under current investigation (see, e.g. Woolhouse & Cross, 2006, for the interval cycle-based model of pitch attraction), and it appears that many of these principles represent abstract, rather than physical (or acoustical) features (Woolhouse & Cross, 2006; note that, in addition to transition probabilities of chord functions, frequencies of co-occurrences, as well as frequencies of occurrences of chord functions and tones also represent statistical regularities, see Tillmann et al., 2008). The processes of serial prediction are likely to be shared between music- and language-syntactic processing (see also below).

That is, the cognitive functions required for the processing of structure in both music and language comprise (at least) the following ones: (1) The computation of structural relations between sequential elements—e.g. the computation of structural relations between words and phrases, or between chords and chord functions, (2) the build up of a hierarchical model of a sentence, a melody, a chord progression, an action, etc. (3) A serial prediction in the sense that a prediction is made about future events (i.e. the structural model is extrapolated into the future, e.g. to prepare for appropriate actions. Therefore, both music- and language-syntactic processing require (4) the operation of Working Memory to store the elements of a sequence, to store and manipulate a structural representation, and to integrate new structural elements into a context, (5) attentional mechanisms, such as prospective attention to sensory events, and (6) possibly imitation, particularly with regards to the learning of syntax.

Serial prediction and ventrolateral premotor cortex

Schubotz and von Cramon (2002) presented individuals with a sequence of tones that followed a simple pattern (low pitch–high pitch–low pitch–high pitch–etc.). The task for the participants was to attend to the sequential order of the tones' pitches, and to judge whether the last three stimuli within a trial matched the stimuli that they expected. This task, thus, involved the analysis, recognition, and prediction of sequential information. In a control condition, the timbre of one of the last three tones did or did not match with the timbre of the preceding tones. In this control condition, subjects were asked to attend to the timbre of the tones, and to detect whether the timbre of one of the last three tones was different. Contrasting the functional magnetic resonance imaging (fMRI) data of the experimental against the control task, activations were observed within the inferior ventrolateral premotor cortex (vlPMC) (within the transition from BA 6 to BA 44), the dorsal PMC, the anterior intraparietal sulcus (IPSa), the left cerebellar cortex, and the supplementary motor area (SMA) (for similar findings see also Schubotz, von Cramon, & Lohmann, 2003; similar tasks in the visual domain appear to involve more superior areas of the vlPMC, Schubotz & von Cramon 2003; see also Wildgruber, Kischka, Ackermann, Klose, & Grodd, 1999). Particularly the vlPMC is not only activated during the build up of serial prediction, but also during the violation of serial predictions (compared to events that do not violate the prediction; Huettel, Mack, & McCarthy, 2002). Thus, extracting and predicting the sequential structure of a string of stimuli activates premotor areas (particularly the vlPMC), presumably because sequences of perceptual events (such as musical sequences and sentences) are transformed into a motor representation that serves further cognitive processing.

Processing complex structural relations and Broca's area

An increase of the complexity of regularities underlying the structure of sequential events appears to correlate not only with an increase of vlPMC activity, but also with an involvement of Broca's area (BA44 and BA45). That is, as the regularities underlying sequential information get more complex, and as establishing the structural relation between elements of a sequence becomes more abstract, Broca's area becomes involved more strongly. Functional imaging studies have shown that Broca's area comes into play for the computation of complex structural relations between sequential elements during the processing of complex syntactic structures in language, during the processing of complex harmonic structures in music, as well as for the hierarchical processing of action sequences (e.g. Koechlin & Jubault, 2006), and for the processing of hierarchically organized mathematical formulas and termini (Friedrich & Friederici, 2009).

Due to the establishment of structural relations between sequential events (i.e. due to the analysis and recognition of structural properties), and due to the fast short-term prediction of upcoming events based on a model of the structural properties of sequences, involvement of Broca's area or vlPMC has been reported for a number of different tasks, in the auditory domain including auditory oddball paradigms (Deouell, 2007), pitch discrimination tasks (e.g. Gaab, Gaser, Zaehle, Jancke, 7 Schlaug, 2003; Gandour et al., 2000), serial prediction tasks (Schubotz & von Cramon, 2002, 2003), as well as music- and language-syntactic processing (Koelsch & Siebel, 2005; Friederici, 2002).

As mentioned above, a number of studies has revealed interactions between music-syntactic and language-syntactic processing (Koelsch, Gunter, Wittforth, & Sammler, 2005a; Steinbeis & Koelsch, 2008; Slevc et al., 2009; Fedorenko et al., 2009). In these studies, chord sequences (Koelsch et al., 2005a; Steinbeis & Koelsch, 2008; Slevc et al., 2009) or melodies (Fedorenko et al., 2009) were presented simultaneously with visually presented sentences while participants were asked to focus on the language-syntactic information, and to ignore the music-syntactic information. Using EEG and chord sequence paradigms, two studies showed that the early right anterior negativity (ERAN) elicited by irregular chords interacts with the left anterior negativity (LAN) elicited by linguistic (morpho-syntactic) violations (Koelsch et al., 2005a; Steinbeis & Koelsch, 2008). The LAN elicited by words was reduced when the irregular word was presented simultaneously with an irregular chord (compared to when the irregular word was presented with a regular chord; see also target article for details). Notably, morpho-syntactic processing critically relies on BA44 and BA45 (Heim, 2008); therefore, one site of neural resources required for music- as well as language-syntactic processing appears to be located in Broca's area.

It is also important to note that morpho-syntactic processing (as reflected in the LAN) and processing of phrase structure (as reflected in an early left anterior negativity, Sammler et al., 2008) usually precedes processes of syntactic integration (Friederici, 2002). Therefore, the term 'shared syntactic integration resource hypothesis' (SSIRH) should perhaps only be used with regard to the 'late' processes of syntactic integration (as reflected electrophysiologically in the P600/late positive component), and not when referring to 'earlier' processes such as syntactic structure building (Koelsch & Siebel, 2005). Moreover, when using the term 'shared syntactic processing resources' (or 'shared syntactic processing resources hypothesis'), it would be useful to exactly specify which syntactic (sub-) processes are referred to.

Working memory

Another cognitive function that is required for the processing of both linguistic and musical syntax is working memory (WM). To investigate WM for verbal and tonal information, two recent studies (Koelsch et al., 2009; Schulze, Zysset, Mueller, Friederici, & Koelsch, 2011) employed an experimental paradigm in which participants were presented with strings of four sung syllables with the task to remember either the pitches (tonal information) or the syllables (verbal information). Interestingly, rehearsal of verbal, as well as rehearsal of tonal information activated inferior vlPMC (encroaching Broca's area), as well as superior vlPMC, the planum temporale, inferior parietal lobe, the anterior insula, subcortical structures (basal ganglia and thalamus), as well as the cerebellum. In non-musicians, the topography of activations was virtually identical for the rehearsal of syllables and pitches, showing a remarkable overlap of the WM components for the rehearsal of verbal and tonal information in non-musicians (for a comparison between non-musicians and musicians see Schulze et al., 2011). When the WM task was performed under articulatory suppression, activations in those areas diminished, while additional activations arose in anterior prefrontal areas (as in the rehearsal conditions, the topography of activations under articulatory suppression was nearly identical for the verbal as compared to the tonal task). These findings indicate that both the rehearsal of verbal (syllable) and tonal (pitch) information, as well as storage of verbal and tonal information relies on strongly overlapping neuronal networks.

WM processes during sentence comprehension also recruit Broca's area, but additionally also involve the inferior frontal sulcus (IFS) in the so-called dorsolateral prefrontal cortex (DLPFC): Using fMRI, Fiebach, Schlesewsky, Lohmann, von Cramon, and Friederici (2005) compared processing of short object wh-questions (such as 'Thomas fragt sich, wen der Doktor am Dienstag nachmittag nach dem Unfall verständigt hat'—'Thomas asks himself, who_{acc} the_{nom} doctor on Tuesday afternoon after the accident called has') with the processing of long object wh-questions (such as 'Thomas fragt sich, wen am Dienstag nachmittag nach dem Unfall der Doktor verständigt hat'—'Thomas asks himself, who_{acc} on Tuesday afternoon after the accident the_{nom} doctor called has'; note that the English translations are a word-by-word translations). The long object questions require more WM resources than the short object questions (because the object and the subject noun phrase are further apart in the long object questions, see words indicated by subscripts), and the direct contrast of these two conditions revealed stronger activations in the IFS (as well as in Broca's area and vlPMC in the precentral sulcus) for long object questions.

Very similar activations of the IFS were also described in fMRI experiments on music-syntactic processing using chord sequence paradigms (Koelsch et al., 2002, 2005b): In that study, chord sequences ending on music-syntactically irregular chords activated the IFS (as well as Broca's area, vlPMC, and several other structures). Although this has so far not been directly tested, it appears highly likely that the IFS activation (and in part perhaps even activation of Broca's area) reported in those studies was due to increased WM load, because the occurrence of music-syntactically irregular chords usually commences a hierarchical processing (requiring a larger amount of information to be integrated over long distances into the music-syntactic context). Activation of the IFS has also been observed in experiments on listening to polyphonic music (contrasted to a silence condition; Janata et al., 2002), and these activations were presumably linked to WM operations that are required for the integration of several complex musical events over time.

Conclusions

In summary, shared 'resource networks' for syntactic processing of music and language are at least to be expected for the computation of structural relations between sequential elements, for the computation of a hierarchical model, for the serial prediction about future events, and for the operations underlying WM. Neural resources for syntactic processing are not only shared for syntactic integration (see the SSIRH of the target article), and future work should aim to specify syntactic (sub-) processes when using the term 'shared syntactic resources'. Interestingly, the resource networks engaged for music- as well as for language-syntactic processing appear to involve sensorimotor-related circuits which provide resources for the production of linguistic and musical information, for the transformation of perceptual (auditory) information into action-related (sensorimotor) codes, as well as for the representation, maintenance, and perhaps even manipulation of information (for details see Koelsch et al., 2005, 2009; Schulze et al., 2011). In this regard, the remarkable similarity for the sensorimotor circuits underlying the production of speech and song (Callan et al., 2006) corroborate the view that the cognitive resources that stem from motor functions and structures are widely shared for the processing of language and music. More empirical work in the field of cognitive science is needed to further specify which cognitive mechanisms are shared, and which differ between music- and language-syntactic processing. Functional neuroimaging studies could then attempt to localize the neural underpinnings of these processes to provide us with a more detailed picture about the functional neuroarchitecture of music- and language-syntactic processing.

References

Bharucha, J., & Krumhansl, C. (1983). The representation of harmonic structure in music: Hierarchies of stability as a function of context. *Cognition*, *13*, 63–102.

Brown, H., Butler, D., & Jones, M. R. (1994). Musical and temporal influences on key discovery. *Music Perception 11*(4), 371–91.

Callan, D. E., Tsytsarev, V., Hanakawa, T., Callan, A. M., Katsuhara, M., Fukuyama, H., *et al.* (2006). Song and speech: Brain regions involved with perception and covert production. *NeuroImage*, *31*, 1327–42.

Deouell, L. Y. (2007). The frontal generator of the mismatch negativity revisited. *Journal of Psychophysiology*, *21*, 147–60.

Fedorenko, E., Patel, A. D., Casasanto, D., Winawer, J., & Gibson, E. (2009). Structural integration in language and music: Evidence for a shared system. *Memory and Cognition*, *37*, 1–9.

Fiebach, C.J., Schlesewsky, M., Lohmann, G., von Cramon, D.Y., & Friederici, A.D. (2005). Revisiting the role of Broca's area in sentence processing: Syntactic integration versus syntactic working memory. *Human Brain Mapping*, *24*, 79–91.

Friederici, A. D. (2002). Towards a neural basis of auditory sentence processing. *Trends in Cognitive Science*, *6*, 78–84.

Friederici, A. D., Wang, Y., Herrmann, C. S., Maess, B., Oertel, U. (2000). Localization of early syntactic processes in frontal and temporal cortical areas: a magnetoencephalographic study. *Human Brain Mapping*, *11*, 1–11.

Friedrich, R., & Friederici, A. D. (2009). Mathematical logic in the human brain: Syntax. *PLoS ONE*, *4*(5), e5599. doi:10.1371/journal.pone.0005599.

Gaab, N., Gaser, C., Zaehle, T., Jancke, L., & Schlaug, G. (2003). Functional anatomy of pitch memory-an fMRI study with sparse temporal sampling. *NeuroImage*, *19*, 1417–26.

Gandour, J., Wong, D., Hsieh, L., Weinzapfel, B., Van Lancker, D., Hutchins, G. D. (2000). A crosslinguistic PET study of tone perception. *Journal of Cognitive Neuroscience*, *12*, 207–22.

Heim, S. (2008). Syntactic gender processing in the human brain: a review and a model. *Brain and Language*, *106*(1), 55–64.

Huettel, S., Mack, P., &McCarthy, G. (2002). Perceiving patterns in random series: dynamic processing of sequence in prefrontal cortex. *Nature Neurosciences*, *5*, 485–90.

Janata, P., Tillmann, B., & Bharucha, J. J. (2002). Listening to polyphonic music recruits domain-general attention and working memory circuits. *Cognitive, Affective, and Behavioral Neuroscience*, *2*, 121–40.

Koechlin, E., & Jubault, T. (2006). Broca's area and the hierarchical organization of human behavior. *Neuron*, *50*, 963–74.

Koelsch, S. (2009). Music-syntactic processing and auditory memory – similarities and differences between ERAN and MMN. *Psychophysiology*, *46*, 179–90.

Koelsch, S., Fritz, T., Schulze, K., Alsop, D., & Schlaug, G. (2005b). Adults and children processing music: An fMRI study. *NeuroImage*, *25*(4), 1068–76.

Koelsch, S., Gunter, T.C., von Cramon, D. Y., Zysset, S., Lohmann, G., & Friederici, A. D. (2002). Bach speaks: a cortical 'language-network' serves the processing of music. *NeuroImage*, *17*, 956–66.

Koelsch, S., Gunter, T., Schröger, E., & Friederici, A. D. (2003). Processing tonal modulations: an ERP study. *Journal of Cognitive Neuroscience, 15*, 1149–1159.

Koelsch, S., Gunter, T. C., Wittforth, M., & Sammler, D. (2005a). Interaction between syntax processing in language and music: An ERP study. *Journal of Cognitive Neuroscience, 17*, 1565–77.

Koelsch, S., Kilches, S., Steinbeis, N., & Schelinksi, S. (2008). Effects of unexpected chords and of performer's expression on brain responses and electrodermal activity. *PLoS ONE, 3*(7), e2631.

Koelsch, S., Schulze, K., Sammler, D., Fritz, T., Müller, K., & Gruber, O. (2009). Functional architecture of verbal and tonal working memory: an FMRI study. *Human Brain Mapping, 30*(3), 859–73.

Koelsch, S., & Siebel, W. (2005). Towards a neural basis of music perception. *Trends in Cognitive Sciences, 9*, 578–584.

Krumhansl, C. L., Bharucha, J. J., & Kessler, E. J. (1982). Perceived harmonic structure of chords in three related musical keys. *Journal of Experimental Psychology: Human Perception and Performance, 8*(1), 24–36.

Krumhansl, C., & Kessler, E. (1982). Tracing the dynamic changes in perceived tonal organization in a spatial representation of musical keys. *Psychological Review, 89*(4), 334–68.

Krumhansl, C., & Toivainen, P. (2001). Tonal cognition. In R. J. Zatorre & I. Peretz (Eds.), The Biological Foundations of Music. *Annals of the New York Academy of Sciences 930*, 77–91.

Leman, M. (2000). An auditory model of the role of short-term memory in probe-tone ratings. *Music Perception, 17*, 481–509.

Lerdahl, F. (2001). *Tonal Pitch Space.* Oxford: Oxford University Press.

Meyer, L.B. (1956). *Emotion and Meaning in Music.* Chicago, IL: Chicago University Press.

Patel, A. D. (2003). Language, music, syntax and the brain. *Nature Neuroscience, 6*, 674–81.

Riemann, H. (1877). *Musikalische Syntaxis: Grundriss einer harmonischen Satzbildungslehre.* Niederwalluf: Sändig.

Rohrmeier, M. (2005). *Towards modelling movement in music: Analysing properties and dynamic aspects of pc set sequences in Bach's chorales* (MPhil Thesis). University of Cambridge. Published as *Darwin College Research Reports 04* (http://www.dar.cam.ac.uk/dcrr/dcrr004.pdf).

Sammler, D., Koelsch, S., Ball, T., Brandt, A., Elger, C. E., Friederici, A. D., *et al.* (2009). Overlap of musical and linguistic syntax processing: intracranial ERP evidence. *Annals of the New York Academy of Sciences, 1169*, 494–8.

Schubotz, R.I., & von Cramon, D. Y. (2002). Predicting perceptual events activates corresponding motor schemes in lateral premotor cortex: an fMRI study. *NeuroImage, 15*, 787–96.

Schubotz, R.I., & von Cramon, D.Y. (2003). Functional–anatomical concepts of human premotor cortex: evidence from fMRI and PET studies. *NeuroImage, 20*, S120–31.

Schubotz, R.I., von Cramon, D.Y., & Lohmann, G. (2003). Auditory what, where, and when: a sensory somatotopy in lateral premotor cortex. *NeuroImage, 20*, 173–85.

Schulze, K., Zysset, S., Mueller, K., Friederici, A.D., & Koelsch, S. (2011). Neuroarchitecture of verbal and tonal working memory in non-musicians and musicians. *Human Brain Mapping, 32*, 771–83.

Slevc, L. R., Rosenberg, J. C., & Patel, A. D. (2009). Making psycholinguistics musical: Self-paced reading time evidence for shared processing of linguistic and musical syntax. *Psychonomic Bulletin and Review, 16*, 374–81.

Steinbeis, N., Koelsch, S., & Sloboda, J. (2006). The role of harmonic expectancy violations in musical emotions: Evidence from subjective, physiological, and neural responses. *Journal of Cognitive Neuroscience, 18*, 1380–93.

Steinbeis, N., & Koelsch, S. (2008). Shared neural resources between music and language indicate semantic processing of musical tension-resolution patterns. *Cerebral Cortex, 18*, 1169–78.

Tillmann, B., Bharucha, J. J., & Bigand, E. (2000). Implicit learning of tonality: A self-organized approach. *Psychological Review, 107*, 885–913.

Tillmann, B., Janata, P., Birk, J., & Bharucha, J. J. (2008). Tonal centers and expectancy: Facilitation or inhibition of chords at the top of the harmonic hierarchy? *Journal of Experimental Psychology: Human Perception and Performance, 34*, 1031–43.

Wildgruber, D., Kischka, U., Ackermann, H., Klose, U., & Grodd W. (1999). Dynamic pattern of brain activation during sequencing of word strings evaluated by fMRI. *Cognitive Brain Research, 7*, 285–94.

Woolhouse, M. H., & Cross, I. (2006). An interval cycle-based model of pitch attraction. In M. Baroni, R. Addessi, R. Caterina, & M. Costa (Eds.) *Proceedings of the 9th International Conference on Music Perception & Cognition (ICMPC9)* (pp. 763–71). Bologna: SMPC and ESCOM.

Chapter 24

Advances in neuroimaging techniques: implications for the shared syntactic integration resource hypothesis

Jessica A. Grahn

The shared syntactic integration resource hypothesis (SSIRH) generates specific predictions about neural overlap in the instantiation of processes required for syntactic integration in music and language. Syntactic integration occurs over time, through communication between areas maintaining domain-specific representations and areas responsible for domain-general processing. Analysing neural overlap and temporal communication requires techniques that enable superior spatial resolution and localization, as well as dynamic connectionist frameworks, rather than interpretation of static activation maps. With recent advances in neuroimaging analysis techniques, we are coming closer to be able to address these questions. For example, multivoxel pattern analysis (MVPA) techniques can make more effective use of information in the functional magnetic resonance imaging (fMRI) signal, whereas examinations of connectivity between different neural areas can tell us more about the dynamic temporal interactions occurring in the brain. What follows is a review of a selection of the techniques in development for functional neuroimaging data, the use of which may be able to provide definitive evidence for or against the SSIRH.

fMRI and pattern analysis

The advantages in fMRI lie in 'its noninvasive nature, ever-increasing availability, relatively high spatiotemporal resolution, and its capacity to demonstrate the entire network of brain areas engaged when subjects undertake particular tasks' (Logothetis, 2008). However, the main disadvantage is that it measures a signal that inherently reflects neuronal mass activity. In addition, the spatial specificity of the signal (most commonly the blood-oxygen-level dependent response) is limited by its 'point spread function', which blurs the measured signal about 2–3 millimetres beyond the locus of neuronal activity. Thus, within the smallest spatial unit measured in fMRI, a single voxel (volumetric pixel), over a million neurons may be present. Conventional fMRI analysis uses mass univariate techniques to identify voxels that show a significant response in certain experimental conditions. Interdigitated networks below the resolution of the voxel cannot be distinguished. In fact, to increase sensitivity to a particular condition, signal is spatially averaged across voxels. Although averaging reduces noise, it also reduces signal, leading to a downweighting of information from voxels with weaker responses to a particular condition. Weakly responsive voxels still might carry some information about what experimental condition is currently being experienced by the participant. In addition, spatial averaging blurs out the fine-grained spatial patterns that could be used to discriminate between experimental conditions.

New techniques such as MVPA take advantage of signal in weakly responsive voxels, by capitalizing on the fact that these voxels will have differing proportions of neurons that may be involved in the different processes of interest. The MVPA approach uses pattern-classification techniques to extract the signal that is present in the *pattern* of responses across multiple voxels, even if (considered individually) the voxels might not be significantly responsive to any of the conditions of interest. The multivoxel pattern of response can be thought of as a combinatorial code with a very large capacity for representing distinctions between cognitive states. Instead of examining the localization of significantly active voxels in both conditions of interest, the pattern of activity across *all* voxels in one condition is correlated with the pattern observed in another condition: areas with high correlations between conditions suggest similar neural operations, whereas those with low correlations suggest differing operations. Considering the SSIRH, the brain 'states' for syntactic integration of musical material versus linguistic material should differ in domain-specific areas of the brain: distinctive patterns should be observed, based on the material being syntactically integrated by the volunteer. By asking where in the brain these distinctive patterns occur, the power of MVPA to clarify the structure of neural representations can be harnessed (Norman, Polyn, Detre, & Haxby, 2006). Areas in which distinctive patterns occur between musical and linguistic conditions are likely to encode domain-specific information.

Perhaps more importantly, MVPA can also be used to discriminate overlapping functional activations (Peelen & Downing, 2007; Peelen, Wiggett, & Downing, 2006). Observations of overlapping activity across stimuli or tasks are frequently used as evidence of overlapping function when comparing fMRI studies. For example, as mentioned in the target article, Broca's area has been found to be commonly activated in both musical and linguistic syntactic tasks (Koelsch, 2002; Tillmann, 2003; Maess 2001), which could be evidence for a shared, domain-general syntactic function. However, when a set of voxels is commonly activated by different experimental conditions, two interpretations exist. The first interpretation is that the area commonly activated between conditions contains neurons that are engaged in a common computational process. This process is thought to be shared by the two experimental conditions (for example, syntactic integration of both music and language), but not by the control conditions (for example, semantic processing). This interpretation is generally the favoured account when overlapping activations are observed.

However, there is an alternative interpretation of overlapping activation (also mentioned in the target article): two overlapping but functionally independent neural populations are present and active within the common region. In this interpretation, a commonly activated area does not indicate a common function. Conventional fMRI analyses cannot discriminate between these two interpretations, yet this is often ignored, and overlapping activations are taken as evidence for overlapping function.

MVPA analyses, however, can be used to discriminate between the two interpretations. A voxel-by-voxel pattern of selectivity to musical or linguistic stimuli can be calculated. In a simple form, this can be accomplished by extracting a t value at each voxel in a neural area of interest for music stimuli (against baseline) and then for language stimuli (against baseline). The t value provides a useful musical/linguistic selectivity index for each voxel, because it combines in a single measure the magnitude of the difference between two conditions relative to the within-condition variance. Then, the pattern of t values in each voxel can be correlated for music stimuli and language stimuli. A positive voxelwise correlation between music selectivity and linguistic selectivity indicates that (1) the two conditions do indeed activate the same neurons and (2) the variation in this selectivity across voxels is stable. Thus, the results of MVPA experiments can support or reject claims about neural mechanisms that are shared across the music and linguistic syntactic domains.

So, how might these approaches be used in the study of the SSIRH? Firstly, fMRI studies of musical and linguistic syntax, conducted within the same subjects, would be useful in determining areas of functional overlap as well as functional separation across the brain (the inferior frontal gyrus seems a likely candidate for overlap from previous work, or perhaps other perisylvian areas (Sammler, 2009)). Koelsch (Chapter 23, this volume) has highlighted several brain areas which may be expected to be involved in the processes required for musical and linguistic syntactical integration. The areas of potential overlap identified using conventional analysis techniques can be further interrogated using MVPA analyses to determine if the common activation can be genuinely interpreted as true functional overlap.

Connectivity

Despite the low temporal resolution of fMRI (on the order of seconds, compared to neural firing which occurs on the order of milliseconds), measurements of neural interaction between brain regions can still be made. In general, we define networks of brain areas that are likely to be involved in a particular task based on static activation maps. For example, Broca's area, or more generally the inferior frontal gyrus, is a potential site for domain-general syntactic integration. If we want to understand the role that this area is playing within a given network, we need to know if and how it interacts with the domain-specific language or music areas when syntactic integration is required.

To answer questions about the interaction between areas we require analyses of connectivity. Many people are familiar with the concept of *anatomical connectivity*: that of a direct neuronal connection between two brain areas; a connection comprised of neuronal axons. In the past, the majority of our knowledge of these anatomical connections came from histological studies of animals, with relatively little direct information in humans. Now, the advent of a new MRI technology, diffusion tensor imaging (DTI), provides visualizations of white matter tracts *in vivo* (Basser, 1994). DTI takes advantage of the fact that the membrane and myelin sheath surrounding axons provides a barrier to the diffusion of water across the membrane. Thus, water diffuses along the direction of axons more than across the membrane and myelin sheath. This 'diffusion anisotropy' can provide estimation of the dominant orientation of axons within a particular section of white matter. DTI studies have already provided information about how musical experience may change anatomical connectivity between brain areas (Bengtsson et al., 2005; Schmithorst & Wilke, 2002), or how differences in anatomical connectivity correlate with language processing ability (Gold, Powell, Xuan, Jiang, & Hardy, 2007; Niogi & McCandliss, 2006).

However, in its current form, DTI methodology is limited, both in spatial resolution, and lack of information about the directionality (retrograde versus anterograde) of the white matter tracts. Directionality is a key consideration in neurobiologically plausible models of cognitive function: whether an area is providing information to or receiving information from another area is certainly non-trivial. Poor spatial resolution, however, is perhaps the biggest problem: multiple fibre directions within a single voxel cannot always be resolved. The presence of branching, crossing, or 'kissing' fibres requires probabilistic solutions or larger-scale trend solutions that may obscure more fine-grained patterns of connectivity. The methods are in rapid development, though, so improvements are likely to occur in both data acquisition and the analysis techniques that can be applied to the acquired data. A more general limitation applies to the conclusions that can be drawn from anatomical connectivity studies: much of the brain is interconnected anatomically (either directly or indirectly), so studies of anatomical connectivity, although informative, cannot indicate which connections are actually being used at any given time to accomplish a particular task, or whether a connection is relevant for the process under investigation. Answering these questions requires analyses of functional or effective connectivity (Aertsen and Preissl, 1991).

Functional connectivity measures the correlations between the concurrent activities of different brain regions. This is a correlative, not causal approach, and can be used in metabolic techniques that measure blood flow as an indirect indicator of neural activity, like fMRI, or in techniques that measure electrical or magnetic signals resulting directly from neural activity, like electroencephalography (EEG) and magnetoencephalography (MEG). Generally, this approach computes covariances or correlations among brain activation time series in different brain regions. An alternative approach is to measure *effective connectivity*, or the influence one neuronal system causally exerts over another, either at a synaptic or cortical level. It is important to remember that functional connectivity may not be due to effective connectivity (e.g. common neuromodulatory input or afferents may mediate the correlation in activity) and, if it is, that effective connectivity may be indirect, through a path comprising several neurons in possibly different regions.

Again, turning to the SSIRH, if areas of genuine neural overlap are found using MVPA analyses, one type of functional connectivity analysis is easily applied, called psychophysiological interaction analysis (PPI) (Friston et al., 1997; Grahn & Rowe, 2009; Kim & Horwitz, 2008). This analysis can determine if the correlations in activity between domain-general and domain-specific areas change depending on whether the context is musical or linguistic. That is, if the activity of one region is regressed on the activity of a second region (in a musical context, for example), the slope of this regression would reflect the influence the second area could be exerting over the first. If one then repeated this regression, using data acquired in a different context (a linguistic context), then the slope might change. This context-dependent change in slope is a psychophysiological interaction. In the syntactic domain, a logical starting place would be extracting activity in Broca's area during musical and linguistic syntactic tasks. Correlations between Broca's area and other brain areas can be examined, to determine which regions show high correlations with activity in Broca's area during musical but not linguistic tasks, and conversely, which areas that show high correlations during linguistic but not musical tasks. This would provide strong evidence for the hypothesized interaction between domain-general and domain-specific systems during syntactic integration. Studies of functional connectivity in syntax have already begun, although not specifically addressing parallels between music and language. One intriguing finding is that connectivity increases between Broca's area and other language production areas for more proficient (compared to less proficient) second language speakers (Dodel et al., 2005). It remains to be investigated whether parallel findings might exist for extensively trained musicians in the musical domain, or to what degree expertise can influence domain-general processes, rather than domain-specific.

Functional connectivity analyses such as these are not limited to fMRI, as similar analyses can be conducted in the electrophysiological domain: coherence (or synchrony) in neural firing between brain areas can be observed in EEG or MEG (Basar, Basar-Eroglu, Karakas, & Schurmann, 1999; Llinas, 1988). Coherence is simply a squared correlation coefficient that provides a measure of the linearity of the relationship between two EEG electrodes at a particular frequency (explained clearly in Shaw, 1981). The frequencies examined generally include delta (<4 Hz), theta (4–8 Hz), alpha (8–12 Hz), beta (13–30 Hz), and gamma (>30 Hz) bands. High coherence in a particular band indicates the contribution of synchronized neuronal oscillations to each electrode, suggesting functional integration between neural populations, whereas low coherence suggests functional segregation. An advantage of EEG or MEG over fMRI is that the high temporal resolution allows the build-up of coherence over time to be observed. This is valuable for the study of syntactic processing, where integration of music or language structures also occurs over time. An important frequency band for linguistic syntactical processing appears to be the lower beta band: increased coherence is observed during syntactically demanding sentences (Bastiaansen & Hagoort, 2006). Coherence is only beginning to be investigated in the music syntactic domain, but the results thus far appear somewhat different from those for language. Synchronization during syntactically irregular musical sequences shows an early decrease in the synchrony within the alpha band and a later decrease in gamma band (Ruiz, Koelsch, & Bhattacharya, 2009). Thus violations of musical expectancy appear to be decreasing the integration between brain areas, rather than increasing it, as occurs for language.

For the SSIRH, one may well predict high coherence between domain-general syntactic areas and domain-specific music or language areas during the relevant context. This coherence may be expected to increase under difficult syntactic conditions (consistent with previous linguistic research) or may decrease when violations of syntax in either domain occur (consistent with previous musical research). Coherence changes between domain-general and domain-specific areas could provide converging evidence of functional connectivity. There are some methodological issues that will need to be addressed before these studies can be run. For example, how one can equate difficulty in musical and linguistic syntax remains an open question. What makes a syntactically difficult musical progression? And is this truly analogous to a syntactically difficult sentence? The answers to these questions may help clarify exactly which processes are shared across the two domains.

If one wishes to take connectivity analyses one step further, with relatively defined networks of interest, one can determine if the activity in a particular area is *causally* influencing the activity in another area, by performing analyses of effective connectivity. Methods of effective connectivity analysis include structural equation modelling and dynamic causal modelling (Friston & Harrison, 2003). These analyses take conclusions from functional analyses one step further, by testing whether neural activity in one area causally modulates activity in another area or other areas. In the current situation, these data could indicate whether Broca's area is indeed playing a top-down role in syntactic integration. Broca's area may bias auditory areas to pick up information relevant to the current musical or linguistic context, or perhaps allow an increase in processing efficiency when incoming stimuli match syntactic predictions. As before, effective connectivity measures also can be conducted in EEG and MEG. The calculation of phase relations in the coherence between brain regions can be taken as an indication of the direction of communication. Evidence from the neuroelectric domain may prove to be crucial, as the greater temporal resolution allows top-down versus bottom-up relationships to be characterized more accurately.

In conclusion, the SSIRH makes several predictions about domain-general processes that would be bolstered by studies finding neural areas that respond similarly during musical and linguist syntactical processes. The presence of significantly activated voxels in the same neural area for both domains may not result from similar activity of the underlying neural populations, therefore conventional analyses of functional neuroimaging data can only serve as a starting point. MVPA can test for similar patterns of activity in a neural area, providing stronger evidence for the activity resulting from similar rather than distinct neural populations. In addition, greater functional and effective connectivity between proposed domain-general areas and relevant domain-specific areas would provide converging evidence for neural interactions that reflect the cognitive operations involved in musical and linguistic syntax computation.

References

Aertsen, A., Preissl, H. (1991). Dynamics of activity and connectivity in physiological neuronal networks. *In Non Linear Dynamics and Neuronal Networks,* pp. 281–302.

Basar, E., Basar-Eroglu, C., Karakas, S., & Schurmann, M. (1999). Oscillatory brain theory: a new trend in neuroscience. *IEEE Engineering in Medicine and Biology Magazine, 18*(3), 56–66.

Basser, P. J. (1994). MR diffusion tensor spectroscopy and imaging. *Biophysical Journal, 66,* 259–67.

Bastiaansen, M., & Hagoort, P. (2006). Oscillatory neuronal dynamics during language comprehension. *Progress in Brain Research, 159,* 179–96.

Bengtsson, S. L., Nagy, Z., Skare, S., Forsman, L., Forssberg, H., & Ullén, F. (2005). Extensive piano practicing has regionally specific effects on white matter development. *Nature Neuroscience, 8*(9), 1148–51.

Dodel, S., Golestani, N., Pallier, C., ElKouby, V., Le Bihan, D., & Poline, J.-B. (2005). Condition-dependent functional connectivity: syntax networks in bilinguals. *Philosophical Transactions of the Royal Society B: Biological Sciences, 360*(1457), 921–35.

Friston, K. J., Buechel, C., Fink, G. R., Morris, J., Rolls, E., & Dolan, R. J. (1997). Psychophysiological and modulatory interactions in neuroimaging. *NeuroImage, 6*, 218–29.

Friston, K. J., & Harrison, L. (2003). Dynamic causal modelling. *Neuroimage, 19*(4), 1273–302.

Gold, B. T., Powell, D. K., Xuan, L., Jiang, Y., & Hardy, P. A. (2007). Speed of lexical decision correlates with diffusion anisotropy in left parietal and frontal white matter: evidence from diffusion tensor imaging. *Neuropsychologia, 45*, 2439–46.

Grahn, J. A., & Rowe, J. B. (2009). Feeling the beat: premotor and striatal interactions in musicians and non-musicians during beat processing. *Journal of Neuroscience, 29*(23), 7540–48.

Kim, J., & Horwitz, B. (2008). Investigating the neural basis for fMRI-based functional connectivity in a blocked design: application to interregional correlations and psycho-physiological interactions. *Magnetic Resonance Imaging, 26*(5), 583–93.

Koelsch, S., Gunter, T.C., von Cramon, D. Y., Zysset, S., Lohmann, G., *&* Friederici, A. D. (2002). Bach speaks: a cortical 'language-network' serves the processing of music. *NeuroImage, 17*, 956–66.

Llinas, R. R. (1988). The intrinsic electrophysiological properties of mammalian neurons: insights into central nervous system function. *Science, 242*(4886), 1654–64.

Logothetis, N. K. (2008). What we can do and what we cannot do with fMRI. *Nature, 453*, 869–78.

Maess, B., Koelsch, S., Gunter, T., & Friederici, A.D. (2001). Musical syntax is processed in Broca's area: an MEG study. *Nature Neuroscience, 4*, 540–45.

Niogi, S. N., & McCandliss, B. D. (2006). Left lateralized white matter microstructure accounts for individual differences in reading ability and disability. *Neuropsychologia, 44*, 2178–88.

Norman, K. A., Polyn, S. M., Detre, G. J., & Haxby, J. V. (2006). Beyond mind-reading: multi-voxel pattern analysis of fMRI data. *Trends in Cognitive Sciences, 10*(9), 424–30.

Peelen, M. V., & Downing, P. E. (2007). Using multi-voxel pattern analysis of fMRI data to interpret overlapping functional activations. *Trends in Cognitive Sciences, 11*(1), 4–5.

Peelen, M. V., Wiggett, A. J., & Downing, P. E. (2006). Patterns of fMRI activity dissociate overlapping functional brain areas that respond to biological motion. *Neuron, 49*(6), 815–22.

Ruiz, M. H., Koelsch, S., & Bhattacharya, J. (2009). Decrease in early right alpha band phase synchronization and late gamma band oscillations in processing syntax in music. *Human Brain Mapping, 30*(4), 1207–25.

Sammler, D. (2009). *The Neuroanatomical Overlap of Syntax Processing in Music and Language: Evidence from Lesion and Intracranial ERP Studies* (MPI Series in Human Cognitive and Brain Sciences, vol. 108). Leipzig: Max Planck Institute for Human Cognitive and Brain Sciences.

Schmithorst, V. J., & Wilke, M. (2002). Differences in white matter architecture between musicians and non-musicians: a diffusion tensor imaging study. *Neuroscience Letters, 321*, 57–60.

Shaw, J. C. (1981). An introduction to the coherence function and its use in EEG signal analysis. *Journal of Medical Engineering & Technology, 5*, 279–88.

Tillmann, B., Janata, P., & Bharucha, J.J. (2003). Activation of the inferior frontal cortex in musical priming. *Cognitive Brain Research, 16*, 145–61.

Chapter 25

Schemas, not syntax: a reply to Patel

Justin London

Introduction

As Ani Patel points out in his chapter 'Language, music, and the brain: a resource-sharing framework,' researchers who study the neurology and psychology of music and language are faced with a puzzle. On the one hand, evidence from neuropsychology seems to indicate that music and language involve separate and specialized parts of the brain. On the other hand, neuroimaging studies seem to show 'significant overlap in certain aspects of musical and linguistic processing' (p. 205). Patel's 'resource-sharing framework' (RSF) is an attempt at solving this puzzle, a solution which teases apart the domain-specific representations versus the shared resource networks that are used for the processing of 'syntactic' information in both domains.

As Patel notes, 'When . . . two domains draw on common brain resources, they do so because these resources provide a particular processing function needed in both domains' (p. 219). This is a compelling argument, though it depends on both (a) the particularity of the processing required, and (b) the nature of the similarities and differences between the domains. In language these sequences are described in terms of syntactic functions and orderings (i.e. subject–verb–object ordering in English, with clearly defined subjects, verbs, and objects). In music, sequences of tones or chords are analogously described in terms of a tone's position in a scale or a chord's function within a key. Patel, like many others, has characterized the relevant representations of both music and language as *syntactic*, that is, as representations of the well-formedness of sequences of sound elements based upon some sense of the grammatical function of each element. Here I will argue that this characterization of music is mistaken, that tones and chords are not really syntactic at all.

Patel is drawn to a syntactic account of melodic and harmonic structure based upon both the common misuse of the term 'syntactic' in music-theoretic discourse, as well as by an over-simplified view of the nature of melodic and harmonic well-formedness. If music is not syntactic in the way that language *is*, then there are implications for Patel's argument, both in terms of (a) what commonalities might underlie the use of shared neural processing resources, and (b) what this might tell us about the nature of both musical and linguistic structure.

On linguistic syntax and musical well-formedness

Let us start by teasing apart the similarities and differences between linguistic and musical organization in greater detail. As noted above, linguistic utterances involve discrete auditory elements that normatively occur in particular orders, and these structures may be described by recursive rules. While the meaning of some phonological elements is context dependent—for example, 'who' as relative clause marker, as in Patel's Figure 22.1, verses 'who' as interrogative, versus 'who' as the onomatopoetic sound of an owl—other phonological elements have fairly fixed meanings (e.g. 'ly' and 'ed' word endings which mark adverbial function and past tense, respectively). Indeed, these elements serve precisely to convey the syntactic function of the word to which they are attached.

Language involves a combination of both syntax and semantics. They are separable, as Chomsky's famous 'Colorless green ideas sleep furiously' example demonstrates (Chomsky 1957, p. 15). This separability has led to the claim that one may have syntactic structures without semantic content, which of course has implications for a syntactic account of music, which lacks referential semantics. But note that in Chomsky's sentence certain functional elements ('less' of 'color'; 'ly' of 'furious'; 's' of 'idea') retain their functional significance. Moreover, the central phonemes ('green', 'idea', 'sleep') also retain some semantic significance—we recognize their senses as adjective, noun, and verb based on their semantic extension, which helps define their syntactic function.

The larger issue regarding linguistic semantics is this: language reflects/describes certain states of affairs in the world, what we commonly think of as the 'meaning' of a sentence: 'The cat is on the mat', or 'Snow is white.'[1]

Thus certain grammatical relationships are not given by language, but by the states of affairs in the world, e.g. the whiteness of snow, or the locations of cats. Thus syntax and semantics, while separable, are not independent. While one can conceive of syntactic structures apart from any particular instance, one cannot parse the syntax of any particular utterance without some appeal to the semantic content of each element.

On now to music. It also is comprised of discrete auditory events that have to occur in particular orders and whose structure may be described (at least partially) by recursive rules. After this initial observation, however, the parallel with language breaks down. First, music lacks context-independent functional markers. While it is true that only certain tones (as defined as steps of a scale) can occur in certain chords (e.g. 'ti' or the leading tone is an element of a V chord), this definition of function is circular, as it is the constellation of such tones which defines the chords themselves (e.g. the V chord is a V chord because it is constructed from the tones 'sol,' 'ti,' and 're' of the scale). Likewise, these scale elements, absent a particular melodic or harmonic context, do not have any intrinsic sonic characteristics; the tone 'F#' by itself is tonally neutral/undefined. Even within a particular context, the 'phonological' aspects of a tone are mutable. For example, Patel claims that 'the 7th tone of the scale ('ti') is very unstable and conveys a sense of restlessness that requires resolution.' Consider, however, the appearances of 'ti' in Figure 25.1 (the F# tones, marked with asterisks).

Let us presume that we already understand that the melody occurs in the tonal context of G-major. The note 'ti' occurs five times in this melody. In the first measure it is a

[1] More precisely, this is of course the 'sentence' or 'utterance meaning', as opposed to the 'speaker meaning'—the aims of our linguistic behaviors in a social/interactive context (Austin, 1962).

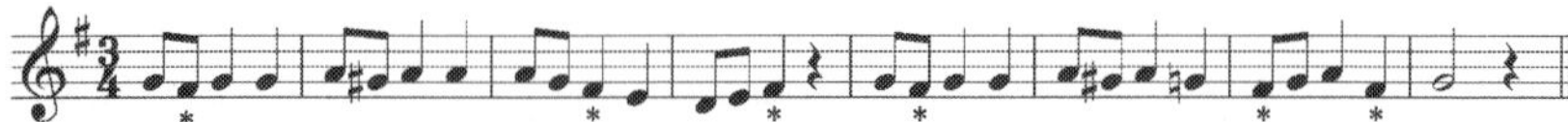

Fig. 25.1 Melody with 'ti' as neighbour, half-cadence, and pre-cadential dominant.

local ornament (a 'lower neighbour') to a repeated G; it has no larger significance within the phrase as a whole. In the third measure it occurs as a part of a descending scale figure; it is no more restless than the tones which precede or follow it. In measure four 'ti' occurs as the last note of the phrase; in this half-cadence it is quite stable, and indeed, a tone of repose. The second phrase, beginning in measure five, is a modified repetition of the first. In measure seven 'ti' occurs twice, and here, finally, do we have instances of 'ti' which match Patel's characterization: as elements in the pre-cadential melodic/harmonic structure, they are indeed restless, and require resolution to the final G.

The story of 'ti' from Figure 25.1 can be extended to more complex melodic and harmonic structures. Note that in the second and sixth measures the note G# appears (analogous to the F#s in measures one and five)—this is a non-scale tone which serves as a local embellishment to the primary note of the melody (A); while chromatic—an altered tonic note, no less—it is no more or less dissonant than the F#s in the preceding measures. Similarly, a single chord has no context-independent syntactic identity. There simply are no musical analogues to the syntactic marking functions of certain phonological elements in language. Rather, in music, the 'function' of a particular tone seems to be almost wholly dependent on context.

Music has no referential-semantic content. This is a well-known problem in musical aesthetics, even in cases where the music is purported to be representational (e.g. as in Berlioz's famous *Symphonie Fantastique*). Without the aid of lyrics or a text (or even the hint given by a title), listeners rarely can identify the person or object a passage is supposed to be about, let alone say what the s/he/it is doing. While musical figures and phrases may have affective and expressive properties, these are 'exemplifications' in the manner proposed by Nelson Goodman (1976)—a swatch of green cloth does not refer to 'green' the way nouns relate to their referents; rather the cloth simply *is* green, and gives us an instance of it. Likewise a melody may be an expression of sadness, in virtue of it having those inherent properties (Kivy, 1989).

To illustrate music's lack of semantic content, consider the word scramble problem. In language, word order conventions may be violated and yet syntax and semantics are still recoverable; one can, with a bit of effort, make sense of the following jumble of words: 'boy felt ball wearing threw the the the hat' ('The boy wearing the felt hat threw the ball'). You cannot, however, do this with tones; one could not reconstruct the melody in Figure 25.1 were the tones similarly scrambled. This illustrates the syntactic 'double whammy' for music: musical elements have no extra-musical semantic content that might help us sort out how they cohere and how they are to be arranged, nor do they contain any sort of function markers, which would allow us to reconstitute the musical phrase absent any semantic content.

Why, then, can one find tree structures describing music, as in Patel's Figure 22.2? As Patel notes, this tree diagrams a relational structure, based upon structural prominence.

As such, these trees are elaborate associational structures, guided by branching rules which show how an event (or series of events) relates to those that have preceded or follow it.

Finally, I would note that Patel employs some problematic descriptions of the elements and rules of western tonal syntax. He defines musical scales and chords as particular subsets of the chromatic scale, and that sequences of tones and chords follow principles 'to which listeners are sensitive' (p. 210). As is common in many music theory textbooks, scales are described as subsets of a universe of twelve chromatic tones, and chords as subsets of those scales. This description makes sense if you are a music theorist or a composer sitting at a piano, and your task is to construct well-formed instances of scales or chords. But we don't listen with miniature pianos in our heads (unless, perhaps, one has absolute pitch). Rather, we hear patterns of tones—perhaps best described as a series of vectors in a musical interval space—and from those patterns we infer a sense of key. We need not have any idea what particular frequency/pitch class serves as the 'anchor' or tonic in order to perceive a key, and indeed, any number of pitches within a key may serve as tonal anchors. Thus there is a bootstrapping problem for scale-based accounts of key recognition, as they presume we hear from the get go pitches-as-scale-degrees (and chords as combinations of scale degrees), when it is the very presentation of a certain series of intervals which allows us, as the music unfolds, to infer a sense of key.

Nor do most listeners, even highly-trained listeners, commonly hear tones in terms of scales and scale-steps. As every music theory teacher knows, while our talented student musicians have a keen sense of key, they are often quite poor at scale degree identification. As DeBellis (1995) has pointed out, learning how to hear melodies in terms of scale degrees is hard work, nor does it necessarily affect or enhance one's sense of key. Yet listeners, both musically trained and untrained, are still 'sensitive' to melodic and harmonic movement and closure, even though we are syntactically unaware.

Music without syntax: Implications for Patel

If musical structure is not syntactic, then what governs its well-for medness? Patel aptly notes that 'In . . . language and music, the structural relationship of incoming elements (such as words or chords) to preceding events must be determined in order to make sense of the sequence'. This seems exactly right, but much hinges on what is meant by 'make sense of'. There are at least two alternatives to a syntactic account of musical well-formedness. The first involves our use of bottom-up, gestalt-like processes to gauge the coherence of melodic sequences and predict their continuation. Most famously proposed by Meyer (1956), a series of tones is well formed if, for example, it is comprised of intervals that are approximately the same size and if they move in a consistent direction. Meyer's work has been extended by recent authors to include effects of specific interval sizes and durations (Narmour, 1990, 1992) and melodic range (Eitan, 1997; Von Hippel & Huron 2000). Psychoacoustic factors, such as the perception of octave equivalence, may also be involved at this stage of musical processing. In addition to bottom-up factors there are, naturally, top-down or schematic aspects to musical well-formedness. These can be in the form of scripts particular to a particular historical style and milieu (e.g. Gjerdingen (2007) on eighteenth-century Italian schemas, or Titon (1994) on melodic formulas used in blues songs of the Southern USA from the 1920s and 1930s), or more generic plans for western tonal music (Margulis 2005).

As noted above, Patel's RSF hypothesis hinges on the particularity of the processing required and the nature of the similarities and differences between mental representations of language and music. Both language and music require listeners to compile (in their working auditory memories) and then assess the structure of auditory sequences in the 3–5-second durational range, sequences that are made of a number of shorter elements, each of which occurs in the 0.2–1.5-second range. Some low-level processing overlap is thus inevitable. What is surprising is that higher-level shared neurological resources (beyond the primary auditory processing areas) are used in language and music at all. Language representations are entangled with our representations of things and events in the world, as well as with representations of language itself. Music does not have these semantic entanglements, though clearly we have representations of music itself. Likewise, knowing a language involves both knowing how to speak it as well as how to understand it (i.e. performance and competence); one need not be able to compose or perform to understand music. So what might be the basis of the higher-level overlap between musical and linguistic processing?

The experimental evidence for resource sharing cited by Patel (Patel, Gibson, Ratner, Besson, & Holcomb 1998; Maess, Koelsch, Gunter, & Friederici 2001) involves expectancy violations. Specifically, these correlate the activation loci of 'out of key' chords with those found in cases of incongruities of linguistic syntax. Two related questions arise with respect to these studies. First, are 'schematic surprises' controlled for in the stimuli which present out of key chords? It is not a trivial problem to compose stimuli that would have harmonic surprises that do not also involve melodic and/or rhythmic incongruities (e.g. an unexpected skip in a melody, or a rhythmic disfluency). Likewise, to what extent do the linguistic stimuli involve purely semantic violations of expectancy, versus script-based or phonetic anomalies? I would expect that there may be problems involved with the musical stimuli (having designed stimuli for other experiments, I am well aware how hard it is to avoid them), though likely not with the linguistic stimuli. The second and larger question is this: might the SRF be one for dealing with surprises/incongruities of any sort that occur in higher-level auditory scene analysis? In order to recognize a syntactic or schematic surprise, one needs to have a grasp of a stream of auditory information of considerable extent—several seconds previous, as well as an equivalent span in prospect. When these sorts of auditory surprises happen, we must reassess what we thought was happening/what we think is going to happen. In doing so, we may draw on representations and knowledge from any number of domains (world knowledge, morphophonemics, discourse conventions, and syntax in language; melodic and harmonic schemas, gestalt pattern recognition, and conventions of musical discourse (c.f. London, 1996)). Such reassessment would require connectivity to not just lower-level auditory processing, as well as lower-middle level musical and linguistic networks, but a broad range of other mental resources. While I have argued that syntactic processing may not be what is shared between music and language, many other aspects surely are.

References

Austin, J. L. (1962). *How to Do Things With Words.* Cambridge, MA: Harvard University Press.

Chomsky, Noam (1957). *Syntactic Structures.* The Hague/Paris: Mouton.

DeBellis, M. (1995). *Music and Conceptualization.* Cambridge: Cambridge University Press.

Eitan, Z. (1997). *Highpoints: A study of melodic peaks.* Philadelphia, PA: University of Pennsylvania Press.

Gjerdingen, R. (2007). *Music in the Galant Style: Being an Essay on Various Schemata Characteristic of Eighteenth Century Music for Courtly Chambers, Chapels, and Theaters, Including Tasteful Passages of Music Drawn from Most Excellent Chapel Masters in the Employ of Noble and Noteworthy Personages, Said Music All Collected for the Reader's Delectation on the World Wide Web.* New York: Oxford University Press.

Goodman, N. (1976). *Languages of Art.* Indianapolis, IN: Hackett Publishing Co.

Kivy, P. (1989). *Sound Sentiment.* Philadelphia, PA: Temple University Press.

London, J. (1996). Musical and linguistic speech acts. *Journal of Aesthetics and Art Criticism, 54,* 49–64.

Maess, B., Koelsch, S., Gunter, T., & Friederici, A.D. (2001). Musical syntax is processed in Broca's area: an MEG study. *Nature Neuroscience, 4,* 540–45.

Margulis, E. H. (2005). A model of melodic expectation. *Music Perception, 22,* 663–714.

Meyer, L. B. (1956). *Emotion and Meaning in Music.* Chicago, IL: University of Chicago Press.

Narmour, E. (1990). *The Analysis and Cognition of Basic Melodic Structures.* Chicago, IL: University of Chicago Press.

Narmour, E. (1992). *The Analysis and Cognition of Melodic Complexity: The Implication-Realization Model.* Chicago, IL: University of Chicago Press.

Patel, A.D., Gibson, E., Ratner, J., Besson, M., & Holcomb, P. (1998). Processing syntactic relations in language and music: An event-related potential study. *Journal of Cognitive Neuroscience, 10,* 717–33.

Titon, J. T. (1994). *Early Downhome Blues.* Chapell Hill, NC: University of North Carolina Press.

Von Hippel, P., & Huron, D. (2000). Why do skips precede reversals? The effect of tessitura on melodic structure. *Music Perception, 18,* 59–85.

Chapter 26

Advancing the comparative study of linguistic and musical syntactic processing

Aniruddh D. Patel

The empirical comparative study of linguistic and musical syntactic processing is a relatively young area of research. The first neuroimaging study of this topic was published a little over a decade ago, using event-related brain potentials (ERPs) (Patel, Gibson, Ratner, Besson, & Holcomb, 1998). While there has been a good deal of research on musical syntactic processing since that time (see Koelsch, 2009 for one review), studies using within-subjects designs to compare syntactic processing in language and music are still relatively rare. At present less than ten such studies have been published. These include ERP studies (Koelsch, Gunter, Wittforth, & Sammler, 2005; Steinbeis & Koelsch, 2008; Jentschke & Koelsch, 2009), intracranial EEG studies (Sammler, 2009), a study of Broca's aphasics (Patel, Iversen, Wassenaar, & Hagoort, 2008), and behavioural studies of normal individuals (Fedorenko, Patel, Casasanto, Winawer, & Gibson, 2009; Slevc, Rosenberg, & Patel, 2009). Notably absent from this list are within-subject functional magnetic resonance imaging (fMRI) studies aimed at comparing patterns of brain activity associated with syntactic processing in language and music. Such studies would advance our understanding of the brain bases of syntax and provide important tests of the resource-sharing framework for music and language (Patel, Chapter 22, this volume).

Given the recent growth of cognitive neuroscience research on music, it seems likely that further comparative studies of linguistic and musical syntax will be conducted soon. Such studies will benefit by attending to a number of issues raised in the commentaries in this volume by Stefan Koelsch (Chapter 23), Jessica Grahn (Chapter 24), and Justin London (Chapter 25).

The importance of specifying cognitive mechanisms

As noted by Koelsch (Chapter 23, this volume), comparative research will benefit from explicit hypotheses about 'which cognitive mechanisms are actually shared between language- and music-syntactic processing (and which are not)'. Focusing on Western tonal music, Koelsch offers a list of cognitive mechanisms involved in music syntactic processing, distinguishing domain-specific mechanisms (such as the extraction of a tonal centre) from mechanisms which might be shared with language (such as the integration of incoming elements into complex hierarchical structures, or the serial prediction of upcoming elements in sequences).

The shared syntactic integration resource hypothesis (SSIRH, see Patel, Chapter 22, this volume) focuses on the integration of incoming elements into hierarchical structures, but I would like to second Koelsch's suggestion that prediction of upcoming elements is another possible mechanism shared by music and language processing. 'Predictive listening' has long been a major theme in music cognition, commencing with the influential theory of Leonard Meyer (1956) on expectancy in music (see Huron, 2006 for a review of empirical data). Prediction is also a growing research topic in psycholinguistics, as empirical evidence accrues that listeners predict (or 'preactivate') upcoming linguistic information during sentence processing (e.g. DeLong, Urbach, & Kutas, 2005). Linguistic predictions are thought to occur at multiple levels (e.g. prosodic, semantic, pragmatic), including structural predictions about the syntactic categories of upcoming words (e.g. Gibson, 2006; Levy, 2008).

Structural prediction is a candidate for a shared cognitive mechanism between language and music. In his commentary, Koelsch states that 'While listeners familiar with (Western) tonal music perceive a sequence of chords, they automatically make predictions of likely chord functions to follow'. In other words, these listeners make implicit predictions about abstract structural categories (chord functions), such as 'dominant' or 'tonic'. Like syntactic functional categories in language (e.g. subject, direct object, etc.), chord functions are structural categories which are assigned by virtue of the context created by a sequence. Thus, for example, the word 'car' can be a subject, object, or indirect object of a sentence depending on the structure of the sentence. Similarly, a G major chord can serve a tonic, dominant, or subdominant function by virtue of the structural context in which it occurs. (This example is not intended to imply any direct mapping between specific linguistic syntactic functions and specific harmonic chord functions, only to point out that both domains have context-dependent structural functions.)

If language and music both involve the prediction of upcoming structural categories in sequences, what is the relationship of the brain networks involved in making these predictions? What brain areas become activated when these predictions are violated? Neuroimaging could be used to address these and other questions about structural prediction in language and music, and thus refine our understanding of how the brain makes abstract structural predictions when processing complex sound sequences.

The importance of advanced neuroimaging techniques

Grahn argues that future fMRI studies on syntactic processing in language and music should go beyond traditional fMRI localization methods. She makes a persuasive case for multivoxel pattern analysis (MVPA) techniques, which examine fine-grained patterns of activation across multiple voxels within a brain region, rather than simply looking for broad regions of activation. Grahn points out that MVPA would be particularly useful for analysing overlapping regions of activation associated with language and music processing. It is tempting to interpret such overlaps as evidence for shared networks involved in music and language. Another interpretation, however, is that 'two overlapping but functionally independent neural populations are present and active within the common region'. MVPA analyses can be used to address this issue by computing voxel-by-voxel patterns of selectivity to musical or linguistic stimuli. As pointed out by Grahn, such analyses would be particularly useful in studying the role of Broca's area (and its right hemisphere homologue) in linguistic versus musical syntactic processing.

Grahn also notes that music-language research should consider interactions between brain regions, not just the locations of active regions. Complex sequences such as music and speech engage multiple brain regions, and may be distinguished more by patterns of brain interaction than by a simple list of regions involved (Patel, 2003). Fortunately modern fMRI methods include techniques for studying neural interactions, such as functional connectivity (which measures temporal correlations between brain activity in different regions) and effective connectivity (which measures the influence of activity in one brain region on activity in another). Grahn notes that such methods could be used to compare patterns of interaction between Broca's region and superior temporal lobe regions during syntactic processing in language and music. I would add that such studies would benefit from approaches that combine the spatial resolution of fMRI with the temporal precision of MEG or EEG, in order to study interactions between brain regions at the timescale of actual neuronal activity (e.g. Freeman, Ahlfors, & Menon, 2009).

The importance of integrating theory and empirical data

London's commentary reminds us that many theorists remain sceptical of links between linguistic and musical syntax. He argues that musical structure and linguistic syntax have several important differences. For example, he notes that language has phonological markers for certain syntactic categories (such as the plural 's' maker in English). In contrast, musical tones lack 'intrinsic sonic characteristics' which signal their structural properties (cf. the earlier section 'The importance of specifying cognitive mechanisms' where it was pointed out that an acoustically identical G-major chord can play a dominant or tonic chord function depending on its context). What London's argument overlooks, however, is that language can also have structural categories which are not signalled by sonic characteristics. For example, the syntactic category of direct object in English (e.g. 'car' in 'We gave our old car to Marta') is not marked phonologically. Rather, 'car' is the direct object of the above sentence (versus, say, its subject or indirect object) only by virtue of the context in which it occurs, i.e. by virtue of its structural relations to other words in the sentence (cf. Gibson, 2006).

Be that as it may, London correctly reminds us that we should be careful about making general claims about the structural roles played by different tones within a musical key. He provides an effective example of how the leading tone in a particular key ('ti') can vary considerably in its degree of perceived restlessness depending on the melodic context in which it occurs (his Figure 25.1). However, this mutability does not invalidate the basic point that pitches in a tonal music context *have* abstract qualities (such as stability and instability, or being in-key or out-of-key) that go beyond their merely psychophysical qualities (e.g. as high/low/loud/soft acoustic events). Such qualities emerge because the pitches of tonal music are not combined in random ways, but instead are combined according to certain structural norms. The resource sharing framework (Patel, Chapter 22, this volume) assumes that listeners develop a sensitivity to these norms via implicit learning of the structural regularities of tonal music (Huron, 2006). It makes no assumption that this sensitivity is rigid and insensitive to local context. Indeed, as implied by London, the various factors that contribute to a tone's abstract qualities in real musical contexts are interesting topics for empirical research.

Stepping back from the details of London's critique, it is worth noting that London is one of several theorists who are sceptical about parallels between linguistic syntax and musical structure (cf. Jackendoff, 2009). Such sceptics have an important role to play in helping us refine our hypotheses about what music and language share in cognitive terms. Indeed, differences between theories of linguistic and musical syntactic structure helped inspire the resource-sharing framework, which acknowledges several formal differences between the syntaxes of the two domains. For instance, linguistic syntax includes word categories, constituent relationships, and point-to-point long-distance dependencies have no obvious analogues in music. Conversely, the pitch hierarchies, harmonic relations, and tension-resolution patterns found in tonal music have no clear counterparts in language. Yet despite these differences, there are similarities at more general levels. For example, both domains create hierarchically organized sequences based on abstract structural categories (e.g. subject, object, tonic, dominant) which can be instantiated by different surface elements (Patel, 2008, p. 267). Furthermore, incoming elements vary in how easy they are into integrate into the existing structure of the sequence. The resource-sharing framework (and more specifically, the SSIRH) posits that difficult structural integrations rely on a shared pool of limited neural resources, and makes predictions that have been empirically tested (see the references in opening paragraph of this essay).

Thus an important challenge for sceptics like London is to engage not only with theoretical arguments but also with empirical data. In other words, sceptics must account for evidence that the processing of tonality in music engages cognitive and neural mechanisms also used in the processing of grammatical relations in language. How does London account for this evidence? He argues that such evidence comes from studies that 'correlate the activation loci of "out of key" chords with those found in cases of incongruities of linguistic syntax.' For London this raises the question of whether what is shared by music and language processing are simply resources for 'dealing with surprises/incongruities of any sort that occur in higher-level auditory scene analysis'.

There are two problems with this idea. First, while many comparative music-language studies have employed structural incongruities in the two domains, at least one study has used well-formed sentences without any linguistic incongruities (Federenko et al., 2009). In this study, syntactic processing demands in language were manipulated by changing the structure of a relative clause within fully grammatical sentences. Hence music-language interactions in this study cannot be attributed to shared mechanisms for dealing with incongruities in sequences.[1] Second, some studies that employ structural

[1] It should also be noted that not all neural studies of musical syntax have used out-of-key chords. For example, Koelsch, Jentschke, Sammler, & Mietchen (2007) showed the early right anterior negativity (ERAN) can be elicited by a structurally unexpected in-key chord.

incongruities in both domains have also employed psychoacoustic incongruities to control for general 'surprise' effects (e.g. Koelsch et al., 2005; Fedorenko et al., 2009; Slevc et al., 2009). For example, Slevc et al. (2009) showed that an unexpected out-of-key chord interfered with the syntactic processing of a sentence, while an unexpected out-of-timbre (but in-key) chord did not have this effect. These results do not support the idea that music and language simply share processing resources for dealing with 'incongruities of any sort' in higher-level auditory scene analysis.

I suspect London would have interesting responses to my comments above, and that his future ideas in this area (like his current contribution) will help me refine my own thinking. More generally, I believe that a lively dialogue between sceptics and proponents of music-language syntax relations, with both sides well informed about theory and empirical data, is essential for progress on this complex and fascinating topic.

Acknowledgements

I thank John Iversen for insightful comments. Supported by Neurosciences Research Foundation as part of its research programme on music and the brain at The Neurosciences Institute, where ADP is the Esther J. Burnham Senior Fellow.

References

DeLong, K., Urbach, T., & Kutas, M. (2005). Probabilistic word pre-activation during language comprehension inferred from electrical brain activity. *Nature Neuroscience, 8*, 1117–21.

Fedorenko, E., Patel, A.D., Casasanto, D., Winawer, J., & Gibson. E. (2009). Structural integration in language and music: Evidence for a shared system. *Memory & Cognition, 37*, 1–9.

Freeman, W.J., Ahlfors, S.P., & Menon, V. (2009). Combining fMRI with EEG and MEG in order to relate patterns of brain activity to cognition. *International Journal of Psychophysiology, 73*, 43–52.

Gibson, E. (2006). The interaction of top–down and bottom–up statistics in the resolution of syntactic category ambiguity. *Journal of Memory and Language, 54*, 363–88.

Huron, D. (2006). *Sweet Anticipation: Music and the Psychology of Expectation.* Cambridge, MA: MIT Press.

Jackendoff, R. (2009). Parallels and nonparallels between language and music. *Music Perception, 26*, 195–204.

Jentschke, S., & Koelsch, S. (2009). Musical training modulates the development of syntax processing in children. *NeuroImage, 47*, 735–44.

Koelsch, S. (2009). Music-syntactic processing and auditory memory: Similarities and differences between ERAN and MMN. *Psychophysiology, 46*, 179–90.

Koelsch S., Gunter T.C., Wittforth, M., & Sammler, D. (2005). Interaction between syntax processing in language and music: An ERP study. *Journal of Cognitive Neuroscience, 17*, 1565–77.

Koelsch, S., Jentschke, S., Sammler, D., & Mietchen, D. (2007). Untangling syntactic and sensory processing: An ERP study of music perception. *Psychophysiology, 44*, 476–90.

Levy, R. (2008). Expectation-based syntactic comprehension. *Cognition, 106*, 1126–77.

Meyer, L. B. (1956). *Emotion and Meaning in Music.* Chicago: University of Chicago Press.

Patel, A.D. (2003). A new approach to the cognitive neuroscience of melody. In I. Peretz and R. Zatorre (Eds.), *The Cognitive Neuroscience of Music* (pp. 325–45). Oxford: Oxford University Press.

Patel, A.D. (2008). *Music, Language, and the Brain.* New York: Oxford University Press.

Patel, A. D., Gibson, E., Ratner, J., Besson, M., & Holcomb, P. (1998). Processing syntactic relations in language and music: An event-related potential study. *Journal of Cognitive Neuroscience, 10*, 717–33.

Patel, A.D., Iversen, J.R., Wassenaar, M., & Hagoort, P. (2008). Musical syntactic processing in agrammatic Broca's aphasia. *Aphasiology, 22*, 776–89.

Sammler, D. (2009). *The Neuroanatomical Overlap of Syntax Processing in Music and Language: Evidence from Lesion and Intracranial ERP Studies* (MPI Series in Human Cognitive and Brain Sciences, vol. 108). Leipzig: Max Planck Institute for Human Cognitive and Brain Sciences.

Slevc, L.R., Rosenberg, J.C., & Patel, A.D. (2009). Making psycholinguistics musical: Self-paced reading time evidence for shared processing of linguistic and musical syntax. *Psychonomic Bulletin and Review, 16*, 374–81.

Steinbeis, N. & Koelsch., S. (2008). Shared neural resources between music and language indicate semantic processing of musical tension-resolution patterns. *Cerebral Cortex, 18*, 1169–78.

Chapter 27

Music, language, and modularity in action

Isabelle Peretz

Introduction

A fundamental question that is currently hotly debated is: What does music share with language? Focusing on this question leads to an emphasis on the similarities between language and music, sometimes to the point of scientists coming to believe that they are the same functions. However, as I have argued for 20 years, the divergences between music and speech are striking (e.g. Peretz & Morais, 1989; Peretz, 2006). These differences have crucial implications for the study of music in general, and its origins in particular.

Imagine you were searching for the genes that are responsible for musicality. Finding the particular gene or genes for a behavioural trait is a challenging task for there are billions of possible loci for these genes in the genome. However, if indeed music and speech are very similar functions that have common origins, a good starting point would be to look for the genes that have already been identified for speech. One good candidate is the FOXP2 gene. The discovery of this gene as related to speech began with the study of the KE family of language-impaired individuals. The KE family has three generations, in which half the members suffer from a speech and language disorder (Hurst, Baraister, Auger, Graham, & Norell, 1990). Around half of the children of affected individuals have the disorder, whereas none of the children of unaffected individuals do. This inherited disorder has been linked to a small segment of chromosome 7 (Fisher, Vargha-Khadem, Watkins, Monaco, & Pembrey, 1998; Hurst et al., 1990). The chance discovery of an unrelated individual with a similar speech deficit has allowed the narrowing down of the disorder down to a mutation of a specific gene, named FOXP2 (Lai, Fisher, Hurst, Vargha-Khadem, & Monaco, 2001). This gene seems to play a causal role in the development of normal brain circuitry that underlies language and speech (Marcus & Fisher, 2003).

Interestingly, the speech disorder experienced by the KE family is not language-specific. It also affects oral movements. Hence, we may wonder if the mutation of the FOXP2 gene also affects vocal abilities such as singing. It does. Alcock, Passingham, Watkins, and Vargha-Khadem (2000a) tested nine affected members of the KE family and showed that they were impaired in rhythm production (and perception) while they performed as well as normal controls in melody (pitch-based) production (and perception). Hence, FOXP2 seems to participate to music rhythm. Hence, music and speech may have common origins after all.

However, pitch-based musical abilities seem governed by distinct genetic factors. The opposite pattern—preserved rhythm but impaired pitch—characterizes amusic (or 'tone-deaf') individuals (e.g. Ayotte, Peretz, & Hyde, 2002). Individuals affected with congenital amusia are impaired on all tasks that require sequential organization of pitch but do not necessarily have problems with time intervals (Hyde & Peretz, 2004). This pitch deficit is most apparent, and even diagnostic of their condition, when amusics are required to detect an anomalous (i.e. an out-of-key) note in a conventional melody (Ayotte et al., 2002). This musical pitch disorder is also hereditary (Peretz, Cummings, & Dubé, 2007). The congenital amusic individuals identified to date have no speech disorder. Thus, the available data are compatible with the idea that there are two innate factors guiding the acquisition of the musical capacity, with one related to temporal sequencing (and possibly related to FOXP2) and the other, pitch sequencing (of which genes remain to be determined).

Thus, as illustrated here, the comparison between music and speech is highly valuable because it provides an entry-point into understanding the genetic factors that contribute to the potentially shared capacity for music and speech and the genetic factors that contribute to music alone. The latter factors, possibly related to pitch-based abilities, may, however, not be unique to music but be involved in speech prosody. This raises the question of what to compare in music and language and how to assess domain-specificity. These two questions are addressed in the present chapter.

More specifically, in this paper, I will expand the modularity position to action rather than to perception. Modularity in perception has been treated in several prior papers (e.g. Peretz, 2001; Justus & Hutsler, 2005; McDermott & Hauser, 2005), including in Patel (Chapter 22, this volume). By action, I mean singing and speaking. Here I will review the literature on these two major modes of vocal expression and discuss their respective modularity. First, I will provide a brief background on the contemporary notion of modularity. Next, I will review the evidence for modularity in speaking and singing as arising from four sources: (1) neuropsychological dissociation; (2) overlap in neuroimaging; (3) interference effects; and (4) domain-transfer effects. Finally, I will contrast the modularity position with the resource-sharing framework proposed by Patel (2003, 2008, Chapter 22, this volume).

Modularity or domain-specificity

Modularity speaks directly to the nature of human evolved cognition. Above all, modularity is a useful framework for directing research and individuating cognitive systems. Unfortunately, the question of modularity has fuelled unresolved debates in the domain of language (Liberman & Whalen, 2000) and of face processing (Gauthier & Curby, 2005). The seeds of this debate are also present in the music domain. Therefore, it is important to address the issue by distinguishing and clarifying some concepts that are often confused when questions of specialization, domain-specificity, brain localization and innateness are considered (see Peretz, 2006, for further discussion). These concepts were connected explicitly in Fodor's (1983) proposal on the modularity of mind, and they have been confounded in many subsequent discussions.

Since Fodor's seminal book, concepts have changed. Of all the characteristics, domain-specificity remains the most important (e.g. Peretz & Coltheart, 2003).

A domain-specific operation is a distinct mechanism that deals with a particular aspect of the input and does this either exclusively or more effectively than any other mechanism. What individuates a module is its functional specialization (Barrett & Kurzban, 2006). Most scientists today would probably agree that the mind involves distinct parts (e.g. one for perception and one for motor control). The key notion is within these large systems, do we have functional specialization for music and speech?

Functional specialization is typically reserved for a whole faculty, such as the music faculty and the speech faculty. However, functional specialization can be very narrow. As narrow as the operation it performs. As argued elsewhere (Coltheart, 1999), there is no theoretical reason for excluding the concept of domain-specificity at the level of components. A domain may be as broad and general as *auditory scene analysis* and as narrow and specific as *tonal encoding of pitch*. Both subsystems perform highly specific computations and hence are domain-specific. That is, both components deal with a particular aspect of music, and they do this either exclusively or more effectively than any other mechanisms. Yet, *auditory scene analysis* is supposed to intervene for all incoming sounds (Bregman, 1990), whereas *tonal encoding of pitch* is exclusive to music.

Thus, domain-specificity does not necessarily imply music-specificity or language-specificity. Rather music-specificity should be examined for each subsystem or processing component. In addition, domain-specificity does not necessarily require special-purpose learning mechanisms. Domain-specificity may either emerge from general learning processes or result from the nature of the input code. I will return to this point later in this chapter (in the section 'The resource-sharing framework').

The question here is to what extent music (and language) processing relies on distinct or shared mechanisms. It remains possible that singing involves no music-specific component. In other words, singing may act as a parasite of speaking. For example, singing may engage the mechanisms for speech intonation. Music may aim at the language system just as artistic masks target the face recognition system. We can stretch this argument further and envisage that music owes its efficacy in relying on the natural disposition for speech. Music may exaggerate particular speech features such as intonation and affective tone, which are so effective for bonding. In this perspective, the actual domain of the language modules is invaded (Sperber & Hirschfeld, 2004). Music could have stabilized in all cultures because music is so effective at co-opting one or several evolved modules. Multiple anchoring in several modules may even contribute to the ubiquity and power of music. Thus, domain-specificity (or modularity) for music and speech requires comparison tests.

Tests of domain-specificity

Tests of domain specificity can be performed in at least four different ways: (1) by searching for neuropsychological dissociations between music and speech in brain-damaged patients or in developmental disorders; (2) by searching for distinct activation patterns elicited by music and speech in the normal brain; (3) by using interference paradigms in the normal brain; and (4) by studying the effects of transfer between musical abilities and speech abilities. Each method has been used in music and speech production tasks and will be reviewed here.

I will focus on production here because I have already addressed this issue in perception in prior papers (e.g. Peretz, 2001; Peretz & Coltheart, 2003) and because Patel (Chapter 22, this volume) deals with perceptual studies as well. Here, I will review the literature that has compared singing and speaking and assess whether there is evidence for music-specificity.

Unlike speaking, the ability to sing is usually considered to be unevenly distributed in the general population. While fine singing is viewed as the privilege of a selected few who are widely prized for their skill, the vast majority would be deprived of singing skills. Such a belief fuels the notion that the musical capacity cannot be innately determined (Pinker, 1997). If genes were responsible for the human musical capacity, then everyone should be able to engage in musical activities. Everyone should be able to carry a tune, unless they are tone-deaf. Singing should be as natural as speaking is. Recently, we showed that contrary to common belief, singing proficiency is widespread. Occasional singers can match the singing abilities of professional singers (Dalla Bella, Giguère, & PeretZ, 2007).

Singing appears as a natural disposition in humans. Singing is universal and found in all cultures. Moreover, singing is a group activity. Its participatory nature, requiring action coordination, is associated to a highly pleasurable experience. This is why singing is a fundamental human ability that is thought to promote group cohesion (Wallin, Merker, & Brown, 2000). In support of the social importance of singing is the observation that mothers universally sing to their offspring and that, in turn, singing abilities emerge early and spontaneously during development. The first songs are produced at around one year of age and at 18 months, children start generating recognizable songs (e.g. Ostwald, 1973; for reviews, see Dowling, 1999). This initial proficiency finds echo in adult singing, which is remarkably consistent both within (Bergeson & Trehub, 2002; Halpern, 1989) and across subjects (Levitin, 1994; Levitin & Cook, 1996) in terms of starting pitch and tempo. Therefore, the adult population seems to possess the basic capacities to sing popular songs with proficiency.

With universality, early and spontaneous emergence, consistency, and social function, singing abilities represent one of the richest sources of information regarding the nature and origins of music behaviour. Moreover, songs are a unique combination of speech and music. Yet, these are separable in many ways, for lyrics and melody rely on separate codes and are even often composed by different persons. Yet, music and text are linked and are most often, if not always, heard and played in a combined form. Thus, the study of singing represents a very rich new area for understanding music cognition as it relates to language because it seems guided by largely unconscious processes (Loui, Guenther, Mathys, & Schlaug, 2008), is a natural alliance between music and speech, and is more natural than most perceptual situations.

Neuropsychological dissociations

A module or domain-specific operation does not need to be neurally distinct or dissociable. It is possible that the neural substrate of a music module be intermingled with the networks devoted to a speech module. In that case, it will never be possible for brain damage to affect just the music module whilst sparing the speech module and vice versa, although the two modules are functionally distinct. In contrast, if the two modules are also neurally separable by involving different areas of the brain, it is possible to observe neuropsychological dissociations. These provide persuasive evidence for the existence of distinct modules. More generally, a mechanism must be neurally separable if the concept of modularity is to be of any use in cognitive neuroscience. The current evidence is consistent with the existence of neurally separable music and speech modules in singing and speaking.

Brain lesions can selectively interfere with speaking while singing remains essentially intact (Hébert, Racette, Gagnon, & Peretz, 2003; Peretz, Gagnon, Hébert, & Macoir, 2004; Racette, Bard, & Peretz, 2006; Schlaug, Marchina, & Norton, 2008; Wilson, Parsons, & Reutens, 2006). This corresponds to the common condition of aphasic patients who can no longer speak but sing. Most cases have preserved singing and prosody (Racette et al., 2006; Warren, Warren, Fox, & Warrington, 2003). Aphasic patients may remain able to sing familiar tunes and learn novel tunes; in contrast, they fail to produce intelligible lyrics in both singing and speaking (Hébert et al., 2003; Peretz et al., 2004; Racette et al., 2006; Warren et al., 2003). This dissociation indicates that speech production, whether sung or spoken, is mediated by the same (impaired) language output system, and that this speech route is distinct from both the (spared) musical and prosodic route.

Conversely, brain damage can impair singing exclusively. Patients may lose the ability to sing familiar tunes but retain the ability to recite the lyrics and speak with normal prosody (e.g. Peretz et al., 1994). The selectivity of the vocal deficit is not limited to non-musicians. Schön, Lorber, Spacal, and Semenza (2004) reported the case of an opera singer who was no longer able to sing pitch intervals but who spoke with the correct intonation and expression. The existence of a specific problem with singing alongside normal speaking is consistent with damage to processing components that are both essential to the normal process of singing and specific to the musical domain.

A typical objection to this argument is that most people are amateurs at music but experts at speech. Hence, music may suffer more than speech in the case of brain insult. When damaged, amateur abilities (e.g. music) would be more impaired than expert abilities (e.g. speech). As amply demonstrated in aphasic patients, the expertise effect cannot account for the recurrent findings of brain-damaged patients who are able to sing effectively whilst being unable to speak. Moreover, in developmental disorders, evidence for a similar double dissociation can be found. Children with specific-language impairments can sing but not speak (e.g. Mogharbel, Sommer, Deutsch, Wenglorz, & Laufs, 2005–2006). Conversely, individuals with congenital amusia (or tone-deafness) cannot sing but speak normally (e.g. Ayotte et al., 2002). In sum, the domain-specificity of music and language processing extends to production tasks.

Such neuropsychological cases constitute the best and most compelling evidence in favour of modularity for music and speech. The double dissociation implies the existence of anatomically and functionally segregated systems for music and speech in which one production system can function relatively independently of the other so that one system can be selectively impaired. Although this assumption remains unchallenged, sceptics have argued that double dissociations are not conclusive. A double dissociation can be simulated in an artificial network that is built with a unitary system. That is, lesioned connectionist systems are capable of generating double dissociations in the absence of clear separation of functions or modules (e.g. Plaut, 1995). However, there is as yet no plausible unitary explanation that can account for the pattern of selective impairment and sparing of musical abilities reported here. Thus, the evidence points to the existence of at least one distinct module for music and speech.

Could this distinct processing module for music be related to pitch production? Indeed, there is no need for all components that contribute to singing abilities to be specialized for music. Only one critical component, if damaged or absent, could account for all the manifestations of music-specificity. For example, all cases of congenital amusia whom we have studied so far seem to suffer from a dysfunction at this level (Peretz, 2008) and as a consequence may sing out-of-tune (Dalla Bella et al., 2009). Moreover, all amusic cases who suffer from a recognition or production disorder as a consequence of brain damage (Peretz, 2006) are systematically impaired on the pitch dimension, not on the time dimension.

In principle, an impairment on the time dimension, particularly in rhythmic entrainment, should also be detrimental to musical activities. Rhythm appears as the essence of music. Moreover, rhythm disorders can occur independently from pitch disorders (Di Pietro, Laganaro, Leeman, & Schnider, 2004; Alcock et al., 2000a; Alcock, Wade, Anslow, & Passingham, 2000b), arguing for the functional separability of rhythm and pitch-based processing of music. It remains to determine to what extent these rhythmic disorders affect musical abilities exclusively. Conversely, preserved rhythmic entrainment may account for the observation that singing at unison (that is along with someone else) improves speech recovery in aphasics while speaking along does not (Racette et al., 2006). Rhythmic factors may also depend on the spoken language. We note that there are more often reports of preserved word articulation in singing in English speakers (e.g. Schlaug et al., 2008) than in French speakers. This might be due to the constraints in text-setting of a stress-language, such as English, to the temporal structure of the melody. More research is needed on the temporal dimension in both singing and speaking, and in chorus singing in particular.

Thus, the current evidence points to musical capacity as being the result of a confederation of functionally isolable modules. To date, however, only abilities related to pitch appear to be uniquely engaged in music. The music-specificity of many other modules remains to be examined (see Peretz and Coltheart, 2003). Nevertheless, the current evidence, essentially based on pitch-related processes, argues against the view that the musical capacity has invaded the speech modules.

Overlap in neuroimaging

Music processing, probably more than language processing, recruits a vast network of regions located in both the left and right hemispheres of the brain, with an overall right-sided asymmetry for pitch-based processing (Peretz & Zatorre, 2005). In this context, it is not surprising that functional neuroimaging of the normal brain reveals significant overlap in activation patterns between music and language tasks. This is also the case of the seven neuroimaging studies in which overt or covert singing and speaking have been compared (Callan et al., 2006; Jeffries, Fritz, & Braun, 2003; Hickok, Buchsbaum, Humphries, & Muftuler, 2003; Özdemir, Norton, & Schlaug, 2006; Saito, Ishii, Yagi, Tatsumi, & Mizusawa, 2006; Brown, Martinez, & Parsons, 2006; Koelsch et al., 2008). Significant overlap is to be expected. Speech and music not only recruit widely distributed networks of brain regions but also involve multiple processing systems that might be shared. The number of networks involved is particularly large in the case of production tasks since the output system also involves the perceptual systems for auditory monitoring. Many of these processing components might be shared between music and speech, especially when singing contains lyrics.

In this context, the identification of distinct activation patterns for singing and speaking are more revealing than overlaps. All but one (Koelsch et al., 2008) of the published studies report distinct areas of activation for speaking and singing (but see below the study of Özdemir et al., 2006, in which increase of activation in a brain region is interpreted as a distinct neural correlate while it may simply reflect an increase in task difficulty). It is beyond the scope of the present paper to list all these potentially domain-specific brain regions. Instead, I will briefly summarize the findings of two studies because these are directly relevant to the work done with aphasics, as mentioned earlier.

In one of these studies, Özdemir and collaborators (2006) used a vocal imitation task for spoken and sung bisyllabic words (e.g. 'money' sung on a minor third). It is worth noting that words were pronounced at an abnormally low rate (e.g. one syllable per second), hence being more similar to chanting than speaking. Areas of activation common to all tasks included the inferior pre- and postcentral gyrus, the superior temporal gyrus (STG), and the superior temporal sulcus bilaterally. More interestingly, singing more than speaking revealed (additional) activation in the right STG and in the primary sensory motor cortex. In addition, singing more than humming showed activation in the right STG, the operculum, and inferior frontal gyrus. This is interpreted as possibly reflecting a distinct route for sung words that is a route that might be used by non-fluent aphasics in singing. However, this might simply indicate that singing with words is a more difficult task than speaking alone or humming alone (Racette and Peretz, 2007). In sum, there was no compelling evidence that singing and speaking involved distinct neural networks.

In contrast, using a well-known song, not just a slowly sung interval as in Özdemir et al.'s study (2006), Saito and collaborators (2006) obtained evidence for a distinct neural network in singing (but not in speaking). They compared singing the lyrics and reciting the same lyrics both alone and along a pre-recorded voice. Both singing alone and at unison activated brain areas that were not involved in reciting the lyrics (but not vice versa: there were no distinct areas associated to speaking). The right inferior frontal gyrus, the right pre-motor cortex, and the right anterior insula were found to be active in singing only (both alone and at unison). Since singing and speaking had the lyrics component in common but not the melody, one may interpret these brain areas as specifically related to melody production. However, there was no melody control condition. Interestingly, synchronized singing as compared to synchronized speaking activated the left anterior part of the inferior parietal lobe, the right posterior planum temporale, the right planum polare and the right middle insula. These specific areas may offer a neural account for the clinical observation that word intelligibility of non-fluent aphasics is enhanced in synchronized singing, as mentioned earlier (Racette et al. 2006).

As an aside, it is noteworthy that there is also more activation in brain regions involved in reward (e.g. nucleus accumbens) in singing than in speaking (e.g. Callan et al., 2006), suggesting a greater emotional component to singing. This is consistent with the fact that singing, more than speaking, is experienced as a highly enjoyable activity in general and in aphasics, in particular. For aphasic patients, singing is often their only spared vocal mode of expression, thereby facilitating proper breathing and increase in volume. This positive experience often motivates them to participate in lengthy and laborious sessions of testing (Racette et al., 2006).

In sum, neuroimaging studies may provide interesting hypotheses regarding the similarities and differences between music and speech, especially when combined with lesion studies, as illustrated here in the case of speech disorders. However, neuroimaging data cannot rival neuropsychological data. This is because neural and functional dissociations have greater inferential power than overlap or associations. Neuroimaging studies are correlational. Moreover, each activated brain area is a vast region that can easily accommodate more than one distinct processing network. Higher resolution may reveal distinct areas. Thus, neuroimaging data alone can hardly be regarded as a challenge to domain-specificity for music (and for language). As attempts for neural separability fail, we should become increasingly sceptical regarding the isolation of music processing components from language processing. In this search for evidence of domain specificity, some tools are, however, more powerful than others. Transcranial magnetic stimulation (TMS), to which we now turn, is one of these more promising tools.

Interference effects

TMS has become a widely used technique in cognitive neuroscience because it is the best available method that produces temporary interference with an ongoing neural process while neuroimaging is correlational by measuring a neural index of ongoing activity. This is important because whereas the other methods can indicate that a given neural response is associated with a behaviour of interest, the TMS method can be used to verify that it is essential, by interfering with it. The logic is similar to lesion studies. Moreover, the TMS has three major advantages over lesion studies: (1) the interference is temporary (reversible); (2) the localization of the 'lesion' can be manipulated experimentally; (3) the local interference can be induced in a normal brain that has no comorbidity due to the brain accident.

When applied in an inhibitory mode to the left inferior cortex in normal right-handed subjects, TMS can create speech arrest while the same stimulation to the right homologous region does not interfere with either speech or singing (Epstein et al., 1999; Stewart, Walsh, Frith, & Rothwell, 2001). On the other hand, singing interference is very difficult to obtain on either side (Epstein et al., 1999; Walsh, personal communication). When applied in a facilitatory mode to the hand motor cortices, speech and singing change the size of the TMS-induced motor evoked potentials of the right and left hand (with corticospinal projections from the left and right hemisphere, respectively; Sparing et al., 2007; Lo, Fook-Chong, Lau, & Tan, 2003). During speech, the right-hand potentials are enhanced whereas the left-handed potentials are increased during singing and humming, relative to the articulation of meaningless syllables. Thus, TMS provides strong evidence for the existence of differentially lateralized mechanisms mediating music and language processing, planning and execution of motor movements.

Similarly, it should be possible to obtain interference and facilitation effects between text and melody in 'normal' singing. This is indeed what we found in a song learning task in both musicians and non-musicians (Racette & Peretz, 2007). Singing both text and melody was more difficult than reciting the text or singing the melody on/la/. Singing both lyrics and tune of a novel song appears as a dual task in which melody and text compete for limited attentional or memory resources.

The interpretation of interference effects between music and language processing as evidence for the operation of distinct mechanisms may appear odd for 'radical modularists'. Indeed, if music and language processing components were completely modular in Fodor's sense, the processing of one domain, say music, should be encapsulated. That is, it should be immune to the parallel processing of speech. As illustrated above, the text and melody in songs interact with each other. It does not imply that melody and text are processed by a common core of mechanisms. On the contrary, the current evidence points to the existence of largely separable components that compete for general attention or memory. Thus, the observation of interference (or facilitation) does not challenge modularity, it only questions encapsulation. The use of information from multiple sources, especially in singing, is to be expected from an efficient system. However, integration of the information does not falsify a specialized use of information by dedicated music and speech systems.

Domain-transfer effects

Recent research has examined transfer effects between musical and language abilities with the idea that such a transfer is mediated by shared mechanisms (see Patel, Chapter 22, this volume). However, effects of music education on music on language processing are poorly understood (Schellenberg, 2006). Nonetheless, speculation abounds about the nature of the observed associations. For example, Patel (Chapter 22, this volume) proposes that musical training improves sensory tuning which in turn benefits the perception of speech.

In principle, this proposal should extend to speaking and singing. Musicians should speak or learn a second language with more proficiency than non-musicians. Such an association has been recently reported by Slevc and Miyake (2006) who showed that native Japanese speakers with high musical aptitude spoke English with a better pronunciation than their peers with less musical aptitude. Conversely, one would expect that speakers of tonal languages would be more musical than speakers of non-tonal languages. To my knowledge, domain-transfer from language to music has never been reported. Nevertheless, there are a number of shortcomings in current studies of domain-transfer effects, as we described in a recent paper (Schellenberg & Peretz, 2008).

First, musical aptitude, music lessons, and musicians are related but not identical concepts. Aptitude refers to 'raw' (untutored) abilities, music lessons involve learning, whereas musicianship is likely to be a consequence of aptitude and training combined with other factors. Duration of music lessons predicts cognitive abilities—including language—among children and adults (Schellenberg, 2006). Nonetheless, comparisons of musicians and non-musicians may yield null or inconsistent results (e.g. Helmbold, Rammsayer, & Altenmüller, 2005). Similarly problematic is the failure to account for musical training when studying aptitude (e.g. Slevc & Miyake, 2006), because musical training improves performance on tests of musical aptitude. In other words, observed associations could be either genetic or the consequence of music lessons.

A second and related issue concerns the nature and specificity of associations between musical experience and cognition. Discussion of 'special links' with language (i.e. Patel, Chapter 22, this volume; Slevc & Miyake, 2006) is misleading when associations between musical training and cognitive abilities are much more general, extending to working memory, mathematical and spatial abilities. Taking music lessons could be one learning experience that improves executive function, and, consequently, test-taking abilities in a variety of cognitive domains. Moreover, inferences of causation are unfounded in correlational studies of domain-transfer effects. Although isolated experimental evidence indicates that music lessons have cognitive transfer effects (Schellenberg, 2004), additional studies with random assignment and appropriate control conditions are essential for identifying the nature of the association between music and language.

This leads to the final issue related to modularity for both music and language. Observed associations between music and language, as that reported by Slevc and Miyake (2006), could just be the product of executive function, domain-general attentional or corticofugal (Wong et al., 2007) influences. In sum, even the optimal design, which would test for domain-transfer effects after training with random assignment, may not give insight into the nature of the shared mechanisms between music and speech. Yet, such studies are very important because they have clinical and educational implications.

The resource-sharing framework

Patel (2003, 2008, Chapter 22, this volume) argues that domain-specificity only applies to representations or knowledge. The operations that operate upon these domain-specific representations can be shared or domain-general. Patel refers to these operations as shared neural resources. In other words, representational specificity is distinguished from processing specificity. In the modular view, domain-specificity refers to both the operation and its output representation. In principle, the resource-sharing framework and the modularity concept are amenable to empirical tests.

For example, the acquisition of tonal knowledge uses general principles, by extracting statistical regularities in the environment. This possibility has been considered for the acquisition of tonal knowledge (Krumhansl, 1990; Tillmann, Bharucha, & Bigand, 2000). Although *tonal encoding of pitch* is music-specific, it may be built on "listeners' sensitivity to pitch distribution, [which is] an instance of general perceptual strategies to exploit regularities in the physical world" (Oram & Cuddy, 1995, p. 114). Thus, the input and output of the statistical computation may be domain-specific while the learning mechanism is not (Peretz, 2006; Saffran & Thiessen, 2006). Once acquired, the functioning of the system, say the *tonal encoding of pitch,* may be modular, by encoding musical pitch in terms of keys exclusively and automatically.

The same reasoning applies to *auditory scene analysis* and to *auditory grouping*. The fact that these two processing components organize incoming sounds according to general gestalt principles, such as pitch proximity, does not entail that their functioning is general-purpose and mediated by a single processing system. They need not be. For instance, it would be very surprising if visual and auditory scene analyses were mediated by the same system. Yet, both types of analyses obey to gestalt principles. It is likely that the visual and auditory input codes adjust these mechanisms to their processing needs. Thus, the input codes may transform general-purpose mechanisms into highly specialized ones. The existence of multiple and highly specialized micro-systems, even if they function in a very similar way, is more likely, because modularization is more efficient (Marr, 1982).

Thus, it is possible that domain-specificity emerges from the operation of a general mechanism, or from shared neural resources as proposed by Patel. However, in practice, it may be very difficult to demonstrate it because the general or 'shared' mechanism under study is likely to modularize with experience (Saffran & Thiessen, 2006).

A developmental perspective is likely to be useful in disentangling initial states from modularized end stage, in both typical and atypical developing populations. Developmental disorders could offer special insight into this debate. Advocates of a 'domain-general' cognitive system may search for co-occurrence of impairments in music and language (and other spheres of cognition, such as spatial cognition). Such correlation may give cues as to the nature of the processes that are shared between music and language. It may turn out that domain-specificity depends on very few processing components relative to a largely shared common cognitive background. These key components must correspond to domain and human-specific adaptations, while the shared background is likely to be shared with animals. Developmental disorders are particularly well placed to yield insight into both parts of the debate: that which is unique to music and language, and that which is not. It follows that a great deal can be learned by comparing impaired and spared music and language and cognition in individuals both within and between disorders over the course of development.

Concluding remarks

Although many questions about speech and music processing remain unresolved, there is evidence that musical abilities depend, in part, on modular processes. However, speaking and singing involve multiple processing components. The details of the functions that these mechanisms carry out, not only their specificity, should be the target of future empirical inquiry. As noted above, developmental perspective is likely to be critical in this debate. Neuroscientific tools such as optical imaging may also facilitate our ability to assess whether distinct brain mechanisms subserve the acquisition of distinct domains of knowledge in infancy (e.g. Pena et al., 2003). It is clear that continued research, rather than rigid theoretical positions, is needed to make progress on the question of domain-specificity and domain-generality.

To conclude, the notion of modularity remains important in contemporary research. First, the modularity thesis informs empirical investigation by the search for specialization. Second, modularity makes plausible candidates for evolved information-processing mechanisms and hence for genetically determined mechanisms. The modern concept of 'modularity affords a useful conceptual framework in which productive debates surrounding cognitive systems can continue to be framed' (Barrett & Kurzaban, 2006, p. 644).

Acknowledgements

Preparation of this paper was supported by grants from Natural Sciences and Engineering Research Council of Canada, the Canadian Institutes of Health Research, and from a Canada Research Chair.

References

Alcock, K. J., Passingham, R. E., Watkins, A. J., & Vargha-Khadem, F. (2000a). Pitch and timing abilities in inherited speech and language impairment. *Brain and Language, 75*, 34–46.

Alcock, K. J., Wade, D., Anslow, P., & Passingham, R. E. (2000b). Pitch and timing abilities in adult left-hemisphere-dysphasic and right-hemisphere subjects. *Brain and Language, 75*, 47–65.

Ayotte, J., Peretz, I., & Hyde, K. (2002). Congenital amusia: A group study of adults afflicted with a music-specific disorder. *Brain, 125*, 238–51.

Barrett, H. C., & Kurzban, R. (2006). Modularity in cognition: Framing the debate. *Psychological Review, 113*, 628–47.

Bergeson, T. R., & Trehub, S. E. (2002). Absolute pitch and tempo in mother's sons to infants. *Psychological Science, 13*, 72–75.

Bregman, A. (1990). *Auditory scene analysis. The perceptual organization of sound.* Cambridge, MA: MIT Press.

Brown, S., Martinez, M. J., & Parsons, L. M. (2006). Music and language side by side in the brain: a PET study of the generation of melodies and sentences. *European Journal of Neuroscience, 23*(10), 2791–803.

Callan, D. E., Tsytsarev, V., Hanakawa, T., Callan, A. M., Katsuhara, M., Fukuyama, H., *et al.* (2006). Song and speech: brain regions involved with perception and covert production. *Neuroimage, 31*(3), 1327–42.

Coltheart, M. (1999). Modularity and cognition. *Trends in Cognitive Science, 3*(3), 115–20.

Dalla Bella, S., Giguère, J.-F., & Peretz, I. (2007). Singing proficiency in the general population. *Journal of Acoustical Society of America, 121*, 1182–89.

Dalla Bella, S., Giguère, J.-F., & Peretz, I. (2009). Singing in congenital amusia. *Journal of Acoustical Society of America, 126*(1), 414–42.

Di Pietro, M., Laganaro, M., Leeman, B., & Schnider, A. (2004). Receptive amusia: temporal auditory processing deficit in a professional musician following a left temporo-parietal lesion. *Neuropsychologia, 42*, 868–77.

Dowling, W. J. (1999). The development of music perception and cognition. In D. Deutsch (Ed.), *The psychology of music* (2nd edition, pp. 603–25). San Diego, CA: Academic Press.

Epstein, C. M., Meador, K. J., Loring, D. W., Wright, R. J., Weisman, J. D., Sheppard, S., *et al.* (1999). Localization and characterization of speech arrest during transcranial magnetic stimulation. *Clinical Neurophysiology, 110*, 1073–79.

Fisher, S., E., Vargha-Khadem, F., Watkins, K. E., Monaco, A. P., & Pembrey, M. E. (1998). Localisation of a gene implicated in a severe speech and language disorder. *Nature Genetics, 18*, 168–70.

Fodor, J. (1983). *The modularity of mind.* Cambridge, MA: MIT Press.

Gauthier, I., & Curby, K. M. (2005). A perceptual traffic jam on highway N170. *Psychological Science, 14*(1), 30–32.

Halpern, A. R. (1989). Memory for the absolute pitch of familiar songs. *Memory and Cognition, 17*, 572–81.

Hébert, S., Racette, A., Gagnon, L., & Peretz, I. (2003). Revisiting the dissociation between singing and speaking in expressive aphasia. *Brain, 126*, 1838–50.

Helmbold, N., Rammsayer, T., & Altenmüller, E. (2005). Differences in primary mental abilities between musicians and nonmusicians. *Journal of Individual Differences, 26*, 74–85.

Hickok, G., Buchsbaum, B., Humphries, C., & Muftuler, T. (2003). Auditory-motor interaction revealed by fMRI: Speech, music, and working memory in area SPT. *Journal of Cognitive Neuroscience, 15*(5), 673–82.

Hurst, J. A., Baraister, M., Auger, E., Graham, F., & Norell, S. (1990). An extended family with dominantly inherited speech disorder. *Developmental Medecine and Child Neurology, 32*, 352–55.

Hyde, K.L., & Peretz, I. (2004). Brains that are out-of-tune but in-time. *Psychological Science, 15*, 356–60.

Jeffries, K. J., Fritz, J. B., & Braun, A. R. (2003). Words in melody: an H2 15O PET study of brain activation during singing and speaking. *NeuroReport, 14*(5), 749–54.

Justus, T., & Hutsler, J. J. (2005). Fundamental issues in the evolutionary psychology of music: Assessing innateness and domain-specificity. *Music Perception, 23*, 1–27.

Koelsch, S., Schulze, K., Sammler, D., Fritz, T., Müller, K., & Gruber, O. (2008). Functional architecture of verbal and tonal working memory: an fMRI study. *Human Brain Mapping, 30*, 859–73.

Krumhansl, C. L. (1990). *Cognitive foundations of musical pitch.* New York: Oxford University Press.

Lai, C. S., Fisher, S. E., Hurst, J. A., Vargha-Khadem, F., & Monaco, A. P. (2001). A forkhead-domain gene is mutated in a severe speech and language disorder. *Nature, 413*, 519–23.

Levitin, D. J. (1994). Absolute memory for musical pitch: evidence from the production of learned melodies. *Perception and Psychophysics, 56*, 414–23.

Levitin, D. J., & Cook, P. R. (1996). Memory for musical tempo: additional evidence that auditory memory is absolute. *Perception & Psychophysics, 58*, 927–35.

Liberman, A. M., & Whalen, D. H. (2000). On the relation of speech to language. *Trends in Cognitive Sciences, 4*(5), 187–96.

Lo, Y., Fook-Chong, S., Lau, D. P., & Tan, E. K. (2003). Cortical excitability changes associated with musical tasks: a transcranial magnetic stimulation study in humans. *Neuroscience Letters, 252*, 85–88.

Loui, P., Guenther, F., Mathys, C., & Schlaug, G. (2008). Action-perception mismatch in tone-deafness. *Current Biology, 18*, R331–32.

Marcus, G. F., & Fisher, S. E. (2003). FOXP2 in focus: what can genes tell us about speech and language? *Trends in Cognitive Sciences, 7*(6), 257–62.

Marr, D. (1982) *Vision.* New York: W.H. Freeman.

McDermott, J., & Hauser, M. (2005). The origins of music: Innateness, uniqueness, and evolution. *Music perception, 23*(29–59).

Mogharbel, C., Sommer, G., Deutsch, W., Wenglorz, M., & Laufs, I. (2005–2006). The vocal development of a girl who sings but does not speak. *Musicae Scientiae*, 235–58.

Oram, N., & Cuddy, L. (1995). Responsiveness of Western adults to pitch-distributional information in melodic sequences. *Psychological Research, 57*, 103–18.

Ostwald, P. F. (1973). Musical behavior in early childhood. *Developmental Medicine and Child Neurology, 15*, 367–75.

Özdemir, E., Norton, A., & Schlaug, G. (2006). Shared and distinct neural correlates of singing and speaking. *NeuroImage, 33*, 628–35.

Patel, A. (2003). Language, music, syntax and the brain. *Nature Neuroscience, 6*, 674–81.

Patel, A. (2008). *Music, language, and the brain.* Oxford: Oxford University Press.

Pena, M., Maki, A., Kovacic, D., Dehaene-Lambertz, G., Koizumi, H., Bouquet, F., et al. (2003). Sounds and silence: an optical topography study of language recognition at birth. *Proceedings of the National Academy of Science U S A, 100*(20), 11702–05.

Peretz, I. (2001) Music perception and recognition. In, B. Rapp (Ed.), *The Handbook of Cognitive Neuropsychology* (pp. 519–40). Hove: Psychology Press.

Peretz, I. (2006). The nature of music from a biological perspective. *Cognition, 100(1)*, 1–32.

Peretz, I. (2008). Musical disorders: From behavior to genes. *Current Directions in Psychological Science, 17*, 329–33.

Peretz, I., & Coltheart, M. (2003). Modularity of music processing. *Nature Neuroscience, 6*(7), 688–91.

Peretz, I., Cummings, S., & Dubé, M-P. (2007). The genetics of congenital amusia (or tone-deafness): A family aggregation study. *American Journal of Human Genetics, 81*, 582–88.

Peretz I, Gagnon L, Hébert S, & Macoir J. (2004). Singing in the brain: Insights from cognitive neuropsychology. *Music Perception, 21*, 373–90.

Peretz, I., Kolinsky, R., Tramo, M., Labrecque, R., Hublet, C., Demeurisse, G., et al. (1994). Functional dissociations following bilateral lesions of auditory cortex. *Brain, 117*, 1283–301.

Peretz, I. & Morais, J. (1989). Music and modularity. *Contemporary Music Review, 4*, 277–91.

Peretz, I., & Zatorre, R. J. (2005). Brain organization for music processing. *Annual Review of Psychology, 56*, 89–114.

Pinker, S. (1997). *How the mind works.* New York: Norton.

Plaut, D. C. (1995). Double dissociation without modularity: Evidence from connectionist neuropsychology. *Journal of Clinical and Experimental Neuropsychology, 17*, 291–321.

Racette, A., Bard, C., & Peretz, I. (2006). Making non-fluent aphasics speak: sing along! *Brain, 129*, 2571–84.

Racette, A., & Peretz, I. (2007). Learning lyrics: to sing or not to sing? *Memory & Cognition, 35*(2), 242–53.

Saffran, J. R., & Thiessen, E. D. (2006). Domain-general learning capacities. In E. Hoff and M. Shatz (Eds.), *Handbook of language development* (pp. 68–86). Cambridge: Blackwell.

Saito, Y., Ishii, K., Yagi, K., Tatsumi, I., & Mizusawa, H. (2006). Cerebral networks for spontaneous and synchronized singing and speaking. *NeuroReport, 17*, 1893–97.

Schellenberg, E. G. (2004). Music lessons enhance IQ. *Psychological Science, 15*(8), 511–514.

Schellenberg, E. G. (2006). Exposure to music: The truth about the consequences. In G. E. McPherson (Ed.), *The child as musician: A handbook of musical development* (pp. 111–34). Oxford: Oxford University Press.

Schellenberg, E.G., & Peretz, I. (2008). Music, language, and cognition: Unresolved issues. *Trends in Cognitive Sciences, 12*, 45–46.

Schlaug, G., Marchina, S., & Norton, A. (2008). From singing to speaking: why singing may lead to recovery of expressive language function in patients with Broca's aphasia. *Music Perception, 25*, 315–23.

Schön, D., Lorber, B., Spacal, M., & Semenza, C. (2004). A selective deficit in the production of exact musical intervals following right-hemisphere damage. *Cognitive Neuropsychology, 21*, 773–84.

Slevc, L. R., & Miyake, A. (2006). Individual differences in second language proficiency: Does musical ability matter? *Psychological Science, 17*, 675–81.

Sparing, R., Meister, I. G., Wienemann, M., Buelte, D., Staedtgen, M., & Boroojerdi, B. (2007). Task-dependent modulation of functional connectivity between hand motor cortices and neuronal networks underlying language and music: a transcranial magnetic stimulation study in humans. *European Journal of Neuroscience, 25*(1), 319–23.

Sperber, D., & Hirschfeld, L. A. (2004). The cognitive foundations of cultural stability and diversity. *Trends in Cognitive Sciences, 8*(1), 40–47.

Stewart, L., Walsh, V., Frith, U., & Rothwell, J. (2001). Transcranial magnetic stimulation produces speech arrest but not song arrest. *Annals of the New York Academy of Sciences, 930*, 433–35.

Tillmann, B., Bharucha, J. & Bigand, E. (2000). Implicit learning of tonality: a self-organizing approach. *Psychological Review, 107*, 885–913.

Wallin, N., Merker, B., & Brown, S. (Eds.). (2000). *The origins of music.* Cambridge, MA: MIT Press.

Warren, J. D., Warren, J. E., Fox, N. C., & Warrington, E. K. (2003). Nothing to say, something to sing: primary progressive dynamic aphasia. *Neurocase, 9*(2), 140–55.

Wilson, S., Parsons, K., & Reutens, D. (2006). Preserved singing in aphasia: A case study of the efficacy of melodic intonation therapy. *Music Perception, 24*, 23–36.

Wong, P. C. M., Skoe, E., Russo, N. M., Dees, T., & Kraus, N. (2007). Musical experience shapes human brainstem encoding of linguistic pitch patterns. *Nature Neuroscience, 10*, 420–22.

Chapter 28

Human subcortical auditory function provides a new conceptual framework for considering modularity

Erika Skoe and Nina Kraus

The central theme to Isabelle Peretz's large body of scientific work is that language and music employ a unique set of neural substrates and networks. Peretz's extensive work with congenital amusia suggests that while pitch is common to speech and music, aspects of pitch processing are unique to the domain of music. While her focus in this book is on vocal production and not perception, her argument takes a wider scope and extends to the general question of modularity. Peretz, by her own account, is not a radical modularist; she does not argue that all aspects of language and music processing are modular. Instead, she acknowledges that language and music are indirectly associated or partially overlapping functions, while still defending the position that music processing invokes specialized operations. Our commentary will spotlight a few key aspects of her argument, in addition to addressing several of her secondary remarks. Our intention here is to expand the theoretical discussion of modularity by presenting work from our laboratory[1] and others that refocus the debate on neural structures outside the cortex.

The debate over the modularity of language and music has been largely cortically centred. The reason is simple: until recently, little was known about how subcortical structures processed behaviourally-relevant signals such as speech and music and how subcortical tuning could be affected by auditory experiences.[2] Subcortical structures, and their interaction with cortical processes, provide a new vehicle for answering old questions, including offering a new perspective on the modularity of music and speech. Zatorre and Gandour (2008) echo this judgement in their review article directed at

[1] To achieve our objectives, many details and key methodological concepts relating to our work will need to be glossed over. We invite the reader to visit our laboratory's website for more information: http://www.brainvolts.northwestern.edu.

[2] For an elegant overview of the auditory brainstem and its changing role in the study of human electrophysiology, see Galbraith, 2008.

rectifying the seemingly contradictory view that speech can invoke both domain-general mechanisms and general-purpose mechanisms. They write:

> The key to reconciling these phenomena probably lies in understanding the interactions between afferent pathways that carry stimulus information, with top-down processing interactions that modulate these processes (p. 1087).

There are many parallels between the arguments laid out by Zatorre and Gandour and Patel's resource-sharing framework. For Patel, music and language involve domain-specific representations, which under certain circumstances invoke identical neural substrates and functional networks. Because Peretz and Patel are both featured in this volume and because Peretz dedicates a section of her article to the resource-sharing model, this manuscript will also serve as an indirect commentary on Patel's framework.

In this commentary, we will review data from clinical populations (language-based learning disorders (LD), autism spectrum disorders, and amusia), and expert populations (musicians and speakers of tonal languages),[3] that speak to domain specificity, resource sharing or their union. As an organizing structure for this commentary, section headings represent summaries or direct excerpts from Peretz's chapter.

'Music specificity should be examined for each subsystem or processing component'

The perception and production of speech and music invoke a vast overlapping network of neural structures that must operate independently and in tandem to achieve normal, non-disordered results. Modularity, therefore, could exist at multiple stages of auditory processing, and as Peretz suggests, a closer examination of each level is in order. To that end, we will be putting subcortical structures (specifically the brainstem) under the proverbial microscope to examine their roles in the modularity of speech and music.

The auditory brainstem, an ensemble of subcortical nuclei belonging to the efferent and afferent auditory systems, has an obligatory role in the processing of all sounds entering the cochlea, making it a common way station in both speech and music processing. Brainstem function can be appraised using scalp-electrodes that detect electrophysiological potentials generated by the synchronous activity of populations of subcortical neurons (Chandrasekaran & Kraus, 2009; Skoe & Kraus, 2010). This response, known as the auditory brainstem response (ABR), provides a means for objectively and non-invasively studying the neural encoding of speech and music. This is because the ABR represents the acoustic properties of the sound stimulus (e.g. pitch, timing, and timbre) with extraordinary fidelity (Galbraith, Arbagey, Branski, Comerci, & Rector, 1995; Akhoun et al. 2008; Skoe & Kraus, 2010). In fact, ABRs look like (see Figure 28.1), and when converted to an audio signal and played back, sound like, the evoking stimulus (Galbraith et al., 1995; Skoe & Kraus, 2010). By comparison, functional magnetic resonance imaging (fMRI) and cortical-evoked electrophysiological responses provide a more abstract representation of the evoking stimulus. Moreover, brainstem function can be meaningfully evaluated in an individual subject. Another appealing aspect is that ABRs to speech and music are correlated with performance on tests of

[3] For a discussion of auditory experts, see Chartrand, Peretz, & Belin, 2008.

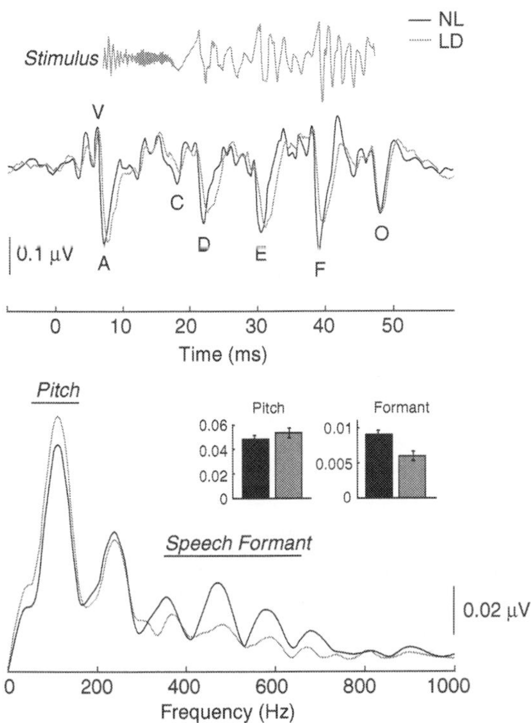

Fig. 28.1 Domain-specificity of the ABR: Subcortical representation of speech is selectively impaired in children with language-based learning disorders (LD). Auditory brainstem response to a 40-ms syllable 'da' in LD (grey) and normal learning (NL) children (black). Top: time domain waveforms with characteristic response peaks labelled. The timing of the LD response is delayed relative to the NLs. The stimulus waveform is plotted above to illustrate the strong visual coherence between the stimulus and response waveforms. Bottom: response spectra (frequency domain waveforms). Spectral peaks corresponding to the first formant of the speech stimulus are significantly reduced in LDs. In contrast, the neural representation of the stimulus pitch (i.e. fundamental frequency) is not abnormal in LD children. Adapted from Banai, K,Hornickel, J., Skoe, E., Nicol, T., Zecker, S., & Kraus, N. Reading and Subcortical auditory function. *Cerebral Cortex*, 19(11), pp. 2699–707. © 2009, Oxford University Press, with permission.

speech and music perception (Musacchia, Strait, & Kraus, 2008; Chandrasekaran, Hornickel, Skoe, Nicol, & Kraus, 2009; Bidelman & Krishnan, 2009; Hornickel, Skoe, Nicol, Zecker, & Kraus, 2009b), yet can be elicited passively without the subject performing a task that unavoidably engages high-order domain-general cognitive functions (e.g. attention and auditory memory). For more theoretical and methodological insights, see Galbraith (2008), Chandrasekaran and Kraus (2009), Kraus and Chandrasekaran 2010, and Skoe and Kraus (2010).

Galbraith was the first to recognize the dynamic nature of sensory processing in the human brainstem (Galbraith et al., 1995), and he laid the foundation for much of the ensuing research (Banai & Kraus, 2008; Chandrasekaran et al., 2009). There is now a wealth of evidence indicating that the brainstem is sensitive to linguistic and musical information. In addition to showing that musicians have heightened subcortical representations of music (Musacchia, Sams, Skoe, & Kraus, 2007) including features that are relevant for melody recognition (Lee, Skoe, Kraus, & Ashley, 2009), ABRs from non-musicians provide evidence that hierarchical representations of musical pitch (i.e. consonance-dissonance continuum) are rooted in subcortical processing (Bidelman & Krishnan, 2009). However, language-specific processes are also evident subcortically. For example, compared to non-speech signals, speech evokes larger ABR amplitudes (Galbraith et al., 1995) and elicits more robust group differences (Musacchia et al., 2007; Swaminathan, Krishnan, & Gandour, 2008). Likewise, we see that language experience primes brainstem tuning in a highly specific manner, as evidenced by enhanced pitch tracking in tonal language speakers for behaviourally-relevant, prototypical linguistic pitch contours (Krishnan, Xu, Gandour, & Cariani, 2005; Xu, Krishnan, & Gandour, 2006). The notion that language-dependent operations might have subcortical origins is also supported by research from Hornickel, Skoe, and Kraus (2009a) who found that the temporal and formant-related elements of the speech signal are preferentially encoded in the right-ear stimulated ABR, but that pitch is not. This finding is consistent with an animal model (King, Nicol, McGee, & Kraus, 1999) and work in the human auditory periphery (Sininger & Cone-Wesson, 2004) and brainstem (Levine, Liederman, & Riley, 1988; Sininger & Cone-Wesson, 2006). Taken together, this line of research suggests that lateralization of speech occurs outside the cortex.

The association between brainstem activity and language function is also evident when language is impaired. A subset of children with language-based learning disorders presents with irregular subcortical representations of timing and speech formants despite normal pitch representations (Figure 28.1) (Wible, Nicol, & Kraus, 2005; Banai et al., 2009; Hornickel et al., 2009b). This pattern is consistent with the phonological processing problems inherent to reading disorders, and the influential theory that reading impairments are symptomatic of a more generalized timing disorder (Tallal et al., 1996; Corriveau & Goswami, 2009). This dissociation of pitch and temporal processing may also explain why children with language disabilities perform poorly on musical timing tasks, but not pitch tasks (Overy, Nicolson, Fawcett, & Clarke, 2003). Work is underway in our laboratory to more fully understand the relationships between literacy and music aptitude and how they relate to behavioural and neurophysiological patterns in this population (see also Anvari, Trainor, Woodside, & Levy, 2002; Tallal & Gaab, 2006).

Domain-transfer effects between speech and music do not necessarily implicate a direct interaction. They may be mediated by a third party such as 'executive function, domain-general attentional or corticofugal influences'

Work from our laboratory fits within the larger scientific literature showing that musical experience has profound effects on the nervous system that extend beyond music. In addition to demonstrating domain-transfer effects between music and speech in vocal production (Stegemöller, Skoe, Nicol, Warrier, & Kraus, 2008), our

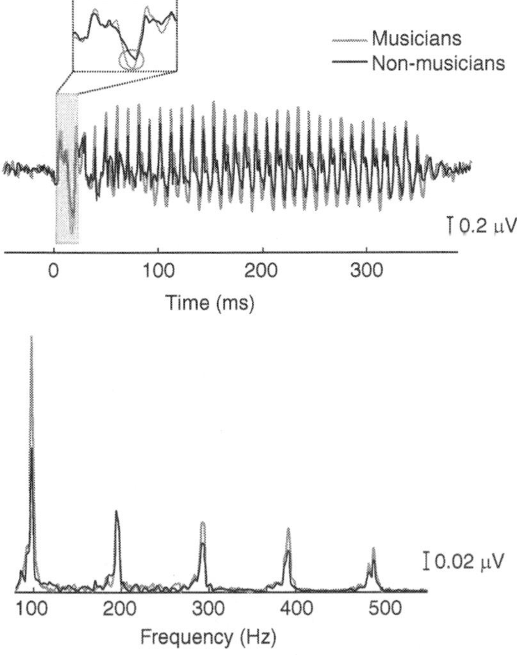

Fig. 28.2 Evidence of domain-transfer effects: musical training is associated with enhanced subcortical representation of speech. Grand average brainstem responses to a 350-ms speech syllable 'da' for both musician (grey) and non-musician (black) groups. Top: amplitude differences between the groups are evident over the entire response waveform. Inset: Musicians exhibit faster (i.e. earlier) onset responses. The large response negativity (circled region) occurs on average ~0.50 ms earlier for musicians. Bottom: musicians have more robust amplitudes of the fundamental frequency (100 Hz) and harmonics (e.g. 300, 400, 500 Hz). Adapted from Musacchia, G, Sams, M., Skoe, E., & Kraus, N. Musicians have enhanced subcortical auditory and audiovisual processing of speech and music. *Proceedings of the National Academy of Sciences* of the USA, 104(40), pp. 15894–98.

research has revealed that musical training is associated with enhanced subcortical representation of linguistic stimuli (Figure 28.2) under both optimal (Musacchia et al., 2007; Wong et al., 2007; see also Bidelman, Gandour, & Krishnan, 2011) and not optimal listening conditions (i.e. background noise) (Parbery-Clark, Skoe, & Kraus, 2009b; see also Bidelman and Krishnan, 2010). Importantly, these subcortical enhancements are not specific to linguistic stimuli and occur to non-linguistic, emotionally-rich vocal sounds as well (Strait, Kraus, Skoe, & Ashley, 2009). This transfer effect may be an indirect outcome of shared subcortical resources for speech and music. Musical experiences may enhance how music is represented in the brainstem (Musacchia et al., 2007; Bidelman et al., 2011; Lee et al., 2009) and as by-product other behaviourally-relevant signals are also fine-tuned. This link between music and speech is reinforced by correlational analysis showing that subcortical enhancements of speech and other vocal signals vary as a function of the extent and onset of musical experience (Musacchia et al., 2007; Wong et al., 2007; Strait et al., 2009).

We have previously argued that this context-general subcortical tuning results from the functional interplay between subcortical structures and high-order cognitive processes, with the corticofugal system serving as the biological mediator of this reciprocal communication (Musacchia et al., 2007; Wong et al., 2007; Parbery-Clark et al., 2009b; Kraus and Chandrasekaran, 2010; for a discussion of these reciprocal processes in an animal model see Malmierca, Cristaudo, Perez-Gonzalez, & Covey, 2009). This argument is grounded in the fact that the auditory system is a two-way street. In addition to the vast track of ascending fibres from the cochlea to the cortex, there is also an extensive chain of descending fibres linking higher neural structures to lower ones (Winer, 2006; Kral & Eggermont, 2007). In the animal model, the corticofugal system works to fine-tune subcortical auditory processing of behaviourally-relevant sounds (Luo, Wang, Kashani, Yan, 2008) by binding together learned representations and the neural transcription of specific acoustic features. This can lead to short-term plasticity and eventually long-term reorganization of subcortical sound encoding (for a review, see Suga, Xiao, Ma, & Ji, 2002). The direct involvement of the corticofugal system in human auditory processing has been demonstrated by Perrot and his colleagues (Perrot et al., 2006) who showed that stimulating the auditory cortex results in suppressed contralateral cochlear emissions. Moreover, the putative role of the corticofugal system in shaping human subcortical activity can also be inferred from training studies (Russo, Nicol, Zecker, Hayes, & Kraus, 2005; de Boer & Thornton, 2008; Song, Skoe, Wong, & Kraus, 2008b; Carcagno and Plack 2011; Song, Skoe, Banai, and Kraus, 2011) and experimental paradigms employing contralateral noise stimulation (Micheyl, Khalfa, Perrot, & Collet, 1997; Perrot, Micheyl, Khalfa, & Collet, 1999). Thus, corticofugal modulation can be seen as a powerful mechanism for guiding neural plasticity, driving language-specific subcortical enhancements, and bolstering transfer effects from music to speech, and possibly vice versa. Likewise, the subcortical deficits we find in children with language impairments (e.g. dyslexia and autism) may arise from faulty or suboptimal corticofugal engagement of auditory activity (Russo et al., 2008; Song, Banai, & Kraus, 2008a; Banai et al., 2009; Strait & Kraus, in press).

While we do see strong correlations between subcortical processing of speech and music, we cannot use the currently available data or methodology to pinpoint whether the putative corticofugal connections between speech and music are direct, or whether they are driven entirely (or even partially) by attention, memory, or other general-purpose cortical functions. The link between brainstem malleability and general cognitive processes is, in fact, a well-grounded idea. For instance, subcortical structures are likely governed by attentional state (Galbraith & Doan, 1995; Galbraith et al., 1998, 2003; Rinne et al., 2008) and shaped by multi-sensory integration (Musacchia et al., 2006, 2007). Thus, because memory, abstract reasoning and attention are common to both speech and music, and because selective auditory attention may mediate broad and long-term learning (Moore, Rosenberg, & Coleman, 2005; Stevens, Fanning, Coch, Sanders, & Neville, 2008; Parbery-Clark et al., 2009a) that results from specific auditory training, brainstem processing of speech and music is likely influenced by top-down cognitive functions via shared corticofugal mechanisms. This suggests that 'a third party' could be involved in the subcortical domain-transfer effects we observe. In this light, corticofugal mechanisms certainly do adhere to Peretz's domain-general characterization. However, while corticofugal mechanisms may affect subcortical processes globally, they can also be highly specific or 'modular'. For example, musical experience and short-term auditory training do not result in a stimulus-independent, generalized gain-effect and likewise, impairment does not necessarily manifest as a pervasive disruption in brainstem processing. What we find instead is that certain sounds or certain aspects of the sounds are impaired (Cunningham, Nicol, Zecker, & Kraus, 2000; King, Warrier, Hayes, & Kraus, 2002; Wible, Nicol, & Kraus, 2004; Wible et al., 2005; Banai et al., 2009; reviewed in Banai & Kraus, 2008) or enhanced (Wong et al. 2007; Song et al., 2008b; Lee et al., 2009; Strait et al., 2009; Parbery-Clark et al. 2009b), with the behavioural relevance and relative complexity or difficulty of the stimulus likely influencing how the sensory system responds (Figure 28.3).

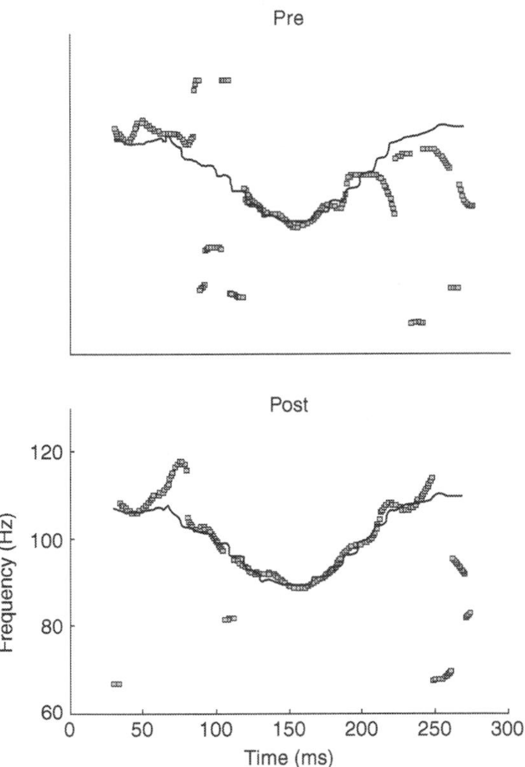

Fig. 28.3 Selective enhancement of pitch-related brainstem function after training. After eight days of lexical-pitch training, native English speaking adults had more accurate subcortical pitch tracking for the most complex pitch contour (i.e. Mandarin Tone 3). A representative example of pre- and post-training pitch tracking is plotted, with the sold black line representing the stimulus pitch contour. Using the same stimulus set, Wong et al. (2007) found that musicians and non-musician groups were also best differentiated by this complex pitch contour. Adapted from Judy H. Song, Erika Skoe, Patrick C.M. Wong, and Nina Kraus, 'Plasticity in the Adult Human Auditory Brainstem following Short-term Linguistic Training', Journal of Cognitive Neuroscience, 20:10 (Oct, 2008), pp. 1892–1902 © 2008 by the Massachusetts Institute of Technology.

Domain-transfer predicts that 'speakers of tonal languages would be more musical than non-tonal language speakers . . . [and] the prevalence of tone-deafness in these cultures should be close to inexistent'

Although formal statistics currently do not exist, we do have first-hand evidence that tone-deafness is not completely absent among tonal-language speakers. We are currently evaluating brainstem function in a native Mandarin Chinese speaker with congenital amusia (female, 30 years old, classified by the Montreal Battery for the Evaluation of Amusia (Peretz, Champod, & Hyde, 2003)). Foxton and colleagues (Foxton, Dean, Gee, Peretz, & Griffiths, 2004) point out that deficits in the ascending pathway may theoretically play a role in congenital amusia; however, this has never been formally investigated. In addition to assessing subcortical pitch encoding in this subject, we seek a better understanding of the complex interaction between simultaneous pitch impairment and pitch expertise, and the crosstalk between different stages of auditory processing. Although we reserve a complete analysis for a different venue, our preliminary results do not provide evidence for pervasive abnormalities in subcortical pitch encoding, which supports the prevailing view that amusia has cortical origins (Hyde, Zatorre, Griffiths, Lerch, & Peretz, 2006; Braun et al., 2008). That said, our data also do not entirely rule out subcortical anomalies. For example, just like there is a spectrum of language impairment, there may be multiple subtypes of amusia with only certain subtypes showing poor subcortical pitch-tracking (Russo et al., 2008) and/or amusia may have more subtle effects on brainstem function than we have been able to observe with our methods.

Now turning to the question of heightened musicality: Despite behavioural evidence for a higher incidence of absolute pitch in Mandarin speakers (Deutsch, Henthorn, Marvin, & Xu, 2006), there has never been a formal evaluation of how absolute pitch affects subcortical pitch tracking. However, recent work from Bidelman and colleagues (Bidelman et al., 2011) comparing pitch tracking of music- and speech-based pitch tokens between Mandarin speakers and native English-speaking musicians and non-musicians, provides the first subcortical evidence for linguistic pitch expertise transferring to the musical domain. Although musicians and Mandarin speakers did not differ in their accuracy of pitch tracking for both speech and music, musicians did show stronger responses than Mandarin speakers did, but only for components of the Mandarin contour corresponding to notes along the musical scale. This suggests a complex interplay of domain-transfer and domain-dependent interactions in the musicians. In addition to elucidating transfer effects from speech to music, a better understanding of these issues would also aid in interpreting amusic pitch tracking.

This brings us to Peretz's point: if domain-transfer effects exist, this should 'eradicate' musical pitch processing anomalies in cultures that use pitch lexically. If we tackle this issue from a corticofugal perspective, we first need a better handle on whether congenital amusia is associated with subcortical deficits. If it is, then the next question is whether the malformation of cortical pitch centres feeds backward to alter subcortical pitch tracking or/and whether music-mediated corticofugal processes are absent or not fully formed in amusics. However, if a large-scale study of amusia reveals no subcortical involvement, then we will need to address whether linguistic pitch expertise is sufficient to overcome or correct any overt subcortical pitch deficits (as might be inferred from Peretz's statement). At this time, there are, of course, still many unanswered questions; nevertheless, we do not view the existence of amusia in tonal language cultures as evidence for the nullification of transfer effects between speech and music.

One anatomical region can contain more than one distinct domain-specific network

While both Patel and Peretz maintain that it is possible for one anatomical substrate to contain functionally separate domain-specific networks, there is no evidence that the processing of speech and music are anatomically segregated within the brainstem (Patel 2011). We have illustrated above how corticofugal influences are both domain-general yet also work to shape aspects of sound processing in a modular fashion. This dual function of corticofugal modulation is the likely vehicle for brainstem structures having both domain-specific and domain-general functions. This suggests that brainstem nuclei could be inherently domain-general but become modularized with experience through the interaction of domain-specific and domain-general corticofugal networks. That is to say, some corticofugal pathways might reinforce modularity while others reinforce shared resources. Importantly, this duality could also account for the different degrees of modularity and/or resource sharing in different impaired and expert populations. These concepts are consistent with the idea that shared mechanisms modularize with experience (Saffran & Thiessen, 2006).

Summary and concluding remarks

Human subcortical auditory function provides a new conceptual framework for studying modularity. There is clear neural evidence for both shared and domain-specific subcortical processes, and our goal here was to try to rectify this apparent dichotomy. We have argued that corticofugal pathways can account for both sides of the coin and have outlined how cortical-subcortical interactions can give rise to both selective neurophysiological dissociations and enhancements, yet also result in overlap in activation between speech and music, and transfer effects. The corticofugal system is quite extensive and the prevailing evidence indicates that the number of efferent fibres far exceed the afferent ones. This intimates a complex architecture with, as we have pointed out here, a multitude of functions and outcomes.

The symbiotic relationship between cortical and subcortical structures leads to what is best described as an 'interaction between shared acoustic features and learned representations' (a phrase coined by Zatorre & Gandour, 2008) taking place at subcortical structures. From an acoustic standpoint, speech and music are highly complex signals with many shared features (e.g. pitch, timbre, and timing). Because the brainstem is the common ascending pathway for both faculties, and furthermore, because the ABR faithfully represents stimulus features, auditory experiences (i.e. learned representations) in one domain can shape the subcortical representation of both domains.

The connection between acoustics and learning is also evident in examples of selective subcortical enhancement and impairment. For example, in language-based learning disorders, the selective (non-pervasive) pattern of subcortical impairment (i.e. timing and speech formants but not pitch) is very much in accord with the behavioural manifestations of the disorder (Banai et al., 2009). Additionally, for speakers of tonal languages, subcortical enhancements occur for learned (i.e. language-specific) pitch contours (cf. Bidelman et al., 2011). Likewise, in musicians we find that subcortical refinement is linked to specific aspects of music learning (Bidelman & Krishnan, 2009; Lee et al., 2009). Taken together, these findings suggest that that music learning does not produce a simple gain effect.

The interaction between acoustics and learning likely encompasses global mechanisms (attention, memory, etc.) as well as *de novo* processes occurring within brainstem structures (e.g. statistical learning) (Dean, Robinson, Harper, & McAlpine, 2008). Although our discussion has primarily focused on top-down processes, the role of bottom-up and *de novo* processes cannot be dismissed (Krishnan & Gandour, 2009). For instance, the segregation of pitch and timing early in the processing stream (Kraus & Nicol, 2005), coupled with the fact that speech perception requires more temporal precision while music requires more spectral precision (Shannon, 2005), suggests that the brainstem could be a precursor for cortical modularization of speech and music. However, the very existence of the corticofugal pathway indicates that this is not an 'either/or' situation; a more realistic view is that both permanent and temporary top-down processes interact with bottom-up and local processes to shape subcortical function over a lifetime (Bidelman et al., 2011; Krishnan & Gandour, 2009; Kraus and Chandrasekaran, 2010). This feedback loop could then reinforce the putative domain-specificity at both cortical and subcortical levels.

Although it is beyond the scope of the commentary to provide a fully fleshed-out model, this commentary could serve as a stepping-stone for a unified account of how brainstem function fits into the debate of modularity and resource sharing. With the help of well-controlled longitudinal (e.g. Moreno et al., 2009) and population-based studies, it may be possible to tease apart: (1) whether subcortical structures are intrinsically domain general and inherit aspects of domain specificity from higher-up structures, (2) which aspects of subcortical pitch processing might be unique to music, (3) whether speech-music interference effects take place subcortically, (4) how music- and speech-learning are linked at a subcortical level, (5) how musical training can possibly strengthen and/or ameliorate impaired subcortical representation of speech and (6) whether amusia is strictly a cortically-based musical disorder or whether it has a subcortical locus and/or non-musical manifestations (Hattiangadi et al., 2005; Douglas & Bilkey, 2007; Nguyen, Tillmann, Gosselin, & Peretz, 2009).

Acknowledgements

This work is supported by the National Science Foundation (NSF 0544846), the National Institutes of Health (R01DC01510) and The Hugh Knowles Center for Clinical and Basic Science in Hearing and Its Disorders at Northwestern University, Evanston IL USA.

References

Akhoun, I., Gallego, S., Moulin, A., Menard, M., Veuillet, E., Berger-Vachon, C., *et al.* (2008). The temporal relationship between speech auditory brainstem responses and the acoustic pattern of the phoneme/ba/in normal-hearing adults. *Clinical Neurophysiology, 119*, 922–33.

Anvari, S. H., Trainor, L. J., Woodside, J., & Levy, B. A. (2002). Relations among musical skills, phonological processing, and early reading ability in preschool children. *Journal of Experimental Child Psychology, 83*, 111–30.

Banai, K., Hornickel, J., Skoe, E., Nicol, T., Zecker, S. & Kraus, N. (2009) Reading and subcortical auditory function. *Cerebral Cortex, 19*(11), 2699–707.

Banai, K., & Kraus, N. (2008). *The dynamic brainstem: implications for APD.* San Diego, CA: Plural Publishing Inc.

Bidelman, G. M., Gandour, J. T., & Krishnan, A. (2011). Cross-domain effects of music and language experience on the representation of pitch in the human auditory brainstem. *Journal of Cognitive Neuroscience, 23*(2), 425–23.

Bidelman, G. M., & Krishnan, A. (2009). Neural correlates of consonance, dissonance, and the hierarchy of musical pitch in the human brainstem. *Journal of Neuroscience, 29*, 13165–71.

Bidelman, G. M., & Krishnan, A. (2010). Effects of reverberation on brainstem representation of speech in musicians and non-musicians. *Brain Research, 1355*, 112–125.

Braun, A., McArdle, J., Jones, J., Nechaev, V., Zalewski, C., Brewer, C., *et al.* (2008). Tune deafness: processing melodic errors outside of conscious awareness as reflected by components of the auditory ERP. *PLoS ONE, 3*, e2349.

Carcagno, S., & Plack, C.J. (2011). Pitch discrimination learning: specificity for pitch and harmonic resolvability, and electrophysiological correlates. *Journal of the Association for Research in Otolaryngology, 12*(4), 503–517.

Chandrasekaran, B., Hornickel, J., Skoe, E., Nicol, T., & Kraus, N. (2009). Context-dependent encoding in the human auditory brainstem relates to hearing speech in noise: implications for developmental dyslexia. *Neuron, 64*, 311–19.

Chandrasekaran, B., & Kraus, N. (2009). The scalp-recorded brainstem response to speech: neural origins and plasticity. *Psychophysiology, 47*(2), 236–46.

Chartrand, J. P., Peretz, I., & Belin, P. (2008). Auditory recognition expertise and domain specificity. *Brain Research, 1220*, 191–98.

Corriveau, K., & Goswami, U. (2009). Rhythmic motor entrainment in children with speech and language impairments: tapping to the beat. *Cortex, 45*, 119–30.

Cunningham, J., Nicol, T., Zecker, S., & Kraus, N. (2000). Speech-evoked neurophysiologic responses in children with learning problems: development and behavioral correlates of perception. *Ear and Hearing, 21*, 554–68.

de Boer, J., & Thornton, A. R. (2008). Neural correlates of perceptual learning in the auditory brainstem: efferent activity predicts and reflects improvement at a speech-in-noise discrimination task. *Journal of Neuroscience, 28*, 4929–37.

Dean, I., Robinson, B. L., Harper, N. S., & McAlpine, D. (2008). Rapid neural adaptation to sound level statistics. *Journal of Neuroscience, 28*, 6430–38.

Deutsch, D., Henthorn, T., Marvin, E., & Xu, H. (2006). Absolute pitch among American and Chinese conservatory students: prevalence differences, and evidence for a speech-related critical period. *Journal of the Acoustical Society of America, 119*, 719–22.

Douglas, K. M., & Bilkey, D. K. (2007). Amusia is associated with deficits in spatial processing. *Nature Neuroscience, 10*, 915–21.

Foxton, J. M., Dean, J. L., Gee, R., Peretz, I., & Griffiths, T. D. (2004). Characterization of deficits in pitch perception underlying 'tone deafness'. *Brain, 127*, 801–10.

Galbraith, G. C., Arbagey, P. W., Branski, R., Comerci, N., & Rector, P. M. (1995). Intelligible speech encoded in the human brain stem frequency-following response. *Neuroreport, 6*, 2363–67.

Galbraith, G. C., Bhuta, S. M., Choate, A. K., Kitahara, J. M., & Mullen, T. A., Jr. (1998). Brain stem frequency-following response to dichotic vowels during attention. *Neuroreport, 9*, 1889–93.

Galbraith, G. C., & Doan, B. Q. (1995). Brainstem frequency-following and behavioral responses during selective attention to pure tone and missing fundamental stimuli. *International Journal of Psychophysiology, 19*, 203–14.

Galbraith, G. C., Olfman, D. M., & Huffman, T. M. (2003). Selective attention affects human brain stem frequency-following response. *Neuroreport, 14*, 735–38.

Galbraith, G. C. (2008). Deficient brainstem encoding in autism. *Clinical Neurophysiology, 119*, 1697–1700.

Hattiangadi, N., Pillion, J. P., Slomine, B., Christensen, J., Trovato, M. K., & Speedie, L. J. (2005). Characteristics of auditory agnosia in a child with severe traumatic brain injury: a case report. *Brain and Language, 92*, 12–25.

Hornickel, J.M., Skoe, E., & Kraus, N. (2009). Subcortical lateralization of speech encoding. *Audiology Neurotology, 14*, 198–207.

Hornickel, J., Skoe, E., Nicol, T., Zecker, S., & Kraus, N. (2009b). Subcortical differentiation of stop consonants relates to reading and speech-in-noise perception. *Proceedings of the National Academy of Science U S A, 106*, 13022–27.

Hyde, K. L., Zatorre, R. J., Griffiths, T. D., Lerch, J. P., & Peretz, I. (2006). Morphometry of the amusic brain: a two-site study. *Brain, 129*, 2562–70.

King, C., Nicol, T., McGee, T., & Kraus, N. (1999). Thalamic asymmetry is related to acoustic signal complexity. *Neuroscience Letters, 267*, 89–92.

King, C., Warrier, C. M., Hayes, E., & Kraus, N. (2002). Deficits in auditory brainstem pathway encoding of speech sounds in children with learning problems. *Neuroscience Letters, 319*, 111–15.

Kral, A., & Eggermont, J. J. (2007). What's to lose and what's to learn: development under auditory deprivation, cochlear implants and limits of cortical plasticity. *Brain Research Reviews, 56*, 259–69.

Kraus, N., & Nicol, T. (2005). Brainstem origins for cortical 'what' and 'where' pathways in the auditory system. *Trends in Neurosciences, 28*, 176–81.

Kraus, N., & Chandrasekaran, B. (2010). Music training for the development of auditory skills. *Nature Reviews Neuroscience, 11*, 599–605.

Krishnan, A., & Gandour, J. T. (2009). The role of the auditory brainstem in processing linguistically-relevant pitch patterns. *Brain and Language, 110*, 135–48.

Krishnan, A., Xu, Y., Gandour, J., & Cariani, P. (2005). Encoding of pitch in the human brainstem is sensitive to language experience. *Cognitive Brain Research, 25*, 161–68.

Lee, K. M., Skoe, E., Kraus, N., & Ashley, R. (2009). Selective subcortical enhancement of musical intervals in musicians. *Journal of Neuroscience, 29*, 5832–40.

Levine, R. A., Liederman, J., & Riley, P. (1988). The brainstem auditory evoked potential asymmetry is replicable and reliable. *Neuropsychologia, 26*, 603–14.

Luo, F., Wang, Q., Kashani, A., & Yan, J. (2008). Corticofugal modulation of initial sound processing in the brain. *Journal of Neuroscience, 28*(45), 11615–21.

Malmierca, M. S., Cristaudo, S., Perez-Gonzalez, D., & Covey, E. (2009). Stimulus-specific adaptation in the inferior colliculus of the anesthetized rat. *Journal of Neuroscience, 29*, 5483–93.

Micheyl, C., Khalfa, S., Perrot, X., & Collet, L. (1997). Difference in cochlear efferent activity between musicians and non-musicians. *Neuroreport, 8*, 1047–50.

Moore, D. R., Rosenberg, J. F., & Coleman, J. S. (2005). Discrimination training of phonemic contrasts enhances phonological processing in mainstream school children. *Brain and Language, 94*, 72–85.

Moreno, S., Marques, C., Santos, A., Santos, M., Castro, S. L., & Besson, M. (2009). Musical training influences linguistic abilities in 8-year-old children: More evidence for brain plasticity. *Cerebral Cortex, 19*(3), 712–23.

Musacchia, G., Sams, M., Nicol, T., & Kraus, N. (2006). Seeing speech affects acoustic information processing in the human brainstem. *Experimental Brain Research, 168*, 1–10.

Musacchia, G., Sams, M., Skoe, E., & Kraus, N. (2007). Musicians have enhanced subcortical auditory and audiovisual processing of speech and music. *Proceedings of the National Academy of Sciences of the USA, 104*, 15894–98.

Nguyen, S., Tillmann, B., Gosselin, N., & Peretz, I. (2009). Tonal language processing in congenital amusia. *Annals of the New York Academy of Science, 1169*, 490–93.

Overy, K., Nicolson, R. I., Fawcett, A. J., & Clarke, E. F. (2003). Dyslexia and music: measuring musical timing skills. *Dyslexia, 9*, 18–36.

Parbery-Clark, A., Skoe, E., Lam, C., & Kraus, N. (2009). Musician enhancement for speech in noise. *Ear and Hearing, 30*(6), 653–61.

Parbery-Clark, A., Skoe, E., & Kraus, N. (2009b). Musical experience limits the degradative effects of background noise on the neural processing of sound. *Journal of Neuroscience, 29*, 14100–07.

Patel, A. (2011). Why would music training benefit the neural encoding of speech? The OPERA hypothesis. *Frontiers in Psychology, 2*, 1–14.

Peretz, I., Champod, A. S., & Hyde, K. (2003). Varieties of musical disorders. The Montreal Battery of Evaluation of Amusia. *Annals of the New York Academy of Science, 999*, 58–75.

Perrot, X., Micheyl, C., Khalfa, S., & Collet, L. (1999). Stronger bilateral efferent influences on cochlear biomechanical activity in musicians than in non-musicians. *Neuroscience Letters, 262*, 167–70.

Perrot, X., Ryvlin, P., Isnard, J., Guenot, M., Catenoix, H., Fischer, C., *et al.* (2006). Evidence for corticofugal modulation of peripheral auditory activity in humans. *Cerebral Cortex, 16*, 941–48.

Rinne, T., Balk, M. H., Koistinen, S., Autti, T., Alho, K., & Sams, M. (2008). Auditory selective attention modulates activation of human inferior colliculus. *Journal of Neurophysiology, 100*, 3323–27.

Russo, N. M., Nicol, T. G., Zecker, S. G., Hayes, E. A., & Kraus, N. (2005). Auditory training improves neural timing in the human brainstem. *Behavioural Brain Research, 156*, 95–103.

Russo, N. M., Skoe, E., Trommer, B., Nicol, T., Zecker, S., Bradlow, A., *et al.* (2008). Deficient brainstem encoding of pitch in children with autism spectrum disorders. *Clinical Neurophysiology, 119*, 1720–31.

Saffran, J.R., & Thiessen, E.D. (2006). Domain-general learning capacities. In E. Hoff and M. Shatz (Eds.), *Handbook of language development* (pp. 68–86). Cambridge: Blackwell.

Shannon, R. V. (2005). Speech and music have different requirements for spectral resolution. *International Review of Neurobiology, 70*, 121–34.

Sininger, Y. S., & Cone-Wesson, B. (2004). Asymmetric cochlear processing mimics hemispheric specialization. *Science, 305*, 1581.

Sininger, Y. S., & Cone-Wesson, B. (2006). Lateral asymmetry in the ABR of neonates: evidence and mechanisms. *Hearing Research, 212*, 203–11.

Skoe, E., & Kraus, N. (2010). Brainstem responses to complex sounds: a tutorial. *Ear and Hearing*, *31*(3), 302–24.

Song, J. H., Banai, K., & Kraus, N. (2008a). Brainstem timing deficits in children with learning impairment may result from corticofugal origins. *Audiology & Neuro-otology*, *13*, 335–44.

Song, J. H., Skoe, E., Wong, P. C., & Kraus, N. (2008b). Plasticity in the adult human auditory brainstem following short-term linguistic training. *Journal of Cognitive Neuroscience*, *20*, 1892–902.

Song, J. H., Skoe, E., Banai, K., & Kraus, N. (2011). Training to Improve Hearing Speech in Noise: Biological Mechanisms. *Cereb Cortex*, [Epub].

Stegemöller, E.L., Skoe, E., Nicol, T., Warrier, C.M., & Kraus, N. (2008). Musical training and vocal production of speech and song. *Music Perception*, *25*, 419–28.

Stevens, C., Fanning, J., Coch, D., Sanders, L., & Neville, H. (2008). Neural mechanisms of selective auditory attention are enhanced by computerized training: electrophysiological evidence from language-impaired and typically developing children. *Brain Research*, *1205*, 55–69.

Strait, D. L., Kraus, N., Skoe, E., & Ashley, R. (2009). Musical experience and neural efficiency: effects of training on subcortical processing of vocal expressions of emotion. *European Journal of Neuroscience*, *29*, 661–68.

Strait, D. L., & Kraus, N. (in press). Playing Music for a Smarter Ear: Cognitive, Perceptual and Neurobiological Evidence. *Music Perception*.

Suga, N., Xiao, Z., Ma, X., & Ji, W. (2002). Plasticity and corticofugal modulation for hearing in adult animals. *Neuron*, *36*, 9–18.

Swaminathan, J., Krishnan, A., & Gandour, J. T. (2008). Pitch encoding in speech and nonspeech contexts in the human auditory brainstem. *Neuroreport*, *19*, 1163–67.

Tallal, P., & Gaab, N. (2006). Dynamic auditory processing, musical experience and language development. *Trends in Neurosciences*, *29*, 382–90.

Tallal, P., Miller, S. L., Bedi, G., Byma, G., Wang, X., Nagarajan, S. S., *et al.* (1996). Language comprehension in language-learning impaired children improved with acoustically modified speech. *Science*, *271*, 81–84.

Wible, B., Nicol, T., & Kraus, N. (2004). Atypical brainstem representation of onset and formant structure of speech sounds in children with language-based learning problems. *Biological Psychology*, *67*, 299–317.

Wible, B., Nicol, T., & Kraus, N. (2005). Correlation between brainstem and cortical auditory processes in normal and language-impaired children. *Brain*, *128*, 417–23.

Winer, J. A. (2006). Decoding the auditory corticofugal systems. *Hearing Research*, *212*, 1–8.

Wong, P. C., Skoe, E., Russo, N. M., Dees, T., & Kraus, N. (2007). Musical experience shapes human brainstem encoding of linguistic pitch patterns. *Nature Neuroscience*, *10*, 420–22.

Xu, Y., Krishnan, A., & Gandour, J. T. (2006). Specificity of experience-dependent pitch representation in the brainstem. *Neuroreport*, *17*, 1601–05.

Zatorre, R. J., & Gandour, J. T. (2008). Neural specializations for speech and pitch: moving beyond the dichotomies. *Philosophical Transactions of the Royal Society London B: Biological Sciences*, *363*, 1087–104.

Chapter 29

What remains of modularity?

Mireille Besson and Daniele Schön

The reading of Isabelle Peretz's (IP) paper (Chapter 27) raises many interesting issues and in this paper we will focus on four main points. First, we will try to clarify what genetics can tell us about the common or distinct origins of music and speech. Second, we will examine the evolution of the concept of modularity from Fodor (1983) to Fodor (2000/2003) and what remains of modularity. We will argue that if modularity exists it can only be at the level of local mental processes (micro level). Third, the definition of cognitive functions is a difficult problem faced by all cognitive neuroscientists in their empirical investigations. We will argue that language and music cannot be considered as entities and that a comparative approach helps defining their constitutive elements. Finally, the inferential power of different approaches will be discussed.

Genetics and the origins of music and speech

In the introduction, IP uses the discovery of the FOXP2 gene as a basis to argue for common (rhythm) and different (pitch) genetic origins[1] of music and speech. She starts by asking us to 'Imagine you were searching for the genes that are responsible for musicality'. This approach can be misleading regarding what genetics can tell us about behaviour because genetics does not allow determining which gene(s) are responsible for which function (there are no genes of memory, of speech, of music or musicality, of criminality or of homosexuality...). Rather genetics can reveal similarities and differences between individuals through variations in the genome sequence (Roubertoux, 2004). For instance, paternity tests, through the comparison of the DNA structure between two individuals (genetic traits) can reveal filiations but not the child's behaviour (behavioural traits). As IP pointed out, the discovery of the FOXP2 gene is revealing in this context because it demonstrates a correlation between the occurrence in the KE family of a mutation of the FOXP2 encoding gene and a developmental disorder that disrupts speech and language abilities.[2]

1 IP does not specify that she is interested in the 'genetic' origin of music and speech but since her arguments are based on FOXP2 we assume this is the case.

2 This is clearly stated in a recent review signed by one of the co-author of the FOXP2 discovery: 'FOXP2 cannot be called the gene for speech or the gene for language. It is just one element of a complex pathway involving multiple genes, and it is too early to tell whether its role in the pathway is special. Furthermore FOXP2 appears to be normal in common forms of developmental language disorder, and these seldom involve the kinds of oromotor deficits observed in the KE family (Markus and Fisher, 2003)'.

As we know, however, correlation is not causality. The ideal proof for causality would be to replace the mutated 'putative disease' allele gene by the 'normal' allelic form and by showing that the normal allele can correct the disorder (or vice versa, that the mutated allelic form can induce the disorder). This is, of course, not imaginable in humans. Causality, in its strongest form, can thus only be addressed in animal models, which is, of course, problematic when searching for a common or different genetic origin of music and speech. Most importantly, causal relationships are always difficult to demonstrate because there is no linear relation between the different levels of biological organization.[3] Thus, there is not necessarily isomorphism between the genotype and the phenotype and mutations in several distinct genes can lead to the same behavioural defect. For instance, mutations in at least 15 human distinct genes are involved in familial hypercardiomyopathy, a congenital disease that will nevertheless show similar aetiology across patients (Richard et al., 2003). Reciprocally, a particular mutation in one particular gene can lead to a variety of disorders. FOXP2, as a developmental gene encoding a transcription factor, obviously acts at a very basic level in the brain (and probably other organs) functional morphogenesis. Its mutated form is therefore expected to have wide consequences (Marcus and Fisher, 2003). If we transpose these notions from a micro to a macro level, the difficulty of the exciting enterprise that tries to establish a causal link between specific brain regions (or specific brain lesions) and specific cognitive functions (or specific cognitive impairments) becomes obvious.

Using genetics to argue for a common (or distinct) origin of speech and music is not a straightforward endeavour for several reasons. First, any complex behaviour rests on the activity of several thousand genes. For instance, around 10 000 genes (among the 15 000 present in the entire genome) are required for the vision function in *Drosophila*. Second, and may be most importantly, most of these genes are also involved in hundreds of distinct behaviour or functions. For instance, the *tubby* mutation in mice induces deafness, neural degeneration, and obesity. Similarly, the mutated FOXP2 allelic form has recently been introduced in the mouse homologue FOXP2 gene. These mice show impaired synaptic plasticity and motor learning, as well as severe reduction in cerebellar growth and postnatal weight gain (Groszer et al., 2008). Thus, while one may argue that that deafness and obesity, or motor learning and postnatal gain weight, share basic common molecular mechanisms, this does not imply that the complex pathways that lead to obesity or deafness are similar. In other words, showing that FOXP2 is involved both in speech articulation and in music rhythm is not necessarily meaningful because all complex (cognitive) functions in the end depend upon a limited number of basic and common molecular mechanisms. FOXP2, as a developmental gene, may be involved in both processes for different (and yet unknown) reasons. Along the same line, the finding that members of the KE family are not impaired in pitch production (and perception) does not necessarily imply that music and speech have different origins. It may be that pitch production (and perception) in music require smaller level of FOXP2 activity than in speech or that the behavioural tests were not sensitive enough to detect subtle changes in pitch abilities. Finally, it is also interesting to note that only 50% of the affected individuals in the KE family show

[3] This is what Roubertoux calls 'degenerated causality'.

language disorders. Therefore, other external or environmental factors (including the genetic background that differs for each member of the family), can modulate the expression of the FOXP2 mediated disorder. It may be that these modulating epigenetic cues exert a larger influence on pitch than on rhythm.

In conclusion, while searching for the genetic basis of functions and behaviours is an extremely important aspect of current research, the genetic evidences for 'common origins' of complex behavioural traits are not straightforward. Nevertheless, FOXP2 is an interesting entry point to dissect some of the molecular mechanisms involved in speech. It is a necessary element of a genetically transmitted programme that allows the development of normal speech abilities. But understanding the genetic origins of language or music is as complex as understanding the brain basis of language or music: in both cases, we are faced with complex, highly interacting, nonlinear systems.

The evolution of modularity: domain-specificity is not modularity

The basic assumption underlying modularity, as defined by Fodor (1983), is that cognitive mental processes are computational (i.e. thinking is a form of computation). Cognitive processes are specific (logico-algebric) computations (i.e. formal—non semantic-operations) on mental representations (i.e. the relationship between the world and the mind) that are structured syntactically (i.e. they obey an ensemble of rules that define the relationship between the different elements).

In his first essay, Fodor (1983) considers cognitive processes as modular if they possess a number of specific properties: (1) domain specific, (2) mandatory, (3) with limited access to the mental representations that they compute, (4) fast, (5) informationally encapsulated, (6) with 'shallow' outputs, (7) with characteristic and specific breakdown patterns, and (8) with a characteristic pace and sequencing of their ontogeny. In this framework, a module is a computational mechanism/system dedicated to the processing of a specific input–output function (i.e. that projects specific inputs onto specific outputs). In other words, a module is a processing device that does its business by using the information available in its own innate database without being influenced by anything else (the extreme example of a modular system is a reflex). In his new book, Fodor (2000/2003) clearly insists that 'informational encapsulation is at the heart of modularity' (2003, p. 107) because this is how modules can be functionally specified. And indeed, informational encapsulation (impenetrability) can be directly tested by using a cognitive neuroscience approach. However, results provide mixed evidence. For instance, results in the visual modality show that low-level visual areas (e.g. V1, V2, V3, and V4) perform some type of featural modular analysis (Sincich & Horton, 2005). By contrast, other results have shown that the presentation of a stimulus in one modality (i.e. vision) can lead to a decrease in regional measures of neural activity in another modality (i.e. audition; Kawashima, O'Sullivan BT, & Roland, 1995) and that, more generally, high-level functions, such as attention or musical expertise can influence lower-level processes, such as pitch encoding, in primary areas and subcortical brain regions (Woldorff et al, 1993; Wong, Skoe, Russon, Dees, & Kraus, 2007). By abandoning the central property of modular systems, informational encapsulation, and by considering that 'domain specificity remains the most important', IP adopts an impoverished view of modularity that loses part of its heuristic value.

Interestingly for our understanding of the evolution of the concept of modularity, Fodor (2000/2003) considers that only local systems can be modular. Global systems are not modular because they are not informationally encapsulated (they do not compute their own function independently of any other information that could possibly be relevant for its implementation). The fact that global systems are context-dependent and use the information available within the entire system to compute their function is taken as a major argument against what Fodor calls the 'massive modularity' of mind (see Pinker, 1997 and Pinker, 1994 for a response to Fodor, 2000/2003). Of course, the problem then is to define local and global systems. Interestingly, IP seems to adhere with the view, advocated by Marr (1982) that computations can be decomposed into a collection of modular, independent, and specialized subprocesses. From a theoretical perspective, this view can be criticized as being open-ended with no empirical failure point: any processes can be decomposed into more refined sub-processes (Van Orden, Pennington, & Stone, 2001). Nevertheless, this approach has a clear heuristic value in cognitive science and provides cognitive scientists with some ways to define cognitive functions (but see below). However, if one agrees with the idea that modularity can only exist at the level of local systems and that local systems are specialized subprocesses, neuropsychological dissociations, neuroimaging (functional magnetic resonance imaging, fMRI) or transcranial magnetic stimulation may not be the appropriate tools to look at such fine-grained level of functional organization. Finally, it is important to end this short and incomplete section on the evolution of modularity by pointing out that even the most basic assumption underlying modularity, that cognitive mental processes are computational, is called into question by Fodor (2000/2003), but this is another story.

The interest of the comparative approach and the importance of defining elementary functions

We are convinced that it is important to compare different cognitive functions using different approaches to better understand how the brain processes information. Indeed, focusing on one single investigation method, on a single brain region, on a single cognitive function, will give a partial view of the functioning of the brain. As noted by Bates (1994) this type of approach most often calls for domain specificity and, as a consequence, for a modular explanation of the brain function under study. By coupling the study of differences with the study of similarities, a comparative approach may provide a more complete picture of which computations are specific and which ones rely on more general cognitive principles. This comparison may be done at the level of the models that describe different cognitive competences (e.g. reading language versus reading music); but it may also be at the level of the relation (independent or interactive) between two different cognitive operations (e.g. language syntactic parsing and music harmonic parsing). For instance the theoretical work of Patel (2003) on linguistic and musical syntax points to the fact that while syntax and harmony may seem very different at first glance they show certain commonalities such as structure integration processes.

Overall, although we believe that it is important to consider music and language processing differences (and no reasonable person would claim 'they are the same functions') we also find it enriching to look for similarities, and consequently to combine the two approaches. As stated above, the definition of cognitive functions is a difficult problem we all have to face. The first problem is bound to circularity, namely the fact that if we have a certain definition of a function (say, harmonic structure processing), then we are going to make inferences about how this function is processed in the brain. If this function has a weak psychological or cerebral validity, we may soon realize that our inferences were wrong. Thus, the point is, how can we best define the cognitive functions we are studying using an experimental approach? Theoreticians might be of great help here. The comparative approach and the search for differences *and* similarities force us to find alternative views of the function in question. For instance, in the example given above concerning harmonic and syntactic processing, one may eventually realize that differences that were taken for granted in the theory are not reflected by corresponding biological differences, and this may in turn change the cognitive theoretical assumptions.

In line with the theoretical arguments developed by Marr (1982) and by Fodor (2000/2003; see above), IP seems to agree with the fact that music can be decomposed into smaller functions and she proposes *tonal encoding of pitch* as a possible candidate. Let us consider more closely this case and see whether it can be further decomposed. If we define pitch as the perceived fundamental frequency of a sound, *encoding of pitch* does not need to be domain-specific. The auditory signal, whatever its origin, is processed in the cochlea and is analysed in the brainstem and in the auditory cortex that show a tonotopic organization: close pitches are represented in topologically neighbouring neurons. There is no reason to believe that the primary auditory cortex is domain-specific (i.e. responds selectively to pitch in music or to pitch in speech). By contrast one may assume that pitch representations undergo quantitatively (and maybe qualitatively) different processing steps depending upon the structure of the auditory signal in the input.

Music builds on a more discrete representation of pitch than speech (totally discrete in the piano, partly discrete in violin or singing due to glides). Moreover, in music, pitch intervals need to be more exact than in speech (higher resolution), the number of pitches used depends on the musical system and is usually rather small (five to seven in average, parsimony) and constant. As noted by Peretz and Hyde (2003), music requires a more fine-grained analysis of pitches (due to higher resolution) than speech. It also allows a structured code of pitch relations (due to discreteness, parsimony, and constancy). Therefore, if the pitch-encoding mechanism is impaired, this will severely affect the perception of music, but it may not affect the perception of speech because speech does not require, even in tonal languages, a half-tone resolution. Thus, finding that a patient cannot sing precisely anymore but has preserved prosody (e.g. Schön, Gordon, & Besson, 2004) cannot be interpreted in terms of modularity of musical pitch. Indeed, one would need to find a patient with impaired prosodic contour perception and preserved musical contour perception, and make sure that such a deficit is not the result of an interaction with another impaired function (e.g. impaired syntax preventing a full understanding of the prosodic structure of a sentence). Indeed, different types of system organization (modular vs. non-modular) can produce identical changes in behaviour (Shallice, 1988; Farah, 1994).

IP suggests ***tonal** encoding of pitch* as a candidate for modularity. But what is exactly tonal encoding of pitch? Tonal encoding is a complex ability that is acquired rather late in infancy and that allows to organize the pitch space into a statistically structured space (Wilson, Wales, & Pattison, 1997; Krumhansl, 1990), based on the succession of the different pitches contained in the input signal. This ability requires that pitch is extracted with a certain degree of resolution. Thereafter, the representation of pitch can be used to code the relation between the current pitch and previous/following pitches. Such a temporal relation bears a notion of memory (or resonance), which is necessary in order to code intervals, intervals that are necessary to code tonality. While interval encoding probably builds on pitch encoding, it is not an 'elementary' function. Indeed, it requires a minimal memory storage capacity (of pitch representations) and the possibility to take into account the relative distances between pitches.

We could go on and parcel again these functions, but it is not the aim of our comment to propose a model of pitch processing in music. What we want to point out here is that *tonal encoding of pitch* is not necessarily a good candidate for domain specificity because it is far from being an elementary function. This does not exclude the possibility (although it is not necessary) that there might eventually be an elementary function, in the processing chain going from the cochlea to the perception of tonal stability, that is domain specific. The caveat we point to is the importance of the definition of elementary functions, both from a theoretical and an empirical point of view.

Elementary set theory and Bayesian inference in neuroimaging

IP, in sustaining the advantage of difference versus similarities, argues that in neuroimaging, 'distinct activation patterns [. . .] are more revealing than overlaps'. We will try to demonstrate that this statement is somewhat problematic. First of all, neuroimaging methods such as positron emission tomography (PET) and fMRI are often based on the assumption of pure insertion described by Donders (1868/1969). The idea is that a new cognitive component can be purely inserted (or subtracted) without affecting the expression of previous ones. While this might be correct, we should not forget that this relies on the strong assumption that processes combine in a serial and additive/independent fashion. This assumption is probably wrong because, most of the time adding/subtracting a component also changes the difficulty level of the task and in turn the attentional resources. For instance, in comparing singing and speaking, as in the study of Saito, Ishii, Yagi, Tatsumi, and Mizusawa (2006) described by IP, the fact that some brain areas are involved in singing but not in speaking, and not vice versa, can simply be due to the fact that singing is more demanding that speaking. Therefore, it might be that all voxels responding to singing are also responding to speaking, but that computing a statistical contrast (subtraction) will show a differential (but *not* distinct) cerebral network (i.e. the top of the iceberg and not the common underlying network). If this was the case, it would be wrong to interpret these areas as 'specific areas': simply on the basis of contrast statistics. Ideally, studies using the subtraction logic, should also have a control condition such as a silence or producing a 'shhh' sound (this was the case in the Saito et al. study but results of these contrasts are not reported in detail). Then, before doing the contrast of interest (e.g. singing–speaking), it would be possible to define the network underlying each experimental condition (exp. cond.–control). This is what we did in a recent study aimed at comparing the perception of speech, melodies, and songs. Interestingly we found that while a direct comparison between experimental conditions (e.g. song–speech) showed a rather large number of suprathreshold voxels that might be interpreted as 'specific areas', the use of a control condition (e.g. speech–control) showed that many of these same voxels were also involved in speech processing (Schön et al., 2005).

Moreover, even if one was to find a region involved in task A and not at all in task B by taking into account all these considerations, the claim for selectivity (i.e. domain specificity) might still be incorrect. In this respect, it is important to recall the concept of inference in probabilistic terms wherein the selectivity of a region depends upon the ratio between the number of times this region has been described as associated to a given function and the number of times it has been found to be associated to other functions (see Poldrack, 2006 for more details). While for primary regions the ratio (and selectivity) might be high, for secondary or more integrative regions the ratio (and selectivity) might be low. Our point here is that care has to be taken before claiming that a given region revealed by a statistical contrast is specific to a given cognitive function.

It is interesting to note that although IP seems to believe that 'neuroimaging data cannot rival neuropsychological data' with respect to 'inferential power', neuropsychological data suffer from similar inferential problems as those described above for neuroimaging data. Indeed, looking at meta-analyses of the neuropsychological literature often shows that a similar symptom can be due to different lesional foci (as mutations in different genes may underlie the same aetiology across patients, as mentioned above) and correlations between lesional sites and cognitive impairments rarely have high values (exception made for primary regions; for instance the correlation coefficient of phonemic and semantic fluency to temporal damage is 0.44 and 0.61, respectively, Henry & Crawford, 2004).

Conclusion

The theory of the modularity of mind did provide a useful framework for empirical research. However, evidence has accumulated, thanks to methodological advances at both the micro (genetics, molecular biology . . .) and macro levels (cognitive psychology, neuroscience, cognitive neuroscience . . .) that, in our view, point to the limits of modularity. Most importantly, advancement of knowledge at various levels of biological organization shows that biological and cognitive processes are largely influenced by environmental factors. Thus, and to only mention two extreme cases, the expression of genes depends upon epigenetic factors (genetic background, molecular environment . . .) and cognitive processes unfold as a function of the context (socio-cultural and personal experiences, motivation, strategies, specific abilities, as well as external environment, stressful, peaceful . . .). It becomes consequently more and more difficult to consider brain and behaviour as linear systems (a strong underlying assumption of several models and methods) that can be decomposed into independent modules and functions. Rather, these functions seem to be highly interactive (Uttal, 2001). One may thus wonder about what remains of modularity.

Acknowledgements

We would like to thank Isabelle Peretz for providing us the opportunity to think about interesting issues. We are particularly thankful to Michel Sémériva for fruitful and passionate discussions about genetics and behaviour. We would also like to thank Petr Janata and Barbara Tillman for interesting comments.

References

Bates, E. (1994). Modularity, domain specificity and the development of language. *Discussions in Neuroscience, 10*, 136–49.

Donders, F. C. (1969). On the speed of mental processes. In W. G. Koster (Ed.), *Attention and Performance II. Acta Psychologica, 30*, 412–31. [Original work published in 1868.]

Farah, M. J. (1994). Neuropsychological inference with an interactive brain: A critique of the locality assumption. *Behavioural and Brain Sciences, 17*, 43–104.

Fodor, J. A. (1983). *The modularity of mind.* Cambridge, MA: MIT Press.

Fodor, J. A. (2003). *L'esprit ça ne marche pas comme ça.* Paris: Odile Jacob. [First published as *The mind doesn't work this way* (2000). Cambridge, MA: MIT Press.]

Groszer, M., Keays, D. A., Deacon, R. M. J., de bono, J. P., Prasad-Mulcare, S., *et al.* (2008). Impaired synaptic plasticity and motor learning in mice with a point mutation implicated in human speech deficits. *Current biology, 18*, 354–62.

Henry, J. D., & Crawford, J. R. (2004). A meta-analytic review of verbal fluency performance in patients with traumatic brain injury. *Neuropsychology, 18*, 621–8.

Kawashima, R., O'Sullivan, B. T., & Roland, P. E. (1995) Positron-emission tomography studies of cross-modality inhibition in selective attentional tasks: closing the 'mind's eye'. *Proceedings of the National Academy of Science U S A 92*, 5969–72.

Krumhansl, C. L. 1990. *Cognitive Foundations of Musical Pitch.* New York: Oxford University Press.

Markus, G. F. & Fisher, S. E. (2003). FOXP2 in focus: what can genes tell us about speech and language? *Trends in Cognitive Neurosciences, 7*, 257–62.

Marr, D. (1982) *Vision.* New York: W.H. Freeman.

Patel, A.D. (2003). Language, music, syntax and the brain. *Nature Neuroscience, 6*, 674–81.

Peretz, I. & Hyde, K. (2003). What is specific to music processing? Insights from congenital amusia. *Trends in Cognitive Science, 7*, 362–367.

Pinker, S. (1994). *The language instinct: How the mind creates language.* New York, HarperPerennial.

Pinker, S. (1997). *How the mind works.* London: Penguin.

Poldrack, R. A. (2006). Can cognitive processes be inferred from neuroimaging data? *Trends in Cognitive Science, 10*, 59–63.

Richard P., Charron, P., Carrier, L., Ledeuil, C., Cheav, T., Pichereau, C., *et al.* (2003). Hypertrophic cardiomyopathy: distribution of disease genes, spectrum of mutations and implications for molecular diagnosis strategy. *Circulation, 107*, 2227–32.

Roubertoux, P. (2004). *Existe-til des gênes du comportement?* Paris: Odile Jacob.

Saito, Y., Ishii, K., Yagi, K., Tatsumi, I., & Mizusawa, H. (2006). Cerebral networks for spontaneous and synchronized singing and speaking. *NeuroReport, 17*, 1893–97.

Schön, D., Gordon, R. L., & Besson, M. (2005). Musical and linguistic processing in song perception. *Annals of the New York Academy of Science, 1060*, 71–81.

Shallice, T. (1988). *From neuropsychology to mental structure.* Cambridge: Cambridge University Press.

Sincich, L.C., & Horton, J.C. (2005). The circuitry of V1 and V2: integration of color, form, and motion. *Annual Review of Neuroscience, 28*, 303–26.

Uttal, W. (2001). *The New Phrenology.* Cambridge, MA: MIT Press.

Van Orden, G. C., Pennington, B. F., & Stone, G. O. *(2001). What do double dissociation prove? Modularity yields a degenerating research program. Cognitive Science, 25*, 111–17.

Wilson, S. J., Wales, R. J., & Pattison, P. (1997). The representation of tonality and meter in children aged 7 and 9. *Journal of Experimental Child Psychology, 64*, 42–66.

Woldorff, M. G., Gallen, C. C., Hampson, S. R., Hillyard, S. A., Pantev, C., Sobel, D., *et al.* (1993). Modulation of early sensory processing inhuman auditory cortex during auditory selective attention. *Proceedings of the National Academy of Science, 90*, 8722–26.

Wong, P. C. M., Skoe, E., Russon, N. M., Dees, T., & Kraus, N. (2007). Musical experience shapes human brainstem encoding of linguistic pitch patterns. *Nature Neuroscience, 10*, 420–22.

Chapter 30

Language, music, and children's brains: a rhythmic timing perspective on language and music as cognitive systems

Usha Goswami

In her elegant position paper, Peretz (Chapter 27, this volume) offers a robust defence of language and music as modular systems, citing detailed evidence from neuropsychology. Extending the modular framework summarized by Peretz and Coltheart (2003, see adaptation in Figure 30.1) to speaking versus singing, she contrasts her modular position with the resource-sharing framework offered by Patel (Chapter 22, this volume). Peretz notes that both Patel's resource-sharing framework and her own modularity framework are amenable to empirical test. Here, I present some relevant empirical data from developmental and animal cognition. While I agree with Peretz that a modular framework is useful for directing research (indeed, I have found her modular framework particularly useful in my own research), I will argue that developmental data do not support strong claims about domain specificity. As argued by Trehub, language and music may result from general perceptual mechanisms that are neither music- nor language-specific (e.g. Trehub & Hannon, 2006). Peretz (Chapter 27, this volume) also notes that data from developmental disorders could offer special insights into the debate about modularity. I completely agree, and I attempt to illustrate this here with respect to rhythmic processing, prosody, and rhythmic entrainment in developmental dyslexia and specific language impairment. An important claim will be that prosody and rhythm rather than syntactic or phonemic aspects of language processing offer the most utility for understanding shared cognitive systems with music.

Initial states and modularized end states: how do cognitive systems develop?

Neuropsychology as a discipline favours modularity, because most neuropsychologists study the selective loss of cognitive skills after developmental trajectories have plateaued (Bishop, 1997; Karmiloff-Smith, 1998; Goswami, 2003). However, the developing brain is not modular. Developmental perspectives reveal that functional specialization is *experience-dependent* (Johnson, 2004). For example, a Japanese baby who hears the phonetic continuum/l/-/r/as always corresponding to one phoneme will develop a single speech sound category for this continuum, whereas an English baby

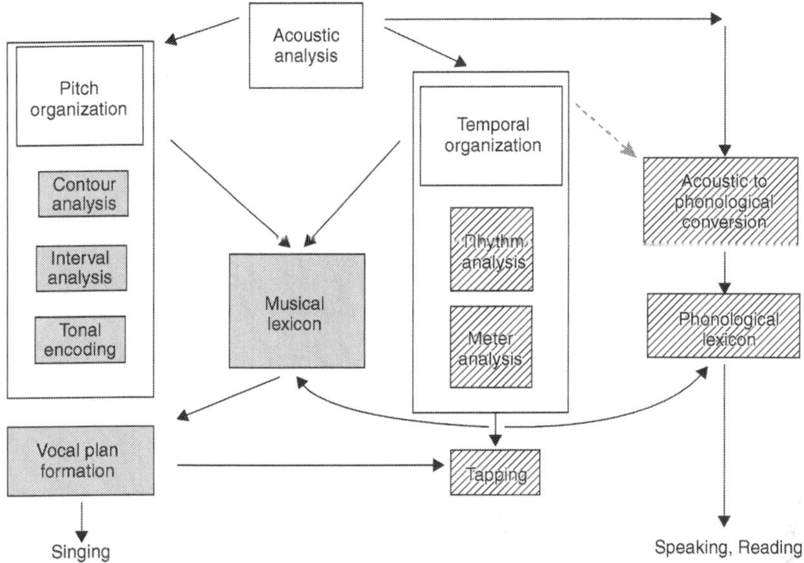

Fig. 30.1 Adaptation of Peretz and Coltheart Model (2003) for Musical Processing. A simplified overview of Peretz and Coltheart's (2003) modular framework, with an amendment of the input to phonology (dashed arrow). The parts of the model that are proposed to be impaired in amusia and specific to pitch organization are shown in grey. These aspects remain to be tested in children with language and literacy problems. Those parts of the model that are proposed to be preserved in amusia, namely aspects of temporal organization such as rhythmic and metrical analysis, are shown in hatched boxes. These aspects are impaired in children with language and literacy problems. Other aspects of acoustic analysis that are reliably impaired in children with language and literacy difficulties are also shown in hatched boxes. Children with language and literacy problems have heritable phonological difficulties.

who hears the same continuum as corresponding to two phonemes,/l/and/r/, will develop two speech sound categories for the same physical input (Munakata & McClelland, 2003). The developmental processes that build apparently specialized neural networks in adult brains remain an integral part of these developed networks (see Ziegler & Goswami, 2005, for an illustration with respect to developmental phonology and skilled reading). Developmentally, processing components and the 'knowledge base' that these components are building are not discrete or dissociable. The more pertinent question for the music/language debate is how the infant brain builds a cognitive system at all. An overview of the current state-of-the-art demonstrates that the infant brain builds cognitive systems on the basis of sensory cross-modal learning of dynamic spatiotemporal structure, initially by low-level perceptual mechanisms (for detail, see Goswami, 2008). Experience of temporal *structure* is critical, as the temporal patterning of inputs to different modalities provides information about whether the inputs are related or not. Further, adult neuroscience studies reveal in detail how the cross-modal processing of inputs that are experienced as corresponding alters the primary sensory processing of those unimodal inputs (e.g. Noesselt et al., 2007). Over developmental time, abstracted dependencies trump the sensory information present in a particular experience. Even the brains of young infants show sustained activity based on abstracted dependencies in the absence of sensory input, for example, when a hidden object disappears unexpectedly (Kaufman, Mareschal, & Johnson, 2003).

For music and language, the key perceptual mechanisms are auditory. Peretz and Coltheart's modular framework (2003, adapted in Figure 30.1) suggests that mechanisms supporting pitch organization versus rhythm organization may contribute to music versus language respectively. Nevertheless, at least some of the auditory neural processes that yield pitch versus rhythmic organization should be common to both. Temporal structure is clearly integral to *both* music and language. By processing aspects of auditory input such as intensity, duration, amplitude and frequency, and correlations and dependencies between such auditory parameters, the infant brain extracts structural properties, of both music and language (Saffran, 2001; Trehub & Hannon, 2006). For example, when language is the input, infant statistical learning mechanisms acquire the phonotactic patterns of language (Saffran, Aslin, & Newport, 1996), the phonetic elements that comprise a particular language (Kuhl, 2004), and language-specific information about prosody, intonation and speech rhythm (Jusczyk, Houston, & Newsome, 1999; Curtin, Mintz, & Christiansen, 2005). When music is the input, infant learning mechanisms rapidly focus on the important pitch and timing relations. For example, infants will recognize the same melody at different pitch or tempo levels (Trehub & Hannon, 2006). Mammals and other animals perceive and produce at least some of these same aspects of auditory input. For example, rats can distinguish Dutch from Japanese on the basis of prosodic (rhythmic) cues (Toro, Trobalon, & Sebastian-Galles, 2003). Chinchillas, budgerigars, and crickets can all recognize 'phonetic' boundaries (Kuhl & Miller, 1975; Dooling, Okanoya, & Brown, 1989; Wyttenbach, May, & Hoy, 1996). Bird song reveals every elementary rhythmic effect found in human music, and whales sing using rhythms similar to those found in human music, and even repeat refrains to form 'rhymes' (Gray et al., 2001). Apes produce calls with pure tonal notes, repetition, rhythm, and phrasing that are reminiscent of the multisyllabic babbling sounds produced by babies at around 8 months of age (ape 'singing'; see Masataka, 2007). For humans, these auditory perceptual mechanisms are supplemented with information gained via action (speaking, singing, rhythmic bouncing of babies by adults, clapping to the beat, dancing), and with information gained via language and teaching. Social interaction plays a key role: we have social brains. Statistical patterns in language 'input' are only learned as part of communication, not from watching TV (Kuhl, Tsao, & Liu, 2003). Similarly, Peretz (Chapter 27, this volume) notes the social importance of singing, and its pleasurable and group-cohesion aspects. She also states that lyrics and music rely on separate codes. However, there is also a very important shared code—rhythmic coordination.

Prosody, rhythm, and pitch in language development

The auditory temporal structure of music and singing can be coordinated (given cross-modal congruence) by aligning rhythmic structure. This will necessitate for example pitch pattern processing, grouping, rhythmic processing and metrical processing. Patel (Chapter 27, this volume) suggests that musical processing may be linked to phonemic processing in language. In my view, developmental data support a stronger link at the level of rhythm and prosody. One reason is that both theoretical linguists and child phonologists are converging on the notion that phonological representation in the pre-literate brain does not involve phonemes at all. For example, Port (2007) reviewed a large body of behavioural data and demonstrated that cherished linguistic beliefs (for example, that words are composed from an inventory of phonemes selected from a set of universal phonetic units) cannot be supported. He proposed instead a theory of language representation based on 'rich phonology'. In rich phonology, representations for words are stored in continuous time as high-dimensional spectro-temporal auditory patterns. By this view, speech processing is auditory rather than linguistic, and words are not represented as sequential collections of phonemes or letter-like segments (as traditionally assumed in both linguistic and literacy research). Port's view is convergent with new theoretical perspectives in child phonology, which argue that children learn language-specific phonotactic templates, or 'prosodic structures' (e.g. CVCV, VCV), based on their specific experiences of adult input and their own babbling practices (e.g. Pierrehumbert, 2003; Vihman & Croft, 2007). Prosodic structures are essentially language-specific exemplars that are stored in rich phonetic and prosodic detail. Like Port (2007), Pierrehumbert (2003) dismissed the classical notion of a universal inventory of phonemes or phones, arguing instead that phonetic perception is dependent on the prosodic context. Hence for the developing brain, prosody and phonology are inextricably linked.

This view of rich phonology is supported by auditory scientists who have argued for 'syllable-centric' rather than 'phoneme-centric' theories of language representation (e.g. Greenberg, 2003, 2006). According to Greenberg's theory (Greenberg, 2003), the prosodic weight of the syllable (its prominence or accent) affects the manner in which its constituents (onset, vowel, coda) are phonetically realized. In other words, prosodic cues (changes in duration, stress, and fundamental frequency) carry important information about how sounds are ordered into words, particularly when the words are multi-syllabic. This fits the developmental data suggesting that prosodic and phonetic perception and representation are inter-dependent in the developing brain. If prosodic phonology is further allowed a role in syntactic development, as proposed by Gerken and her colleagues (e.g. Gerken, 1994; Gerken & McGregor, 1998), then impaired prosodic processing could also play a role in speech and language impairments as well as in phonological impairments (see Corriveau, Pasquini & Goswami, 2007; Corriveau & Goswami, 2009). (Note in passing that Peretz's examples of double dissociations in speaking and singing all preserve prosody, see the section 'Neuropsychological dissociations'). Meanwhile, auditory neuroscience is showing that traditional models of the auditory structure of speech (based on the spectrogram) may have lead to an over-emphasis on the importance of frequency discrimination for language development. According to the classical model of speech perception (e.g. Blumstein & Stevens, 1981), invariant acoustic features in the speech signal such as spectral energy peaks (formants) were the correlates of phonemes. Yet experiments with adult listeners showed that speech was intelligible even when no formant structure was present

(Remez, Rubin, Pisoni, & Carrell, 1981), and that intelligibility relied on the slower amplitude modulations in the lower frequency regions (1–16 Hz) (Drullman, Festen, & Plomp, 1994). These slower amplitude modulations are the acoustic consequences of the relatively slow movements of the vocal tract that babies experience when they babble syllables (Nittrouer, 2006).

A different way of modelling auditory structure comes from Hilbert (1912), who showed that any sound can be factored mathematically into the product of a slowly-varying envelope (also called modulation) and a rapidly varying fine time structure (see Smith, Delgutte, & Oxenham, 2002). Smith et al. (2002) created auditory 'chimera' for sentences and melodies using the envelope of one sentence or melody and the fine time structure of another. They found that while the envelope was dominant with respect to speech intelligibility, the fine structure was dominant for perceiving a tune. The brain may process the envelope and fine structure information independently before binding them together (Boemio, Fromm, Braun, & Poeppel, 2005). Such data are clearly relevant to the modular framework shown in Figure 30.1. Basic auditory processing of the amplitude envelope of an auditory signal may be more important for language processing, while processing of the fine structure may more important for musical processing. Developmentally, these data suggest that perception of the slowly-varying amplitude envelope information should be central to setting up a phonological lexicon in infancy. A child with reduced sensitivity to amplitude envelope cues is likely to have subtle impairments in the representation of the speech signal and thereby in the perception (and production) of linguistic information. On the other hand, a child with reduced sensitivity to fine structure might be expected to have impairments in musical processing. We have extensive data with respect to the first of these hypotheses, which I will now outline.

Amplitude envelope processing in developmental dyslexia and specific language impairment

Peretz has engagingly described amusic brains as being 'out of tune but in time' (Hyde & Peretz, 2004). When I first came across her work, it led me to think about whether children with developmental dyslexia or specific language impairment (SLI) have brains that are 'in tune but out of time' (e.g. Thomson & Goswami, 2008; Corriveau & Goswami, 2009). As illustrated in the adaptation of Peretz's modular framework (Figure 30.1), the parts of her model that are proposed to be impaired in amusia versus in children with language and literacy problems are different and complementary. Developmentally, they are unlikely to be completely dissociated. For example, Foxton and colleagues have reported difficulties in processing pitch contour in developmental dyslexia (Foxton et al., 2003). Nevertheless, the primary auditory difficulties for children with reading or language problems appear to involve rhythmic processing (Goswami et al., 2002; Richardson, Thomson, Scott & Goswami, 2004; Muneaux, Ziegler, Truc, Thomson, & Goswami, 2004; Thomson, Fryer, Maltby, & Goswami, 2006; Corriveau, Pasquini, & Goswami, 2007; Pasquini, Corriveau, & Goswami, 2007; Thomson & Goswami, 2008; Corriveau & Goswami, 2009; Goswami, 2009; Goswami,

Gerson, & Astruc, 2010). To summarize a large body of data, we have been comparing typically-developing children's processing of the rise time, duration, intensity and frequency of non-speech tone-like stimuli with that of children with developmental dyslexia or SLI. We have found that the difficulties in phonological processing found in both of these developmental disorders are strongly associated with inefficient basic auditory processing of amplitude envelope structure, with rise time (the rate of change of the amplitude envelope at onset) being particularly important. Rise time is the critical auditory cue for rhythmic timing in language and music, across languages from different rhythm classes, in both perception and production (Morton, Marcus, & Frankish, 1976; Gordon, 1987; Hoequist, 1983; Scott, 1998). In our studies, duration detection can be impaired as well, intensity detection is usually preserved, and findings for frequency discrimination have been mixed (e.g. there is usually no difficulty with *rapid* frequency detection, see for example Richardson et al., 2004).

Individual differences in the severity of the rise time impairment are strongly predictive of the degree of phonological impairment in developmental samples, suggesting that accurate rise time perception is particularly important for developing the high-quality phonological representations of language required for the acquisition of literacy. Classically, rise time has been most closely associated with the perceptual experience of speech rhythm and stress. It is therefore fundamental to prosodic perception, which as we have seen, is intimately connected developmentally to phonological representation. In fact, carers speak to infants in a special prosodic register called motherese or infant-directed speech (IDS), which appears to help with phonological learning (e.g. in segmenting words from the speech stream, Echols, 1996). Traditional theories of prosodic perception assumed that changes in fundamental frequency, duration and amplitude governed the aspects of auditory grouping, rhythm and prominence that comprise prosody, with fundamental frequency playing the dominant role (e.g. Fry, 1954). More recent investigations using natural speech have suggested that amplitude and duration cues play a stronger role in prosodic prominence (Greenberg, 1999; Kochansky, Grabe, Coleman, & Rosner, 2005; Choi, Hasegawa-Johnson, & Cole, 2005). Children with processing inefficiencies for amplitude rise time and duration (as in our data) would therefore be expected to show difficulties with prosody (e.g. Goswami et al., 2010).

The developing brain, language, and music

These developmental data suggest that auditory cues like rise time and duration are fundamental to the perception of rhythm and prosody, and are also fundamental to phonological representation. Basic auditory processing of rise time affects the development of phonology, language and literacy. These processing difficulties never go away, as even remediated adults with dyslexia who had gained entry to a top world university showed impairments in the rise time tasks used for testing children, and showed continuing difficulties with phonology (Thomson et al., 2006; Pasquini et al., 2007). Given the research on rise time and rhythmic behaviour, a basic auditory impairment in rise time perception should also affect the coordination of motor behaviours with an external rhythm, for example tapping to a beat. This skill seems far removed from literacy and language, nevertheless we have shown that children with developmental dyslexia and SLI (and adults with remediated developmental dyslexia) are indeed impaired in rhythmic entrainment tasks such as tapping to a metronome (Thomson et al., 2006; Thomson & Goswami, 2008; Corriveau & Goswami, in press). So a very low-level aspect of auditory temporal structure (rise time) has general consequences for rhythmic behaviours that may be considered integral to musicality (such as keeping time with a beat), as well as specific consequences for language development (as illustrated here). As Peretz notes in her paper, rhythm appears as the essence of music. In my view, this gives music education a unique role to play in the potential *remediation* of phonological disorders in children.

Early interventions that involve music may be very helpful for children with the kinds of basic auditory processing impairments described here. This is because music has an overtly rhythmic structure. Developmentally, these children have subtle rather than incapacitating deficits in basic auditory processing. The rise time impairment documented here makes the developmental mechanisms that build the language system less efficient, but a language system still develops. The developed system relies on phonological representations that are less well-specified than those developed by a non-dyslexic brain. If rhythmic processing skills could be enhanced at the beginning of the developmental process, by musical experiences that involve rhythmic coordination such as playing simple instruments in time with others (e.g. chime bars), singing to music, or marching in time with syllables, this extra experience may help with rhythmic organization and have positive effects on the developmental trajectories for language and literacy.

Indeed, such rhythmic activities have long been part of a rich nursery education. The rise time research provides insights into the potential causal mechanisms whereby such activities carried out within the cognitive system of music might have specific developmental effects on the cognitive system of language. At a neural level, potential mechanisms have already been demonstrated by Wong and colleagues (Wong, Skoe, Russo, Dees, & Kraus, 2007). Wong et al. demonstrated that adults who had received extensive musical training as children (which was assumed to involve increased musical pitch usage) showed more accurate pitch tracking of linguistic stimuli (Chinese tones), as measured by the frequency-following brainstem response. Neural responses to the amplitude envelope structure of the linguistic stimuli were not measured. Nevertheless, this study demonstrates *in principle* that musical experience can affect basic neural circuitry, an effect that should also hold for rhythmic musical experience and phonological awareness. Indeed, Phillips-Silver and Trainor (2005, 2007) recently showed that making rhythmic movements affected the auditory perception of ambiguous rhythms for both adults and babies.

And of course, musical activities are fun. Motivation and engagement are important for successful learning by young children. The pleasurable aspects of music-making and dancing mean that rhythmic coordination skills are likely to be learned almost as a by-product of emotional engagement and having a good time. Systematic research investigation of such interactions would enable deeper insight into the resources that may be shared by music and language as cognitive systems.

Acknowledgements

We would like to thank the head teachers, teachers, children, and parents of all our participants. This research was supported by funding from the Economic and Social Research Council (ESRC), grant RES-000-23-0475, awarded to Usha Goswami, and the Medical Research Council (MRC), grant G0400574, to Usha Goswami. Requests for reprints should be addressed to Usha Goswami, Centre for Neuroscience in Education, Downing St., Cambridge CB2 3EB.

References

Bishop, D. V. M. (1997). Cognitive neuropsychology and developmental psychology: Uncomfortable bedfellows. *Quarterly Journal of Experimental Psychology, 50A*, 899–923.

Blumstein, S. E., & Stevens, K. N. (1981). Phonetic features and acoustic invariance in speech. *Cognition, 10*, 25–32.

Boemio, A., Fromm, S., Braun, A., & Poeppel, D. (2005). Hierarchical and asymmetrical temporal sensitivity in human auditory cortices. *Nature Neuroscience, 8*, 389–95.

Choi, J-. Y., Hasegawa-Johnson, M., & Cole, J. (2005). Finding intonational boundaries using acoustic cues related to the voice source. *Journal of the Acoustical Society of America, 118*(4), 2579–87.

Corriveau, K., Pasquini, E., & Goswami, U. (2007). Basic auditory processing skills and specific language impairment: A new look at an old hypothesis. *Journal of Speech, Language & Hearing Research, 50*, 1–20.

Corriveau, K., & Goswami, U. (2009). Rhythmic motor entrainment in children with speech and language impairment: Tapping to the beat. *Cortex, 45*, 119–30.

Curtin, S., Mintz, T. H., & Christiansen, M. H. (2005). Stress changes the representational landscape: Evidence from word segmentation. *Cognition, 96*. 233–62.

Dooling, R.J., Okanoya, K., & Brown, S. D. (1989). Speech perception by budgerigars (Melopsittacus undulates): The voiced-voiceless distinction. *Perception & Psychophysics, 46*, 65–71.

Drullman, R., Festen, J. M., & Plomp, R. (1994). Effect of temporal envelope smearing on speech perception. *Journal of the Acoustical Society of America, 95*, 1053–64.

Echols, C. H. (1996). A role for stress in early speech segmentation. In J.L. Morgan & K. Demuth (Eds.), *Signal to Syntax: Bootstrapping from speech to grammar in early acquisition* (pp. 151–70). Mahwah, NJ: Lawrence Erlbaum Associates.

Foxton, J., Talcott, J. B., Witton, C., Brace, H., McIntyre, F., & Griffiths, T. D. (2003). Reading skills are related to global, not local, acoustic pattern perception. *Nature Neuroscience, 6*, 343–4.

Fry, D. B. (1954). Duration and intensity as physical correlates of linguistic stress. *Journal of the Acoustical Society of America, 26*, 138.

Gerken, L. (1994). Prosodic structure in young children's language productions. *Language, 72*, 683–712.

Gerken, L., & McGregor (1998). An overview of prosody and its role in normal and disordered child language. *American Journal of Speech – Language Pathology, 7*, 38–48.

Gordon, J. W. (1987). The perceptual attack time of musical tones. *Journal of the Acoustical Society of America, 82*, 88–105.

Goswami, U. (2003). Why theories about developmental dyslexia require developmental designs. *Trends in Cognitive Sciences, 7*, 534–40.

Goswami, U. (2008). *Cognitive Development: The Learning Brain.* Hove: Psychology Press.

Goswami, U. (2009). Mind, brain, and literacy: biomarkers as usable knowledge for education. *Mind, Brain, and Education, 3,* 176–84.

Goswami, U., Gerson, D., & Astruc, L. (2010). Amplitude envelope perception, phonology and prosodic sensitivity in children with developmental dyslexia. *Reading & Writing, 23,* 995–1019.

Goswami, U., Thomson, J., Richardson, U., Stainthorp, R., Hughes, D., Rosen, S., et al. (2002). Amplitude envelope onsets and developmental dyslexia: a new hypothesis. *Proceedings of the National Academy of Sciences of the United States of America, 99*(16), 10911–16.

Gray, P. M., Krause, B., Atema, J., Payne, R., Krumhansl, C., & Baptista, L. (2001). The music of nature and the nature of music. *Science, 291,* 52–4.

Greenberg, S. (1999). Speaking in shorthand – A syllable-centric perspective for understanding pronunciation variation. *Speech Communication, 29,* 159–76.

Greenberg, S., Carvey, H., Hitchcock, L., & Chang, S. (2003). Temporal properties of spontaneous speech–a syllable-centric perspective. *Journal of Phonetics, 31,* 465–85.

Greenberg, S. (2006). A multi-tier framework for understanding spoken language. In S. Greenberg & W. Ainsworth (Eds.), *Listening to Speech – An Auditory Perspective* (pp. 411–33). Hillsdale, NJ: Lawrence Erlbaum Associates.

Hilbert, D. (1912). *Grundzüge einer allgemeinen Theorie der linearen Integralgleichungen.* Teubner: Leipzig.

Hoequist, C. A. (1983). The perceptual centre and rhythm categories. *Language & Speech, 26,* 367–76.

Hyde, K. L. & Peretz, I. (2004). Brains that are out of tune but in time. *Psychological Science, 15,* 356–60.

Johnson, M. (2004). *Developmental Cognitive Neuroscience* (2nd Edition). Oxford: Blackwell.

Jusczyk, P. W., Houston, D. M., & Newsome, M. (1999). The beginnings of word segmentation in English-learning infants. *Cognitive Psychology, 39,* 159–207.

Karmiloff-Smith, A. (1998). Development itself is the key to understanding developmental disorders. *Trends in Cognitive Science, 2,* 389–98.

Kaufman, J., Csibra, G., & Johnson M. H. (2003). Representing occluded objects in the human infant brain. *Proceedings of the Royal Society of London B (Suppl.), 270,* S140–43.

Kochanski, G., Grabe, E., Coleman, J., & Rosner, B. (2005). Loudness predicts prominence: Fundamental frequency adds little. *Journal of the Acoustical Society of America, 118* (2), 1038–54.

Kuhl, P. K. (2004). Early language acquisition: Cracking the speech code. *Nature Reviews Neuroscience, 5,* 831–43.

Kuhl, P. K., & Miller, J. D. (1975). Speech perception by the chinchilla: Voiced-voiceless distinction in alveolar plosive consonants. *Science, 190,* 69–72.

Kuhl, P. K., Tsao. F. -M., & Liu, H. -M. (2003). Foreign-language experience in infancy: Effects of short-term exposure and social interaction on phonetic learning. *Proceedings of the National Academy of Sciences, 100,* 9096–101.

Masataka, N. (2007). Music, evolution and language. *Developmental Science, 10(1),* 35–39.

Morton, J., Marcus, S. M., & Frankish, C. (1976). Perceptual centres (P-centres). *Psychological Review, 83,* 405–8.

Munakata, Y., & McClelland, J. L. (2003). Connectionist models of development. *Developmental Science, 6,* 413–29.

Muneaux, M., Ziegler, J. C., Truc, C., Thomson, J., & Goswami, U. (2004). Deficits in beat perception and dyslexia : evidence from French. *NeuroReport, 15*(8), 1255–59.

Nittrouer, S. (2006). Children hear the forest. *Journal of the Acoustical Society of America, 120,* 1799–1802.

Noesselt, N., Rieger, J. W., Schoenfeld, M. A., Kanowski, M., Hinrichs, H., Heinze, H-J., *et al.* (2007). Audiovisual temporal correspondence modulates human multisensory superior temporal sulcus plus primary sensory cortices. *Journal of Neuroscience, 27*, 11431–41.

Pasquini, E, Corriveau, K., & Goswami, U. (2007). Auditory processing of amplitude envelope rise time in adults diagnosed with developmental dyslexia. *Scientific Studies in Reading, 11*, 259–86.

Peretz, I., & Coltheart, M. (2003). Modularity of music processing. *Nature Neuroscience, 6*, 688–91.

Phillips-Silver, J., & Trainor, L.J. (2005). Feeling the beat: Movement influences infants' rhythmic perception. *Science, 308*, 1430.

Phillips-Silver, J., & Trainor, L. J. (2007). Hearing what the body feels: Auditory encoding of rhythmic entrainment. *Cognition, 105*, 533–46.

Pierrehumbert, J. (2003). Phonetic diversity, statistical learning and acquisition of phonology. *Language & Speech, 46*, 115–54.

Port, R. (2007). How are words stored in memory? Beyond phones and phonemes. *New Ideas in Psychology, 25*, 143–70.

Remez, R. E., Rubin, P. E., Pisoni, D. B., & Carrell, T. D. (1981). Speech perception without traditional speech cues. *Science, 212*, 947–49.

Richardson, U., Thomson, J., Scott, S. K., & Goswami, U. (2004). Supra-segmental auditory processing skills and phonological representation in dyslexic children. *Dyslexia, 10*(3), 215–33.

Saffran, J. R. (2001). Words in a sea of sounds: The output of infant statistical learning. *Cognition, 81*, 149–69.

Saffran, J. R., Aslin, R. N., & Newport, E. L. (1996). Statistical learning by 8-month-old infants. *Science, 274*(5294), 1926–28.

Scott, S. K. (1998). The point of P-centres. *Psychological Research/Psychologische Forschung, 61*(1), 4–11.

Smith, Z. M., Delgutte, B., & Oxenham, A. J. (2002). Chimaeric sounds reveal dichotomies in auditory perception. *Nature, 416*, 87–90.

Thomson, J. M., & Goswami, U. (2008). Rhythmic processing in children with developmental dyslexia: auditory and motor rhythms link to reading and spelling. *Journal of Physiology-Paris, 102*, 120–29.

Thomson, J. M., Fryer, B., Maltby, J., & Goswami, U. (2006). Auditory and motor rhythm awareness in adults with dyslexia. *Journal of Research in Reading, 29(3)*, 334–48.

Toro, J. M., Trobalon, J. B., & Sebastian-Galles, N. (2003). The use of prosodic cues in language tasks by rats. *Animal Cognition, 6*, 131–36.

Trehub, S. E., & Hannon, E. E. (2006). Infant music perception: Domain-general or domain-specific mechanisms? *Cognition, 100*, 73–99.

Vihman, M., & Croft, W. (2007). Phonological development: Towards a 'radical' templatic phonology. *Linguistics, 45*, 683–725.

Wong, P. C. M., Skoe, E., Russo, N. M., Dees, T., & Kraus, N. (2007). Musical experience shapes human brainstem encoding of linguistic pitch patterns. *Nature Neuroscience, 10*, 420–22.

Wyttenbach, R. A., May, M. L., & Hoy, R. R. (1996). Categorical perception of sound frequency by crickets. *Science, 273*, 1542–44.

Ziegler, J. C. & Goswami, U. (2005). Reading acquisition, developmental dyslexia, and skilled reading across languages: A psycholinguistic grain size theory. *Psychological Bulletin, 131*(1), 3–29.

Chapter 31

Towards the role of working memory in pitch processing in language and music

Leigh VanHandel, Jennie Wakefield, and Wendy K. Wilkins

In her article in this volume (Chapter 27), as well as elsewhere, Peretz discusses the concept of domain specificity and its relationship to music and language processing. Along with Patel (Chapter 22, this volume), Peretz's concern is whether, and to what extent, music and language processing rely on shared mechanisms within the brain. One of these shared resources is working memory, which has received increased attention in cognition literature.

This response describes a recent behavioural experiment carried out at Michigan State University which indicates that working memory plays an important and multifaceted role in the processing of pitch in language and music, and illustrates the need to further explore the relationship between the mechanisms of working memory and pitch processing in language and music.

The Tone Project

The Tone Project was an investigation of linguistic and musical tone processing that began with a consideration of congenital amusia as described by Peretz and colleagues (Ayotte, Peretz, & Hyde, 2002 and elsewhere). We were interested in the general observation that individuals who have difficulties with distinguishing pitch contours in music are not generally thought to have any sort of problem with pitch distinctions in language.

There have been suggestions that this music–language difference could be due to the fact that linguistic pitch contours, such as those involved in sentence prosody, are less subtle than those relevant for music (Peretz & Hyde, 2003). We were interested, therefore, in constructing a study in which musical and linguistic pitch contours could be closely matched, in order to carefully examine the similarities and differences in these two closely related cognitive domains.

Further, because it is known that pitch, generally referred to as tone, can be a distinctive contrastive feature in so-called tone languages, we investigated tone perception in music and language and in two distinctively different languages, English (a stress-using language) and Mandarin (a contour tone language).

The study

We recruited 48 native speakers of English and 48 speakers of Mandarin Chinese. All reported normal hearing, normal language skills and acquisition, and were not music majors or professional musicians, although some subjects did self-report having some musical training. Instruction and practice for each task was provided in the native language of each subject, and order was random within tasks and counterbalanced across tasks. Data presentation and response collection was done via e-Prime.

Our experimental paradigm was influenced by the nature of the same-different melody tasks developed initially for the testing of acquired amusia, and then used (in the form of the Montreal Battery of Evaluation of Amusia, the MBEA) in testing for congenital amusia. Our experiment consisted of four same/different tasks using two-note dyads, longer melodies, individual two-syllable words, and longer sentences.

The linguistic stimuli consisted of speech samples, recorded by native speakers of the language, of two-syllable words or multi-word sentences. Target words were recorded one syllable at a time and then combined into words.

For the Chinese stimuli, they were manipulated to remove any redundant phonetic information that might normally accompany pitch contour changes. (For detailed information on the manipulations of the Chinese stimuli, see Meng, Rakerd, & Wilkins, 2005.)

For English stimuli, the manipulation and synthesis involved decomposing stress into its component parts (pitch contour, syllable duration, vowel quality alterations, and loudness), allowing the pitch contour to vary but keeping all other features of stress identical across the two syllables.

The two-syllable word pitch contours were manipulated to match the pitch intervals in the music dyad stimuli. The sentence-level contours were maintained so as to be as natural as possible, and only the pitch of the target word was altered. Subjects made same/different judgements with respect to stimulus pairs that were either identical or that were minimally different and involved only the single localized pitch distinction.

The music tasks consisted of same/different pairs of melodic two-note dyads and relatively short melodies. The pitch intervals used for the dyads were matched to pitch contours used for the word pairs. For the melody task, some melodies were borrowed directly from the MBEA, while others were modified versions composed specifically for this study so that we had a sufficient number of stimuli without repeating any. The melodies were selected or written to be studied in comparison to the sentence-level pitch contours.

Studying the role of working memory

When doing a same/different task such as those in the MBEA and our study, there are two types of errors that can be made. One error is if a subject calls two stimuli different when they are actually the same; this is a *false alarm*. The other possible error is if a subject calls two stimuli the same when they are actually different; this is a *miss*.

Our subjective experience of the MBEA led us to doubt that the mistake of a *false alarm* on 'same' stimuli was equivalent to the mistake of a *miss* on 'different' stimuli. We believed that a mistake of a *miss* is not necessarily an inability to recognize a pitch distinction; instead, it would seem to be a problem with remembering the first stimuli while listening to the second. We thought it might be revealing to consider subjects' working memory abilities in addition to their pitch discrimination capabilities; to test these, we selected one verbal working memory task and one spatial working memory task, not knowing which, if either, might be relevant.

To study verbal working memory, subjects were administered a reading span task via computer that required them to respond via paper and pencil. Subjects were presented with a letter flashed on the screen, followed by a distractor sentence which they had to judge (via computer input) for meaning and sense. This pattern would then repeat. After two to five iterations of the pattern, subjects were asked to write down the letters they had seen in order. The letters used were Roman alphabet letters for both language groups, but the sentences were translated to Chinese for the Chinese subjects.

The spatial working memory task, a symmetry span test, was also administered via computer and also required subjects to respond using paper and pencil. Subjects were instructed to recall both the direction and length of an arrow originating from the centre of concentric circles. The length of the arrow was always short (to the inner circle) or long (to the outer circle), and the direction of the arrow varied throughout the full 360 degrees in 45-degree increments.

Subjects were shown this figure on the computer, immediately followed by a distractor task, which was also a spatial task involving identifying whether letters had been shown in a rotated or mirror-imaged and rotated version. Subjects answered the distractor task via computer, and after between two to five iterations of this sequence, subjects were asked to draw the direction and length of the arrows they had seen on their paper response sheet.

Results

The study resulted in 47 sets of usable data for the English subjects and 46 for the Chinese.

For Chinese speakers, performance scores for accuracy were higher on language than on music tasks for both the words/dyads and sentences/melodies tasks, with no correlation between performance scores on language and music tasks (Table 31.1).

Table 31.1 Accuracy scores, t-tests, and intertask correlations for Tone Project behavioural study

		mean	std dev	t-stat	p-value	corr	p-value	n
Chinese	Dyads	91.01	10.11	4.047*	0.000	–0.015	0.921	46
	Words	97.67	4.42					
English	Dyads	94.34	7.45	4.270*	0.000	0.464*	0.001	47
	Words	86.17	14.78					
Chinese	Melodies	88.14	9.47	5.169*	0.000	0.107	0.479	46
	Sentences	95.87	4.79					
English	Melodies	83.38	10.07	2.854*	0.006	0.289*	0.049	47
	Sentences	76.87	15.20					

In contrast, native English speakers had a higher level of accuracy on music tasks relative to language for both the words/dyads and the sentences/melodies tasks, and demonstrated a strong positive correlation between performance on music tasks and language tasks. This suggests that English speakers process musical and linguistic pitch information in similar fashion for both short and long stimuli, in contrast to the Chinese speakers, whose processing strategies diverge for music and language tone processing.

The finding that Chinese subjects performed much better on the language tasks than the English subjects was exactly what we expected; given that Chinese is a tone language, and that we were studying pitch discriminations, the language task was trivial for the Chinese speakers. However, the Chinese subjects' sensitivity to pitch in language did not seem to translate to music; the Chinese subjects did not perform as well as English subjects on the dyads task, though they did perform better on the melodic task than the English subjects. This may indicate that the Chinese subjects process pitch information differently for short stimuli than for longer stimuli.

As mentioned, subjects were also given tests of working memory designed to determine the effect of specific types of working memory on both the language and music tasks. We hypothesized that if subjects were relying on working memory to complete the tasks, their performance scores would positively correlate with one or more working memory performance scores, and that partialing out the effects of working memory might change the intertask relationships.

Towards the role of working memory

In the original characterization of congenital amusia (Ayotte et al., 2002), those who performed at three standard deviations below the control group mean on at least two of the six subsets in the MBEA were categorized as having congenital amusia.

We were also interested in comparing high and low performers, but we realized that using only a subject's total score was not giving a complete picture of performance. For example, it would be possible for a subject to correctly identify 100% of the *same* stimuli but only correctly identify 60% of the *different* stimuli, or having a 40% *miss* rate. This would result in a subject's overall score of 80% correct not reflecting the wide disparity in performance on the two types of tasks. Indeed, we disaggregated our data and found that high performance on the *same* stimuli was not a guarantee of high performance on the *different* stimuli, and that using only the total score hid some people who had no trouble with the *same* stimuli but who struggled to correctly identify the *differents*.

Rather than deciding a priori how to group our subjects, we used a k-means based cluster analysis, using as input both the same and different scores for dyads, melodies, words, and sentences, as well as the scores on the working memory tasks. A k-means cluster analysis looks for patterns among the subjects, and groups together those who performed similarly.

Three natural groups for each native language resulted from the cluster analysis. Even though the data for determining the clusters had included the results for the same/different tasks for all music and language tasks and the working memory scores,

Table 31.2 Performance scores on the *different* tasks by cluster group

English	Group 1 (n=11)	Group 2 (n=30)	Group 3 (n=6)
Dyads	96.7 (4.9)	93.5 (8.0)	72.4 (12.3)*
Melodies	82.5 (14.4)	89.7 (11.9)	71.3 (15.4)*
Words	85.9 (18.0)	81.1 (19.3)	29.2 (25.8)*
Sentences	65.8 (20.5)	70.1 (20.4)	16.3 (16.9)*
Chinese	**Group 1 (n=15)**	**Group 2 (n=21)**	**Group 3 (n=10)**
Notes	81.6 (18.3)	96.5 (5.5)	55.7 (9.1)*
Melodies	95.6 (8.2)	97.4 (5.9)	75.1 (14.2)*
Words	100 (0.0)	98.8 (3.7)	100 (0.0)
Sentences	97.8 (4.5)	95.1 (5.3)	92.8 (8.4)

% correct score on *different* tasks (std. dev).
Items with an asterisk are significant from the other within-language groups at $p < 0.05$.

the results of the cluster analysis isolated one group of subjects in each language who had overall performed poorly on the *different* music tasks.

Table 31.2 shows each group's mean performance and standard deviation for the *different* tasks; in each case with an asterisk, the group's performance on the different stimuli for that task was significantly lower (at $p < 0.05$) than the other groups' mean performance. The English subjects in Group 3 performed significantly lower than the other two groups on both the music and the language tasks, while the Chinese subjects in Group 3 performed significantly lower on the music tasks alone, reinforcing the interpretation that Chinese subjects may have been processing the music and language tasks differently. Even for the Chinese subjects who struggled with the music *different* tasks, the language tasks were trivial; while the Chinese Group 3 did perform slightly less well on the *different* sentences task, it was not significantly different from the other groups.

These results made us want to look specifically at the profiles of people who were scoring well or poorly on pitch in the context of the longer melodic task—that is, the on the task most like the MBEA—but for obvious reasons we didn't want to rely only on the total percent correct scores.

For each subject we tallied their responses to the melodic stimuli in four ways: total % correct, % correct of the *same* stimuli, % correct of the *different* stimuli, and a d′ score, a single accuracy score that reflects a balance between *same* and *different* scores. We submitted these four measures to another k-means cluster analysis, this time basing the clusters only on subjects' scores on melody tasks.

This k-means cluster analysis provided a high group and a low group for both English and Chinese; Table 31.3 shows the mean and standard deviations for the two groups resulting from the these four melody scores. For each task, the mean for the low group is significantly different (at $p < 0.001$) than the mean for the high group of the same language.

Distinguishing the low and high groups for melody did not create natural classes with respect to our working memory tasks; the individual working memory scores are not significantly different in the low and high groups overall based on this grouping.

Table 31.3 Melody and working memory scores for high and low cluster groups

	English		Chinese	
	High (n=31)	**Low (n=16)**	**High (n=35)**	**Low (n=11)**
Music melody:				
Melodies (% total)	89.1 (6.3)	71.1 (7.0)*	92.6 (5.0)	74.8 (8.0)*
Melodies (% same)	87.1 (10.6)	68.0 (14.7)*	87.9 (10.2)	74.9 (12.1)*
Melodies (% different)	91.2 (10.2)	74.9 (14.9)*	97.3 (5.4)	74.9 (13.8)*
Melodies (d′)	3.39 (1.27)	1.42 (0.76)*	4.16 (1.02)	1.56 (0.71)*
Working memory:				
Verbal	86.4 (12.9)	85.3 (11.8)	82.3 (11.7)	82.5 (8.2)
Spatial (length)	77.6 (13.5)	76.3 (11.6)	84.1 (9.9)	83.8 (14.4)
Spatial (direction)	66.4 (17.4)	64.5 (12.9)	75.3 (13.3)	77.3 (14.5)

* Difference between English high/low and Chinese high/low significant for each score at $p < 0.001$.
There are no significant differences between groups for any working memory or language task scores.

However, we found that when we partialed out the subjects' scores for the spatial working memory test regarding arrow length, there was a distinction between the low and high groups in both languages in terms of a music-related d′ score and a separate working memory score, namely arrow direction.

For the English subjects who struggled with the melody task, the melody d′ score shows a significant positive correlation with the spatial working memory task focusing on arrow direction, while for their Chinese counterparts, we see a significant positive correlation between the music dyads task d′ score and arrow direction on the spatial working memory task (Table 31.4). While these relationships are different, they both illustrate a relationship between a music-related task and a spatial working memory task, in this case direction.

With these same low and high groups, we also looked at the effect of controlling for performance on the spatial direction task (rather than the spatial length task). For the

Table 31.4 Intertask relationships

Controlling for effects of spatial (length) working memory			
	Music	**Working memory**	**Partial correlation**
English low	Melodies (d′)	Spatial (direction)	0.576*
Chinese low	Dyads (d′)	Spatial (direction)	0.640*
Controlling for effects of spatial (direction) working memory			
	Language	**Working memory**	**Partial correlation**
Chinese low	Sentences (d′)	Verbal	0.815*
Chinese low	Sentences (d′)	Spatial (length)	0.678*

* $p < 0.05$.

low-performing Chinese subjects, the d′ score for the sentence task is highly significantly positively correlated with both the verbal working memory task and arrow length in the spatial working memory task.

As discussed previously, the results shown in Table 31.2 implied that Chinese subjects who were prone to *miss* errors were differentially processing the short stimuli and the long stimuli. Table 31.4 illustrates that the subjects in the low-performing Chinese group are, in fact, using different working memory strategies for the two significant interactions. For the short condition, the dyads task showed a significant correlation with scores on the direction element of the spatial task, while the words task did not have enough variance to be able to determine any relationship. (Recall that even the low performing Chinese subjects scored at or near 100% on the words task, as shown in Table 31.2.) For the long condition, the low-performing Chinese group demonstrated a significant correlation between the sentences task and both the verbal memory task and the length element of the spatial task.

Discussion

Our results indicate that research on tone or pitch discrimination are probably not applicable cross-linguistically, or at least not for stress and tone languages. We believe that it is likely that speakers of stress-based languages like English process pitch in language and music in a more similar fashion than do speakers of tone languages.

Our results also indicate that specific types of working memory seems to be a factor in pitch discrimination tasks for both language and music for at least a subset of subjects. Therefore, research on any element of pitch discrimination must take into account subjects' working memory abilities not just for music recall, but for other types of working memory. While we don't yet know what the full role of working memory is in pitch discrimination, we do know that partialing out working memory scores changes the intertask relationships, and we know that it interacts differently with pitch discrimination in low and high scorers. Further study into the role of various types of working memory on pitch discrimination is clearly needed.

We have also shown the importance of disaggregating subjects' data; *false alarms* appear to have different origins than *misses,* and this phenomenon needs to be studied more carefully with respect to language and music. In addition, the disaggregation allows a cluster analysis to group subjects naturally to highlight intertask relationships that might otherwise have been hidden.

Much of Peretz's discussion in this volume focuses on the relationship between a specific type of music (singing) and language action (i.e. the actual act of speech); it remains to be seen what the role is of working memory in a study of the relationship between speech production and vocal music production.

Acknowledgements

This work was supported by a Michigan State University Incubator Grant. We thank Dennie Hoopingarner, David McFarlane, Deborah Moriarty, Brad Rakerd, Frederick Tims, Kyle Grove, Matthew Husband, Yuanliang Meng, and Denise Travis for their invaluable assistance in this project.

References

Ayotte, J., Peretz, I., & Hyde, K. (2002). Congenital amusia: A group study of adults afflicted with a music-specific disorder. *Brain, 125*(2), 238–51.

Meng, Y., Rakerd, B., & Wilkins, W. (2005). Disaggregating co-occuring phonetic features: Examples from speech synthesis of Mandarin Chinese. Paper presented at the Michigan Linguistics Society, East Lansing MI, October 2005.

Patel, A., Foxton, J., & Griffiths, T. (2005). Musically tone-deaf individuals have difficulty discriminating intonation contours extracted from speech. *Brain and Cognition, 59*(3), 310–13.

Peretz, I. and Hyde, K. (2003). What is specific to music processing? Insights from congenital amusia. *Trends in Cognitive Science, 7*(8), 362–67.

Schellenberg, E.G., & Peretz, I. (2008). Music, language and cognition: unresolved issues. *Trends in Cognitive Sciences, 12*(2), 45–46.

Chapter 32

Modularity in music relative to speech: framing the debate

Isabelle Peretz

A central question in psychology and neuropsychology concerns the parts or processes of which the mind/brain is composed. In this debate, modularity has been and continues to play a determinant role. As I wrote in the conclusion of the target article, the notion of modularity remains important. First, the modularity thesis informs empirical investigation by the search for specialization. Second, modularity makes plausible candidates for evolved information-processing mechanisms and hence for genetically determined mechanisms. The modern concept of modularity remains a useful conceptual framework in which productive debates surrounding cognitive systems can continue to be framed (Barrett & Kurzban, 2006).

In their comments of my paper, Besson and Schön question the usefulness of the modularity frame. They choose to address four points. The first is that genetics cannot tell us very much about modularity because the relations between genes and behaviour is not straightforward. I agree that the paths from genes (and environment) to cognition via neurobiology are not simple. However, I think these issues are tractable, as illustrated by the study of the KE family and FOXP2, and as fully developed in the special issue of *Cognition* entitled 'Genes, Brain and Cognition: A Roadmap for the Cognitive Scientist' and edited by F. Ramus (2006). The second point raised by Besson and Schön concerns the property of encapsulation of a modular system, which has been abandoned by most cognitive scientists (e.g. Coltheart, 1999; Barrett & Kurzban, 2006), arguing that we adopt an 'impoverished view of modularity that looses part of its heuristic value'. On the contrary, I would argue that lack of encapsulation, by which other systems may interact and influence the computation of a module, does not challenge modularity nor its heuristic value. Interaction of multiple systems and use of information from multiple sources do not falsify a hypothesis of specialized use of information by dedicated systems. Integration simply promotes efficiency in complex systems. Finally, I will certainly not dispute the fact that it is important to define elementary functions. I rather refer to Barrett and Kurzban (2006) who make a compelling case for the definition of the modular (elementary) function in terms of its (evolved) specialization. Nor will I argue that distinct activation in neuroimaging studies indicates specificity (or modularity). As I have written, increase of activation in a distinct brain region is often interpreted as a distinct neural correlate while it may simply reflect an increase in task difficulty. In sum, I agree with most cautionary comments made by Besson and Schön. However, I strongly disagree with their argument that post-Fodorian modularity is vacuous.

In their comments, Skoe and Kraus provide a useful reminder and compelling case for considering that cortical modules do not function in isolation from subcortical neural systems. They remind us of the importance of top-down processing or corticofugal influences on the early tuning of brainstem responses to auditory input. In reviewing the relevant and impressive literature that deals with this issue, Skoe and Kraus also show that complexity can be tackled with rigor and high precision.

Goswami provides yet another, welcome addition to my paper by drawing attention to the role of prosody and rhythm in both music and speech from development and animal cognition. She further responds to my invitation to test modularity by examining developmental trajectories. In her comments, Goswami agues that developmental data do not support domain specificity. Rather, she proposes that prosody and rhythm, rather than syntactic and phonemic processing of speech, are most useful in the comparative study of music and speech in development. These predictions should be tested in future studies. In this respect, I am particularly grateful to Goswami for bringing to my attention a study in which auditory chimera were created by interchanging sentences for melodies in using the envelope of one sentence or melody and the fine time structure of another (Smith, Delgutte, & Oxenham, 2002). It would be very interesting to test how musical pitch disorders affect the processing of such auditory chimera.

To conclude, I would like to join my voice to Goswami who rightly points out a fundamental and too often overlooked difference between music and speech, particularly in its expressive mode, which accounts for the observation that singing (and dancing) is much more engaging and pleasurable than speaking. Systematic research of the sources of this musical enjoyment would enable a deeper insight in the comparative study of music and speech.

References

Barrett, H. C., & Kurzban, R. (2006). Modularity in cognition: Framing the debate. *Psychological Review, 113*, 628–47.

Coltheart, M. (1999). Modularity and cognition. *Trends in Cognitive Science, 3(3)*, 115–20.

Ramus, F. (2006) Guest editor. Genes, brain and cognition: A roadmap for the cognitive scientist. *Cognition, 101*.

Smith, Z., Delgutte, B. & Oxenham, A. (2002). Chimeric sounds reveal dichotomies in auditory perception. *Nature, 416*, 87–90.

Section 5

Conclusion

Chapter 33

Music as a social and cognitive process

Ian Cross

Music: discursive category or biological universal?

Music, in recent Western thought, is a discursive category. It is a term that can be applied to a cluster of behaviours, artefacts, experiences, and institutions within contemporary and historical Western societies, and provides the basis for an orderly taxonomy—and orderly or disorderly exegeses—of cultural products and behaviours. It expresses a normative ideal that is specific to particular cultural contexts. Music may thus only be understood largely, or even exclusively, in terms of the dynamics of historical and cultural process (Kramer, 1995). Most humanistic and musicological thinking about music adheres to this view, which implies that there is virtually no room for approaches to understanding music that attempt to treat it as comprehensible in terms that are not reducible to the effects of social or historical agency.

Nevertheless, music does appear to have scientific, and especially, biological foundations, and at least some aspects of music are understandable by the application of scientific method. Music, as sound, appears susceptible to explanation in terms of physics (Campbell & Greated, 1987); as perceived sound, it should be capable of being elucidated by means of psychoacoustics (Helmholtz, 1885); and as perceived patterns of sound and action that cannot be derived directly from the physical signal and that yield pleasure, at least some aspects of it should be understandable from the perspectives of the cognitive sciences and neuroscience (Hallam, Cross, & Thaut, 2009; Patel, Chapter 22, this volume; Peretz, Chapter 27, this volume). For music to be an appropriate subject for scientific investigation, we must be able to claim that music exhibits characteristics that are expressible in terms that are independent of historical or social agency. Music must be at least partly understandable in terms of generally applicable scientific theories. While many musicologists (see, e.g. Kramer, 2003) would strongly contest the idea that this is either desirable or possible, it certainly seems to be the case that many aspects of music are indeed amenable to scientific investigation. Over the last few decades, there has been an explosion of scientific studies of music—building on work conducted since the middle of the nineteenth century—and we now know a great deal about the principles underlying music cognition, and over recent years, about the ways in which those principles manifest themselves as processes in the brain.

However, it might be that while musicologists' objections to music as the object of scientific study are beginning to be overcome, the unacknowledged role of humanistic conceptions of music in shaping the course of scientific investigations of music has undermined the generalizability—and hence the scientific status—of those investigations. Almost all scientific studies of music have focused on music from Western societies, and have implicitly assimilated into their concepts and procedures many of the features of music as understood in those societies. The vast majority of studies have focused on music as an aural phenomenon, something that is listened to; they have tended to treat music as embodying types of structures that are salient in Western theories of music; and they have, often implicitly, conceived of music as fulfilling only one simple function, that of affording pleasure.

It can be argued that music, as a focus of scientific enquiry, has all too often been a shadow of the discursive category that constitutes music for Western intellectual culture, particularly when the focus is on listening as 'the' mode of engagement and on structures which may, in the exemplars employed, be atypically characteristic only of music of the Western common-practice period. This argument would suggest that what has constituted the focus of the scientific study of music is, at best, a subset of the prospective phenomena that may constitute music and, at worst, a completely unrepresentative and contingent set of sounds, artefacts, and behaviours that is specific to one (albeit hegemonic) culture in one particular historical period. In this worst case, the scientific study of music would be telling us almost nothing; the culture-specificity of its object of study would undermine its generality to the extent that it could scarcely be called 'science'. In the best case, science has explored only a small fraction of what there is to be known about music, and requires radically to re-evaluate its fundamental premises in order to develop adequately comprehensive scientific accounts of music.

While this argument presents a vastly over-simplified account of the scientific study of music, there is more than a grain of truth in it. Ethnomusicologists have long focused on the exploration of structures, institutions, behaviours, and sounds in non-Western societies that appear, from the viewpoint of Western culture, to constitute 'something like music' (e.g. Wallaschek, 1893). While this 'something like music' is largely recognized on the basis of foregrounding of patterns in pitch and rhythm, there is certainly more to 'something like music' than would be evident from its manifestations and descriptions in Western culture. It sounds different, appears to exploit different types of structures, fulfils a startlingly wide range of functions, and more often than not is something that involves the active and interactive participation of all members of a culture (Blacking, 1976). A science which explores music as patterned sound that has hedonic value is evidently exploring only a subset of prospective musical behaviours. But if this is the case, what would be the superset?

It could be that 'music' is simply an epiphenomenal and pleasurable outcome of human biology, a contingent and ephemeral exploitation of capacities that have arisen for other purposes (such as language, auditory scene analysis, emotional expression, motor control, etc.—for such a view see Pinker, 1997). If this were the case then we could expect that 'something like music' might be accessible to all humans, irrespective of their cultural background, but that 'something like music' should have no particular function in any society other than simple enjoyment. We might also expect that societies should exist in which something like 'music' has never arisen. The superset of all music would then be extremely variable and would be largely determined by the ways in which different societies license the exercise of the heterogeneous human capacities upon which the pleasure-value of 'something like music' is parasitic.

Alternatively, we could suppose that 'something like music' is universal and accessible to all humans, and shares at least some characteristics in addition to its pleasure-value across cultures, 'music', in the sense in which it is used in Western societies, representing a subset of the possible range of manifestations of music (Nettl, 2000). This latter position can be defended on the basis of what is known from the ethnomusicological record, on the basis of which it should be possible to develop at least an operational definition of 'music' that has some universal applicability and hence is susceptible to scientific exploration.

Ethnographies of 'something like music'

In order to give a sense of the scope of prospective musical behaviours across cultures, a range of non-Western examples of behaviours that are recognizably 'music' will be considered. These examples are taken from geographically and historically separated societies that have, and have had until very recently, no common point of contact, within which 'something like music' can be thought of as an indigenous activity that is, in different ways, accessible to all members of each society.

Starting with an historical example from the USA, Bruno Nettl (one of the most eminent living ethnomusicologists) suggests that music, for the Blackfoot group, seems to fulfil and to have fulfilled several different functions. In 1966 it was still used in games between men's societies, preceding and following the contests, but its historical roles (particularly pre-1900) were more widespread. As Nettl (1967, p. 152) notes, 'musical performance [was] associated with all kinds of activity . . . [having to be] performed with practically every activity, religious or secular, in order for that activity to be regarded as properly carried out'. Any important act could not be carried out without its proper songs, which, for Nettl (1967, p. 152), acted as 'an authenticating device': 'without it no important act was a truly Blackfoot act'. Notably, however, the contexts in which it appears to have been used—such as the transfer between persons of a medicine bundle (a wrapped package used in shamanistic ritual), or in the approach to an encampment of another tribe—are contexts where acts are taking place that either do not have outcomes that are determinable in advance or that signal significant potential changes in social status. Nevertheless, music appears here to be interwoven into other aspects of everyday life; it is—or was—not something distinct from normal social intercourse, but an intrinsic part of that intercourse.

A very different form of music is encountered in Podstavsky's (2004) account of the role of music in traditional Hausa society in Nigeria. Here, musicians are of very low status—indeed, Podstavsky notes that the word for musician, or more properly, for singer, *maroki*, derives from the Hausa term for begging, *roko*. The *maroka* are and were dependent on patrons for largesse, but they 'flout social conventions in an ostentatious display of license, and the liberties they take with patronage, even of the highest rank, are not less expected of them than are praise, flattery and self-abasement [. . .]' (Podstavsky, 2004, p. 348) Nevertheless, as Podstavsky suggests, 'if *maroka* are permitted so many liberties, it is not despite their lowly condition, but because of it. . .'

(Podstavsky, 2004, p. 348). In effect, in traditional Hausa society, singers—*maroka*—are bound to powerful patrons (who are generally male but may be female, and may be corporations rather than individuals). *Maroka* are themselves of low status, being almost extrasocial, and are licensed not only to praise but also to comment and critique (in a sense, as the lowest of the low they have nothing to lose!). But they and their music again appear to have a significant role in ambiguous or doubtful situations, such as when social structures require to be re-affirmed (for instance, when a chief's power needs re-affirming—either for his own ego or for the reinforcement of his followers' confidence in the chief), or when collective actions require to be motivated.

On yet another continent, Simon's (1978) account of the musical practices of the Eipo pygmies of Irian Jaya (the Indonesian-held territory of Papua), show that music in this more-or-less neolithic, exogamous, patrilineal, and patrilocal clan-based society again permeates critical phases of social action. Music—again, more properly, song—in this culture falls into four categories according to the occasion in which it is manifested; it can be used for self-entertainment during various daily activities, in ritual dancing, and in the activities surrounding either death or illness. Self-entertainment music is termed *dit*, while that involved in ritual dancing is termed *mot*; as Simon (1978, p. 442) notes, 'The third category (laments) and the fourth (singing at the curing ceremony) are not considered music or singing, and therefore these musical activities have no special term'. Yet again, in this culture music appears to be critically involved at moments of social—or even individual—uncertainty. While the solitary *dit* songs may occur sporadically, and can be thought of as fulfilling psychical or magical functions for an individual (in effect, self-regulatory), the social *mot* songs, performed at feasts or dances, have a primary function of social stabilization; 'they maintain the social forces of the . . . men . . . they strengthen the friendship between allied villages . . . [and] . . . also serve as a kind of marriage market' (Simon, 1978, p. 443). The curing songs and laments appear to have both self-regulatory and social functions in helping manage change or transition in the states of individuals and in their roles and significances within the society.

The Kamayurá is a very small Amazonian group with around 300 members, living in the headwaters of the Xingu River, a tributary of the Amazon in Central Brazil; their culture is presently under severe ecological stress, and indeed under threat of extinction. Hill (1979) provides an account of their musical practices which focuses on three distinct sets of activities: *jaqui* dances, *taquara* dances, and *kwarìp* ceremonies. *Jaqui* dances are performed only by the men, take place at the beginning of the dry season (in April) and invite forest and river spirits to enter the Kamayurá village to 'bring the fish'. *Taquara* dances are held when the Kamayurá wish to rid the village or household of evil spirits that may result from contact with outsiders. *Kwarìp* ceremonies occur at the beginning of the rainy season in late August, are held only when a man of high prestige has died, and consist of two parts, a funerary rite and a celebratory festival. As Hill (1979, p. 428) notes, 'the two categories of social relations represented individually in the structurally opposed *jaqui* and *taquara* dance are simultaneously expressed in the first part of the *kwarìp* ceremony'; in effect, three forms of musical practice are employed in the management of relationships between the environment and the community (*jaqui*), between the community and outsiders (*taquara*), and within the community and between the community and the outside world as the community changes over time (*kwarìp*). Again, in this tiny and marginal Amazonian society, music is an integral component of collective action in situations where potential outcomes—in terms of future relationships between the group and its environment, and within the group and between the group and other groups—are uncertain.

A final example from yet another continent illustrates the ways in which music can appear recognisable but can yet bear a weight of meaning that is quite alien to the expectations of members of contemporary Western cultures (see example). This example comes from the Northern Territory of Australia, and is reported by Allan Marett in his 2005 volume *Songs, Dreamings, and Ghosts: the Wangga of North Australia*. Marrett states that around the small coastal settlement of Wadeye in the 1940s and 1950s, the establishment of a mission station led local groups to come to the mission regularly for food assistance. This frequently led to actual violence, as several of the groups had long been in conflict with each other, although these groups inhabited very much the same areas of the country. Elders from the three main language groups collectively created a system of tripartite ceremonial reciprocity, in which the each group would, in turn, sing songs using their own song-forms but all referring to local places and to commonly-held cosmological principles. So the wangga-owning group would sing wangga for the dhanba- and lirrga-owning groups, the dhanba-owning group would sing dhanba for the wangga- and lirrga-owning groups, and so on. As Marrett notes (2005, p. 23), in Wadeye, 'The tripartite ceremonial system . . . continues to function to the present day and is pointed to as a source of ongoing stability within the community'. Marrett (2005, p. 35) also notes that '. . . song texts often contain elements of ambiguity that permit a variety of different exegeses', and it appears likely that it is this ambiguity that allows the tripartite ceremony to maintain a degree of social harmony across the three groups. Here, we have a state of affairs where music has consciously been employed by the participants to manage a situation—the co-presence of groups, each of whom claim that their locale is part of *their* own ancestral heritage—that has the potential for violent conflict; again, music is central to a situation where the dynamics of inter-group relations are dangerously uncertain.

Each of the societies from which these examples are drawn display different types of social organization, inhabit different physical and ecological environments, and provide seemingly quite different manifestations of music. While all share modulation of pitch and the use of periodically-based rhythmic structures, manifested in song—and, more often than not, dance—otherwise all take quite distinct forms and fulfil quite different functions in these different cultural contexts, few if any of which are simply reducible to 'entertainment'. Nevertheless, there are at least two general tendencies that are evident in all these examples. Music is generally interwoven into other aspects of everyday life, and music tends to be employed to manage situations involving change or transition in the states of individuals and in their roles and significances within a society (Cross & Woodruff, 2009). One can draw a very general hypothesis from examples such as these (and, indeed, many more): that 'music', as a communicative medium accessible to all members of a society, has a central role in the management of situations of social uncertainty, situations where outcomes are unclear, on the edge.

It is obvious that language also has a hugely significant role in managing situations of social uncertainty, as a medium for instruction, negotiation, collective agreement, or the imposition of individual or collective will. However, unlike enactive language, music as an interactive behaviour leaves no apparent traces or residues in the form of goal-directed behaviours or consensual agreement as to current or future behaviour—other than the agreement that the music has been enacted, though precisely *what* has been enacted may remain unclear. Music seems a much less purposeful and consequential form of interaction than does language. If it is functioning so as to help manage situations of social uncertainty, the relationships between music and the generic processes of social cognition require to be explored in order for music's putative social functionality to be understood.

Recent approaches conceive of the processes involved in social cognition as automatic, orienting responses that rely on the behaviours of others—particularly facial expression of emotion, or eye gaze direction—to be informative about the environment, whether physical or social (Adolphs, 2003; Frith, 2008), and to guide behaviour. When interaction is communicative, there is a generic tendency towards mirroring of action, which can be thought of as underpinning shared intentionality (Tomasello, Carpenter, Call, Behne, & Moll, 2005). In communicative interaction, there is also evidence for the use of continual (pragmatic, attitude-, and intention-signalling) acts of 'communicative scaffolding', such as eye gaze signals in controlling turn-taking, or eye contact in signalling communicative intention to manifest new and relevant knowledge (Hari & Kujala, 2009); these signals are not limited to the eyes as indicators of attentional focus, but may also involve more complex ostensive orofacial, brachiomanual, or postural gesture (Kendon, 2004) which may be deliberate but are frequently subconscious. In real-time social interaction, then, there is thus a complex cycle in which we abstract information from the acts of others which guides our own behaviours, which will in turn form part of the social environment from which the others abstract information that guides their own behaviour.

Much of the research that has explored these types of interactive situation has focused on circumstances in which interactions are goal-directed and hence volitional or involving conscious awareness. However, there is considerable evidence—particularly from the explorations of 'mirroring' in communicative contexts—that non-conscious and, particularly, affective, processes play a crucial role in sustaining, and perhaps enabling, efficacious social interaction (Singer & Lamm, 2009). Affective mirroring, whether in the form of mimicry of affective expression (facial, vocal, gestural, or postural), or emotional contagion, appears largely automatic or reflexive. It has been proposed that either of these processes is likely to precede empathy, an affective state elicited by observing the affective state of another person, and which we are aware is brought about by the other's state or situation; empathy may precede sympathy which may, in turn, precede prosocial behaviour.

A framework for exploring the functional efficacy of music

How, then, do the types of process that enable music to be functional as a medium for managing situations of social uncertainty relate to these more general processes involved in social interaction? To start with, we shall sketch some of the features that appear likely to endow music with the capacity to deal with social uncertainty. One attribute that characterizes music in almost all accounts is the way in which it simultaneously appears ambiguous—its meaning is not consensually determinable—yet it seems also to present raw, basic and unmediated meaning (Tolbert, 2001). Music seems to mean like it sounds, yet participants are unlikely to agree on its precise meaning. A further consistent feature is that music enables participants to orient their attention and behaviours around a common temporal framework, usually by foregrounding a periodic pulse (Clayton, Sager, & Will, 2005). It can be suggested that music's sense that a meaning is being presented, yet maintenance of indeterminacy in the meanings that can be derived from it—which elsewhere I have termed *floating intentionality* (Cross, 1999)—together with its capacity to induce a sense of connection between participants by establishing a commonly experienced temporal framework, makes music an excellent medium for non-conflictual interaction. Music's floating intentionality allows different participants to derive different significances from the ongoing musical event while each feeling that the meanings that they are experiencing are somehow intrinsic to the music; as these different significances are not made manifest between the participants, potentially divergent interpretations are never in conflict. Moreover, music's provision of a periodic temporal framework acts as a foundation for the coordination or entrainment of participants' actions and perceptions, leading to a sense of mutual affiliation. Exploitation of these two features endows music, as a communicative medium, with a particular efficacy in managing situations of social uncertainty.

This still leaves unresolved the questions of how music can simultaneously evince fixity and multiplicity of meaning, and of how it relates to the types of process involved in social interaction described above. Elsewhere (Cross, 2008), I have proposed that we can analyse the sources of meaning in music in terms of at least three dimensions reflecting aspects of biologically-grounded communicative systems that have different levels of generality, the first shared with other species of animals, the second common to all humans and the third specific to each culture.

We can account for the feeling that music means like it sounds in terms of the first of these dimensions which can be termed the *motivational-structural*. The rationale for hypothesizing this dimension of meaning in music derives from some recent theories of animal communication (Owings & Morton, 1998; Rendall, Owren, & Ryan, 2009) which postulate that, through processes of evolution, animals have come to be sensitive to the acoustical structure of biologically-significant signals, which act to modulate their emotional or *motivational* states. A form of relationship between the acoustical structure of signals and the motivational states of perceivers appears general across a wide range of species (though modulated by species-specific constraints), and it is no surprise that there is evidence that human listeners are similarly sensitive; in experiments on the ways in which listeners respond emotionally to music, perhaps the only consistent finding tends to be that certain 'primitive' global features of music—such as tempo, register, or intensity—are reliably associable with changes in arousal (see, e.g. Schubert, 2004; Gomez & Danuser, 2007). These relationships between acoustical structure and motivational state allow music to be experienced as though it were 'honestly' conveying quite specific information; indeed, from these considerations, music appears to be acting like an 'honest signal', a signal that reveals, to the receiver, qualities of the signaller that are relevant to the communicative situation (after Szamado & Szathmáry, 2006). Nevertheless, music's 'honesty' is more apparent than real; at most, the motivational-structural dimension of music's significance may constrain the range of possible interpretations rather than determining any single interpretation.

A second dimension of meaning in music can be termed the *socio-intentional.* The workings of this dimension are rooted in parameters that are universally evident in the pragmatics of human communicative interaction (see, e.g. Kendon, 2004; Gussenhoven, 2005) and are shared with language, being concerned with the sense of communicative intent that can be inferred from what could be termed prosodic and gestural cues (Ogden, 2006). These types of meaning are communicated by and inferred from features such as the overall pitch contour of a musical phrase (rising or falling) and its overall range (broad or narrow), and afford inferences about attitudes and emotions of the producer of the musical signal (see Huron, Kinney, & Precoda, 2006). The operation of this dimension of musical meaning is unproblematically evident in contexts in which music involves interactive participation. Here, music can be thought of as exhibiting features that are common to linguistic dialogue, being exemplified in specific contoural and accentual structures, call and response patterns, or antecedent-consequent phrase structures. This dimension is likely to underlie the inter-cultural accessibility of music, the fact that we are able to make at least some sense of the music of a culture with which we are completely unfamiliar.

A third dimension of musical meaning stems from the ways in which musical activities and their traces come to have particular significances in specific cultural contexts. These significances are the result of active participation in, and engagement with, the dynamics and specificities of particular cultural contexts and processes, as well as of individual life histories. They are shaped by the conceptions and uses of music that exist within a specific cultural framework, by the contingencies of cultural formation and change, by enculturative, formal and personal learning processes, and by associations of music with episodes in and aspects of an individual's life history. Examples might include the ways in which a particular song may have a range of significances for different groups at particular periods in time (such as *Nkosi Sikelele Africa*, composed as a hymn in 1897, but gaining particular significance during the years of apartheid in South Africa), or the ways in which particular genres of music may have particular—though often transient—significance for adolescents in constructing their own identities.

These three dimensions of musical meaning are probably always simultaneously present in any musical interaction or experience. As an example, we can consider a famous instance of the use of music in film: the passage of violin 'stabs' during the shower scene in Hitchcock's *Psycho.* These can be considered at one and the same time to be eliciting emotion in the audience by virtue of embodying the acoustical characteristics of the signal produced by an animal in an extreme situation, by articulating (in overall downward contour across multiple phrases) a sense of diminution of effort, and at the same time a particular cultural code—post-tonal musical structure—that is likely to signify unfamiliarity and strangeness (the music was written by Bernard Hermann, whose own musical interests were profoundly modernist). All the significances are simultaneously accessible, and while one may be foregrounded for a particular listener on a particular viewing the others persist in the background, colouring the overall experience. At the same time, this example points up one other aspect of music that must be considered, which is that it rarely, if ever, constitutes an unattached or independent domain of experience. It is almost always embedded in a broader social context—here, the unveiling of a cinematic narrative—which will shape the ways in which its meanings are interpreted, while at the same time being re-shaped by the meanings accessible within the musical domain. As the ethnomusicologist Philip Bohlman (2000, p. 293) has put it, 'Music accumulates its identities . . . from the ways in which it participates in other activities'.

Music not only manifests this network of dimensions of musical meaning embedded in social context, it presents, across cultures, a temporal framework within which participants can experience their actions and perceptions as commonly organized in time. Across cultures, music is characterized by patterns of temporally regular events, allowing participants to align their experiences in time with the musical signal and with each other—in other words, to *entrain* their perceptions and actions (Clayton, Sager, & Will, 2005). Entrainment, in this sense, is a feature of music that appears more-or-less universal (even when a regular pattern of pulses is not present in the phenomenal musical surface, as, for instance, in the *alap* section of a North Indian musical performance). It is also a feature of the ways in which humans engage attentionally with temporal sequences of events; the experience of sequences of events that are regularly spaced in time is likely to involve a periodic modulation of attention that aligns with the temporal structure of the stimulus (see, e.g. Large & Jones, 1999). Moreover, humans appear to be particularly attuned to each other's capacity to act and produce sound at regular time intervals; studies by Tommi Himberg have shown that individuals interacting musically will continually adjust the timing of the signals that they produce in ways that adapt what each participant is doing to what each other is doing, a continual process of mutual temporal co-adjustment (Himberg, 2006).

It is possible that this capacity is unique to humans, despite the attention that has recently been paid to relationships between the capacity of a species for vocal learning and entrainment (Patel, Iversen, Bregman, & Schultz, 2009) and the thesis concerning the origins of human entrainment capacities in great ape drumming behaviours that Fitch puts forward in this volume (see Chapter 9). Humans exhibit entraining behaviours spontaneously and consistently and appear motivated to do so, whereas entrainment in non-human species has only been observed in a very few instances and may well be based on processes that are not the same as those that underlie human inter-individual entrainment. Indeed, a recent paper comparing the performance of humans with that of rhesus macaque monkeys when tapping along with a metronome (Zarco, Merchant, Prado, & Mendez, 2009) found that humans tended to anticipate—tapped in advance of—the beat while the macaques reacted to the beat, tapping almost in response. Moreover, humans required minimal training—if any—to undertake the task, while of the three macaques used in the experiment, one took 25 months to master the task. It is likely that entrainment underpins not only musical interaction but also shapes aspects of linguistic interaction (see, e.g. Krahmer & Swerts, 2007). This feature of human communicative interaction, entrainment, affords interacting individuals the sense that they and all other participants are experiencing their interactions within a common temporal framework, endowing a collective musical behaviour with a profoundly affiliative sense of shared purpose or meaning.

Hence music integrates multiple sources of potential meaning within a framework for interaction that is likely to align participants' expectations, attentional and affective states (see also Bharucha, Curtis, & Paroo, Chapter 16, this volume); types of possible meaning attributed to the ongoing flow of musical activity are likely to be similarly constrained for all participants, but definite meanings are not made publicly attributable. Music, in communicative interaction, provides cues as to our affective attitudes to, and levels of engagement with, our co-participants. These cues are typically embodied in the acoustic signal but are also present in the actions and expressive behaviours that occur while making music together, helping to co-construct the collective musical activity as it unfolds in time. The specific significances of these cues are rarely, if ever, resolved; in effect, music in interaction embodies the preconditions for propositional meaning without itself embodying propositions, allowing us to abstract our own narratives from the progress of our musical interactions.

In this respect, music exemplifies a condition of ambiguity (see Cross, 2005), a feature that can be claimed to be the ground state of communication—and of the cognitive processes involved in social interaction. We have to detect and decode the meanings of our interactions with others, and in the real world we might fail, with prospectively negative consequences for ourselves and others. But in musical interactions, we are provided with a framework that is, at root, affiliative; our interactions are hypothetical, bounded, suspended in pretence. Engagement with each other in music absolves us of the need to resolve the ambiguity of our involvement with each other—and with ourselves. Yet at the same time we have a sense that we *know* what the music means; it means like it sounds. Our musical actions and intentions appear to have no ends beyond the moment, or beyond the conventions that frame our musical interactions. Yet it can be suggested that they do have consequences, in that the envelope of our musical attachment may provide us with a means of carrying beyond the immediacy of our interactions a sense of involvement with, and understanding of, others. Indeed, recent research by Tal-Chen Rabinowitch (see Cross, Laurence, & Rabinowitch, in press) has provided some preliminary evidence that the regular participation of young children in forms of musical group interaction that require them to attend and respond to what each other is doing can lead to an enhanced disposition towards empathy.

Implications and conclusions

One key implication of this view of music as an efficacious communicative medium is a need to re-assess our understandings of how music relates to other communicative media, in particular, how music relates to language. While we could adopt the position that language and music are distinct domains—or even modules—of mind, brain and behaviour (see Peretz, Chapter 27, this volume), it would seem more parsimonious to hypothesize that both might draw on common resources (see Patel, Chapter 22, this volume). Music appears distinct from language in foregrounding pitch and (entrainable) rhythm, facilitating affective expression and a sense of connectedness but not expressing secure or consensual meaning. But music, in most of its cross-cultural manifestations, is essentially song, articulating words, albeit endowing them with a fluidity of meaning by foregrounding the expressive and affiliative dimensions of pitch and rhythm. Furthermore, music is typically an integral component of larger contexts for social interaction that may shape and constrain participants' interpretations of music's possible meanings.

Conversely, pitch and rhythm are generally interpreted as constituting background aspects of language that may be drawn on in the service of embodying and articulating semantically decomposable propositions, generally taken to be the primary role of language. However, language may also foreground pitch and rhythm to facilitate affective communication and engender a sense of mutual affiliation between interlocutors; speech in socially interactive contexts (as opposed to language abstracted as symbolic notation) almost always involves elements that could be construed as 'musical' in terms of its intermittent foregrounding of entrainment and semantic non-specificity (as in phatic communion—see Coupland, Coupland, & Robinson, 1992). It also appears to share features with music in the extent to which it embodies, in speech signals, cues as to degrees of communicative engagement, by exploiting features that we might think of as characteristic of music such as pitch contour and rhythmicity. Indeed, in at least some cultures it is very difficult to draw a hard and fast line between music and language. As Jerome Lewis (2009, p. 383) notes in respect of the communicative culture of the Mbendjele pygmies of Central Africa, while in the forest women accompany each other's speech with sung sounds, both ideophones and expletives, which contribute to increasing the volume and distinctive melodiousness of their conversations, a form of communicative interaction that appears to be neither speech nor music but somewhere in between. Similarly, in his study of music and communication amongst the Amazonian Suyá, Anthony Seeger identifies a range of types of communicative interaction that, in his words (Seeger, 1987, p. 51), '. . . demonstrate how the separation of speech and music distorts both of them'.

So there is some good evidence for considering music and language as overlapping in many of their features: as drawing on the same pool of communicative resources. At the same time, they do appear to be distinguishable in at least three ways, the first two of which have conventionally taken as of most significance though it can be suggested that the third is likely to be the most definitive.

Language and music can be distinguished semantically in terms of their capacity to embody articulate propositions. Language can express semantically decomposable propositions—complex, well-formed utterances that can be decomposed into constituent and dependent, and implicative and entailing, simple propositions. Music simply cannot do this; its capacity to mean is not understandable in the same way as is that of language (see, e.g. Scruton, 1987; Davies, 1994; Cross & Tolbert, 2009).

Language and music can be distinguished structurally in terms of the extent to which affective/rhythmic or syntactical/semantic features are foregrounded (see responses to Bharucha et al., Patel, Peretz, and Fabb & Halle, this volume). While theories of syntax have been applied with some success to a subset of possible musics—principally, to

Western tonal music of the common-practice period (see Lerdahl & Jackendoff, 1983; Bharucha et al., Chapter 16, this volume; Wiggins, Chapter 18, this volume)—it remains to be seen whether or not some type of structure analogous to linguistic syntax is truly characteristic of a wider range of musics.

Finally, language and music can be distinguished in terms of the communicative contexts within which they tend to be efficaciously deployed. Language—more properly, speech—tends to have primacy in situations where goal-directed behaviour requires to be co-ordinated; in other words, language is efficacious in getting people to do things. Music, on the other hand, figures largely in situations where the goal is getting people to experience other people *as* people with whom one might get together and do things; in other words, music is efficacious in facilitating social interaction as a context for possible social action. In effect, language can be thought of as mobilizing shared intentionality for goal-directed behaviour, while music can be interpreted as mobilizing shared intentionality per se. Music and language can thus be interpreted as context-specific manifestations of a common substrate for human communicative capacities.

This approach to understanding music also has implications for the cognitive sciences and neuroscience of music. It suggests that we need to extend our explorations well beyond the bounds of listening; we need to explore music as interaction and in social context. While there is some indicative evidence that language and music do indeed draw on common resources, we need to move beyond the constraints of current methodologies and conceptions of what could and should constitute music and language in order fully to investigate their commonalities, as well as the features that differentiate them, in both behaviour and in brain. There is an urgent need to develop more ecologically valid and culturally sensitive means of investigating relationships between music, language, cognition, and brain.

References

Adolphs, R. (2003). Cognitive neuroscience of human social behaviour. *Nature Reviews Neuroscience, 4*(3), 165–78.

Blacking, J. (1976). *How musical is man?* London: Faber.

Bohlman, P. (2000). Ethnomusicology and music sociology. In D. Greer (Ed.), *Musicology and sister disciplines* (pp. 288–98). Oxford: Oxford University Press.

Campbell, M., & Greated, C. (1987). *The Musician's Guide to Acoustics.* Oxford: Oxford University Press.

Clayton, M., Sager, R., & Will, U. (2005). In time with the music: The concept of entrainment and its significance for ethnomusicology. *ESEM counterpoint, 1*, 1–45.

Coupland, J., Coupland, N., & Robinson, J. D. (1992). 'How are you?': Negotiating phatic communion. *Language in Society, 21*(2), 207–30.

Cross, I. (1999). Is music the most important thing we ever did? Music, development and evolution. In S. W. Yi (Ed.), *Music, mind and science* (pp. 10–39). Seoul: Seoul National University Press.

Cross, I. (2005). Music and meaning, ambiguity and evolution. In D. Miell, R. MacDonald, & D. Hargreaves (Eds.), *Musical Communication* (pp. 27–43.). Oxford: Oxford University Press.

Cross, I. (2008) Musicality and the human capacity for culture. *Musicae Scientiae*, Special Issue, 147–67.

Cross, I., Laurence, F. & Rabinowitch, T-C. (in press) Empathy and creativity in group musical practices; towards a concept of empathic creativity. In G. MacPherson and G. Welch (Eds.) *Oxford Handbook of Music Education.* Oxford: Oxford University Press.

Cross, I. & Tolbert, E (2009) Music and meaning. In S. Hallam, I. Cross & M. Thaut (Eds.) *Oxford Handbook of Music Psychology* (pp. 24–34). Oxford: Oxford University Press.

Cross, I., & Woodruff, G. E. (2009). Music as a communicative medium. In R. Botha & C. Knight (Eds.), *The prehistory of language* (Vol. 1, pp. 113–44). Oxford: Oxford University Press.

Davies, S. (1994). *Musical meaning and expression.* Ithaca, NY: Cornell University Press.

Frith, C. D. (2008). Social cognition. *Philosophical Transactions of the Royal Society B-Biological Sciences, 363*(1499), 2033–39.

Gomez, P., & Danuser, B. (2007). Relationships between musical structure and psychophysiological measures of emotion. *Emotion, 7*(2), 377–87.

Gussenhoven, C. (2005). *The phonology of tone and intonation.* Cambridge: Cambridge University Press.

Hallam, S., Cross, I., & Thaut, M. (Eds.). (2009). *Oxford Handbook of Music Psychology.* Oxford: Oxford University Press.

Hari, R., & Kujala, M. V. (2009). Brain basis of human social interaction: From concepts to brain imaging. *Physiological Reviews, 89*(2), 453–79.

Helmholtz, H. (1885). *On the sensations of tone as a physiological basis for the theory of music* (A. J. Ellis, Trans. 2nd ed.). London: Longmans, Green.

Hill, J. (1979). Kamayura flute music: A study of music as meta-communication. *Ethnomusicology, 23*(3), 417–32.

Himberg, T. (2006). Co-operative tapping and collective time-keeping – differences of timing accuracy in duet performance with human or computer partner. In M. Baroni, A. R. Addessi, R. Caterina, & M. Costa (Eds.), *Proceedings of the 9th International Conference on Music Perception & Cognition* (pp. 377). Bologna, Italy: 2006 ICMPC.

Huron, D., Kinney, D., & Precoda, K. (2006). Influence of pitch height on the perception of submissiveness and threat in musical passages. *Empirical Musicology Review 1*(3), 170–77.

Kendon, A. (2004). *Gesture: visible action as utterance.* Cambridge: Cambridge University Press.

Krahmer, E., & Swerts, M. (2007). The effects of visual beats on prosodic prominence: Acoustic analyses, auditory perception and visual perception. *Journal of Memory and Language, 57*(3), 396–414.

Kramer, L. (1995). *Music and postmodernist thought.* London: University of California Press.

Kramer, L. (2003). Musicology and meaning. *Music Times, 144*(1883), 6–12.

Large, E., & Jones, M. (1999). The dynamics of attending: How people track time-varying events. *Psychological Review, 106*(1), 121–56.

Lerdahl, F., & Jackendoff, R. (1983). *A Generative Theory of Tonal Music.* Cambridge, MA: MIT Press.

Lewis, J. (2009). As well as words: Congo Pygmy hunting, mimicry, and play. In R. Botha & C. Knight (Eds.), *The cradle of language* (Vol. 2, pp. 381–413). Oxford: Oxford University Press.

Marett, A. (2005). *Songs, Dreamings, and Ghosts: the Wangga of North Australia.* Hanover, CT: Wesleyan University Press.

Nettl, B. (1967). Studies in Blackfoot Indian musical culture. Part I: Traditional uses and functions. *Ethnomusicology, 11*, 141–60.

Nettl, B. (2000). An ethnomusicologist contemplates universals in musical sound and musical culture. In N. Wallin, B. Merker & S. Brown (Eds.), *The origins of music* (pp. 463–72). Cambridge, MA: MIT Press.

Ogden, R. (2006). Phonetics and social action in agreements and disagreements. *Journal of Pragmatics, 38*(10), 1752–75.

Owings, D. H., & Morton, E. S. (1998). *Animal vocal communication: a new approach.* Cambridge: Cambridge University Press.

Patel, A. D., Iversen, J. R., Bregman, M. R., & Schulz, I. (2009). Experimental evidence for synchronization to a musical beat in a nonhuman animal. *Current Biology, 19*(10), 827–30.

Pinker, S. (1997). *How the mind works.* London: Allen Lane.

Podstavsky, S. (2004). Hausa entertainers and their social status: A reconsideration of sociohistorical evidence. *Ethnomusicology, 48*(3), 348–77.

Rendall, D., Owren, M. J., & Ryan, M. J. (2009). What do animal signals mean? *Animal Behaviour, 78*(2), 233–40.

Schubert, E. (2004). Modeling perceived emotion with continuous musical features. *Music Perception, 21*(4), 561–85.

Scruton, R. (1987). Analytical philosophy and the meaning of music. *Journal of Aesthetics and Art Criticism, 46*, 169–76.

Seeger, A. (1987). *Why Suyá Sing: A Musical Anthropology of an Amazonian People.* New York: Cambridge University Press.

Simon, A. (1978). Types and functions of music in the Eastern Highlands of West Irian. *Ethnomusicology, 22*(3), 441–55.

Singer, T., & Lamm, C. (2009). The social neuroscience of empathy. *Annals of the New York Academy of Sciences: the year in cognitive neuroscience 2009, 1156*, 81–96.

Számadó, S., & Szathmáry, E. (2006). Selective scenarios for the emergence of natural language. *Trends in Ecology and Evolution, 21*(10), 555–61.

Tolbert, E. (2001). The enigma of music, the voice of reason: 'Music,' 'language,' and becoming human. *New Literary History, 32*(3), 451–65.

Tomasello, M., Carpenter, M., Call, J., Behne, T., & Moll, H. (2005). Understanding and sharing intentions: the origins of cultural cognition. *Behavioral and Brain Sciences, 28*(5), 675–91.

Wallaschek, R. (1893). *Primitive Music.* London: Longmans, Green & Co.

Zarco, W., Merchant, H., Prado, L., & Mendez, J. C. (2009). Subsecond timing in primates: comparison of interval production between human subjects and Rhesus monkeys. *Journal of Neurophysiology, 102*(6), 3191–202.

Index